Self-Confidence

You Deserve to Have Self-Confidence!

James R. Fisher, Jr., Ph.D.

Published in the United States of America

1. Psychology / Social & Cultural Psychology
2. Psychology / Industrial & Organizational Psychology 14.02.17

For

Ken Shelton of Executive Excellence,
A true Renaissance Man of our time

Table of Contents

INTRODUCTION

YOU DESERVE TO BE SELF-CONFIDENT

We all have our own idea of what confidence is. Confidence is often defined in terms of believing in something or trusting someone else. For example, "We had every confidence in the staff." That is not how it is defined in these essays.

Confidence here is defined as belief and trust in oneself. It is being comfortable in one's own skin and therefore equal to the tasks at hand. Confidence has nothing to do with feeling certain.

Nor does a confident person display superiority or preeminence in any way. On the contrary, the confident person recognizes his limitations, but is resolute in developing himself within those parameters. He knows that he may sometimes falter, prove less than equal to the task, but he will not get down on himself. Instead, he will learn from the situation and add it to the bank of his experience in moving forward.

Confidence is not something learned in a book, taking a course, attending a seminar, or following a set of rules. Confidence is a mindset, a state of mind.

Norman Vincent Peale published *"The Power of Positive Thinking"* (1952) after WWII, which was a collection of inspirational essays. It captured the mind of the time looking for a simple formula to regroup and go forward after the terrible trauma and sacrifice of that Great War.

Dr. Peale advised his readers in this self-help book that confidence can be attained by positive thinking through practice, training, and knowledge by talking to people. It was a rote agenda that fit the natural American inclination to optimistic thinking.

This rationale has survived despite a retinue of seemingly constant anxious and depressing issues. It is all right to see the glass half full, but it is equally all right to wonder about how to fill the other half of the glass. The confident person is dedicated to that quest.

Confidence cannot be taught. It can only be experienced. Confidence is the accumulative effect of learned experience. In chemistry, the valence of the atom determines the vigor with which atoms combine with other atoms of the opposite charge. The higher the valence the greater the activity.

Confidence mirrors this physical chemical phenomenon. To state it another way, the confident person embraces rather his anxieties rather than retreating from them. I learned this first hand as a chemical sales engineer making cold calls to prospects in the field. At first, I didn't want to make the calls. My hands would sweat, my temples would ache, and I was afraid I would stutter, embarrassing myself and looking stupid. But I had no choice. I had a young family to feed and I was a long way from my home roots. So you could say I had motivation.

Once I broke the ice, once I made that first call, and then the next, and the next after that, I learned an important lesson about confidence. My contacts were at first as nervous as I was, apprehensive that I was there to take advantage of them. We worked through this awkward stage by talking and listening, developing common ground, and getting to know each other. In the process, we found we were not buyer and seller adversaries, but partners attempting to some a problem.

It is natural for us to put up a shield of resistance as self-protection when we encounter a stranger no matter what the circumstances. Time and good intentions reduces the icy distance but not before encountering some combative resistance.

Remember others have to break through their own wall of distrust. The irony is that it becomes easier for us once we break through our own self-distrust. Once we establish self-trust, it is catching dissolving the distrust of others without a word.

Once I had that insight, I was on my way to self-confidence.

Confidence comes from feelings of well-being, a product of self-awareness and self-acceptance, not self-absorption. The mind, body, spirit are focused on giving, not getting. This is learned behavior through experience. It is where the unknown and unpredictable are encountered, where criticism and disappointment are endured, where surprise and failure are the ingredient of success.

Experience can build to confidence if we are willing to learn from every nuance of that involvement.

By nature, I am shy, introverted, reclusive and introspective. In the field, I found this not to be a handicap but an asset because I had a natural inclination to read people and the situation. Also, I was more comfortable listening than talking. I didn't understand it at the time but listening eases the discomfort of others by putting them in control giving them power over the situation.

By asking questions and directing the conversation to your purpose, you put yourself in control by not controlling the conversation. The traditional belief is that the extrovert makes the best salesperson, executive, public speaker, and leader. That has not been my experience.

Those happiest in the quiet of thought are apt to get inside words spoken, gestures made and protests expressed because they are listeners, not talkers; learners, not tellers. Perhaps that is why I started out to be a chemist. Soon after, I realized I did not think like a bench chemist and lacked the mechanical dexterity to set up experiments, but did have a conceptual sense.

The first challenge of self-confidence is self-discovery, that is, the personal struggle within. Confidence must first be felt before it can be leveraged to advantage. Since confidence is not a static measure, our confidence may fluctuate in the performance of our tasks or in our role relationships with others from day to day, but the intuitive experience that gave you that self-confident edge through self-discovery is always there, Like anything else, it has to be nurtured.

THE FISHER PARADIGM©™ & SELF-CONFIDENCE

This realization led to the *Fisher Paradigm©™* which is an intuitive diagnostic tool based on a simple formula: *the definition of a noun, which is of a person, place or thing.*

It can serve in any situation, but especially where there is a degree of uneasiness or tension. It is the prehensile reptilian brain being engaged.   The heart is racing, the mind close to panic. Our reptilian brain comes to the fore. It is a survival mechanism man has relied on throughout human history. It gives us instant insight into the situation with an ability to calibrate the discomfort and even the danger. Yes, our whole body and mind feels the situation. It involves thinking with our whole body, not just our mind. This means allowing ourselves to feel the situation instantly with that evaluating signaling how we should act.

This paradigm is divided into three separate dimensions:

- The personal or the person, which is described as the *Personality Profile.*

Personality is our acquired self. It is the learned behavior that sets us off from other people so that others can say, "Oh, that is

Jim Fisher," because that is how they see me acting. *Personality* is subject to change as circumstances change, and a person is apt to act differently in private than in public as we all wear masks, and these masks are part of our personality.

Personality involves the constant changing of these masks that we all wear. Moreover, our personality in private may differ again in public as the circumstances change or as our emotional state changes. The point is that personality is not static and our intuitive senses can detect fluctuations in ourselves and in others so that we may deal with them accordingly.

- *Place* takes on a territorial imperative in terms of our familiarity with a place and our comfort level. We carry a sense of place with us wherever we go. In popular parlance, we are apt to say we can move from New York City to Tampa, Florida but we carry our psychic baggage with us. That baggage, of course, is our personality.

If we are in a place of ease, our self-confidence, caring and carefreeness come to the fore. Conversely, if the place is not familiar and our ease level deserts us, our awareness is heightened and our reptilian brain comes into play. It calibrates the unease and danger level of the situation or simply our discomfort with the unfamiliar.

We know some people are comfortable wherever they go, never seeming to meet a stranger, then there are others who are uncomfortable wherever they are. This is a peculiar way is an index of our self-awareness and self-acceptance or lack of the same which are the necessary precursors to self-confidence. We will always have difficulty with self-confidence is we cannot find it within ourselves to be our own best friend.

Some people are never comfortable in their own skin no matter where they are or with whom they find themselves. *Place* is designated as the *Geographic Profile.*

In other words, we carry our personal baggage accompanies our geography. Our baggage includes our belief system along with our values, interests, and biases. *Place* is obvious in our speech patterns, syntax, semantics, use of words and comfort level with ideas.   It is also apparent nonverbally expressed in our countenance, demeanor, and our carriage. *Geographic Profile* is an index of our cultural DNA.

- Our *Demographic Profile* or things relate to our essence. Essence is our *real self*, or our gene pool. Essence cannot be changed or modified. Essence simply is. Essence determines whether we are short or tall, light or dark skin, intelligent or not. It is our genetic DNA.

We can change our personality but we cannot change our essence. We can deny it, mask it, or fabricate it, but we cannot change it. It is for this reason that it is our *Demographic Profile.* It is what we are but not necessarily who we are.

As permanent and fixed as our essence is, this can be misread especially by a strong and convincing personality. For example, we may assume someone is intelligent because he reads books, can quote authors impressively, and carries the patina of brilliance. Politicians use this device, so do academics, as do gurus and experts of every ilk.

One of the most intuitive lessons to learn about the *Demographic Profile* is that intelligence is not an I.Q. score. Intelligence is what it does. Measure the *Demographic Profile* in terms of the person's actual history, experience, and character and how he handles adversity and disappointment as well as success. The *Demographic Profile* is the report card we receive every day of our existence.

"It wasn't quick thinking; it was everything else!"

To give a quick glance of how the mind, body and soul reacts to a sense of danger, consider this example. I was making an organization development (OD) intervention in the Fairfax County Police Department, Fairfax, Virginia. A riot had broken out in Herndon in the African American section of that community after a white police officer shot and killed an unarmed black youth in a 7-Eleven store after an altercation.

When I interviewed plain clothed detectives about that incident, and asked sensitive questions, they would invariably adjust their shoulder holsters through their suit coats.

Later, I was invited by an Iowa government official to dinner and a play, who was in the Nation's capital on Iowa State business. He had earlier attended a seminar I had given in Kansas City and extended the invitation after learning that I was an Iowa native.

My hotel in Fairfax City was twelve miles from Washington, D.C.   A Fairfax County police officer provided my transportation. After the play, the police officer said he would pick me up about 1 a.m. I said, "No problem," as I am a walker.

Walking down Pennsylvania Avenue of the Nation's capital at this early hour, I thought of a U.S. Senator from Mississippi who had been stabbed and robbed and nearly died in this area. Three youths walking parallel to me on the other side of the street, several lanes comfortably separating us, brought this memory to the fore, but not yet with noticeable apprehension.

Two blocks later these youth raced ahead and crossed the street to my side and were jiving and kibitzing as I closed the distance between us. My prehensile antennae went up as my mind said, *this can't be happening!*

Somehow I reacted intuitively and continued to walk jauntily towards them. When I was two yards from them I adjusted my mock shoulder holster, as I had seen those plain clothes detectives do in my interviews, and said, "Little late, isn't it boys, going to be hard to get up for school."

The three faces froze, looked nervously at each other, then they allowed me to pass. When I was five yards past them, they said in unison, "There goes the fuzz," and laughed nervously.

When I told the Fairfax County police officer what had happened, he said simply, "I'll tell you one thing. You're one lucky bastard. That quick thinking may have saved your life."

It wasn't quick thinking. It was the *Fisher Paradigm*©™ that kicked in.

CONFIDENCE and SELF-ESTEEM

Confidence and self-esteem are not the same thing, although often erroneously linked as synonymous. Self-esteem is more the equivalent of self-respect. It is earned by doing something that in turn registers on the psyche with self-approval.

Confidence is developed through experience as a learner not a knower, as a listener and not a teller, as an observer and not an obtrusive evaluator.

Self-esteem is colored with the biases we hold for other people and can be quite disruptive if we are not self-aware. Simply put, self-esteem is how we feel about ourselves, or would like to give the impression we feel, and is therefore value intensive. We can have high self-esteem and low competence, or low self-esteem and high competence. Self-esteem and competence are not necessarily correlative. The point is to be weary of mixing the two.

This collection of essays endeavors to establish this fundamental premise: failure is as much a part of success as confidence is a product of experience. We all make mistakes; we all register failures; we do so because we are all human. If in our life's adventure, we flunk an academic course or flunk out of school; are fired from a job; are rejected by a loved one or find ourselves very much alone, we are on the cusp of being introduced to ourselves, perhaps for the first time. Chances are we have been on automatic pilot. It is time to focus and pay attention evaluating where are and how we got to this place and space, and what we plan to do about it, now. It is often when we hit bottom that the road less traveled to self-confidence is the road we are already on.

Every experience is a learning experience telling us something about ourselves and where we are and saying:

You are in the wrong place and space with the wrong people to realize your true potential. It is time to move on to where the culture and circumstances better fits your talent and temperament. It is telling you that the time is now.

Good luck in that endeavor and always be well,

James R. Fisher, Jr., Ph.D.

March 15, 2017

ONE

SELF-CONFIDENCE

MOST IMPORTANT SALE YOU'LL EVER MAKE!

"When young, we trust ourselves too much, and we trust others too little when we are old. Rashness is the error of youth; timid caution when old. Manhood is the isthmus between the two extremes, the ripe and fertile seas of action when, only, we can hope to find the head to contrive, united with the hand to execute."

Caleb Colton, Nineteenth Century English Clergyman

"Trust men and they will be true to you, treat them greatly and they will show themselves great."

Ralph Waldo Emerson, Nineteenth Century American poet and essayist

WHY MOST IMPORTANT SALE?

"With confidence, you can do anything your mind envisions." This is the opening lines of my first book, *Confident Selling* (1971). *"Confidence,"* I write, *"is the antidote to fear; fear rooted in self-ignorance. With self-understanding comes confidence followed by tolerance for our own false steps and*

failures. As we face down our fears, we rise above obstacles we once thought were utterly beyond our control."

Now, why would I say that? Why would I write about confidence, fear and control in the same paragraph? The simple reason is that I had learned:

- *If I thought it, the deed was already half done.*

This could be taken as arrogance to the extreme. There is a litany of reasons to discourage us from doing what our hearts and minds tell us we can do.

- *But you see that is the problem; people are afraid to believe in themselves.*

Therefore, they do not take that first step. They wait for approval from others. They wait for someone to push them over the line into action. They wait until the line becomes a wall. They hang out with people who say they are where they belong while envying those with the confidence to move on. They wait for confirmation that they are on the right track when they are not on any track at all.

- *You know who these people are. They hang out together.*

They are waiting for the right time to make a move. They are waiting until they have enough education, or money, or support, or love and affection to take the risk.

- *They wait until one day they run out of life.*

They are *the gonna be's* and the *gonna do's*, and are always going to do these things tomorrow. They never make it because they never made the most important sale in their lives, belief in themselves come hell or high water.

BUSINESS OF CONFIDENCE – GROUND FLOOR

Confidence often identifies with one's hero or some simpatico person. Reading is not only a gauge to explore the unknown but a window to knowing the self.

BUSINESS OF CONFIDENCE – IDENTITY

Someone may asked you, *"Who are you?"* Then before you have a chance to answer that someone asks another question, *"What are you?"*

It could be the questions of a parent, friend, wife or husband, boss or teammate. We sometimes not only confound ourselves but others with whom we seem to be. Identity is personal and is largely the product of what we do (our work), what we enjoy doing (our leisure), who we hang out with (our friends), what organizations we belong to and support (church, school, club), as if stenciled on our foreheads. Ask yourself these two questions: Who Am I? What am I? How you answer them will give you a sense of your comfort level with your identity.

BUSINESS OF CONFIDENCE: WHAT IS CONFIDENCE?

Confidence is not having a sense of superiority, or inferiority; confidence is being engaged.

- *Confidence is the ability to act to completion on something of value to you.*

Confidence is not about half measures, not about looking for approval, or reasons to succeed. Likewise, it is not about finding excuses to abort the chase or back down from the target.

- *Confidence is about commitment. Commitment involves involvement and involvement means you are already half way there so stay the course!*

It doesn't mean going to the "right schools," having the "right teachers," having the "right pedigree," working for the "right companies," or hanging out with the "right crowd." It can be all or none of these. They are incidental to the process. Nor is it about pursuing the favorite career-of-day because everyone says that is what you should do.

- *You know in your heart what you love to do, so do it with a vengeance!*

Confidence is being well acquainted with your own history, with your failures, successes, your false steps and disappointments, your surprises, your embarrassments, as well as your triumphs. Confidence is not mechanistic but a process of growth, a growth that never peaks, but may have several valleys.

- *Yes, one's confidence dips and vacillates, but that only strengthens your resolve.*

Confidence has a lot in common with moral courage rather than physical courage. I see young people today building up their muscles and flashing tattoos all over their bodies as billboards of personal identity when it is just the opposite. It is playing to the crowd identifying with the herd.

- *Confidence is quiet. It is engaged. It has no need for show, or need for kudos.*

That does not mean that confidence does not have a goal. Indeed, the confident person wants to make the sale:

The completion of his work to a satisfying degree; the completion of his dissertation to a Ph.D.; the winning of the love of his life; the finding of the job that he seeks; the successful launching of his children into life; the advancement to the position sought; the feeling of love and fulfillment in life.

There are many obstacles to these desires and they are primarily self-imposed because of the lack of confidence or the will to work through difficulties to their full realization.

Bullies can discourage people from continuing to pursue these goals, bullies from the outside or bullies from the inside; bullies disguised as friends or advisers.

BUSINESS OF CONFIDENCE: BULLIES FROM INSIDE AND OUTSIDE

- *"To have a friend you must be a friend starting with yourself."*

We are more inclined to trust secondary sources, including the views of friends and family more than our own counsel. We allow ourselves to be bullied by others. We think of a bully as the neighborhood tough in which everyone cowers. We outgrow that tough during our early years. But we face bullies in the system every step of the way throughout life.

You meet them in teachers and preachers at school and church, in employers and colleagues at work, in pundits and politicians on the tube, in newspapers, magazines and television news, in psychiatrists, psychologists, family physicians and friends who claim to be in the know on what is best for you. It this becomes your quintessential self, then you are owned by them, and a stranger to yourself.

- *When confidence is compromised, there is no chance for the authentic self.*

Many of these secondary sources may mean you no harm, but they are not you, and they are not privy to the length and breadth of your experience. We are also bullied in the military as anyone knows who has gone through basic or boot training in the US Army or the US Navy, the Marine Corps or the US Coastguard.

Strangely, this kind of bullying can put you in touch with yourself. Some never before experienced the discipline that is fundamental to a military experience. Many have found themselves not only realizing greater maturity but better self-understanding. In the military, you are treated fairly and consistently in the protocol of what it means to be a fighting man.

There are no bullies that equal academic bullies, as they have little power and prestige other than the grade or possibly withholding the degree at their discretion.
Mean spirited academics want to break your will, and make you grovel at their feet, if they feel you are the sort that they despise or simply dislike. Consequently, there are many "all but the dissertation" (ABDs), having completed the course work to a doctorate but unable to have their committee accept their final paper.

They have the power over you that you have willingly given them. Once you surrender your power, the expectation is that they will treat you with kindness and caring; that they will be supportive and appreciative of your interests; that they will be fair and considerate goes out the window.

- *Unfortunately, power corrupts and absolute power corrupts absolutely.*

Too frequently, those in charge in the workplace exploit this power, control and authority advantage with reckless abandon. For the attention, we have the world that we have today.

- *A factory mentality of academia and industry has no place in the 21st Century.*

Our only hope is to have the courage to take charge and map out an agenda consistent with our intuitive strength and the natural guidance system of our internal moral compass. Should we do that, not only will we be more engaged and happy, but everyone else around us will be engaged with the same synchrony. *Confident Thinking* (2014) concludes with this suggestion:

It is a time when we can no longer depend on others to decipher the road maps of our mind. Our mind has become homeless. That mind, Milton reminds us, is its own place, and in itself can make a heaven of hell, or a hell of heaven. The choice is ours to make. May you make that connection and soar to grace, greatness and fulfillment."

TWO

WHO IS IN CHARGE?

You want to be happy, to forget yourself, and yet the more you try to forget yourself, the more you remember the self you want to forget. You want to escape pain, but the more you struggle to escape pain, the more you inflame the agony. You are afraid and want to be brave, but the effort to be brave is fearing trying to run away from itself. You want peace of mind, but the attempt to pacify it is like trying to calm the waves with a flat iron.

We know that worry is futile, but we go on doing it because calling it futile does not stop it. We worry because we feel unsafe, and want to be safe. What we have to discover is that there is no safety, that seeking it is painful, and that when we imagine we have found it, we don't like it.

There is no safety or security. One of the worst vicious circles is the problem of the alcoholic. In very many cases, he knows quite clearly that he is destroying himself, that for him liquor is poison, that he actually hates being drunk, and even dislikes the taste of liquor. It gives him the "horrors," for he stands face to face with the unveiled basic insecurity of the world.

Alan W. Watts, *The Wisdom of Insecurity: A Message for an Age of Anxiety* (1951)

We all know the nursery rhyme of Humpty Dumpty sitting on, and falling off the wall, *"and all the kings horses and all the king's men couldn't put Humpty Dumpy together again."*

Whether we admit it or not, we are all broken, split apart in some fashion with our head separated from our body, while being driven by fear, and in the cage of memory. The contemporary mind has been haunted by the feeling that in some mysterious way the one struggling for security is nearer to hell than heaven, that the mazes of self-deception, and self-mockery hide behind the masks that we assume.

St. Augustine has something to say about this split-mindedness:

The past is not dead, it is not even past . . . we cannot properly say that the future or the past exists, or that there are three times, past, present, and future. Perhaps we can say that there are three tenses, but that they are the present of the past, the present of the present, and the present of the future. This would correspond, in some sense, with a triad I find in the soul and nowhere else, where the past is present to memory, the present is present to observation, and the future is present to anticipation.

NO ONE PROMISED YOU A LIVING! NO ONE OWES YOU A JOB!

In an uncertain world, where job security is vital to our self-interests, we often do all the wrong things to put ourselves back together again. Instead of taking calm inventory of our situation, we panic or become traumatized when made redundant; when our place of work closes; when the skills we have that once were in demand are no longer; when we are asked to take a 10 percent cut in wages and benefits for the company's survival; and are barely making ends meet as matters now stand. How could this happen when we've done nothing wrong? Turns out we've done a lot wrong, starting with waiting for someone to rescue us from our predicament and ourselves.

Author Alan W. Watts sees such circumstances consumed with anxiety looking at nature backwards:

When we try to stay on the surface of the water, we sink; but when we try to sink we float; likewise, when we try desperately to save our job we lose it.

Insecurity, he maintains, is the result of trying to be secure in a topsy-turvy world in which the normal order of things seems completely out of order. Everything is turned inside out and upside down. Suddenly, circumstances have forced us to be in charge of our lives and no one has prepared us for that ordeal, leastwise ourselves.

We think we live in a time of unusual insecurity. This is not the case at all. In the past hundred years, or throughout the past twentieth century, long established traditions have broken down continuously: the traditional family, social life, government, economic order, religious beliefs, values, ethics, and most notable of all, morality.

We have seen society stagger out of the *Industrial Age* only to be caught in a breathless dance in the *Information Age*, as manufacturing assembly lines have become a shadow of that former benchmark. The assembly line was the early watershed moment of the twentieth century. It created mindless jobs requiring little or no skills, while giving birth to the working middle class.

For the first time in history, working men and women in mass could afford to purchase homes and company automobiles at a discount and live in comfortable circumstances, conditions working people never before dreamed of experiencing.

Then in the late twentieth century information technology spirited the working middle class away from the comfortable status of *Machine Age Thinking.* This found robotics increasingly replacing assembly line workers, while now most jobs required quick minds and agile fingers to master computer keyboards as work was being transformed from brawn to brains, obliterating the blue-collar working class.

There is no longer any certainty if certainty ever existed. Yet, certainty remains a myth perpetuated by a society deep in denial. Academic, political, religious and commercial institutions have denied this reality by failing to pay attention. Workers denied it by failing to learn new skills. Companies denied it by failing to press for change as the workforce was being transformed from 80 percent blue-collar to 80 percent college trained white collar.

Elementary and secondary schools as well as universities continued to teach curriculums locked into 1945. Even as private and public workplaces continued to be managed as if the color of the workers' collars had not changed. If blame is the game, there is more than enough to go around, but that doesn't get us off the dime.

That said for far too long the majority were willing to put up with lives largely doing jobs that were boring and inconsequential, content in earning the means to seek relief from the tedium with periodic respites of drinking and partying in expensive pleasure, or going on shopping sprees with reckless abandon. Saving for a rainy day was not in the specifications.

People were drunk with optimism seeing the weather ahead full of sunshine and promise with no dark clouds. To suggest otherwise would be to be branded a pessimist or "negative thinker." As a consequence, neither workers nor employers were looking ahead. It wasn't anybody's job!

We often refer to assembly line blue-collar working jobs as boring. Nothing can compare to the boredom of managers and administrators who spend 50 to 75 percent of their working day in inconsequential meetings. These meetings take away from meaningful work, and consistently have no purpose other than that the meetings were routinely scheduled. Meeting for meeting's sake is a corporate disease that has been institutionalized to produce a report that few are likely to ever read.

A survey of a monthly sales report went out to affiliates and manufacturing facilities in 13 countries involving some 14,000 employees. When asked, first, if they were aware of the report, second, if they had read it, and third, if it was useful, most confessed that they didn't even know the report existed. Yet, several people spent a good deal of time each month preparing this report. Further inquiries found that the report was redundant as all the information was now accessible electronically.

Speaking of redundancy, consider the performance appraisal process. This process is designed to bring managers and workers together to assess performance and create a developmental roadmap for workers to build on their assets and manage their liabilities. Any organization has 15 percent hard chargers, who manage themselves, 70 percent followers who are management dependent, and 15 percent who are foot draggers, or essentially beyond salvation.

In this one instance, a facility of some 4,000 professional workers and 350 managers dedicated several hundred hours to the performance appraisal process. Six workers were found to be declining in rating, and four were designated to need improvement. All others received automatic merit increases.

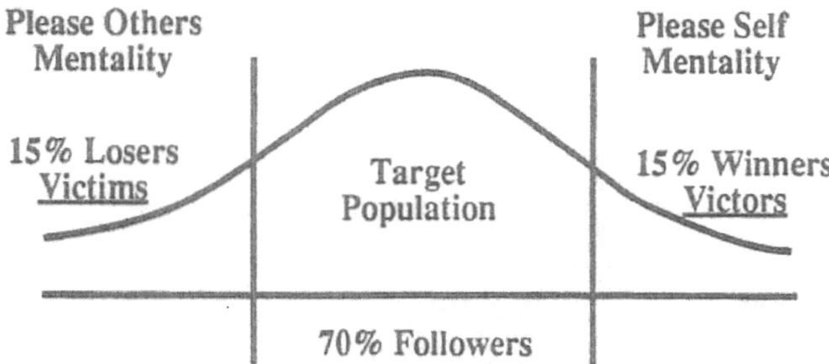

- Winners will contribute regardless of management style.

- Followers will move in the direction of the dominant culture.

- Losers will seldom contribute no matter what the style or culture.

Given the normal bell curve breakdown of the working population, at least some 600, or 15 percent of the workforce should been considered possible poor performers and treated accordingly. This is another indication of the company lock stepping to a routine that is counterproductive with the company taking two steps backward for every step forward.[1]

Performance appraisal did these workers no favors. That company is only a shadow of its former self today. Hundreds of these workers, once well paid and comfortably employed in what were supposed to be lifetime employment jobs, are now out of work. Unfortunate, this is a promise no company can guarantee or should. At best, what a company can do is pay a worker what he is contracted to do.

In an ideal world, these workers – engineers, administrators and managers – would have acknowledged this and taken charge of their situation. Unfortunately, they had no incentive to do so. Poor as they might perform they had job security and their income was not in jeopardy. In many cases, 20 percent of the workforce was doing 80 percent of the productive work, yet there were no protests from these contributors. Nobody wants to make waves when the tsunami has not yet hit the shore.

Alas, we don't live in an ideal world. Workers have come to be dependent on the company to do for them what they would not do for themselves. When the company fails, workers derive satisfaction accusing the company of failing in its function, unwilling to see their tacit complicity in the act.

When a company is struggling, and needs the full support and cooperation of its workers, often management keeps this fact from the workers, or the workers misread management's reluctance to share this information, become moody, call in sick, or go on strike on the job by engaging in counterproductive passive behaviors, cutting off the hand that literally feeds them.2

In the 1950s, after World War II, General Motors' blue-collar workers earned as much as many practicing physicians in the medical field. I was often a guest in their Detroit homes, and played baseball with their kids during my summer visits.

In many households, both parents worked for GM, Ford or Chrysler, and spent as much as they made. It was evident in their fine brick homes and new automobiles in their driveways. Their children expected to follow their parents working for the "Big Three" right out of high school with no break in the continuum.

Then came the late 1960s. The Rising Sun of Japan entered the automotive market and cut deeply into these automakers' customer base and profits, producing better, cheaper and smaller automobiles. Tom Brokaw delivered an NBC television "white paper" on June 24, 1980 with the resounding lament, *"Japan Can! Why Can't We?"*

Japan was using American technology that American manufacturers scoffed at as being too costly, too time consuming, and not necessary.3 What was the technology? It was statistical quality control, involving production workers in decision-making teams, where they were asked to identify and solve chronic work related problems.

Detroit's automotive hemorrhaging, fifty years later, has still not stopped despite now using these quality control tools. The auto industry's workers and managers could not escape the controlling mindset of 1945 management nostalgia when it could do nothing wrong. In 2008 with the near total collapse of the United States economy, and with it much of the Western world, GM and Chrysler had to be "bailed out" by the federal government with the rationale "they were too big to fail." It is now 2017 and there is little evidence that much has been learned from this meltdown.

Brett Farve, former NFL quarterback for the Green Bay Packer, has it about right: *We get paid for practicing all week, playing on Sunday should be for free.*

Yet, one of the main complaints of professional athletes is the reverse of this: they hate practice, don't think they need it, and believe they get paid for Sunday's performance only. Many workers in other professions display this same attitude. They acquire a quality degree that they think speaks for itself: "Why do we have to take orders from someone less qualified than we are?"

They don't want a job; they want a position with an automatic pass to a satisfying career. After all, they reason, why else would we dedicate four, six or eight years to a university education? The reality is that is the wrong question.

A CASE IN POINT!

A survey was conducted of 1,000 engineers in a high tech company. The demographic profile revealed staggering results. Of the engineering population: 72 percent were over 35; 50

percent over 45; and 15 percent over 55. Fully 60 percent were working on technology developed long after they had left university. Despite this technical gap, they were doing little if anything to upgrade their skills.

Complicating the picture, it was evident that job performance decreased precipitously as job complexity increased for veteran engineers. Yet, their salaries continued to increase. At age 45, salaries for veterans peaked reaching a plateau with no noticeable decline for the balance of their careers. This represented, in some cases, a $20,000 differential with neophyte engineers, many of whom had advanced engineering degrees with state-of-the-art technical acumen.

Concomitantly, engineers ages 21 to 39 represented a spiraling upward linear curve of increasing job performance and job complexity, but modest salaries compared to veterans. In an environment dedicated to the gospel "pay for performance," they clearly weren't.

What did they do about it? They complained among themselves, or retreated into the *"six silent killers"* of passive behaviors.[4] In a word, they took no initiative or action to redress the issue. They were being paid a dollar more an hour than they felt they could afford to rock the boat or quit.

- Engineers choose an engineering education because they have talent for and an interest in solving technical problems.

- Research indicates that this gives engineers only a 3 to 5 year window of competence before their technical talent starts to erode if they are not exposed to a significant continuing education program.

- The burden in the past has rested on engineers for continuing engineering education, which is another way of saying it is not likely to have been initiated.

- Engineers who have become key contributors to long-term programs are often protected from more diverse experience and therefore suffer greatly when programs reach completion, or assume the next iteration in sophistication. They are likely ill prepared to take on new engineering assignments.

- Engineers, who cannot contribute meaningfully, may become anxious, frustrated, angry, hostile, passive, and eventually alienated from work and their associates, exhibiting the tendency to coast and drift into apathy.

- Engineers, once realizing they can't keep up, may also show initiative by going back to school, asking for specialized training, attempting to find on-the-job mentors, or going to another company. This is more the exception than the rule.

Confrontation, managing conflict, indeed, interpersonal relations are not high on the list of preferred activities of engineers. The social content of the job is the least appealing to many engineers.

By creating an assessment center process, and then sharing the results with management, it was possible to convince management of a need, which resulted in the inauguration of a comprehensive *Continuing Technical Education Program.*

Management initially pledged $1 million for this program, which has grown in sophistication to where technicians can now earn their engineering degree in cooperation with the University of South Florida's School of Engineering, while attending engineering classes and laboratories at work. This is possible because many engineers have advanced engineering degrees.

Meanwhile, veteran engineers continue to upgrade their skills concurrent with new technologies. Once the seed was planted, engineers took control of the technical education program with a rotating engineering chair providing its continuity and enhancement. This was accomplished with no interference from management. Engineers now owned the program and the process.[5]

THE NEW REALITY: Self-Confidence is Self-Directed!

A job is a sacred trust between employee and employer. It is a contract, a bond. We have moved into a climate where workers must exercise more control over the process than ever before. For far too long employment in most cases was to be other directed, that is, reactive to management's instruction; depending on the company to take care of you as your second home. The result has been for workers to devolve into *learned helplessness* dependent on management and counter dependent on the company for their well-being. This has suspended most workers in terminal adolescence, a luxury no company can any longer afford.

Opportunities are limited only by our perceptions of their horizons. Prudent workers in this new climate of self-dependency will make the appropriate assessments of where they are, who they are, what they do well (strengths) and where they need help (weaknesses) and seek to exploit their strengths and to assess what they need to do to work on their weaknesses.

Self-directed individuals will create their own career roadmap, not wait for management to create one for them. Likewise, they will seek out mentors and exploit the opportunities available. They won't wait for opportunities to present themselves, but will create them by taking the initiative. They will study their jobs as owners, not renters, and assume the role of leadership of their function.

They won't waste energy or time campaigning for the next position at the expense of what they are being paid to do. Nor will they spend countless hours chatting on the Internet or cell phones, texting or tweeting, entertaining themselves when they should be working. They won't bad mouth colleagues or the company as they are too busy bringing new life into their function.

They won't look for fantasy jobs beyond their recognized limits. Fantasy jobs are positions in which they have no stomach for the pain, frustration, commitment, sacrifice, or risks involved to realize the return. Boring as their present job might appear to some, it is stimulating to them as they are learners, not tellers; listeners, not tellers; students of what they do, not complainers.

In this new reality, some see others less able prospering because they are less afraid to venture outside the box and embrace the unknown. They are not only students of what they do, but find ways to complement the skills of associates so that they might be equally successful. They look for opportunities to make the company stronger without fanfare.

They are not on the make but on the making. They are systemic thinkers consistent with Russell Ackoff observations:

If you take a system apart to identify its components, and then operate those components in such a way that every component behaves as well as it possibly can, there is one thing of which you can be sure. The system as a whole will not behave as well as it can. Now that is counterintuitive to Machine Age thinking, but it is absolutely essential to system thinking. The corollary to this is that if you have a system that is behaving as well as it can, none of its parts will be.[6]

If this describes you, and your approach to work, there is no reason to worry. Should the company be forced to downsize or relocate, it would find a place for you; if not with that company certainly with another. You are poised to look at opportunities in your industry because the misfortune of one is likely to lead to the good fortune of another.

This new reality forces many companies to make hard choices. Some workers critical of the company's relocating plans refuse to admit they wouldn't move under any circumstances. They insist on the company providing security for them when the company is in a survival mode teetering on bankruptcy. Not to worry, these workers expect to be treated from birth to death by the company as surrogate parent to meet their economic and emotional requirements at any cost, reality be damned!

This is not to make light of the fact that many lives have been disrupted if not destroyed by plant closings. By the accident of their birth, workers today have come of age in a transitional and transforming period when the definition of work itself is in a state of change; when a place of employment is no longer an assumed fixed place; when brains are much more in demand than brawn; when the role of worker and manager are in flux; when working hard has been replaced by working smart; when a manufacturing based economy has been eclipsed by a service based economy; when information technology disrupts provincial stability with global fluidity.

It was bound to happen. It just happened during your working years. Now, you must deal with it, or it will deal with you.

Much criticism has been directed at companies such as Walmart and others who have forced their suppliers to manufacture their finished products in China and India. The downside is that it takes away jobs in the United States. The upside is that it produces cheap consumer goods that the less fortunate can afford to purchase. It is an old cliché, but the world is in fact getting smaller and more interdependent. In time, as the standard of living of third world countries improve, somewhere down the road equilibrium will be reached. Then cheap labor will not be the bargaining chip that it is today.

That trend has started and is gaining momentum. The dominance of the West is now being challenged by the emerging economic powers of the East. The days of the fictive belief in the economic and political dominance of one nation over others seems to be in the twilight. The combination of technology and population growth is forcing yet another reality on workers. The onus is on them to be contract consultants and their own agents in a most competitive, but opportunistic marketplace, where it will be necessary to hone workers' skills and match them to the demands of that marketplace. Here is one story.

NOT FOR EVERYONE!

When he was a boy, he discovered he was dyslexic. School was difficult for him, and he had to work harder than most to earn average grades. The problem wasn't any less difficult in high school, as schoolwork remained a challenge. He met it with every ounce of energy he could muster without complaint. Some thought college was too high a hill for him to climb, but he persisted, and graduated with a B.S. degree in Criminal Justice from Michigan State University.

His first job out of school was as a police officer in Tampa, Florida. That soon appeared a dead end as he could see seniority controlled his destiny. So, he went back to school at the University of South Florida, and earned an MS degree in Criminal Justice. He continued to be a police officer, gradually separating himself from it to become an assistant professor in Criminal Justice at the university.

As a professor, he met a number of rising legal minds in the community. This sparked his interest in the law. He took to studying law at night school. Reading was always a challenge, now it was the main requirement as law school meant reading scores of books. Undaunted, he persevered and graduated with a law degree, and promptly committed himself to taking the bar examination. He studied so hard that he lost weight, but it paid off, as he passed it on his first try.

Everything changed. He became a junior lawyer of a law firm in which much of the work was pro bono or handling cases others took a pass on. By nature kind and generous, unassuming and even humble, he noticed that in his new work environment that there was a distinct pecking order, which included preferred billing hours, client exploitation, and amoral arrogance. He remained stoic, as unhappy as he was, and refused to complain. Instead, he studied diligently for his Doctor's in Jurisprudence, which he again passed on his first try. At this point, he changed law firms.

The new law firm was more of the same. Only here the partners were treated like royalty, or as "crown princes or princesses." They talked about him behind his back because he didn't spend the hours billing as they did. What's more, to their chagrin, he didn't seem to feel guilty about it. He couldn't see billing clients excessively because you could, feeling this was as good as fraud. So, he moved on again, this time opening his own law firm.

He invited more than one hundred lawyers and former clients and friends to celebrate the new opening but only a handful showed up. It had to hurt, but he said nothing, going about his business working as hard as ever to make a go of it. The firm prospered.

Fortunately, years earlier, he had purchased five acres of prime real estate on Thonotosassa Lake, in Hillsborough County, Florida, which had a large house, and a smaller one on the property. He moved into the larger one and rented out the smaller one.

The economy changed and with it his law firm's fortunes. Business deteriorated and then things got so desperate that he had to split his property down the middle and sell half. He also sold the little house on his side of the five-acre split. This kept him solvent, but barely so. Not dissuaded, he was still not through pushing the envelope.

He decided to create an entertainment center in Ybor City, Tampa, Florida, a Cuban community of historic significance modeled after the French Quarters in New Orleans. Never a timid spender on projects, he brought in a cadre of entertainers and investors from St. Louis. They seemed interested until it was clear there were no guarantees. He scuttled that project, and looked about for another. None were on the horizon so instead he bought an office building, renovated it, and then rented a good share of it out to small businesses, while keeping his law practice afloat.

Some twenty years ago, he married a model and now has a family of two children, a boy and a girl, both are in college. A family is what he always wanted, as his parents and brother had died, and only a sister was left.

It was during this period that he met a number of entrepreneurs who were restless for a project, but lacked the capital to seed it. He had the capital. Starting on a small scale, and paying his partners and his small staff out of his pocket, he operated the business like this for several months, nearly to the point of going broke again.

Then, with his partners, he created a website and the business took off. It grew every week. More people were brought on staff. Additional expertise was needed, so he sold part of his interest, bringing in another partner, still remaining the majority stockholder. His generosity continued. Operations were opened in other locations, and they took off as well. But again, his generosity and over optimism came crashing down on him as the economy changed and so did regulations.

During his affluent days, he designed an estate on his property of eye catching delight. He had sold his little house, and now had to buy it back at twice what he paid for it, and did this without complaint or regret. The new estate was in the Miami style with a two story white alabaster house with twenty foot windows overlooking the lake with a French stucco patio, an entertainment center, a gymnasium, and bar, a winding marble staircase, the floors a combination of marble and carpeting, a large contemporary kitchen, ornate fireplace, and enough original artwork to fill a gallery, gated with a quarter mile landscaped serpentine driveway with fountains and dolphin sculptures snaking along the way, a tennis court and swimming pool, three car attached garage, and a separate four car garage for his automobile collection, which included an auto workshop. He had a pier built on the lake with a cover boat hangar for his boat, and two wave runners, and other toys of a man with the disposable income to recapture his youth at age, fifty.

He is now sixty five, and was set back again even prior to 2007 – 2008 economic meltdown as were many others, and has never regained his momentum. But his optimism has not faded. Nor has his fondness for taking risks or looking for new opportunities. He opened a new business in 2014, and with the same enthusiasm and élan that is part of his DNA.

He could be described as a visualizing investment capitalist for he has been doing what many dream of doing, but never find the courage. It could also be said that given his propensity to design his own estate without the expertise to do it right indicates more of a capacity to do it on the cheap with a kind of arrogance that he has knowhow when clearly he doesn't. Moreover, his capacity to absorb failure and defeat philosophically and move on, while seemingly admirable in one sense seems quite the contrary in another sense.

Self-Confidence is displayed in having a moral center and an internal guidance system that when violated by others in any demonstrable way results in a counter reaction as indicative of that person's dignity.

Two questions come to the fore: who are you; what are you? The estate of this man's own design has aged as he has aged with the visual weariness of his optimistic perspective. While seemingly being self-directed, he has clearly been neither self-aware nor self-accepting, holding to dreams other people might envy. This is like building sand castle in the air, an odyssey where there is no real sense of what he would really like to do, or who he would like to be as his actions indicate more of a need to please others than to please himself.

Envy may be defined as wanting what other people have; jealousy fearing what you already have but fear of losing. In a peculiar way, this man seems to be driven by both.

Contrast his bumpy ride through life with other people who never metaphorically ever get out of bed. He is a handsome powerfully built man, but never shows anger, a man more generous than anyone you have ever met, and a man who frustrates others with that generosity because he feels compelled to buy allegiance and support and camaraderie which while not being characteristically healthy is never sustainable.

A conflicting sense of this impressive generosity is also evident as he is a notoriously poor tipper to waiters and waitresses in restaurants who live on customer generosity. Now, why do you believe that this is so?

He is a family man in the truest sense of the word, and has a beautiful wife and two adoring children. But he frustrates them, too, because he is not into work as work is defined; is not into security as it is defined; and certainly is not into a logical, consistent, rational approach to making a living as some would expect from him.

My sense is that he was burned out on work early in life, working at his father's automobile dealership after school and of a Saturday for hours washing and polishing cars, leaving little time to play sports or just hang out with other friends.

Parents can stimulate or kill our appetites for life in many different ways. I suspect this was what killed his work ethic as we know work. Again, he is a man who would never utter a negative word about his parents, or the ordeal he has suffered at their hands. It is not his nature. Yet, it is important to understand what motivates and demotivates us in everyday life. Our parents were not saints but struggling to get beyond the scars they absorbed from their own youths. This is not to castigate or cast aspersions, but to understand. Self-Confidence is impossible without this understanding.

Should you see him on the street, chances are he'll be in a polyester warm-up suit, or an open polo shirt and stone-colored Timber Creek Wranglers and loafers or sandals. He seldom is seen in a coat and tie, although when forced to wear a suit he does so reluctantly for it is clear that such attire is terribly uncomfortable.

He once belonged to a fashionable country club but didn't play golf where he was known to swim a hundred laps at the club's Olympic sized pool for warm-up to a workout with his body builder physique without the necessity of steroids.

One day he overheard say to another about him: "Why doesn't he work like the rest of us? It's not fair." He heard but said nothing. Whatever he might have said would be uncharacteristic of him and then if he had said anything it wouldn't have made any difference.

How do you explain someone who has overcome mountains of difficulty, and only creates new mountains of difficulty, seemingly in a never ending drive to what, no one knows?

Few of us have the courage or the appetite much less the energy required for such a life on the edge. Most people want to play it safe and dream of winning the Lotto. They don't think of creating their own wealth, or heaven forbid, once earned, to put it into immediate jeopardy as has this man.

The irony, and paradox if you will, is his quest is for money when money is not that important to him. What he wanted, achieved, then lost more than once, was to be master of his own time. When he was enjoying a seven figure income, he could have invested, but he didn't. He is a man of modest appetites but a profligate spender seemingly clueless as to his own motivation. Could it be for that the reason he didn't invest because those that do think constantly of little else than money? Interestingly enough, he is often broke and nearly always deeply in debt but doesn't seem to lose a step or any sleep over the fact. He is the antithesis of self-confidence because he is not charge of his life or himself yet I suspect many reading this might envy him.

THE WISDOM OF INSECURITY

Alan W. Watts explains insecurity as a given that we best accept. Once we do, he insists, we miraculously overcome insecurity anxiety. We are able to act and do, to be and take the initiative, to take control. Insecurity, Watts discovered, is a mania for control of things we cannot control at the expense of the things we can, but don't.

Control all starts with recognizing the only person, circumstance, situation, or predicament that we can change, if we but find the will to do so, is ourselves. No other. None. Nada.

Many of us are waiting; waiting for the boss to change; waiting to be promoted; or waiting to retire. We think others are the problem. Absent our nemesis, we think, our anxiety will vanish. Our waiting never ends, because we cannot allow ourselves to realize it could be "me" that is the problem.

We attempt to escape through pleasure only to find it kills what we love. We delight in music, in its rhythm and flow, but should a note or cord be held beyond the flow, the rhythm destroyed, and so would be our comfort. But the discordant sound is part of the rhythm, the atonality of life.

We want certainty when life is full of dissonant music. Our anxiety is not new. Read *"The Confession of St. Augustine"* (397 A.D.), the Bishop of Hippo, a man who straddled the fourth and fifth centuries, and you hear your own mind spinning while you straddle the 20th and 21st century:

I am toppled back to earth, weighted with heavy burdens, plunged into compelled ways, netted, wailing strongly but strongly netted still. So great is compulsion's heavy baggage. Here I can abide but do not wish to; there, I wish to abide but cannot – miserable either way.[7]

How many of us have been in this state of mind when our careers have gone awry; when an expected raise or promotion did not occur; when out of the blue we were made redundant, or shockingly surprised to be fired; when we thought our job was secure, and our contribution appreciated and were instead given a pink slip; when our world crashed and burned and we thought we had finally realized security?

Those experiencing the greatest difficulty adjusting to new circumstances live in the illusory world of false expectations, not the reality of the times.

This is most troubling for workers who live only to make money. They are forever worrying about losing their jobs, and frequently do. Instead of earning a living, they are living an earning, and thus when the time comes to relax they are unable to do so. They are likely to be bored and miserable when they retire, because all they know is work and making money. They think nothing of returning to work and taking a position away from a younger person. Their whole identity is work. Their essence is tied to making money.

The sad irony is that many have more money than they could ever spend the rest of their lives. Money isn't the point, they say, but they have made it so. They are a machine that has no other function than to make money when they no longer need to make a living. There is no one to master or to be mastered, no one to rule or to surrender to.

The purpose of life is what we do. When what we value is only money, we are bound to live in misery when money no longer has a purpose. Watts sees such people caught in their own honey:

It is as if we were divided into two parts. On the one hand there is the conscious "I," at once intrigued and baffled, the creature who is caught in the trap. On the other hand there is "me," and "me" is a part of nature, the wayward flesh with all its concurrently beautiful and frustrating limitations. "I" fancies itself as a reasonable fellow, and is forever criticizing "me" for its perversity – for having passions, which get "I" into trouble, for being so easily subject to painful and irritating diseases, for having organs that wear out, and for having appetites, which can never be satisfied.[8]

The wisdom of insecurity is that truth, life, change, movement, and beauty are many names for the same thing. The rhythm of life in all its uncertainty produces its own music and makes all things lovable.

Life and death, career and retirement, security and insecurity are all simply ways of looking at the same thing through different eyes. We are at once all builders and destroyers, growing and dying, reaching high and low notes, all in the rhythm of life. I could not write these words if I had not known pain and loneliness, love and wonder, failure and success, pride and humiliation, science and religion.

It is difficult to realize job security when we compartmentalize work from life, and life from work; when we drive a wedge between the head and the heart; between thinking and feeling; when science, which covers the empirical realm of what is (fact) and why does it work that way (theory) is separated from religion, which questions the ultimate meaning and moral imperatives of why we are here; when pain and pleasure are on a collision course instead of being treated as normal fare.

It may sound absurd but the highest pleasure is to be unconscious of one's own existence, to be absorbed in interesting sights, sounds, places, and people; to be lost in life. In that mindset, there are no thoughts of what's in it for me, no concerns about carrying other people's load, and no worry about getting credit for this or that.

On the other hand, one of the greatest pains is to be self-conscious, to be constantly worrying about what other people think of us, and thus to be totally oblivious to the richness of life found through self-involvement in the greater community.

If we are obsessed with security, traumatized with the possibility of losing our job, then we are back to Humpty Dumpty, suffering split-mindedness between "me" (self-demands) and "I" (role demands); between the job at hand and anxiety concerning that function.

If I am afraid of losing my job, my efforts to feel and act bravely in the face of that possibility are moved by fear, for I am afraid of fear. That is to say my efforts to escape from my insecurity drive me deeper into it moving me into the vicious circle of collapsing possibilities, compressing my perspective, shrinking my options, and giving me a blinding headache. I know because I've been there. Unless we break this cycle it can surely become a self-fulfilling prophecy.

CREATING JOB SECURITY IN AN UNCERTAIN WORLD

You can no longer expect to place your faith in a company. Companies are struggling against the most competitive odds to stay afloat in a shrinking world. You must rouse yourself from this fixation and take charge of your work, which is the only way to take charge of your life.

You can do this by creating your own job security by taking small steps. These are some that might be considered:

- *Embrace the reality of your situation.*

It no longer is enough to do your job, to put in your time and let management worry about the health of the company. You are the company! Without you, there is no company. Managers and workers are the arms and legs, brains and backbone of the same body. Nothing of sustaining value happens unless this body works together and moves in the same direction. There is no point in complaining. Ask yourself: why am I frustrated? What can I do about it? Needy people need not apply.

- *Pay attention to what is going on beyond the rhetoric and rah rah!*

Long before a company is in crisis, there are indicators that something is awry. New competitors are on the horizon, orders fall off, quotas aren't met, and schedules are late. It suddenly gets very quiet. Some of the hard chargers resign.

The rumor mill goes into high gear. Workers who pay attention know when the workplace culture gets a cold. It is not enough to generate feedback, but to take personal action. You don't wait for management to resurrect a survival strategy, or for the workplace to develop pneumonia. You create innovations in your own function. Once this momentum starts on a personal level, it flows out in concentric rings touching all operations, and then miracles do sometimes occur. But it starts with attention and proceeds directly to action on a personal basis.

- *Organize your work and work your organization.*

Transparency is "in," as the vertical organization collapses into horizontal teams, where managers and workers are on the same page. Transparency is also in as the boundaries between disciplines blur and specialists promote user-friendly tools for all.

At the same time, and this is new, workers and managers have more discretionary control of what they do than ever before. The problem is not that this power suddenly exists. The problem is that it has always been there, but few have taken advantage of this fact, first by using it, and second, by using it effectively. Functions and disciplines have complementary relationships, but to benefit from them requires creative initiative. Put another way, it means asking for help when it is required.

- *Promote the mature adult in your personality and take action.*

The purpose of a company is what it does. The function of your job is what you do. The company's mission and your function must be clear, understood and mutually supportive. If they are not, it is your responsibility to make your case politely and as often as necessary, instead of infrequently and violently.

The company is a human group made up of conflicting, contradictory and sometimes colliding issues, all of which can be resolved with mature adult dialogue. *Managed conflict* is actually the glue that holds the company to its task, not harmony. A company that works hard to create the myth of harmony is a company in trouble. Confusion is bound to occur periodically; failure is parent to success; and sustained success is endemic to a *Culture of Contribution* where problems are never denied but worked through and out.[9]

Shakespeare has Macbeth saying: *And you all know, security is mortals' chiefest enemy.*

It continues to be so, but need not, especially in work if we recognize the wisdom of insecurity, and embrace its possibilities. All problems contain their own solution, and the highest happiness is found in our awareness that impermanence and insecurity are inescapable and inseparable from life and work.

There is a new movement afoot. Maturity is gripping the workforce despite all the uncertainties of the times, perhaps because of them. Workers are remaining resolutely committed to the job, rolling with the punches. These workers, which are only a small contingent, are massing to become a large army as they show the way to go forward with the basic requirement of taking charge, leaving the cage of being taken care of behind.

Notes:

1. James R. Fisher, Jr., *Six Silent Killers: Management's Greatest Challenge*, TATE Publishing, 2014, Chapter 9, The Culture of Contribution. 2. Ibid, Chapter 6, *The Mad Monarchs of the Madhouse.*
2. Ibid, Chapter 5, *Echoing Footsteps.*
3. Ibid. *The Mad Monarchs of the Madhouse*
4. James R. Fisher, Jr., Ph.D., *"Combating Technical Obsolescence: The Genesis of a Technical Education Program."* Presented at the World Conference of Continuing Engineering Education in Orlando, Florida, May, 7. 1986.
5. Russell L. Ackoff and Fred E. Emery, *On Purposeful Systems*, Intersystem Publications, Seaside, California, 1972, p.1.
6. Garry Wills, *Saint Augustine's Memory*, Viking, 2002, pp. 7-8.
7. Alan W. Watts, *The Wisdom of Insecurity*, Vintage Books, 1951, p. 39.
8. Op. Cit., Dr. Fisher, *Culture of Contribution.*

THREE

THE SUBTEXT OF LIFE & ITS MEANING

"There is general denial of the subtext of life. It is contained in a kind of culture that exists apart from the kind transmitted by schools and universities, a kind of culture that once flourished in typical neighborhoods across the country, but is now gone. It helped to stem lawlessness, greed, corruption and other social diseases. It was a kind of social resistance that is lacking today, something upheld by average citizens, but by people in authority as well. There was a subtext of restrain undefined, unwritten, unspoken, but nonetheless felt, practiced and experienced.

"Today, the gap between people's dreams and experience is too large. People have resorted to living life on the edge, running without thinking, on automatic pilot in the rhythm of the content and context of things without a sense of restrain or penalty.

"We see this in general apathy as people react to the lead stories on television nightly news and in the headlines of morning newspapers regarding murder, mayhem, rape, fraud, and malfeasance with irritations but little more. It is the ghost in the room and not the elephant.

"The mind is homeless. It lacks roots. Most people aren't from where they came. A kind of isolation from a sense of place and space breaks people down and leaves them untethered. Easily forgotten is that shameful acts are committed by people who are themselves wounded human beings.

"Once upon a time, they were children, little ones running down the street at the start of school with their backpacks bouncing in cadence to their happy feet. They were on their way to school and on their way out into life. One wonders watching this parade if there goes a thief, a wife beater, an addict, a drug dealer, a murderer, a rapist, an embezzler, a gang member, a prostitute, a pimp, or some other drag on society, someone on the fringe that will garner those lead stories that we essentially ignore.

"Is this predetermined? Quite the opposite. But only if people use their intelligence and good will to get beyond surface issues of class and race, status and wealth, education and profession, immigration and ethnicity, religion and ideology, language and culture to consider the subtext of life to uncover what destroys social restrain and how to repair the damage.

"The world gets better or worse one person at a time. Apathetic or psychopathic behavior occurs because people are not acquainted with the subtext of their own lives and therefore are enslaved to surface issues. It was the same a hundred years ago and is likely to be so a hundred years hence."

James R. Fisher, Jr., *"Fragments of a Philosophy"* (unpublished)

THE PRICE OF A CELEBRITY CULTURE – AN AVERSION TO SUBTEXT

Great talent wastes its gifts when it loses contact with its subtext. Richard Burton was the greatest Shakespearean actor of his generation but sold out to Hollywood. Norman Mailer saw himself as heir apparent to Ernest Hemingway, but sold out to the false bravado and high jinx of that writer, and thus became a caricature of himself.

Albert Einstein was the exception. He had similar celebrity pressures as his most productive years were before he was thirty, and he lived into his seventies. He ignored this pull of celebrity because he was well acquainted with its subtext. It was not false modesty, but the realization that he had been lucky in his discoveries. He was lucky because he got beyond the content and context of Newtonian physics to explore the subtext that was not readily apparent, a subtext that physicists for more than two hundred years had not visited because they thought the work of physics had been completed.

Einstein was a dreamer and could see himself riding a light beam in the darkest recesses of the universe and played with that image in his mind until his thoughts rearrange themselves into his *"Theory of Relativity."*

Talented people ultimately sell themselves out to the celebrity culture that always threatens to embrace them. They are adored for all the wrong reasons. It is the herd mentality on display, the self-indulgent and hedonistic desiring to experience the wonders of genius, if only vicariously, by having power over that genius with flattering attention.

Sycophants do not appreciate the talented; sycophants only appreciate basking in its reflected glory. Thus the talented unwittingly compromise their genius by failing to recognize and therefore being able to resist that symbiotic connection and sycophants' mocking embrace.

The quest for celebrity is apparent in critics who can't write; performers who can't act; people with little more than good looks to be television journalists; or novelists with one idea to capture in scores of books. The chiaroscuro of content and context pulsates with monotonous consistency as brand not brilliance reduces tastes to the lowest common denominator. Gore Vidal was a decent enough writer whose celebrity was his angst. This found him a guest on the couch of late night television shows. Hundreds have since copied him.

It was a different problem for John Updike. Literary critic Grandville Hicks of the *Saturday Review of Literature* once said that Updike wrote like an angel but had nothing to say. Updike mastered a beautiful lyrical style, and became the darling of *The New Yorker* magazine, but was less attentive to subtext of the lives he created. He seemed satisfied to create thematic caricatures, which are apparent in *"Couples"* (1968) and with his *"Rabbit"* (1960s) series.

Updike approached the sex revolution from his Protestant Calvinistic stiffness as well as the feminine and civil rights movements on a tactile level without getting caught up in the tangled web of that contradictory subtext of American life. He had an opportunity, which he didn't explore, of penetrated the radical abandonment of the common good for personhood that collapsed around that narcissistic generation.

The accident of his clicking with *The New Yorker* and falling into a profession not sought, goes a long way to explain the problem. He first wanted to be a graphic artist, a cartoonist, where linearity of content and context is featured. He gravitated from that to study as a painter, mastering the techniques of texture and graphic composition, but unable to grasp the subtext that was the making of a Picasso, taking up his pen to write novels, short stories, and criticism of art with the fluid ease of a New England Puritan.

Kurt Vonnegut, Jr., from the middle of the United States, had a different problem. He lived in the subtext and tried desperately to reach an audience in content and context. The strain became the perplexity of his life. This frustration shows in his last book *"Armageddon in Retrospect"* (2008). There he challenged the Mona Lisa being a perfect painting while celebrated for its imperfection.

"Listen," Vonnegut writes, *"her nose is tilted to the right, OK? That means the right side of her face is a receding plane, going away from us, OK? But there is no foreshortening of her features*

on that side, giving the effect of three dimensions. And Leonardo could so easily have done that foreshortening. He was simply too lazy to do it."

I don't think so. I prefer to think Da Vinci lived in a casual subtext. He didn't suffer the anguish or doubt of Michelangelo. He had little time for pathos preferring to dance with ideas perceived, awed by the athleticism of men running, birds flying and fish diving to the deep and imagined in his mind being one with them.

That is how he came to envision the airplane, human anatomy, the submarine, automation and other devices that rose from his subtext to break through the world of content and context. It was enough for him to surface such issues and let posterity work out the details.

"No wonder she (Mona Lisa) has such a cockeyed smile," Vonnegut adds. But that is precisely it. She is meant to be enigmatic. The smile is a reflection of what is going on beyond the surface. It is the mystery of her that haunts us to this day. Were the painting as Vonnegut proposed, it is doubtful it would be a masterpiece.

There is a reason why the Bronte sisters, Jane Austen, Shakespeare, Dostoyevsky, Tolstoy and Joyce are still read. They dealt with the subtext of their stories while telling the surface story on the popular level of content and context. Hemingway escaped all his bravado, if only briefly, while dealing primarily with subtext in *"The Old Man and the Sea"* (1952) and won the Nobel Prize for the gamble.

Over the last sixty years, I have seen a tectonic shift from subtext to content and context as the issues that drive behavior have been pushed aside to celebrate the superfluous.

With the lack of restrain, without the tension to sublimate creatively beyond the banal in an effort to create only our brand, art has been reduced to making ourselves giddily rich for the effort. Consequently, we have failed as a society to produce great writers, composers, painters, and architects. This is the *"Age of Mediocrity"* where we celebrate such opportunists as Steven Jobs and Bill Gates as if they were geniuses when their skill was superfluous in harnessing the content and context of inventions created decades earlier as entrepreneur.

Noise has become the predicate of music, exhibitionism that of art, featureless glass buildings that of architecture, the shocking and bizarre popular comedic entertainment while political intercourse has been reduced to the behavior of spoiled children. We have become a surface and disposable culture with no gravitas with a dull and damaged if not permanently dysfunctional affect.

The reader may argue what about the great electronic breakthroughs, what about Internet? Alas, what could be a better example of the charge?

Computers have been around for more than sixty years, but have been perfected and made available to support people's lives at the content and context level as never before. We have innovations, not inventions; replications, not creative subtext; fads and fantasies, not transcendental liberation. We are locked into mediocrity as if it were an inescapable chronic plague.

Steven Jobs and Stephen Wozniak were making electronic games when Jobs happened on the personal computer at Xerox, which management refused to fund, and so Jobs stole it.

Bill Gates won the software contract with IBM by default when the wife partner of a husband and wife company wanted more assurances. Gates required none at the time as he basically had only his boldness to sell. He quickly acquired the software from another fledgling company for peanuts and was off to the races. Two decades later, because he understood the importance of subtext, he is the richest man in the world on a foundation of other people's ideas. While understanding this about him, it should be pointed out that he is also one of the most generous philanthropists in human history.

DOUBLE-EDGED "CUT & CONTROL" HISTORY OF HUMAN CULTURE

We experienced a global economic meltdown (2008) that terrified advanced societies from one end of the globe to the other, a meltdown that to this moment is viewed in terms of content and context with hardly a glance at the subtext of the calamity. The Dow Jones Industrials on Wall Street have past 21,000 and wealth catchers in 2017 have already forgotten the calamity of nine years ago. There appears no escape from living high now and paying for it later. There is no sense of the folly of this in subtext.

 Economics has proven as faulty a profession as has management. Some years ago, I wrote:

"We desperately need minds with a natural affinity for culture in the boardrooms across America, as well as in every other walk of professional life. We need poetry in commerce, government and industry.

"Engineers, economists, and political scientists have done about all the damage we can stand, perhaps more than we can absorb.

"Economists, for one, readily admit they are operating in a fog. From former Chairman of the Federal Reserve, Arthur Burns ("The rules of economics are not working quite the way they used to.") to Milton Friedman ("I believe that we economists in recent years have done vast harm by claiming more than we can deliver."); from former Secretary of Treasury Michael

Blumenthal ("I really think the economic profession is close to bankruptcy in understanding the situation, before or after the fact.") to Juanita Kreps, former Secretary of Commerce, when asked if she would go back to Duke University upon leaving government ("I wouldn't know what to teach.").[1]

Economists have always been enamored of algorithms and mathematical models, analysis at the content and context level, which is clean and neat, while management has treated people as things to be managed rather than persons to be led. Now they all have egg on their faces.

Geopolitics has also proven a faulty profession. Little time has been devoted to the subtext of why the Twin Towers of New York City were destroyed. Instead, there was a visceral and spontaneous response (2003 invasion of Iraq) at the content and context level with the United States launching a preemptive military action on the false pretense of Iraq having "Weapons of Mass Destruction" (WMDs); in other words, with little if any appreciation of the subtext such a precipitous act. This action has led to a domino effect as the Middle East is now ravaged in war with the festering emergence of Al-Qaeda and ISSI as a consequence. Islamic terrorism has been addressed in terms of content and context – current United States President Donald Trump believes he can eradicate this movement without an iota of understanding of the subtext of this movement's motivation – as there is little evidence that learning has taken place.

If you are wondering why this is included here, remember the macro sense of things is only a reflection of our micro sense of things. Self-Confidence is not possible if a country as well as an individual is self-aware and self-accepting in that awareness of itself as a limited entity for not until that level of tolerance is realized can the subtext of life that touches everyone surface and be understood and acted upon properly. Otherwise, chaos only generates more disorder, pain and displacement.

A predisposition to react rather than reflect is characteristic of the content and context limitations that appear endemic to the puerile American character. Consequently, the United States and its future are in economic and political peril without an appreciation of the subtext of life. What preoccupies American economic and political life at the moment? It is the outrage, visceral hatred and pervasive polarity of the American people after the surprising election of the first businessman as the President of the United States. There is no room for subtext when spoiled brats rule the roost.

The great recession of 2008 behind us, but what is ahead? Inflation? Economic depression? The world sits on the precipice of its faulty axis with little appreciation of what matters most, which is buried in the subtext.

*   *   *

We glory in instant communication where everyone has a cell phone, iPad, computer, or laptop, busying oneself with the twaddle of white noise. Electronics have become a form of addiction in this *Information Age*. No longer is drunk driving the only major cause of deaths on our highways and byways, but people texting on their electronic contraptions.

No one seems to be looking at the downside of this paradigm shift, which has elevated content and context to the status of a new religion. We have cut existence away to a new sense of reality that has no pause in the virtual community.

It has been a "cut and control" journey throughout man's history with something gained for something forever lost. The hunting and gathering period 12,000 years ago has often been depicted as a matriarchal society or a society controlled by women as there were no boundaries.

There is some evidence to suggest this. Archeological evidence suggests that pre-agricultural humans of the hunting and gathering period were much more gender egalitarian than modern societies. Women then as now lived longer than men, and humans are one of the few species whose females live for quite a long time after child-bearing age. Since men might be much more likely to die young from hunting accidents or skirmishes with other tribes, it would make sense for women to serve the collective memory of the tribe.

Also, pre-agricultural humans likely didn't understand how exactly sex and pregnancy were related, and even if they did, they almost certainly weren't sexually monogamous, so one's parentage was always questionable. That said even in our species' earliest days, the structure of human society could be dramatically different from place to place as communal norms were relative.

Agriculture led to a patriarchal society with men giving up their nomad existence to settling down raising crops and owning property with boundaries now having significance.[2]

This led to an industrial society where owners ruled and cities grew. This broke up the cohesive harmony and domestic culture of life on the farm as young families flocked to the cities to work. They found themselves living in cramped unsanitary tenement houses imprisoned in blatant squalor and crushing poverty, slaves to inanimate machines.

The gap between haves and have nots grew, as society moved swiftly through the modern management class to and through the postmodern era of capitalists, as managers first replaced owners, and they in turn were replaced by indifferent stockholders who valued profits above people.

This elevated finance, an industry that produces nothing but exchange rates, to the ultimate power broker of investment bankers and venture capitalists. They became the significant differentiators as power shifted from people to property to products to floating capital.

This all came down as a crushing nightmare in 2008 when the wonder of electronic transfer of complex derivatives sped out of control as capital was leveraged thousands of times greater than its capacity to honor its debt as the "cut & control" journey of 12,000 years found the subtext of life once more breaking through the content and context of existence. Man keeps pushing forward blindly and incomprehensively, and then wondering what he has done wrong.

The answer is not to be found in assessing blame, or looking at the matter in terms of right and wrong, which attracts content and context consideration, but why does man so uncompromisingly move away from the subtext of his existence?

ALL TOO HUMAN

Should a person work around the globe, he would see the subtext of life is the controller, where the undercurrent of life and society are manifested with the spontaneity of behavior free of controls. Yes, there are surface controls of content and context which have little to do with actual human behavior as they are essentially ignored. This is the puppet master of each of our individual fates.

Imagine a rubber band with a certain elasticity. We know a new rubber band has an elasticity that diminishes with use. With the human psyche, we don't consider it of a certain elasticity, or of a limited flexibility that deteriorates with use and age. We instead possess the arrogance and hubris to believe in our fluidity; in our capacity to embrace and master circumstances no matter how outlandish and profligate our behavior. We don't believe we have nine lives like a cat but ninety-nine lives, and of course that is where the fallacy lies.

Think of all the people who garner the headline stories, people caught in shameful acts. Now think of all the people who lie for them: parents, grandparents, siblings, relatives, and friends. Not only that, think of these same people bailing them out of their difficulty, feeling sorry for them, buying their cheap excuses for their shameful behavior, and you have the making of an emotionally and psychologically crippled culture. You have the current culture that we now enjoy.

We have a person cold in the morgue killed by a hit and run driver who goes to his maker experiencing no sense of social justice as his killer carries no responsibility for his early demise. This is multiplied thousands of times over and includes drive-by shootings of gang members at war with each other unconcerned at the collateral damage they cause in the death of innocent shoppers or children playing in the streets.

Take the young man who went to the bachelor party of a friend who was about to be married. He didn't drink and so when the party got rowdy he chose to leave and walk the two miles home. It was eleven o'clock. He worked his job religiously, didn't make much money, lived alone in a modest apartment, read books, and would discuss them intelligently and critically with his friends. Then one day, only 42, he was no more.

It was assumed some drunken fool hit him, knocked him a hundred feet into the air and leaving him to die on the side of the road, his shoes left at the point of impact. Chances are the person killing him was so intoxicated that he didn't know he hit the man. The shoes however were fifteen feet off the road. His death is a cold case now fifteen years old, which is unlikely to ever be reopened.

Being one who has no sympathy for drunks; no sympathy for people who smoke themselves to death; and no sympathy for drug addicts, it is because I have no sympathy for people who are unaware of the subtext of their lives, and how it has managed and mangled their existence. Friends and family don't have the courage to remind these people of their addiction but instead make excuses for them having such dependence. There is complicity here. We never go badly alone. We have a lot of enabling contributors to this behavior, and too often they are members of our own families who manage to avoid such compulsions.

It is in the subtext that the health and elasticity of life is lost never to be discovered. Nor will I accept that alcoholism and drug addiction are diseases. They are choices. They are people who choose to ignore their reduced elasticity, which is apparent in the subtext of their lives. Through artificial stimulation they promote the illusion that they can still maintain the same flexibility and elasticity that they have always enjoyed despite their reckless behavior. The subtext of life reminds us we are dying a little every day and therefore should make the most of our days, not hide from them in content and context oblivion.

The subtext of life will not allow us to fool ourselves. The embezzler knows he is committing a crime but deludes himself that he will never get caught, justifying the behavior in rationalizations: his wife is dying of cancer, his sons need money for prep school, and he has the right to a better lifestyle given the many years of service in which he has been taken for granted and shown little respect.

Rationalization is the product of content and context but never the subtext of the matter, which is the fear that life in a zero sum game and amounts to nothing else. The embezzler's elasticity is gone, and so he says, "Why not?"

Bernard Madoff bilked investors and companies of billions of dollars with his Ponzi scheme while denying the subtext of his life. He is not a bad man but a little man with an obsessive need to please others and feel important and vital in their eyes, but why? The answer is buried in his subtext.

Then there are people who have buried terrible secrets of their past deep in their subconscious as if they had never happened. Often, according to social scientist Billy G. Gunter's "deficiency motivation theory," the criminal aspires to be a police officer, the psychosexual pervert the religious fanatic, the conflicting sinner the priest, the person with an inferiority complex the psychologist, guru, pundit or soothsayer, the plotting student the scholar, the jackal the entrepreneur.

What is incredible about this is that the motivation is so convincing that many times it materializes with the paradoxical effect of their problems and confusions becoming ours with our blind receptivity to their angst.

Sin is the armor of the proselytizer with the voice and zeal of salvation, but it is not our sin that disturbs him, but his. A flock is formed as the evangelist's subtext becomes that of the converted as no one sees the folly in this.

The flock is badgered to repent or they will be damned. By whom? By God, of course, because the crusader is the self-anointed self-appointed messenger of God. The individual caught up in this charade may forget he has a right to question the authority and legitimacy of the messenger, but that would be tantamount to blaspheme, would it not? What we cannot question is our decreasing elasticity, which limits what we can and cannot do. If anyone can save it, that savior is ourselves.

*   *   *

In this climate of generating a plethora of solutions looking for problems, coaches, counselors, psychologists, psychiatrists, sociologists, political pundits on television and radio gurus have surfaced with these networks and the social media of the Internet while making billions of dollars and these personal experts making millions, while defining the problem continues to receive scant if any attention as it always buried in the subtext.

Should you freeze frame a collection of these programs twenty or thirty years ago and juxtapose them with what happened on the airwaves yesterday you would see little variance because they are not dedicated to the problem solving, but to providing worry beads to an anxious unengaged nation in entertaining content and context to buffer it from awareness of its collapsing reality.

The irony is that there are exceptions to this. There is a woman in her fifties who is still carrying her other siblings well into their adulthood forgiving them for their improprieties and transgressions, which has stunted their growth and development resulting in none of them becoming truly adults in any sense of the word.

Now, when she has come into a hard patch in her own life, her siblings are not there for her. They are insensitive and unsympathetic to her ordeal, angry that she has little time to listen to them now, and no longer has the wherewithal to bail them out of their self-imposed financial miseries.

Has this made her bitter? No. Has this made her vindictive? No. Has this found her angry? No. It has made her resilient. The subtext of her life has proven to have much greater elasticity than one would expect. It came about when she stopped denying its existence and finally said, "Hey that is where my strength lies. Hey, that is why I am so understanding of my siblings. Hey, that is why I can tolerate my parents. Hey, that is why I am me!"

With that resilience, she discovered she could refocus and reenergize her efforts to go forward accepting the inevitable bumps in the road. That is what she is now doing. She finds she is a learner not a knower, a doer not a thinker, a problem solver but in the subtext of intuition not cognitive analysis. It is working for her.

She has two beautiful children who are a projection of her. She married a person like her siblings. She is the best thing that has happened to him. He gets into one economic strafe after another. Will he ever grow up? I don't think so. Will he ever examine the subtext of his life? Not on a bet. Will he continue to repeat the same errors? Undoubtedly. Am I being cruel and unsympathetic? I don't think so.

In subtext, there is a strong moral imperative to effectively utilize one's inherent ability with little time or energy wasted on suffering fools poorly including one's own follies.

Doubtless we fail this moral imperative many times in our lives repeating the same errors failing to acknowledge or learn from our deficiencies. A writer is aware of this elasticity going from supple to brittle but he soldiers on depositing words, ideas, philosophies and projections of what he has learned hoping those so inclined might find succor.

Does this mean that most people need to be liked? No, but it does mean there is no place for being malicious. Most people derive little satisfaction seeing other people being dominated, diminished or failing. Then does that mean that is it important to respect people? Again, respect as with trust must be earned as it is equally true that self-acceptance (or liking oneself as one is) is necessary before one can be genuinely accepting of others as they are found. With our moral suasion we have a sense of dignity and a need to be needed, but that dignity and need is fragile and must be supported by action. Otherwise, it can result in the blind violence of people who feel on the surplus heap of humanity with nothing to lose as we have seen in the terrorist movement of recent years.

There is a crisis in dignity which is most acutely felt by the working (or unemployed) middle class that has been badly served for decades by public education and in lackluster fashion by federally funded job training programs.[3]

We find two Americas in the subtext of American life. Today, the top and the bottom of American society live in separate worlds. They do not attend school together; do not socialize together; and they do not work together. They hardly know each other. As a result, few people in either of these two Americas even recognize the social trends that are widening the cultural gulf between them. Moral suasion is the cultural fixation on gaining four-year degrees at any cost, which leaves 40 percent of

America's youth who attempt to fulfill this journey, but fail accruing only punishing debt for the attention. Moreover, less than 10 percent of births out of wedlock are to college-educated women while more than 50 percent occur to women with a high school education or less. Children born out of wedlock are unlikely to grow up with a father. These children are likely to have mental health issues but less likely to enjoy regular employment or a sustained employment history.[4]

Donald J. Trump was swept into the presidency with the message "Make American Great Again" with people from the heartland coming out in droves who had never voted before interpreting his message as "Make America Dignified Again" with stable family life, job and personal security, peace and prosperity and a sense of belonging to a strong community with an opportunity to work hard for something worthwhile.

SUBTEXT UP CLOSE AND PERSONAL

The content and context of Seamus Devlin would suggest that he is mainly intuitive because that is what he likes to project, but the subtext of his life suggests that he is a cognitive, analytical, critical, and conceptual person. The fact that the subtext has come to the surface in the evening of his years is representative of another quality, the need to leave something of value behind.

Devlin's life has been one of being structured, disciplined and demanding of himself as well as of others with little give – little elasticity – displayed. The irony of this subtext is that he is more comfortable in chaos than order, more energized in confusion than in certainty.

- Item: He was a US Navy hospital corpsman on the flagship of the sixth fleet in the Mediterranean participating in annual maneuvers with some 100 other American ships and 50,000 men. A gun mount on a destroyer escort "hang fired," that is, the breech was not secure with the blast torching the 13-man crew, badly burning several. The injured were brought to his ship and treated in the ship's hospital. Three died while they were being attended; the others were flown to the burn hospital in Germany.

Doctors from other ships were brought on board. It was general chaos. None of these doctors had experience with badly burned trauma cases nor did any of the corpsmen. Some could not deal with the sight, the smell or the carnage of burning flesh. By default, although of junior status, he assumed a senior role to fill the void and received an accommodation. He was 23-years-old, and learned something about himself that day that he didn't know before. Highly emotional on the surface, only to discover he had a calm subtext that surfaced in crisis. This subtext would resurface throughout his life in chaotic situations.

Given awareness of our limited elasticity, knowing we all have a breaking point, and that our elasticity can go from resilient to brittle to snapping without warning, it is useful to review how we act and react in certain situations. Our elasticity may surface or desert us when we are emotional exhausted or hypertensive leading to a mental breakdown or a resurgence of effort and commitment. Be wary of the psychiatric labels that are indiscriminately used to describe our state such as schizophrenia, bipolar disorder, or some other "mental disease."

Dr. Thomas S. Szasz in *"The Manufacture of Madness"* (1970), *"The Myth of Mental Illness"* (1974) and other books, himself a psychiatrist, sees modern psychiatry using its ideology and insanity plea as a convenience to avoid confrontation with the hard moral conflicts and social problems of the day. Clear speech, what he calls the *"second sin"* is missing in the prognosis. Broadly speaking, Szasz is addressing subtext.[5]

Of course, we all talk to ourselves; we all have dreams of loss, confusion and betrayal. That is part of the subtext that is the driver of behavior. Some people are made uncomfortable because they think you can read their minds. You can't. But you can read their behavior, which is quite apparent for anyone paying attention.

You don't do this with eye contact, which is supposed to indicate sincerity, for eyes lie. We have all become very good liars. Some people can even control their emotions to the point of passing a polygraph test with ease.

By actively listening to what people say and channeling this into the rhythm of what they do will give you assess to how genuine or disingenuous they are. You see in this in gestures, the care of the nails, the texture of the skin to whether they are or aren't what they wish to project. Our faces are roadmaps of self-indulgence. The subtext of our lives oozes up through the pores to confirm or contest the content and context on display. We all become eventually what we are.

There are palpable warning signs before a person commits suicide; before a person takes that first dollar out of the till that doesn't belong to him. There is no such thing as an innocent cup of coffee between a man and a woman married to other people. All of these indicators are there and all of them are rejections of the subtext of life.

When the subtext is ignored or rejected, life becomes a lie. There is no possibility for understanding the authentic self.

My nickname is *"Rube,"* which is commonly translated to mean a farmer, rustic, unsophisticated, an ignoramus. The sobriquet has delighted me as a source of pride.

At a dinner in New York City, someone once confronted me. *"I understand your nickname is 'Rube.' Is that true?"*

"Yes."

"Are you comfortable with that?"

"Quite, why do you ask?"

"You're not offended?"

"No."

"Then you're a country bumpkin?"

"If you like."

"That doesn't offend you?"

"No, why should it?"

"Do you like being called 'Rube'?"

"I love being called 'Rube'!"

"Why is that?"

"Because it's a name associated with the most wonderful time in my life growing up in the middle of the country in the middle of the century when I was catching baseball for the Courthouse Tigers as a kid.[6]

"There was no activity I loved more. I took pride in that. I would watch catchers in the Industrial League with a dreamy like concentration. And I loved putting on the 'tools of ignorance' (catcher's equipment) knowing I was the best catcher around for my age. I am Rube. Rube gave me my first taste of excellence and how to achieve it." That seemed to end the conversation.

Coming from a farm state, I must confess that I've never actually been on a farm. My people in Ireland as well as America have always been city dwellers. My da was born in Chicago as were his parents, but his mother died in childbirth and his father took off never to be seen again. He was reared in Clinton, Iowa, a small industrial city on the Mississippi River by his grandmother. My siblings and children gravitated to metropolitan areas with no farmers in our family tree.

The subtext of the connection, however, is real. I have the down-to-earth values of the farmer, a love of the seasons of the year, of the fertilizing, planting and growing of ideas, the earthy norms that identify a person with a particular place and space, the sense that a man's word is his bond, the humility that Nature knows best, and that we are all connected. We are caught in the subtext of our geography, which we carry in our demography wherever we go.

Notes:

1. James R. Fisher, Jr., *Work Without Managers: A View from the Trenches*, The Delta Group Florida, Tampa, Fl., 1991, pp. 253 – 254.
2. Sir James George Frazer, *The Golden Bough: A Study in Magic and Religion*, Simon & Schuster, Boston, 1996; Roger Lewin, *In the Age of Mankind: A Smithsonian Book of Human Evolution*, Smithsonian Books, 1988.
3. Arthur C. Brooks, "The Dignity Deficit: Reclaiming Americans' Sense of Purpose," *Foreign Affairs*, March/April 2017, p. 115.
4. Ibid, p. 116.
5. Thomas S. Szasz, *The Manufacture of Madness*, Delta Books, NY, 1970; *The Myth of Mental Illness*, Harper & Row, NY, 1974; *The Second Sin*, Anchor Books, NY, 1974.
6. James R. Fisher, Jr., *In the Shadow of the Courthouse: A Memoir of the 1940s Written as a Novel*, AuthorHouse, Bloomington, IN, 2003.

The sobriquet "rube" was given to me because I was never allowed to come out to play after dinner "until my meal" settled, which meant that sides had been chosen up, and the only thing I could do is be steady catcher for both sides. Also, at the time, Rube Fischer was a pitcher for the New York Giants in Major League Baseball, and Rube Walker was catcher for the St. Louis Cardinals. The name seemed a natural.

FOUR

SELF-REALIZATION & SELF-DEFEAT

"The perception of one's life space grows and sharpens; one more fully experiences both the outer world of events, and the inner world of feeling. One develops the attitude of perceiving oneself, of being an object to oneself, of utilizing the intelligence in order to view one's own activities and being, and to make continued changes in the light of such intelligence."

Samuel J. Warner, *Self-Realization and Self-Defeat* (1966)

THE LASTING IMPRESSIONS OF EARLY CHILDHOOD

We are imperfectly formed. The best minds have throbbing doubts and play special havoc with their lives. Stephen King sublimates his terror into spine tingling novels of horror. His horror becomes our entertainment. King doesn't deny his demons. He puts them to work.

As a small child, cartoonist Gary Larson was frightened out of his wits. His impish brother locked him in the basement, turned off the lights, and then taunted him with imagined horrors. Larson never forgot his trauma. It put him in touch with his *Far Side* comic strip.

The late Irish–American actor Charles Durning confessed, "There are many secrets in the depths of our souls that we don't want anyone to know." A producer, noting Durning's intensity, once remarked, "Charlie, if you hadn't been an actor, you would probably have been a murderer. Within you is a boiler ready to explode." Durning admitted:

"There's terror and repulsion in us, the terrible spot that no one knows about—horrifying things we keep secret. A lot of this is released through acting."

This actor's journey took him from poverty through the *Great Depression* and World War II, where he was a much-decorated combat soldier on the Western Front, unto fame and wealth.

The late novelist Michael Crichton, like Somerset Maugham, a physician turned prolific author, compared his bouts of depression to the weather. *"Suns out today, cloudy today, cloudy this month."*

Crichton admitted to an interviewer of contemplating suicide, but never thought to take action because *"I have too much respect for depression."* The Harvard educated doctor envied the insouciance of his friend, actor Sean Connery, who admitted to having ulcers at sixteen. Connery saw Crichton's creative standards so high that they intimidated him.

Crichton, who earned more than $22 million for the successful filming of his book, *Jurassic Park*, admitted to having a never ending fight with himself. This was not a war to be more, or to have more, but to distill from his considerable talents something meaningful. That price is high, too high for most of us for it demands one embrace constant suffering and struggle to realize a perfection always beyond our grasp.

OUR CREATIVE SECRET GARDEN

Metaphorically, we all have rocks in our heads, snakes in our secret gardens. Our snakes, sunning themselves on these rocks, symbolize our fantasies and wicked thoughts.

To deny their presence is to throw our lives off balance, out of control, as if stumbling unconsciously on one and being pierced by its deadly venom. What we do is one thing; what we think is quite another. No one is absolutely good or absolutely evil, but a combination of both. If we ignore one at the expense of the other, we are bound for trouble. To respect our wickedness gives us an advantage.

Others less self–accepting may stumble on their snakes at any time, whereas we, ever alert, gingerly step around ours. We can even use them, on occasion, as creative inspiration to stimulate our visionary powers. Fantasies are an important source of energy, not so much to be acted on as to add dimension to our vision, to widen our horizons.

Creative artists are well acquainted with their snakes. They call them many names—curses, blessings, demons, crosses, redeemers, gods, devils, swords, punishment, inspiration—to name only a few. Many purposely provoke them to a frenzy state to reach beyond the norm.

Painter Vincent Van Gogh, now celebrated, did this with regularity. He called it his insanity. Van Gogh was essentially ignored during his lifetime. Could his insanity be the seeds of his genius? He sold but a single painting, and that was to an art dealer friend of his brother's.

While he battled his snakes, he painted magnificently. You sense his anguish in his excruciating precise brush strokes, the brilliance of his soul in his bold use of color. All the while he entertained the constant torment of doubt. Yet today his paintings sell for tens of millions of dollars. They depict the agony and ecstasy of an unquiet soul, and speak to our rootlessness and unsatisfied searching, to our excruciating refusal to give ourselves the benefit of the doubt.

Consider the creative process as metaphor: The artist's snakes stare at him with their lidless eyes, tails posed ready to strike, vibrating with the rattle of death, their swollen wedged heads and long slithering tongues, hypnotic, as they take measure of the artist, their vulnerable prey. Now, they strike! In a flash, meaning implodes between conflicting forces of passion and intellect, madness and reason, pain and ecstasy, doubt and conviction, as the artist's talent explodes into one of exquisite beauty.

Mystical thinker J. Krishnamurti once wrote of this in a compelling way.

There was this painter who went out every day, set up his easel and canvas, organized his paints, then contemplated his subject, a solitary tree penciled against the sky on a small bluff by the sea. Day after day he did this without ever touching paint to canvas. A passerby observed this strange behavior on several occasions and was finally prompted to ask,

"Sir, are you a painter?"

The painter replied, "Yes, indeed, I am a painter."

"Pardon my boldness, sir, but I come this way several times a week. I have yet to see you place a single brush stroke to your naked canvas."

The painter smiled. "That is also true." Sensing the stranger's confusion, he added, "I will paint the tree when the tree and I are one, but not before."

"Surely you jest?" quipped the stranger. "That is not possible."

"For you, my good man, perhaps not," countered the painter, "for the artist it is not only possible, but necessary."

Art is created only when the artist and the subject merge. Realism is not the aim. The artist's interest is in what he sees with his mind's eye. Form in his painting is substance. The forces of self-realization and self–defeat melt into a common force of expression. Conflict is resolved in creation. That is the power of art. It is a difficult process, taking great patience, endurance and, yes, immense suffering. There is no art without pain.

Art takes a heavy toll. Few are willing to pay the price. Ernest Hemingway paid the price, as did Wolfgang Amadeus Mozart. Their benediction is immortality. Neither man ever grew up. Hemingway died at the chronological age of 61, while Mozart was but 36. They both played dangerously with their lives, the way young people do whom expect to live forever. The more pain they endured from their play the greater their art soared. They celebrated an adolescent zest for the illusory with naked bravado.

The creative process is a constant contest of the self with the secret self. It is not restricted to the artist. Anyone who attempts to create something instead of reacting to what others create experiences this.

The process may be likened to an animal tamer trying to control a vicious predator set to devour him, with but a whip and chair as his defense. The tamer mocks the beast. He hits it viciously with his whip to bring out its anger, and then turns his back on the beast and walks away in defiance of the creature's savage nature. Suddenly, as if struck by inspiration, the animal tamer pirouettes to face off with the beast again, capturing it in a mid–air strike before striking with the full impact of mortality in the balance.

At that precise moment, when the beast is about to devour him, a thought materializes, previously hidden in the primordial recesses of his reptilian brain. Such bold and courageous persistence, more than strenuous effort, keeps the artist in touch with himself and the fact that he is always both the animal tamer and the beast at large. For the moment, he has tamed and exploited the subtext of his soul.

- Nor is living on the edge exclusive to artists. Many seek residence there because it suits them.

- They are bored with their lives, relationships, jobs, possessions, with their reason for being.

- They are people in gilded cages often living on beautiful estates, trapped inside themselves.

- They have all the visual hallmarks of happiness as a marketable product: fine clothes, homes, cars, jobs and adoring friends with whom to play.

- They are trapped inside the mannerisms of their frigid public roles, incapable of expressing their true feelings, or what they are.

- They have successfully closed the gap between their public and private lives, as form becomes substance.

- Looking good is chosen over doing good; personality over performance; and career over family. Such people do not simply perform their corporate job. They become their corporate job. This is their entire identity and it doesn't belong to them.

Dennis Rodman, the controversial ex-professional basketball player for the Chicago Bulls and San Antonio Spurs, embodies the torment when form wars with substance. Rodman colors his hair orange, green and other shades as his mood varies. He also sports many body tattoos and outlandish dress off the court—shiny tank top, metallic hot pants and a rhinestone dog collar being common apparel.

Rodman also has dressed in flowing white of a drag queen bride. He sees this less as being risqué and more as a way to push the envelope of acceptability. An extremely gifted athlete, Rodman is however a rebel without a cause, a reluctant celebrity, who fights the system which labels him difficult.

He finds this unfair, and rightly so, because he sees himself trapped in the caricature of a one-dimensional black basketball player. No one in the NBA could rebound, before or since, with the critical theatre of Rodman and so there is toleration for his eccentricity.

But the war goes on with–in him as he sees himself more than the job. He even dreams of suicide. *"Sometimes I dream about just taking a gun and blowing my head off,"* he confesses in *Sports Illustrated* (May 29, 1995). A multimillionaire, he lives temperamentally on the edge as an artist not unlike those in other art forms, fighting the continuing war between self–realization and self–defeat.

THE VANILLA REVOLUTION

Corporate society, which has dominated our lives for more than a century, is not wicked. It is simply monochromatic and anachronistic. Its dominate flavor is vanilla making us all essentially the same. Samuel J. Warner writes:

"Our culture provides increasing pressure towards conformity and stereotype, as witness the clothes we wear and the thoughts we express, for there are intrinsic dangers in being original or 'different.' But the wine of life requires the ingredient of freedom to deviate from the herd-path; and each person generally uses his intelligence so as to conform only so far as he must. Not so the self-defeat; for as he often opposes without rational basis, so does he frequently bend the knee unnecessarily, when external realities do not really demand it of him."

At least corporate society has had the privilege of being able to say at the end of its era of influence, it made its own mistakes. Many might say it was courageous. It chose the technological path exclusively, which proved a misguided one, largely for its failure to understand and deal wisely with the fall out and unintended consequences of Mach Speed change. But there you have it!

Corporate society chose its fate. As for the average citizen, who went along for the ride without complaint, he cannot make such a claim. He trusted corporate society to know what was best for him. He placed his confidence in its wisdom to be equal to all its challenges.

For the past century, generation after generation served corporate aims religiously trusting its dictates and designs as the way to self-realization and the good life. Corporate society's destiny became our destiny.

Now, with the scandalous decline of corporate society into *corpocracy*, the average citizen cannot even say he made his own mistakes. He feels betrayed, but betrayed by what or by whom?

Corpocracy in this collection refers to the corporate bureaucracy, which has come to be increasingly covertly manipulative, dissembling and exploitative, while corporate policy vigorously attempts to project an overt image otherwise.[1] What dignity is there in that?

So what do most people do when faced with living in a breakdown culture? Many embrace danger as a lark. They cannot seem to focus on anything real. Everything seems to slip out of focus, to be just beyond their grasp. Since they cannot feel, it is impossible for them to think as they exist as if autopilot drones of corporate society frozen in its cyclic torment unable to escape.

Anyone who has not felt betrayed may think this extreme. The experience is frightening when the pain is in the mind, not the body; when life takes on the characteristics of a charade; when people feel forced to find something real and meaningful by living on the edge to get in touch with their feelings, even if it portents disaster.

The artist is bent on self-realization through the painful process of creation. There has never been a place for the artist in corporate society, so he has always been an outsider. Corporate society holds the bored artisan to its bosom, not the renegade artist. Ultimately, the corporate insider gravitates to self–defeat through adolescent self–indulgent practices. There is little sense of purpose to what he is doing. He is doing *whatever* mainly "for the hell of it," or to escape monotony.

Compliance is the key to corporate society. Those who comply with its inanities are given comfort and made complacent. This suspends persons in adolescence and insulates them from the pain of reality and therefore the need to grow up and take charge of their lives. Suspended in adolescent dependence, unable to focus on anything real for very long, they are driven by excitement, danger and the unexpected.

Shock is their therapy. They are captives to their fears, not driven by either their passions or convictions. They are most with themselves when they are free–falling from airplanes as parachutists; deep sea diving for fauna several fathoms into the ocean's cavity; punishing their bodies daily in some sauna or commercial workout gym; or engaging in the madness of the triathlon. In each instance, they are carrying the corporate banner while running from the only mortality that they own.

No longer finding vicarious satisfaction as spectator of such violent sports as football, hockey and race car driving, these adult children suspended in permanent adolescence, now embrace these sports in the virtual reality electronic games. This is a new multi-$ billion industry with tournaments and gambling on outcomes as if they were real. It is madness now accepted as the norm of corporate society for grown-ups to act forever as if twelve-year-olds without contempt or complaint.

The uniform of *corpocracy* requires advocates to wear the blinders of compliance and complacency and to behave as if unilinear pixels on an electronic screen following the dictates of corpocracy's civil religion.

INDIVIDUALISM AS THEATRE

Corporate society never understands how working people think, feel or breathe. Once workers of spiritual depth are exposed to the subliminal intensity of this cultural environment, they quickly forget their spiritual roots and become heretics to their core values.

Corporate capitalism thrives on this all-embracing ideology. There is no room for individualism, but this does not stop individualism from being preached as dogmatically as a Papal Encyclical.

Evidence of captivity to this free-floating anxiety is personal identity. In the 19th century, the concern was for the loss of one's immortal soul. In the 20th century, it was for the loss of one's individualism. In the 21st century, there is no such concern as personal identity and dignity is now a remnant of history.

When Americans were individuals, when the home was one's castle, when there existed ethnic and neighborhood pride, when people were poor but didn't know it, when religion was a private affair, and one's personal life was sacred, individuals shared an exclusive spirit in their hearts with room for eccentricity. Now, all of that is gone, replaced by *corpocracy*, or the demands of corporate society.

Americans are programmed by sublimating fear that compromises their creativity and finds them running from anxiety to depression escaping into computer games and PlayStations while treating their mobiles as worry beads frantically texting and tweeting most of their waking hours, which fails to allow their latent talent to bloom. Americans have become afraid of life!

Consider the absurdity of the murder/suicide of John Littig, 47, and Lynne Rosen, 45. They had a popular self-help radio show in New York City with the title *"The Pursuit of Happiness."* They urged listeners to embrace spontaneity, which apparently included suicide.

This suicide happened in June 2013 leaving the Freudian question: Why fear life or something known for death, which is unknown? Freud answered his own question saying self-destruction won over self-realization.

The secret weapon of the artist is to know what he is running from as well as running toward. Chances are he is running from the sentimentality of hope and toward the reality of courage. Courage is the haven of identity while hope is its mirage.

Courage gives the artist the capacity to find beauty by releasing his beast. This takes more perspiration than inspiration. Courage is the patient pursuit of a dream. The bored are on a treadmill as they run in place dreaming of the miraculous. They deny the beast *with-in*, only to run into its nightmare. The self-help couple couldn't help themselves.

The bored drive too fast, punish their bodies with too much or too little exercise, too much or too little food or drink, party until they drop, embark on chance relationships with meaningless affairs, anything to escape making a decision or having a heart-to-heart with themselves. What the bored do is never fulfilling, only draining. Running on impulse, they are overwhelmed by the mundane.

John Littig was a motivational speaker; Lynne Rosen was a workshop facilitator and life coach, speaker and consultant. Elsewhere in this book, the reader is warned that such people package their demons and sell them as a consumer product, suggesting the buyer beware! People who put themselves on a pedestal as experts are likely to be more strangers to themselves than their gullible clientele.

Notes:

1. The German magazine, *Wirtschaft Woche* (January 16, 1987), featured the cover story, *Amerikas Krankheit* ("The American Disease"). The article alluded to the fact that America's corporate society was rampantly running out of control. Claiming this was formerly confined to government bureaucracies, but now was a rash across American business, industry, education, the media and the religious. This corporate disease was designated *"corpocracy"* with these characteristics:

   - *Management is insensitive to its employees;*
   - *Management supports company politics at the expense of productivity;*
   - *Secretiveness is the measure of communications;*
   - *The principal product of work is paperwork;*
   - *Endless meetings are the way – when in doubt hold a meeting;*
   - *An internal focus is maintained as potential markets are ignored;*
   - *Short-term planning and thinking is preferred to embracing long term challenges – plan, plan, and plan some more;*
   - *Individual initiative is never supported as you never know where it might lead;*
   - *Management has isolated itself from employees by building mahogany towers between them;*
   - *A covert hostility to innovation is maintained while it is overtly praised and supported.*

FIVE

THE CAGE OF HUMAN INATTENTION AS A CLOSED SYSTEM

We get ourselves in situations in which we feel there isn't anything we can do to make it better. The more we try to do something the more we become blind to the reality of the situation. We are trying to do something which, in the nature of the thing, is impossible to disentangle ourselves, and therefore we develop a sense of *chronic frustration.*

Chronic frustration is like living in a cage, forever running around the cage to get out, only staying forever in the cage. When feeling so trapped, we are like the gerbil on the wheel in the cage, running faster and faster and going nowhere. In jargon of the 1970s, we are trapped in the "rat race," the everlasting pursuit of ends, going around and around afraid to stop, or to take a "time out" for fear circumstances will overwhelm us.

The most acceptable way to escape the wheel and the "rat race" has been euphemistically called "burn out," the result of burning the candle at both ends until there is no longer any wick and we have no choice drop off the pace or completely drop out to allow recovery. The least acceptable way is to abandon the "rat race" altogether. Then we are seen as a "quitter." Should we simply become ill, and have to be hospitalized or committed to our bed, that is acceptable in the corporate world.

In the 1970s such people were called "drop outs," and not necessarily in charitable terms. A brilliant doctor I know dropped out in her forties, leaving medicine and her marriage entirely and becoming a sculptor never to be heard from again. So, how did she get out? That is the wrong question.

What has to be understood is that only the person feeling so trapped can decide rather or not the trap is unacceptable. She is the observer as well as the observed when it comes to this, and it is her burden to decide what she is going to do about it with no apologies. The lady in question here was one of the top ten members of a class of some 300 in high school, and finished near the top of her graduating class in medical school, but has never appeared at a high school reunion; nor has she ever returned to the university of her medical training. She had the confidence and the courage to make a life changing mood with apparently no fallback position.

In another case with which I am familiar, a man in his mid-thirties making a good income decided to resign his executive position although married and the father of four pre-teenage children with no other income than what he had saved, which was modest.

What did he do? He took a two-year sabbatical, played tennis, read books, and wrote one, and then when nearly broke went back to school full time for six years to earn a Ph.D. in a totally different field than his earlier training consulting on the side to keep the family in beans.

Armed with his Ph.D., he did some consulting and teaching as an adjunct professor, then joined a client in a staff position, eventually promoted to executive status, retiring again in my 50s to write books.

Obviously, there was no plan to his strategy but every indication that he wished to escape his programming, relying on his wits to land on his fee, which he did. It is included here to suggest that chances are we have more options than we think if we simply trust in ourselves to be ready when the opportunity presents itself.

There was the boy, a poor high school student, so poor that his parents took him to a psychologist. After examining the boy, the psychologist said, "He has not found what he is looking for; once he finds it, he will be fine."

His parents looked skeptically at the counselor. The psychologist smiled, "Did you notice that your son hasn't missed a day of high school?" The parents shook their heads as it never occurred to them. "When your son finds what interests him, you will know it."

Years later, the young man was working in a high tech company as an hourly employee when he visited a friend who had a new computer. The friend explained to him how it worked – we are talking about the early 1980s. Thereafter, his fascination grew. He bought his own computer; then was confounded with his limitations in computer literacy. Sent for his high school records, enrolled in a junior college earning an associate degree; then transferred to a Big Ten University pursuing a degree in computer science. Today, he own his own computer consulting firm and remains fascinated with everything in that digital world.

The key to breaking free from the mundane to something more stimulating and engaging is to act; to do something. When you say to yourself, "I am trapped. I cannot get out of this," you are describing the trap precisely. But if you trust yourself and have the confidence to take a chance on yourself, you are going to say instead, "I am trapped no more. I'm going (to change jobs, move, seek new friends, change professions, go back to school) to embrace my freedom and see where it takes me."

Yes, you will encounter doubt, but you will be embracing not denying your fear. You will be trusting your instincts to do the right thing. You will be listening to yourself not what other people are saying what you should and shouldn't do. When you do this, you will be moving beyond your *chronic frustrations*.

Chronic frustration represents the cage you have created. It is no longer a trap. You are aware of it and are now involved in the process of escaping its bondage. By design or default, by the choices you have made, you will see you are precisely where you expected to be but want to be no longer. Everything will be nakedly apparent. All the pieces of your life will now make sense as to how you got to this point and why it is time to move on.

This is not happening to you. This is "you." You're not its victim, but its designer. So, instead of asking, "How do I get out of this," the question simply disappears. You step out of the cage and move on, as the people shown here were able to do.1

Notes:

1. James R. Fisher, Jr., *WHO PUT YOU IN THE CAGE?"* (2015) an Amazon Kindle paperback.

SIX

BE YOUR OWN BEST FRIEND!

"To have a friend you must be a friend, starting with yourself."

James R. Fisher, Jr., *The Reader's Digest*, June 1993

THE CRIPPLE GEINIUS OF OUR TIMES

Paternalism, benign or otherwise, has run its course. So have emotionalism, disordered enthusiasm and sentimental rhetoric. Grand schemes devoid of personal experience and uncritical acceptance of the views of others have too often been substituted for reason and have led instead to our being un-grown-up in our approach to life. The source of the problem is our failure to listen to ourselves, to look for answers in our own experiences rather than elsewhere, to be our own best friend.

The dry light of reason supported by science has changed the boundaries of consciousness where sensible man can verify himself without parental or institutional authority as to what is best for him. It starts by being his own best friend. Inequality, hierarchies, paternalism and nationalism have lost or are losing their clout as liberal rationalism is coming into its own, starting with the individual.

Immanuel Kant has written:

"Beings who have received the gifts of freedom are not content with the enjoyment of comfort granted by others."

We have seen and are seeing what comfort provided by others does to us. It leads to complacency but also wreaks havoc upon our conscience. The most distinguishing characteristic of being human is the freedom to act, to choose between what is self-enhancing or self-negating. Unless a person is author of his own acts, he cannot be held responsible for them. Where there is no responsibility, there is no morality.

Inanimate life does not make choices. It behaves as it does by the causal forces of nature, which are outside its control. This is not so if we are in control of our minds and bodies. In *Meet Your Own Best Friend* (2014), I write:

We are all authors of our own footprints in the sand, heroes of the novels inscribed in our hearts. Everyone's life, without exception, is sacred, unique, scripted high drama, played out before an audience of one, with but one actor on stage. The sooner we realize this the more quickly we overcome the bondage of loneliness and find true friendship with ourselves.

We have, as free men, the right to act rightly or wrongly, virtuously or viciously according to our lights, but we have limited control of our physical, chemical, biological and physiological internal guidance systems. So, if we choose to be at the mercy of causal forces, rationalizing that we have no control choosing to "go with the flow," then we might as well be a turnip.

Although causal laws may affect our bodies, they need not affect our moral center and its compass. This is our guidance system for action.

The external world is dealt with by science. The internal world, which should be free to make choices, is a function of voluntary actions and the foundation of morality. If there is no such freedom, there can be no possibility of moral law.

The case for being your own best friend is a moral one. Morality cannot be imposed upon us, but we can, indeed, impose morality on ourselves to act rationally and freely in our own best interests.

This will be, by extension, in the best interests of everyone we touch without exception.

We have reached the point with the rush of history and the calamity and complexity that it has enjoined to demonstrate autonomy (self-governance), meaning giving rules to ourselves, and the freedom from being coerced or from being determined by something or someone else we cannot control.

The ideas expressed here are meant to demonstrate that we are ends in ourselves, and not means to some arbitrary ends of someone else. This is so because we are the ultimate authors of the rules that guide us and to which we freely submit. To suggest that this is narcissistic or egoistic is to miss the point.

Should we be made to submit to something that is not consistent with our rational nature, but inconsistent with it, we degrade ourselves as persons, and allow ourselves to be treated as dependent children rather than as grownups, as mere animals or objects to be manipulated and managed as things to the satisfaction of others.

To deprive ourselves of the power of choice is to do to ourselves the greatest imaginable injury. No matter how benevolent the intention with which benevolence is presented it does us irreparable damage to our individual spirit.

Paternalism is the antithesis of being your own best friend. The effort here is not to make you more assertive against institutional paternalistic authority, but to offer you a framework for viewing your own reality differently by stepping outside external dependencies to experience internal integrity with the ethical authority consistent with your nature. What you do beyond that is up to you.

To be civilized is to be grown up, to behave responsibly to others and not allow anyone to treat you as a child, or to barter your freedom away from you with the promise of compensation and entitlements to satisfy your need for security and comfort. Nor should you allow flattery to be used against your nature to think or behave contrary to internal integrity and self-regard.

Our corporate society has relegated its citizens to dependent children, which is a manifestation of soft despotisms and destroyer of freedom. Writing 174 years ago (1843), Immanuel Kant had this to say:

"The man who is dependent on another is no longer a man, he has lost his standing, he is nothing but the possession of another man."

To attempt to do for others what they best do for themselves is to weaken their resolve, and diminish them as persons. The same holds true of ourselves. We have seen what has happened to our world as a result of this faulty doctrine in the 20th century. The fact that it lapses into the 21st century indicates how little self-regard is on display.

The intellectual movement of the 17th and 18th century, known as *The Enlightenment,* rose during an age when reason, not revelations, came to be valued as the ultimate source of true knowledge. The natural sciences were on the rise, technologies were developing, and philosophies of the mind were in vogue. *The Enlightenment* ushered in the decline of traditional religion, some would say its demise. Among other things, *The Enlightenment* encouraged reasoned skepticism of the precepts of religion. By stressing the power of human thought, a dismissive attitude developed for the spiritual as the emphasis was placed on objective verification of what could be known. As pointed out earlier with the *"cut & control"* phenomenon, when something of value is gained something is also lost as well. Spiritual identity and comfort has been the collateral damage in the wake of the fragmentation of religious conviction.

Modernity is the culture of separation and science leads the way with materialism obliterating the transcendental. Secular society has little time and gives even less attention to matters of the soul. With all the brilliance of science there seems however little room for wisdom as our fractured world strives on dignity deficits in a patchwork of scientific discoveries and technological inventions.

Corporate society, as expressed through technology, is too clever by half. Typical is the experience of a scientist who attempted to make synthetic rubber. Overnight the beaker solidified. He couldn't extract the material by conventional means, so he burned it off. The heat generated was so intense that he measured it. Thus solid propellant fuel was created, a happy accident, making the jet age possible.

We are also happy accidents. We come into the world and into a time in which man has mastered his environment nearly to the point of his extinction. The distinguished American entomologist Edward O. Wilson captures this sentiment in the first sentence of his biography, *Naturalist* (1994): *"I have been a happy man in a terrible century."*

The strangers we first encounter—our parents and immediate family—have much to do with how we are formed. We see, hear, watch and behave like them. We imitate what we see, hear and observe. These strangers reinforce or correct our interpretation of that experience with either applause or scolding. Our initial role in life is that of entertainer. From this we develop a high need to please others; to put a smile on their faces; to control them by giving pleasure; by manipulating them through exploitation of their weaknesses; and thus coming by default to exploit ourselves.

By the time we enter school we are professional pleasers. Now we are exposed to another set of strangers, teachers, who tell us what is true, important and what is not. We are compliant and pliable. What we see, hear and observe at school may not complement what we experience at home, seeding a budding conflict. When we attend church, Sunday school or the Temple, we learn of God and about oral history that is our culture. If we are not careful, what and who we are has been so identified and programmed into us that we are nearly total strangers to ourselves when we leave the home, and go out into the world on our own. The damage may be so great that it may require a lifetime to rectify that situation, which obviously many fail to do.

SEVEN

LOVE WHAT YOU DO!

There is no true and more abiding happiness than the knowledge that one is free to go on doing, day by day, the best work one can do, in the kind one likes best, and that this work is absorbed by a steady market and thus supports one's own life. Perhaps freedom is reserved for the man who lives by his own work and in that work does what he wants to do.

R. G. Collingwood (1889-1943), English philosopher and historian

FINDING THE POWER THAT RESIDES WITHIN

The most important marriage in life, and the one that so often is chosen more by accident than design, is one's life work. Yet, what one does one becomes. Work provides identity as much as it provides a means of sustenance. It can either be love made visible or the darkest kind of self-enslavement.

"Man must work," writes 19th century American clergyman Henry Giles, *"but he may work grudgingly or gratefully; he may work as a man, or as a machine. There is no work so rude that he may not exalt it; no work so impassive that he may not breathe a soul into it; no work so dull that he may not enliven it."*

Eric Hoffer, the longshoreman turned philosopher, loved manual labor because monotonous routine gave him ample time to think. He never worked without a small notebook and pencil in his pocket. An idea would spring into his mind, and he would jot down a couple of words to expand on later in the comfort of a lunch break, the sun beating down on his brow and his happy

95

hand dancing across the page. This is how he came to write his stunningly successful *The True Believer* (1951), a book that caught the attention and fascination of CBS Nightly News commentator Eric Severide.

Severide conducted a series of television interviews with Hoffer, resulting in the author becoming a national celebrity and financially secure writer. Did he quit his day job of working on the dock? Not on a bet. A reporter found it quite remarkable that a man with no formal education could write so profoundly.

"I can do that," Hoffer confessed, *"because my work on the dock is so impersonal. My mind is not taxed. I have the passion and energy to learn."*

His work blessed him and he blessed his work with many of his books still in print. He once wrote a piece for the Sunday Parade magazine in which he celebrated the glory of routine manual labor.

Hoffer, an immigrant, blind at six with his sight not restored until he was nineteen, discovered a love for the printed word, not in a classroom, but in the public library, a place accessible to everyone. He looked for the largest book with the smallest print, he says, with no clear understanding what he had chosen. It was a book of essays by the French essayist Michel de Montaigne (1533 – 1593). He delighted in the taste of Montaigne's words, his skeptical philosophy, and the rhythm of his mind.

This book opened his mind to view the world differently, not as he had, or thought he would prefer, but as he found it. A reporter asked, *"What is your system for generating ideas?"* Hoffer chuckled, having become used to others wanting a simple formula for him to explain his sudden fame. He confessed politely that he had no system; that his ideas came to him eclectically, like reading while standing on a corner, surprised by some interesting author that might pass by. We are all enriched today for the attention he gave that corner.

Not every worker is a writer, but every reader is a worker. James Hillman, author of *The Soul's Code* (1996), believes everyone without exception has a vocation. We associate vocations with the religious, but Hillman insists we all have vocations. It is in discovering and working on our vocation that we realize the true essence of our character, as well as our separate and unique individualism.

A person can be sullied, paradoxically, by too much or the wrong kind of formal education. Novelist Kurt Vonnegut, Jr. noted his wife could have been a distinguished novelist but for having taken too many writing courses.

President Franklin Delano Roosevelt once quipped to Interior Secretary Harold Ickes about Lyndon Johnson, then a twenty-eight-year-old congressman from Texas with a teacher college education, *"You know, Harold, that's the kind of uninhibited young pro I might have been as a young man if I hadn't gone to Harvard."* Johnson, of course, went on to become President of the United States.

It is so easy to put on hold what we would dream of becoming only to miss the rich experiences we have along the way. So often a person looks back over a long life, and sees those wonderful times he had, but never appreciated, because he was too busy looking ahead. More likely he saw those times as drudgery because they were things he had to do, not realizing they were making him into the person he would become. Emerson writes:

There is a time in every man's education when he arrives at the conviction that envy is ignorance; that imitation is suicide; that he must take himself for better or worse as his portion; that though the wide universe is full of good, no kernel or nourishing corn can come to him but through his toil bestowed on that plot of ground which is given to him to till.

The power which resides in him is new in nature, and none but he knows what that is which he can do, nor does he know until he has tried. Not for nothing one face, one character, one fact, makes much impression on him, and another none. This sculpture in the memory is not without pre-established harmony.

The eye was placed where one ray should fall, that it might testify of that particular ray. We but half express ourselves, and are ashamed of that divine idea which each of us represents. It may be safely trusted as proportionate and of good issues, so it be faithfully imparted, but God will not have his work made manifest by cowards.

Each chip whittled off the shapeless granite of one's being eventually produces a divine sculpture in the tradition of Michelangelo, as each seemingly insignificant job contributes to one's ultimate character and completeness. Emerson warns:

A man is relieved and gay when he has put his heart into his work and done his best; but what he has said or done otherwise shall give him no peace. It is a deliverance which does not deliver. In the attempt his genius deserts him; no muse befriends, no invention, no hope.

A person is what a person does, not eventually, but now. Whatever the job, be it part-time to assist in financing oneself through college, or a second job to add necessary income to the family budget, if it is done in love, it will blossom in kind. Conversely, if it is belittled as many part-time jobs are, it will scorch the soul and produce venom and contempt.

How others see one's work is as visible as a framed picture. A person came to me who was fired from a part-time job, a jewelry store in a shopping mall. She claimed the job was a no-brainer.

"I worked my ass off for this moron and this is what I get for it," adding the ethnic slur, kike under her breath to describe the owner.

"That's it!" I said.

"What's it?" she replied, confused.

"That term you just used that you didn't think I heard. That is why you got fired."

Self-righteously, she waved her cigarette in the air as if it were holy incense, saying each word with measured distinction. *"I never said that word once to a living soul in that place."*

"You didn't have to, the owner sensed it, and that was enough."

She folded her arms across her chest. I continued, *"Your attitude was showing just as much as that sweater you're wearing shows off your figure. You insulted his dignity, and quite frankly, you deserved what you got."*

I would like to report she learned from that experience, but unhappily, she did not. She has wandered through life like a tumbleweed blowing hither and yon while blaming the wind and everything else for her misfortune except herself.

Love and work are mutually inclusive. Kahlil Gibran calls work *"love made visible."* Together, love and work embody a synchronicity that merge work and play into one. Steve Jobs and Stephen Wozniak turned their love of gadgets into making video games. They didn't stop there. They went on to set the world on its head by bringing out the personal computer, "Mac," creating Apple, Inc.

They taught us a lesson about ourselves in doing so. They exposed the fact that companies can become blindsided and mind blinded just as readily as we as individuals can be shackled to an unbearable routine. Once a set formula freezes a company or individual in a frame, it is nearly impossible to grasp opportunities although they exist right under foot.

This happened to Xerox. The lab people at Xerox created essentially the computer that Apple, Inc. would eventually market. Xerox engineers were unable to persuade senior management that their personal computer was a marketable idea. Xerox has never fully recovered from that faux pas.

So often in this competitive world, where compare and compete psychology dominate, companies are seldom fully appreciative of their naked assets, which are not found in P&L statements, but in the ingenuity of their people.

Such companies are imprisoned in the corporate cage of old beliefs and practices, old attitudes and procedures, while taking comfort in that absurdity, *"If it ain't broke, don't fix it!* As author William L. Livingston IV notes in his book *Friends in High Places* (1990), such companies maintain a strategy of *ready, fire, aim!*

There is nothing plain or simple about a job or career. Animosity, although thought to be concealed, sticks out like an ugly blemish on the skin, as was the case with the jewelry clerk.

Attitude is always in full view. Without a word spoken, nonverbal indicators leave no doubt. President Roosevelt spotted a comer in Lyndon Johnson, and he was proven right.

THE ROLE OF THE MENTOR & SELF-MENTORING

The mentor senses potential in the neophyte. It could be something remembered of his own earlier self, or in the case of Roosevelt a melancholy regret. It is alleged that President John Fitzgerald Kennedy once confessed that if he could change three things, it would be his parents, his religion and his wife. History reveals Kennedy wasn't much into being mentored, as he couldn't distance himself from these conflicting intimacies, compounding the problem by seeing that his brother, Robert, was appointed Attorney General of the Justice Department, and then surrounding himself with other like-minded nepotistic thinkers.

Mentoring isn't the romantic ideal it is thought to be, but a projection of the doer's visualization of the unfinished novice in terms of the doer's own struggle.

What the mentor sees in the tenderfoot is neither showing nor hidden, neither a false self nor a true one. It is the mature perspective of a doer against the possibilities observed in an emerging one. Reality is the work performed at the moment. Promise is just that, promise. What Roosevelt saw in the clumsy, crude, amoral and aggressive Lyndon Johnson was a side of himself he kept hidden in his patrician gentrified roots.

A mentor perceives the folds of complexity, the topsy-turvy implications that are truth unexplored, that the unfinished doesn't know exist.

We don't know who we are until someone tells us. That is the important role of the mentor. No one gets to where they want to go, alone. Everyone needs help. But the help is often rejected because it is ill conceived or falsely perceived. Either the would-be-mentor is too timid or too bold, too circumspect or too subtle in the offering of help. It is not easy to be a mentor. On the other hand, exposure is crucial to the neophyte.

The tenderfoot works to attract attention to himself where influence resides. Lyndon Johnson's "uninhibited" style got the attention of the patrician President Roosevelt and paved his way to becoming a legislator in the US Congress of some distinction.

There was a colleague of mine at university who had a passion for farming. He came from an Iowa farm family of nine generations. His father, seeing conglomerates swallowing up independent farms in the district, was determined to save his son from that humiliation by seeing that he became a professional man. To please his father, he studied hard, got fair if not impressive grades, but his heart was always in farming.

One night in a college bull session, I said, "Mark, farming is your father's vocation. You talk of farming like it was a hobby. Don't you see the difference?" Meekly, apologetically, in a little boy's voice although twenty, he said, "Why can't it be both?" Why not indeed?

My friend stayed in school and took a law degree. I wonder how happily so. Many, such as Bill Gates, Steven Jobs and Stephen Wozniak, turned the love of tinkering into a springboard to fabulous careers. Jobs and Gates were college drop outs with the courage to pursue their avocation turning it into vocations. They did this as pioneers before the potential for the personal computer and software was known. With tinkerers, serendipity is always in the air.

When International Business Machine (IBM) offered Gates a contract loaded with constraints, he did not hesitate to sign. "Big Blue," however, failed to see the potential of this new technology. So, IBM didn't tie Gates down to licensing agreements.

Thanks to the IBM contract, Gates and his associates had the capital to create Microsoft, Inc. They purchased the rights to what would become MSDOS and then conceived Microsoft Windows. The rest is history. Like Xerox, IBM was blindsided by its failure to visualize cutting edge technology on the horizon.

One's avocation can indeed become one's vocation if one is not limited by facts. Eric Hoffer writes:

The war on the present is usually a war on facts. Facts are the toys of men who live and die at leisure. They who are engrossed in the rapid realization of an extravagant hope tend to view facts as something base and unclean. Facts are counterrevolutionary.

People, then, who pursue their avocation as a vocation are rebels with a cause, a cause perhaps not too clear in their minds, but a cause certainly not blinded or mesmerized by facts.

Think how the personal computer left giant IBM in the dust, a dust that has not yet settled, as "Big Blue" is still struggling to match the pace of the Steve Jobs' and Bill Gates' of the world.

IBM, as with General Motors (GM), was obsessed with facts: balance sheets; P&L statements; stock prices; customer preference. IBM failed to see the future in the personal computer. GM failed to see the future in the compact car until Europe, South Korea and South East Asia came to dominate that market.

GM is still in love with the SUV and large trucks that increasingly resemble military tanks. Consider this in the face of perennially fluctuating crude oil prices. These block-like gas guzzling cars and trucks still roll off the assembly line taking comfort in the fact that crude oil prices are around $55 whereas they have been more than $100 per barrel.

Nor has GM made much of a concession in its car design to the narrow streets of Europe and Asia. Surveys show Americans prefer "big" machines even as the American marketplace for "big" continues to shrink. Facts:

- It is facts that blind and confine, but not for rebels. The giants are in a reactionary mode; the rebels in attack mode. Young Davids are striking down Goliaths nearly every day. And why? They are not lock stepping to a system where departure from the norm is locked out.

No longer is the knee jerk reaction justified, "I have to make a living." Nor is it necessary to pretend that the marriage of love and work are not negotiable. Anyone can have a love affair with what they do. All it takes is the courage to make appropriate choices. There is little excuse for taking a job because the benefits are too good to pass up.

Corporate welfare is shrinking and will continue to do so. Entitlements, which have seldom been tied to performance, are a luxury companies can no longer afford. Nor is there much point in basing what you do on what other people think. Even if their opinions are important to you, they don't have to take residence in your head. Save your energy, and in the process save your mind as well. In terms of the job market, you have literally landed in paradise. Never has there been greater diversity, mobility, opportunity and flexibility in the job market than now.

Consider this: People often confess that they hate their jobs. When asked what they would prefer doing, they look aghast as if they have no idea. They forget that luck is a matter of preparation meeting opportunity.

AN UNEXAMINED LIFE IS NOT WORTH LIVING

When people tell you, they can't wait to retire, ask them what they plan to do in retirement. Invariably, they will answer with the inanity, "I plan to travel." You can only travel so much. So you ask, when you get traveling out of your system, what then? They look at you with that puzzled expression that tells you they haven't thought about that. Then to stir the pot a little more, you ask with a smile, "What have you always dreamed of doing if you only had the chance?" Many it would seem are even afraid to dream.

Someone asked my wife one day, "How do you feel about Jim sitting around reading and writing all day? Doesn't that get on your nerves?" She replied, "I would prefer that to having him sit in front of the television all day drinking beer and eating chips."

Devlin, mentioned in an earlier chapter, retired the first time in his mid-30s after completing an executive assignment for an American chemical company in South Africa. He had seen apartheid up close and personal, as well as executive corruption and malfeasance, and the insensitivity of his religion (Roman Catholicism) being adverse to a changing world, and decided to take a "time out." He never gave a thought to whether he could afford it or not. He knew it was what he had to do.

With a wife and four young children to support, and modest savings, he did little else for two years but read books, write and publish one, along with several articles for newspapers and magazines.

When nearly broke, he went back to school full time, year around for six years to earn my master's and doctor's degrees, keeping the family together at an uncertain socioeconomic level by consulting on the side.

This economic departure from affluence to mere subsistence was a shock to the family, especially his eldest son, not yet a teenager, who had aspirations to one day be a tennis great. This resentment of his father was carried into his mature years, yet it did not stop him from earning a six-figure income doing what he had always loved, playing and teaching of tennis. The others, less resentful, managed to find their way as well, but not all, however, doing what they loved.

This is shared knowing some will flinch trying to fathom the audacity or the insanity of his conduct. Not only has it worked for him, but for his family, as they were forced to be self-reliant and self-directed, and consequently, have earned their own dignity and identity.

One should feel no guilt for doing and being what makes one happy and productive. Doing what pleases oneself is a way of staying out of the cage of convention where misery is the common complaint. Two things to note:

- You should not be afraid to be free and to love what you do; nor should you be afraid to enjoy your work as if it were play.

- If you can muster the will and find the courage to make appropriate choices, you will find yourself listening to the rhythm of your own heart and not be saddled with a second hand life following the "right choices" preferred for you by others. You will be making choices consistent with the content of your character and talent.

Before you can please others you must first please yourself. Unfortunately, we are not programmed to seek self-contentment, yet that is the way we function best. Too often we unwittingly assume the role of the victim and take residence in our cage, then blame others for the confinement.

SELF-REGARD COMES WITH THE CURRENCY OF JOY NOT WITH THE BANKRUPTCY OF DESPAIR

It is much easier to be miserable at work resenting the company for not providing the desired satisfaction than to realize you are the company. If you don't feel you are the company, you are in the wrong company. The company and job are blameless.

We are living in the corporate world of modernity; a universe of states and corporations governed by administrative bureaucracies themselves subdivided into smaller and smaller units where decisions and choices are exercised by individual non-initiatives. Inaction, in such an institutional environment, becomes action; the absence of active choice substitutes for choice itself. In this climate, no one is responsible because no one is in charge. Leaderless leadership has found a home.

Consequently, you are never going to have the independence, control, flexibility or potential earning power working for someone else. There is a limit to what a company can provide. The German sociologist Max Weber wrote about this one hundred years ago and we have still not outgrown his bureaucratic model.1

If you are in school, stay in school, and get your degree. The pay gap between college graduates and everyone else reached a record high in 2013 based on the analysis of *Labor Department Statistics* by the *Economic Policy Institute* in Washington, DC.

- Americans with four-year college degrees made on average, 98 percent more an hour in 2013 than people without a degree. Although a college education can cost as much as $500,000, without a college degree will cost a person about $500,000 in lost earnings. So, from a zero sum perspective, college is relatively free to the holder of the degree.

On the other hand, despite all the hype to the contrary, most companies do a fair and equitable job paying for performance in what has been a fifteen year disappointing economic climate with rising inequality among those with and without college degrees. For younger readers, the decision not to attend college for fear it's a bad deal is an economically irrational decision given these statistics.

Employers typically get a bad rap for not hiring, not investing, not expanding. Start a business and be an employer for a short while, and you will understand how difficult it is to stay in business, and what a crap shoot it can be reading the economic tea leaves wrong.

A company can only do so much for its workers. A more important job is for workers to invest in themselves, which increases their capabilities to ride the economic roller coaster that the economy can sometimes prove to be. Companies no longer have the wherewithal to assume the role of surrogate parent that they did during the booming period (1950 - 1980). Entitlements and union contracts put them in a corporate cage of which they still have not escaped.

A company today must stay lean and mean or it goes into bankruptcy. A prudent company recognizes the pivotal change in the distribution of power and control and deals with it proactively. The irony is that it costs companies far less when *true pay for performance* is swapped for huge entitlements. Knowledge workers want to contribute, but too often that brainpower is ignored for *business as usual practices.* This finds these workers reverting back to passive behaviors. Will and power are an individual affair, but a company can leverage this to mutual satisfaction if conscientiously engaged.

DO YOU HAVE A DREAM JOB IN MIND?

Several years ago, I was having dinner in Amsterdam with my European executive colleagues. The conversation got around to our "dream job." There were five of us, all in comfortable economic circumstances with solid educations in technology, but not one of us in our dream job.

One wanted to be a farmer, even though he had never farmed in his life, another wanted to be a large newspaper editor, yet had never published an article, a third wanted to be a radio personality but had no media experience, a fourth wanted to be a general, but had never been in the military, and then there was me, who wanted to be a writer.

Before joining this company, I had had one book published and a score of articles in trade journals. While with this company, I had written more than a dozen monographs, and was working on a book, which would become *Work Without Managers* (1991).

What we dream is often as incredulous to our conscious mind as those obsessed with retirement, and thinking only of "traveling." Dreams rarely materialize into real experience, but they often become preoccupations.

As such, they encounter no risks or pain, no failure or disappointment, nor do they require any preparation or engagement. In my case, I was working the problem treating my work as a laboratory for my writing. For me, dreaming was the other side of reality.

Dreamers can confuse need with want, as need touches the soul and want only the appetite. Need and want are worlds apart. We need an automobile for transportation but we want a $150,000 golden buggy. As basic as this is, many confuse the two.

If you could imagine work as an expression of happiness, everything else might look quite differently. Happiness husbands our energy, which is always spiraling down. German philosopher Martin Heidegger puts it plainly: *As soon as you are born, you are old enough to die.*

Imagine the freedom this realization provides. You appreciate every moment. You have no time for being petty, vengeful, or self-pitying. You are open to all possibilities. You don't wait for circumstances to be just right, you take charge! You invest in the future by doing what is fulfilling in the present. You realize life is short, and failure is life's greatest teacher. Failure is a wake-up call to the sleepwalker who marvels, once awake, that he is on the threshold of success.

POWER AND WILL REVEALED

Abraham Lincoln had so many failures that books are devoted exclusively to them. Something within, however, kept him on task. He didn't let his lack of formal education hinder him; his failure in business; his failure to be elected to the US Senate; his failure to keep the nation whole once elected president leading to the Civil War; his failure to keep his favorite son alive; and his failure in marriage to provide his family with a sanctuary of tranquility.

He however persevered. When his generals failed him; when members of his cabinet talked derisively behind his back; when his wife became a yoke around his neck; when the war was going badly, he kept true to his role demands. He was forgiving and understanding and had no time to carry a grudge. Yet, he was a melancholy man subject to fits of depression. Perfection is not parent to a cause, but its child. He understood this and kept to his appointed task of healing the nation.

Power and will as Schopenhauer has shown is confrontational, conflicting, and contradicting. Lincoln, despite his mild manner, had a despotic will. He took command on the battlefield when his commanding general postured but failed to engage the enemy, relieving popular General George Brinton McClellan of his command. He reactivated a general, a reputed drunk, to the position, a man who also had a reputation of getting things done. General Ulysses S. Grant was a soldier with a will to win often at any cost, which was kindred to his own spirit.

Power and will defy convention and the expected and go against the grain of established practices. You cannot read of Lincoln's presidency without appreciating his constant thinking outside the box, or the magnitude of the draconian measures taken to assure final victory. This was demonstrated in General Ulysses S. Grant's bloody campaign through the mid-South and General William Tecumseh Sherman's deep-South scorched earth policy through Georgia on his "March to the Sea."

Without Lincoln's hard choices as president, we would not be the nation we are today. Hard choices rise out of the will to power in the crucible of confrontation, conflict and contradiction, having little to do with harmony's way.

Choice defines us. It can be no other way. We cannot be namby-pamby about our choices, and expect our will to prevail. Nor can we expect to be all things to others and be true to ourselves. We cannot worry about how decisions will rest with others if they are right with us. Choices may be conflicting with others, but that is all right as long as they are not conflicting with what, where and who we are.

Find love in some kind of work and you will find love in life. What could be more compelling and a greater reward?

Notes:

1. See Felix Merz, *Max Weber's Theory of Bureaucracy and Its Negative Consequences,* Grin Verlag, Germany, 2011. This is a seminar paper that builds on the sociology of Robert K. Merton's functional analysis of Weber.

EIGHT

CHOOSING A PROFESSION & TAKING CONTROL OF YOUR LIFE

What one thinks one becomes.

James R. Fisher, Jr., *Fragments of a Philosophy*

My son, Alex, is not sure where he wants to go to college, or what to do when he grows up. I'm still working for an insurance company, still working on what I want to do when I grow up, too.

Single parent, *46, college graduate*

I had dreamed of becoming a scientist in general, and a paleontologist in particular, ever since a Tyrannosaurus skeleton awed and seared me at New York's Museum of Natural History when I was five years old. I had the great good fortune to achieve these goals and to love the work with fully sustained joy to this day, and without a moment of doubt or any extended boredom.

Stephen Jay Gould, *Rock of Ages: Science and Religion* (1999)

EVERYONE'S LIFE IS UNIQUE, SCRIPTED HIGH DRAMA

Philosopher Arthur Schopenhauer (1788 -1860) believed "the will" existed independently of one's perceptions. In essence, he argued that all human actions and knowledge were constituted by the human will:

It is only in reflection that to will and to act are different; in reality they are one.

This all-encompassing human will, as characterized by Schopenhauer, is a blind force striving to power. It reveals itself to everyone directly as the in-itself of the person's own phenomenal being. Schopenhauer points out that when you reach an advanced age and look back over your lifetime, it can be seen to have had a consistent order and plan, as though composed by some novelist. Events that when they occurred might have seemed accidental and of little import in retrospect turn out to have been indispensable factors in the composition of a consistent plot.

So who composed this plot? Schopenhauer again suggests that just as an aspect of ourselves in which our consciousness is unaware, composes our dreams, so, too, our whole life is composed by the will within to bring that life of ours to completion.

Many readers, especially younger readers, might have difficulty fathoming this philosophy. Indeed, they might reject it out of hand as totally absurd. But I can tell you it rings true to me after eight decades of living.

As a child, I had a natural inclination to wonder that was fed by my Irish Roman Catholicism. As a youngster, I read the dictionary as if it were a novel in the interest of developing the tools to express that wonder. As a student, I was attracted to dead authors that kept reassuring me that I was on the right track. Even my passion for athletics as a youth never deterred me from this predisposition to wonder and to attempt to express this wondering in words.

My da derailed me temporarily from this proclivity as his dying words jolted me, which were: *"Your mother tells me you want to be a writer. Jimmy, how can you be a writer when you don't even write a good letter."* Then he added soberly, *"If you persist in this madness, you'll starve to death, mark my words."*

His influence was so great that when a professor in undergraduate school wanted to recommend me for the *Honors Program in the Humanities*, instead of the sciences, which I was pursuing, I declined. The professor, however, planted the seed and introduced me to many authors that I would perhaps never otherwise have read.

By the serendipity of my professional career, I was taken to places around the world to experience all levels of society and working situations. This provided me with the empirical data that would give my writing the legs of support that it would need.

My da was right in that I have never made a living as a writer. I write because Schopenhauer's words have proven true for me. Writing is part of my constitution. It is my vocation as avocation.[1]

English celebrated dramatist Ben Jonson (1572 - 1637) once said: *"Only an idiot would endure the hardship of writing without concern for the coin."* I take exception to this having published hundreds of journal articles and thousands of missives on my website and blog that have connected with readers about the globe.

Psychologist James Hillman has a theory consistent with Schopenhauer. He calls it his *"acorn theory."* Hillman proposes that each life is formed by a particular image, an image that is the essence of that life and calls it to its destiny, just as the mighty oak's destiny is written in the DNA of the tiny acorn.

This theory gets beyond the missteps of youth and the collision of character with desire, family pride, guilt and the influence of others, as there is almost a mystical need within for self-expression and therefore self-realization. Hillman insists that this is our "calling," our vocation in the center of our being waiting to be answered.

The question being asked is: what is in your heart to do, to be and to have, and why? 2 You need only listen to that will stirring from deep within you. It will be what you love but have been afraid to wish for, finding it too fanciful to be realized.

THE ACORN AND THE O'REILLY FACTOR

Provocative television journalist Bill O'Reilly has painted houses, driven a taxi cab, did odd jobs while going to high school and college, then a high school teacher, and ultimately going to Harvard Business School and earning an MBA. O'Reilly's career has been a winding road but always a consistent essence.

Born in New York City in 1949, O'Reilly is currently a staple on Fox television with his popular *"The O'Reilly Factor,"* where he confidently declares, "The spin stops here!" Now, an incredibly successful author with his *"Killing Lincoln,"* and other killing books in this series selling in the tens of millions, his television career started modestly after leaving teaching and has involved stints in many television news outlets around the country before reaching his current status of having the most popular news program on cable television. His Hillman acorn is, indeed, now a giant oak.

As a correspondent, he won several Emmy Awards before moving to *Inside Edition*, a popular "infotainment" program. Then when FOX News launched its conservative attack against the liberal networks (NBC, ABC, CBS) and cable news (CNN, MSNBC), he was hired to launch *The O'Reilly Factor*, which features conservative commentary and interviews and quickly became the most watched cable news program on television.

Besides *Killing Lincoln* (2011), he is authored *Killing Kennedy* (2012), *Killing Jesus* (2013), and *Killing Patton* (2014). Earlier, he published *The O'Reilly Factor* (2000) and *The No Spin Zone* (2001) as well as the novel *Those Who Trespass* (1998), all bestsellers.

 Few would deny his acorn has produced a giant oak, as he has undoubtedly listened to his own heart and smiled with understanding but with some rancor when, despite his popularity, he has never gotten his just due from the liberal media as he considers himself a balanced and fair journalist.

THE HEART HAS ITS REASON

One of the first missteps we make in choosing a career is leading with our head instead of our heart. Reason looks at what careers pay the most, how long it takes to become qualified, what degrees are the least intellectually demanding, what universities have the most successful students, and on and on.

Meanwhile, there is an unconscious blind force within us that has its own intentions that protects us from ourselves. The head is looking for an insurance policy guaranteeing a good outcome, which includes rapid promotion, generous disposable income, and a good benefit package. The best-laid plans often go awry, but something always seems to save us from being blindsided. Some of us call it "our guardian angel," others instinct, still others a matter of self-preservation, or a sixth sense.

At the same time, we all know people who disregard this guardian spirit, this blind force of the will, and are instead given to being self-destructive, accident-prone, or forever hyper as if perennial children. Should this be the case we will fail to grow up to be the tree our acorn has destined us to be.

Still others blame this failure on their chromosomes projecting the failure on the seed of their parent's whose genetic code failed to give them an advantage of being tall and beautiful, bright and flawless. Parents are also blamed, by the same people for what they did or didn't do for themselves in their early years, now long past. The more we are of this mindset the more our biography is the story of the victim. What such individuals fail to realize is that the victim is the flipside of the hero.

Regrettably, our culture reinforces this victim complex in the popular press, cult psychology, and even all these scientific queries that claim it is a "gene" issue that causes us to be fat, lazy, and antisocial or mean.

We love justifiers who take us off the hook. We want to believe it is not our fault that we are unhappy; have failed to grow up; or failed to find our niche. We are in a cage with more than enough justification to explain away ourselves to ourselves without any help from authorities.

There has been a craze over the last several decades on self-fulfillment and self-development. Over the last forty years, authors have become household words to those who subscribed to the idea of finding one's "inner child," never one's "inner adult."

Author Wayne Dyer (1940 - 2015) became one of the premier pioneers of the self-help industry publishing more than forty books, including *Your Erroneous Zones* (1976) and *Pulling Your Own Strings* (2011). He filled a niche raising more than $100 million for PBS Television, where he gave regular seminars to millions of viewers. At the same time, the 1970s was the era of the personal trainer that spawned an industry doing for the self-indulgent what Dyer and others pointed out that they best do for themselves.

Americans did go to college and did earn degrees, but once employed expected employers to take care of them in the style to which they had become accustomed. Daniel Yankelovich writes a scathing report of this mindset:

The predicaments of self-fulfillment seekers arise from the defective strategies they deploy to achieve these ambitious goals. These strategies are defective, first, in their economic premises. The typical self-fulfillment strategy presupposes that economic well-being is a virtual citizen's right, automatically guaranteed by both government and economy.

A strategy built on the presumption of ever-expanding affluence is bound to run into trouble even in a country as abundant as our own. The most serious defect, however, is psychological.

People unwittingly bring a set of flawed psychological premises to their search for self-fulfillment, in particular the premise that the self is a hierarchy of inner needs, and self-fulfillment an inner journey to discover these. This premise is rarely examined, even though it leads people to defeat their own goals and to end up isolated and anxious instead of fulfilled.[3]

Reading life backwards enables us to see how early passions were in fact premature indicators of behavior now. It suggests that growth is less cultural and more genetic, that development makes sense only when it reveals a facet of the original impression. Obviously, we progress and regress from day to day, see some faculties develop and others wither. Our person, however, is not a process. As Picasso says, *"I don't develop. I am."*

The *"code of the soul,"* as Hillman puts it, is in our character. We are born with a character unique, as well as a *distinct calling.* We may postpone or miss our *calling* and deny our character and suffer for it. But this defining image, call it a *"second self,"* saves us constantly from making bad choices or nudges us gently when we should go for it if we would but listen. The cage becomes our home when we don't.

John LeCarre is a successful novelist of the espionage genre. He is also something of an apologist. In reading his life backward, it is clear that he wants to leave the impression it was all by chance, an accident, and not by design. He writes:

I began writing because I was going mad with boredom. Not the pathetic, listless kind of boredom that doesn't want to get out of bed in the morning, but the screaming, frenetic sort that races around in circles looking for real work and finding none.

I had tried teaching "backward" children, and most of them were suffering from exactly what I was suffering from: boredom. They had sat at the back of their classes, and been bored stiff. I had tried teaching at Eton, but at Eton I often felt younger than the boys, and quite as much in need of a good tutor as they were. And I certainly wasn't ready to see straight down the corridor to the end of my life: housemaster at forty, retirement at sixty, cottage in Devon, and on God, let me please go gentle into that good night.

While teaching I had dabbled in commercial art during the school holidays, but not with much success. To satisfy me, everything I drew or painted should have explained the meaning of life. But you don't get many opportunities to express your soul when you are knocking out children's book jackets at eight pounds a crack.[4]

The next chapter of his life was the world of Whitehall and MI5 as a low-level clerk in His Majesty's government's spy business. He reflects,

I toiled from morning and often till late into the evening at the dossiers of people I would never meet: should we trust him? Or her? Should their employers trust them? Might he be a traitor, spy, lonely decider, or a suitable case for blackmail by the unscrupulous opposition? Thus I, who seemed to have no adult understanding of myself, was being asked to sit in judgment on the lives and loves of others. I was not versed in the ways of the world, only my own. The only tools I possessed were the possibilities of my own nature.

These were of many sorts in those days, and the imaginative bridges that I built to my paper suspects earned me a reputation for, of all things, perspicuity. Nothing could be further from the truth. All I was doing was inventing people out of the meager clay of telephone taps, purloined mail, and investigators' reports. What else I gave my suspects came from myself. It wasn't good intelligence work, but in that mediocre world it could easily pass for such. And it turned out to be excellent training for the career I had not yet consciously embarked upon: named that of the novelist.[5]

The paradox of this author was to escape the falseness of his life by discovering life's truth in writing fiction. He was obsessively involved in the *content* and *context* of life, finding it boring, when the *subtext*, beyond his consciousness was screaming to be addressed. He did so ultimately in creating a fictitious world of dissembling and dissemblers. He found his niche by stumbling into an artistic creative life, but chooses to find this incomprehensible and only a chance affair.

By the strength of his intellect, he forced himself to observe humanity with clinical objectivity. Moody and self-estranged by nature, LeCarre was a sentimental man long in exile from himself, which only strengthened his deep love of his native England, a nation he felt failed to keep pace with a changing world.

He fed hungrily on his school days through the character of George Smiley, its beauty, its rational ease, and the mature slowness of its judgments. The glory days of England were gone but he could freeze-frame them in prose. Unconsciously, his life as a spy was his laboratory for the profession that chose him, that of the novelist.

*　*　*

Were you to take a moment to read your life backwards, my guess is that you would see similar patterns to John LeCarre's unfolding: that is, the false steps, the anxiousness, the self-rebuke, then the recovery, the surprised changes of direction, a collection of syncopating detours, finally arriving precisely where you are now. Where you are now is most likely where you were meant to be.

The picture in the frame shows its face at an early age. Some fill in the frame with their passions; others look to what brings attention to them in spite of their passions. The former are inner-directed; the latter are outer-directed.

Golda Meir, who led Israel during the 1970s, found her picture in the frame in the fourth grade while in the Milwaukee public school system. She organized a protest group against requiring poor people to purchase schoolbooks they couldn't afford.

Stephen Jay Gould loved dinosaurs as a boy of five telling everyone he was going to be a paleontologist. When he still indicated such passion when he was ten, other children made fun of him, calling him a "baby." It didn't deter him, going on to become one of the world's great scholars in that discipline.

Yehudi Menuhin, the renowned violinist and conductor, asked for a violin at four. When he was given a toy violin with metal strings, he erupted into tears. He wanted a real violin!

James Hillman's "acorn theory" insists each child is a gifted child; every child has a *calling*. So, if we're not allowed to organize a protest group, feed your passion for dinosaurs, or acquire a real violin, and your life spirals into unanswered prayers, whom do we blame? Your parents? Hilton has something to say about that:

121

The fantasy of parental influence on childhood follows us through life long after the parents are faded into photographs, so that much of their power comes from the idea of their power. Why do we cling to the parental fallacy? How does it still parent us, comfort us? Are we afraid to admit the daimon (angel) into our own lives, afraid that it might have called us once, might still be calling, so we hid out in the kitchen? We retreat to parental explanations rather than face destiny's claims.[6]

COMPENSATORY ADJUSTMENT

Just as the blame game doesn't work to our advantage when it comes to choosing a profession, compensating for real or imagined shortcomings is not the way to emotional satisfaction in a career. Sometimes there is more than a grain of truth to clichés. For example, an excruciatingly shy person of fragile physique and diminutive size may assert himself to compensate for a sense of inferiority by a menacing superiority.

That was the picture in the frame of *Generalissimo Francisco Franco*, who ruled Spain with an iron fist for more than thirty years. At fifteen, tiny and baby-faced, he entered the Infantry Academy at Toledo and was handed a light weapon instead of a heavy rifle. He boldly announced, *"Whatever the strongest man in my section can do, so can I."*[7]

Adolph Hitler had a similar history. He wanted to be an architectural designer and painter but couldn't pass the entrance exam at the Academy of Art in Vienna. One of his pretentious schemes was to design Berlin as the premier city of the world in grandiloquent architecture. He spent as much time with this obsession as with the war. Incidentally, for his failure to win entrance into that school, he blamed his Jewish examiners. His revenge materialized into the *"Final Solution,"* also known as the Holocaust.

Psychologist *Alfred Adler*, the founder of individualistic psychology, claims 70 percent of art students have optical anomalies, and that many great composers such as *Mozart, Beethoven* and *Bruckner* had degenerative hearing. Adler further claims that challenges of illness, birth defects, poverty, or other unfavorable circumstances contribute to high achievers.

American Noble Laureate *James Watson*, co-discoverer of the double helix of DNA, admits to an average intelligence to the brilliance of his English Nobel Laureate colleague, *Francis Crick*. Watson's intrusive personality and natural curiosity noted the significance of the x-ray of coal by the cryptographer *Rosalind Franklin*. Her "photograph 51" indicated a distinct double helix for the genetic nature of coal, which was the double helix of DNA.[8]

Compensating adjustment may be the stimulus for higher achievement, but not necessarily inner-directedness. *Professor Emeritus Billy G. Gunter* of the University of South Florida, prefers to call this *"ambient deficiency motivation."* He argues we are inclined to be attracted to what we lack: for example, a criminal's desire to be a police officer, a mortal sinner a priest, and so on.

Chances are there is a cultural drive imminent within most Americans to amount to something, to exercise power and influence, all characteristics of *outer-directedness*. The United States of America in particular and many Western societies in general are *outer-directed societies*. Perhaps it is a manifestation of the Calvinistic *Protestant Work Ethic*. In any case, by compensating for real or imagined weaknesses within such people transform inabilities into empowerment and control.

We see this displayed in some chief executive officers of corporations. They exhibit a single mindedness to reach their Mount Olympus thinking in terms of strengths, and ignoring their weaknesses. Unfortunately, too frequently they compound the problem by surrounding themselves with likeminded support people, who tend to magnify their deficiencies. Consequently, the residue of early childhood embarrassments or assumed wrongs can be detected in the quality of their leadership.

Compensatory adjustment has little to do with passion, inspiration, or the élan of self-forgetfulness. It amounts to putting a person in somebody else's frame robbing the individual of an authentic identity and unique life. Superiority emerges from our lower rather than our higher centers.

George Washington became America's first president, not because he was as brilliant as *Thomas Jefferson, John Jay, Alexander Hamilton or James Madison*, but because he understood the heart and mind of ordinary citizens of the new republic. Many wanted to make him a monarch, or president for life, but he would have none of that. He had a vision and a mission, which had no room for self-aggrandizement. He was the perfect leader because he was the complete follower.

Abraham Lincoln, unlike *Washington*, elicited neither the respect nor the admiration of those around him, yet they were both *inner-directed leaders*. Every member of Lincoln's presidential cabinet felt superior to him culturally, intellectually and politically. They saw him as a country bumpkin, unsophisticated and unfinished. True, he rose out of the soil of mid-country where conflicting values and beliefs were painfully in evidence. His own wife was a southerner with biases similar to her people with a sense that she married below her station.

What *Lincoln* showed, as did *Washington* before him, is that almost every extraordinary life encompasses a vision, an ideal that calls them to the fore. It is often a vision that eludes them like a ghost in the night, or an unknown sense that this is why they were born. Adversity, criticism, fraudulent claims against them, even embarrassing defeats fail to deter them from their course.

The vision is bigger than they are, a vague presence that walks with them all their days. They persist simply because the *calling* is not an echo chamber from the disenchanted, but a drum roll from within. Extraordinary people are not different people. That is a myth. Where they differ is that they are driven by motivation whereas others are driven by distraction.

Imagine, if you will, a world in which a profession is chosen only on the basis of the greatest earning power, the most prestige, greatest distance from the hoi polloi, or the best opportunity to power and influence.

Then imagine further if that professional determines their decisions only on the basis of polls, employee surveys, profitability, and customer preferences irrespective of ethics, morality, or long-term consequences. Such a professional, should that be the case, would epitomize *outer-directedness.* For these compensatory adjustments, the attention is likely to kill the spirit, as there is no apparent authentic inner life, while feigning glory in the cage of mediocrity.

We live in a time when we allow pundits, soothsayers, gurus, experts, statisticians, scientists, celebrities, mass communicators, educators, and the religious to simplify the extraordinary complexities of modern life, and prescribe piecemeal what we should think, feel, believe, eat, drink and how we should behave without so much as a fair thee well protest.

How many reading this believe a cell phone is an absolute necessity; a new automobile every three years a prudent move; who are down on their favorite team if it has a losing season; who only read books on the bestseller list; and watch television shows currently in the top ten; who escape their own lives through soap operas, celebrity games, people magazines and films of the rich and famous; and who think Bill Gates is a genius because he is the richest man in the world?

People say television is garbage, but any television program needs a 37 percent share of the television audience to stay on the tube, and some programs display some pretty horrific stuff, so somebody must be watching.

If someone asks you, what you think about rap music, hard rock, virtual reality television, funky clothes, and you are not into that culture, chances are you will pause, not only not to offend but to give the impression you are "with it." The same goes for tattoos. And so, we consider the prudent thing to do is to say nothing or lie.

Everybody is in a hurry. Time is money! So, we hurry. We can't stand to be alone; can't stand a noise free environment where there is no radio, no television, no talking, just silence. Silence is imposing, threatening, intimidating, and boring. This suggests that we are unable to stand our own company.

We want to fit and to fit in. We want to belong. We want to choose a profession where we will be accepted, admired, even envied, and then others will want our company. Then we will be somebody. But alas, *"the someone"* we want to be is likely to have little room for *"the someone"* that we already are.

In other words, we have no room for ourselves. We want to belong to everyone else without belonging to ourselves. We have turned off the light *of inner-directedness* and are bouncing off the walls in *outer-directedness* psychologically blindfolded. We need to appreciate the importance of our own lives before we can choose a profession that will fit us, bring us satisfaction and peace, and most of all, fulfillment.

We don't seek self-fulfillment by going after it, as the gurus would suggest. We find it by staying home and getting acquainted with ourselves as ourselves. We discover the poetry of our soul, not in a scientific report, but liking, and yes loving who we are, not who we are going to be, but who and what we are right now.

Our Western mind is programmed to time. We have trouble stopping the clock. It is inconceivable to us to think in terms of *psychological time* when the only time we appear to understand is *chronological time.* Consequently, our minds are geared to *chronological time.* It convinces us we have plenty of time to change to more appropriate and sustaining behavior; that we are too young to have a career or worry about growing up and taking responsibility for ourselves. Say, you are seventeen and haven't given it much thought, or seventy and think it is too late to worry about such things. In both cases, you would be wrong.

At seventeen, we're not supposed to know our own mind when we may know it perfectly well, but are afraid to assert such knowledge. I know a lad who was forced by his farmer parents to be a dentist, when he wanted to be a farmer. He became a dentist, and most unhappily so, and dreamed all the way to retirement to be a farmer, which he now is at the age of seventy.

There is an artist who at 16 preferred painting to schoolwork and now at age 19 is selling her paintings for upwards of $100,000. She scoffs at the idea she is a genius. She sees her *Maker* working through her, and gives *Him* all the credit. At this moment, her *inner-directedness* is healthy and in charge.[9]

RESTRUCTURING PERCEPTIONS

The first order of business, it would seem in this business of choosing a profession consistent with one's *calling*, is to be introduced to oneself as a unique human being. This amounts to restructuring perceptions relative to two primary sources: our desires and our *interests*.

From an early age, each of us are "turned on" by certain things and "turned off" by others. Not infrequently, what is a turn off to us is equally a turn off to our peers, and perhaps our parents as well. The tendency is to unwittingly deaden our desires to be consistent with those important to others, failing to realize these desires may however importance to us.

We're back into the "fitting in" business again. Neglect of what really moves us can lead to all passions spent. Then there is little fun and even less humor to existence. We are leading a secondhand life. Mythologist Joseph Campbell, echoing the Buddha tradition, puts it simply, *follow your bliss.*

Ironically, rejection of our normal desires leads to an obsession with "finding ourselves." We become self-help junkies with a tranquilizing addiction for soothing anodynes for our troubled souls, which go into cold storage.

Our heads become filled with quotation marks around such words as performance, growth, creativity, threshold, continuum, response level, integration, synergy, identity, development, readiness, synchronicity, validation, boundaries, coping mechanisms, programming, operant conditioning, variance, subjectivity, adjustment therapy, verifiable results, value-free analysis, test results, emergence, hope, preference tests, biofeedback and limits.

Closely tied to interests are our *values.* The source of our values are perceptions including spiritual sensitivity to our relationship to Our Creator, or our personal, social and professional relationship to others. Seldom do we think in terms of our personal relationship to ourselves. These form our character and personify our motives, which, in turn, express our *interests.* Just as desires can be deadened by attack, so also can our *interests.*

The well-motivated person is interested and passionate about something. It can be life, work, study, nature, people, science, sports, literature, religion, philosophy, something. The more intense the interests the more purposeful the behavior.

Should a person's interests be constantly rained on, the spark can be lost, and apathy replaces interests, and with it purposefulness.

Extrinsic interests often become expressed as "what is in it for me?" With such interests, a line is drawn between the head and the heart, between work and play, between things we have to do and things we wants to do. In a most compelling way, the person's orientation becomes *outer-directed* rather than *self-directed* or *inner-directed.*

Intrinsic interests dominate the *inner-directed* person. These refer to interests in and of themselves. Play and work are mutually inclusive. All the things the person does on or off the job are considered self-renewing. Work is viewed as love made visible. Contrast this with the person who does what he does because these things must be done or because of what they may lead to down the road.

Obviously, a combination of *intrinsic interests* and *extrinsic interests* drive most people. That said there is a healthy relationship between what is expected and what is accomplished in the person who is constantly growing.

GROWING DOWN WHILE GROWING UP!

Using Hillman's metaphor, like the acorn, we grow down establishing solid roots in our core personality, and out of that core personality *inner-directedness.* Then, we are ready to grow up to embrace our opportunities. What seems fundamental to career selection and success is recognition of who is in charge and why. This is the difference between being in a reactive mode having others dictate the choices we make in life, and being proactively in charge.

When we avoid the burden of choosing a career, we are like a willing passenger in somebody else's vehicle. We have no idea where we are and no control over where we are going. Given this situation, it is easier to plead the victim than the victor; play the blame game than launch ourselves into another direction; more convenient to say we are too old, can't afford the risks, or are saddled with too many responsibilities than to admit we lack the courage to take charge.

It is admittedly difficult to develop a solid core personality with conviction when we grow from the outside in rather than the inside out. Parents, peers, priests and professors are bombarding our psyches with what is right and proper for us to do and be, and we often are listening with rapt attention to them, while disregarding that little drummer inside suggesting a different cadence and direction.

Not only can we lose our momentum we can become absolutely stuck. Our anxiety level increases as we fight a war between pleasing others and pleasing ourselves. This is a conflict that can never be won. It is a stalemate not unlike the recent wars we have had in Vietnam, Iraq and Afghanistan.

Am I suggesting it is a national problem? Indeed, I am. We have become a leaderless society with no one in charge, staying the same, missing the changes, burning up energy in relentless polarity, leaving the future up for grabs. We cannot solve a national malaise, but we can resolve it at the personal level by establishing that we will be engaged; that we will listen to our heart and what it tells us, and that we will politely disregard the voices of distraction.

It is so easy to drift unconsciously into a job and make it a career as if we were sleep walking through life. Wishes are the dreams we dream when we are awake. Never be afraid to dream. If you can visualize a career, you are already in the frame but don't know it. Relax and let it happen, and it will.

If you look at friends and colleagues happy in work, chances are you will find they are self-pleasers without making a case for it; creatively involved in work without worrying about conforming to an arbitrary standard; performing at a high level rather than worrying about making an impression.

You sense they have a moral center guided by a moral compass. Such people have discovered that what serves others serves them as well. Moreover, they have no reluctance to say "no" when it is prudent to do so, and to say "yes" when it serves the situation. Nor do they have any trouble abandoning ship when the culture is not conducive to their purposes. They don't make waves but quietly move on to a more appropriate climate.

They behave in this way because they don't confuse motivation with money, or mindset with mentality:

- *Motivation is a drive within.* It is concerned with the "why of behavior," and consists of two facets, motives and incentives. Motives are found in the person's character or value system, while incentives relate to the work environment including pay, fairness issues, and so on. Motives and incentives are the two sides of the same coin, which are fueled by our desires and lubricated by our interests. What motivates us may not be what others desire for us.

- *Money is a common justification for doing and being whatever.* Money is a poor motivator. It can demotivate if we are paid too much or too little for what we are doing. A justifiable raise has a short-duration as an incentive. When money is the only arbiter to performance, it can derail desire and diminish interests.

- *Mindset is the way a person thinks things seem to appear, not how they actually are.* Perceptions can be flawed. Since the workplace culture represents an attitude, if your mindset is not in sync with the culture, either it is wrong for you or you are wrong for it.

- *Mentality is not an intelligence quotient but an index of the prevailing norm.* Is the workplace supportive of learners or knowers, listeners or tellers? Are doers consulted for answers because they are thinkers as well? If so, it is a place where problems will be confronted and solved, not avoided and denied. It is a place for learners to grow.

The seed you plant is pride in what you do, passion in the doing, patience when growth and development are slow, persistence in staying focused on plan, recognizing you are the fertile soil that must grow down to grow up, not unlike the acorn that must let go of its code to become the giant oak.

Notes:

1. James R. Fisher, Jr., *In the Shadow of the Courthouse: Memoir of the 1940s Written as a Novel,* TATE Publishing (2nd Edition), 2014. It is the portrait of a young man as he struggles to grasp his place in space.
2. James Hillman, *The Soul's Code: In Search of Character and Calling,* 1996.
3. Daniel Yankelovich, *New Rules: Search for Self-Fulfillment in a World Turned Upside Down,* 1981, p. 10.
4. John LeCarre, *Call for the Dead: The First George Smiley Novel* (reissue of 1961 novel, 2004), p. xii.
5. Ibid, p. xiii.
6. Op. Cit., Hillman, p. 20.
7. Ibid, p. 23.
8. Brenda Maddox, *Rosalind Franklin: The Dark Lady of DNA,* HarperCollins Publishers, 2002. See also James Watson's *The Double Helix,* New American Library, 1968.
9. Alexandra Nechita's paintings have been compared to Pablo Picasso. But in 1996, she told Oprah that she didn't emulate anyone else's style. "I didn't even know who Picasso was" when I started to paint. "I just wanted to enjoy myself and just painted this way because I wanted to be different."

NINE

TEACHING SMART PEOPLE HOW TO LEARN!

10,000 HOURS? REALLY?

After returning from an Alaskan cruise, it occurred to me that my fellow Americans are members of a fat nation consumed with white noise and sloppy language however finding some solace in Malcolm Gladwell's witty pop psychology books. The genius of this author is that he manages to touch cultural nerves as if he is everyone's ventriloquist.

Gladwell did this with *Tipping Points: How Little Things Can Make a Big Difference* (2000), then *Blink: The Power of Thinking Without Thinking* (2005) and then again with *Outliers: The Story of Success* (2008).[1]

In statistics, an "outlier" is an observation point that is distant from other observations. An outlier may be due to variability in the measurement or it may indicate experimental error; the latter are sometimes excluded from the data set.

Gladwell takes us on an intellectual journey through the world of *"outliers"*—the best and the brightest, the most famous and the most successful. He asks the question: what makes high achievers different? Of course, we all want to know this because we want to imitate and mimic them if only in a cameo sense.

Then he hits us with reality saying, and rightly so, that we pay too much attention to what successful people are like, and too little attention to where they are from: that is, their culture, their family, their generation, and the idiosyncratic experiences of their upbringing. This is where he parts company with me because the focus is on them (still) and not on ourselves and our own circumstances. Along the way, he explains the secrets of software billionaires, what it takes to be a great soccer player, why Asians are good at math, and what made the Beatles the greatest rock band.

This is all found intriguing and mind catching, not so much for what it purports to advocate, but for the readiness with which the reader is inclined to buy into the provocative premise that follows: that is, that high achievers spend a minimum of 10,000 hours dedicated to a singular pursuit, and then, voila, they have arrived. I don't think so. Serendipity as much as sagacity is likely the Mother of Good Fortune. His explanation for writing the *Outlier* is enlightening:

In the case of Outliers, the book grew out of a frustration I found myself having with the way we explain the careers of really successful people. You know how you hear someone say of Bill Gates or some rock star or some other outlier—"they're really smart" or "they're really ambitious?" Well, I know lots of people who are really smart and really ambitious, and they aren't worth 60 billion dollars. It struck me that our understanding of success was really crude— and there was an opportunity to dig down and come up with a better set of explanations.

At heart, his premise suggests he equates "success" with wealth and celebrity, which is pretty close to the lowest common denominator of our society, and not to the passion expressed in *staying focused* and *paying attention* no matter what, on something loved for and of itself.

Where would television be without all its awards winning shows, without all these aspiring people wanting to be "stars" on a profusion of amateur hours, without late night television parading these people across the stage, including presidential candidates vying for the office of President of the United States, without television network and cable news covering domestic politics in combination with wars, sports and entertainments as if interchangeable to boost ratings and sell books?

The 21st century is in a *New Gilded Age* to rival Tammy Hall and the Gilded Age of the 19th century. A few showman and unethical souls dominated that earlier period. Meaningful growth and development need not be in the glare of the public eye. Take a boy named Dirk.

A FULFILLING LIFE OFF STAGE

In high school, he was a four-sport athlete, making all-state along the way, also finishing in the top ten percent of his graduating class, but hardly a brain. The valedictorian of his class flattered him by asking him to be his roommate at the university.

They took many of the same college prep courses together in high school so he agreed but had the feeling he would be embarrassed rooming with someone far superior to him in intellect. It didn't happen. The valedictorian was a premed and he a chemistry major with a bent towards literature.

What he learned from that association was just how hard his roommate worked. He worked hard, too, but not like a machine. They were both in the top 3 percent of the class with his roommate enjoying an outstanding career in medicine while he had a more modest career as an international corporate executive. Were they outliers? I don't think so.

Years later – now retired in his mid-thirties – he decided to earn a Ph.D. in the soft sciences to better understand the corporate bureaucracy that had given him fits. Without preliminary preparation, he took the *Graduate Record Examination* (GRE) at the age of 38 or nearly two decades since college, and managed to score well enough to be accepted into the Graduate Program of the Social & Behavior College of a land grant institution.

Two of his professors, knowing his background, asked him where he had taken his prep course for the GRE. This astounded him because he didn't know such a course existed, and then thought it would surely cloud the integrity of the examination but said nothing. One of the professors went on to say he took the exam "three times," each time with a higher score. "It was a $3,000 investment, but well worth it!"

What amazed Dirk is that neither of these professors could believe anyone would register a sufficient score to be accepted into graduate school without such preparation. Here were two professors who believed in the necessity to master a test rather than to be confident that they had acquired sufficient knowledge to be ready for graduate school on the strength of their previous education. Were they outliers?

When he was a sophomore in college, there was a core course, *"Modern Literature, Greeks and the Bible"* that everyone was required to take whatever their major. Dirk had liked to read but wasn't into classical literature. His background was more oral history, as his family and clan were Irish American in a subculture that would have had trouble putting 10,000 hours together collectively into anything. No "outliers" there.

As it happened, he had to take a makeup examination in this course on the biographical novel of the Irish author James Joyce's *"Portrait of the Artist as a Young Man."* His professor chose to make it an oral examination, and was asking him questions, which he was answering when he stopped suddenly: *"May I tell you what this book meant to me?"* The professor paused, then smiled, and waved his cigarette as if to say "go on."

When he finished, the professor said, *"You understand Joyce. How do you explain that?"* He answered, *"I am Joyce. My Irish Catholic life has been consistent with his including the church's tyrannical authority and the bullying of my pastor."*

The professor asked him what he was majoring in, which he told him. He looked at Dirk suspiciously and asked, *"What the hell are you doing in science?"* He answered defensively that he was good at science.

After a long pause, studying the student, smoking pensively while looking out the window, he said he wanted to recommend him for the *University's Humanities Honors Program*, which had an international reputation. The recommendation, he said, was not only based on this oral exam, but the original quality of his written papers which while showing some naïveté were cuttingly distinctive on such writers as Dostoyevsky and Tolstoy, whom it was clear he had never read before. *"Now, I meet you on this one-on-one session and find you're the real deal!"*

For a long moment, he just stood there, transfixed, not knowing what to say, so he didn't say anything, but picked up his books and left. He went home and told his Irish Roman Catholic father what his professor had recommended.

His father put down his newspaper, looked him in the eye and said, *"Dirk, can I ask you a question?"* He nodded nervously. *"You're not a goddamn fag are you?"*

The shock to my system was immediate. He felt like a deer in the headlights of a car bearing down on me. Unconcerned with his son's discomfort, his father continued.

"On my trains, I see these guys reading books like you're reading looking unkempt, sloppy, dirty long hair, ratty clothes, hanging on each other, and you want to be like them?"

His father left school at the end of the seventh grade, and had little patience with him in any case. It was his mother who covered his back, and she was standing in the doorway of the kitchen smoking, listening. It was the 1950s and his Irish American culture couldn't have been more homophobic. He stayed in chemistry. His mother didn't protest.

Years later, now in his fifties, still with the writing bug, he retired once again and wrote many books mainly based on his working years spending many times 10,000 hours in such effort It would become more of an avocation than vocation, returning pretty much to where his sophomore humanities professor said he should have been when only twenty-years-old.

His humanities professor was right about one thing. He would continue to be an innovative writer but never a popular or well-known author. How many thousands of others out there are like Dirk, people who are dedicated to writing, painting, and sculpting, people who are not chasing Gladwell's "success," but who have spent many times 10,000 hours doing what they love. Billionaires and celebrities don't necessarily have more significant lives.

10,000 Hours: A READER'S DISCLOSES:

On my blog (peripaticphilosopher.blogspot.com), reference is made to Malcolm Gladwell's *Outliers*.   I found this book intriguing, not so much for what it purports to advocate, but for the readiness with which readers were inclined to buy into his provocative premise -- 10,000 hours. A reader offered this response:

As a 37-year-old, I figured that I have lived roughly 324,120 hours, so 10,000 hours would only be 1/30th of my life, or 10,000 would be about 32 hours of that life. My question to myself is, how come I'm only good at whatever I do, and not great?

Perhaps the "correct type of practice" that Gladwell mentions is the key. When I played guitar in my teens I noodled a lot without really learning anything new--I probably hit close to 5,000 hours, but really only 1,000 were used to improve. The rest was self-indulgent repetition. I could say the same for my running career, my triathlon experiences, chess, jazz piano playing, my years as an English major, and even my career as a teacher.

In each of these endeavors, I notice a quick peak where I get better than 80% of my colleagues/peers, but then can never seem to get through the last 20%.

My flaw is the plateau effect that comes from slipping into complacency. As I look back at everything that I became good at, but not great at, I see a pattern of becoming tired, frustrated, and easily distracted. Or probably more importantly, I just wanted to move on to something else.

So at what I hope is at least the midpoint, (and hopefully less than a mid-point), in my life, the question becomes do I now take 10,000 hours and learn to do something really well, or do I accept that the time to do this is now behind me?

P.S. I come from a Catholic background as well. Joyce came as easily to me as it did to you. I could also say the same for Mark Twain because I grew up in Missouri and New Orleans.

DR. FISHER RESPONDS:

Mr. Gladwell is a clever fellow. No doubt about that. He is able to ponder the obvious and work out what it means, then translate that meaning into works that capture the imagination of the general reader. He is careful not to be too overwhelming. This explains his mnemonic of 10,000 hours. It captures the reader's attention especially when associated with highly successful people. Notice how he stays away from scientists and philosophers who are unlikely to be either billionaires or celebrities.

This does not make him wrong for cultivating the obvious or in suggesting the benefit of 10,000 hours when dedicated to some interest. *Great* is a relative term that we have come to toss about in a cavalier style. Clearly, *"The Outliers"* are people he expects us to see as "great."

Adroit writers are careful to direct the reader's attention to a simple but well thought out premise. How many equally dedicated people passed this 10,000 hour, and do not become great?

That is not the question Gladwell presumes the reader to ask. As you point out, he expects the reader to ponder, "Why not me?" This leads the reader to put himself in the frame as you have done. That is why I shared my brief biography. We plow the fields, man the machines, serve the customers, carry the burdens of society, and create the world that billionaires and celebrities enjoy. They don't create us.

It is interesting that the *Outlier* is focused on *chronological time* which is *Machine Age Thinking*, when the *Information Age* deals mainly with *chronological time*, or real time, the only time we experience. *Information Technology* didn't invent this time. It has had no choice but to grow consistent with *psychological time.*

My experience has been that success is not a *linear chronological curve*, but a *disruptive, interruptive psychological* fluctuating curve. Failure is a natural part of this progression with periodic eruptions of success.

The psychological challenge is to embrace the risk and pain of this everyday process, which is necessary to work our way through the failure phase to be ready when success is on our horizon.

We do not learn when we are riding high with achievement. We learn when our achievements fall off or disappear. It is then that we take stock. Only then can we understand the meaning of this impasse, this difficulty. The answers are waiting in the silence of things we once took for granted. Circumstances have forced us to take a "time out!" Alert to the silence, we stop and listen and come to know. This is when learning takes place.

WHY SMART PEOPLE FAIL

A high Intelligent Quotient (IQ) or a high Scholastic Achievement Test (SAT) score is just that, an indicator of having a high acumen to test taking while implicitly conforming to those cultural norms.

Intelligence is not a quotient or a test score. Intelligence is what it does.

There are more smart people perhaps than ever before. Yet many of them are failing to make the progress necessary to compete successfully in life. Even though they may have high test scores and even receive impressive grades, this is no guarantee that they will compete successfully in life.

Less talented individuals develop balance between their *essence* (their owned assets) and *personality* (their acquired assets) to make progress in life. They know one thing and that is that *failure is the ticket to success.* Indeed, failure is the road to success for it involves pushing the limits to growth and development.

Abraham Lincoln had much more familiarity with failure than success. His great asset was that he was a learner not a knower, treating each failure as s "bump in the road." Often during the *American Civil War,* defeat stared him in the face but he never lost his focus on "one nation," and that perseverance carried him and the nation to victory and with it the end of slavery of the American Negro.

 In *The Baseball Hall of Fame*, failure is a measure of success. Great baseball players fail to hit safely seven out of the ten times they are at bat. Imagine, seven out of ten times they fail to be productive.

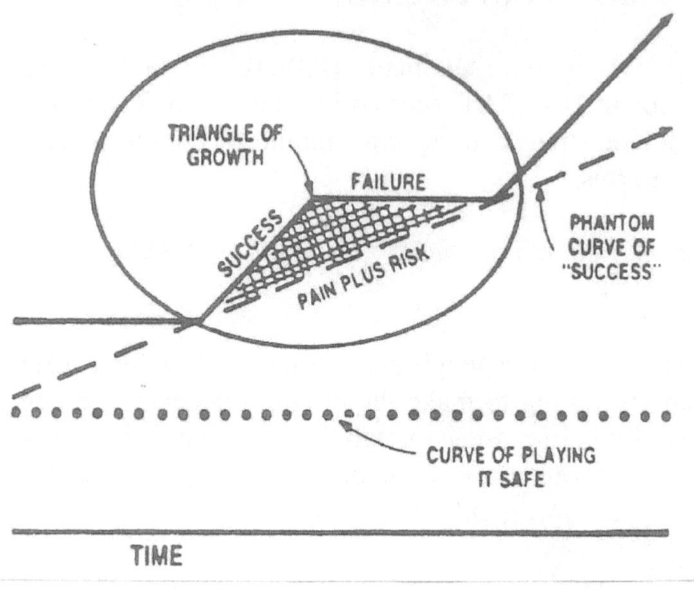

Failure is not unlike a kind of dying. We have to regroup and will ourselves through difficult periods. Failure shatters our defense system, our sense of self. We may go through:

- *Shock* and disbelief.
- *Fear* of "what will I do now?"
- *Anger and blame; anger* at feeling betrayed; *blame* directed at others, not at oneself.
- *Shame* for letting others down giving them the power to judge us.
- *Despair* in feeling alone, abandoned, depleted, and isolated from the group.

But if we are wise and embrace our failure and take inventory of where we are and how we got to this place, something good can happen. We can discover a new sense of what is important.

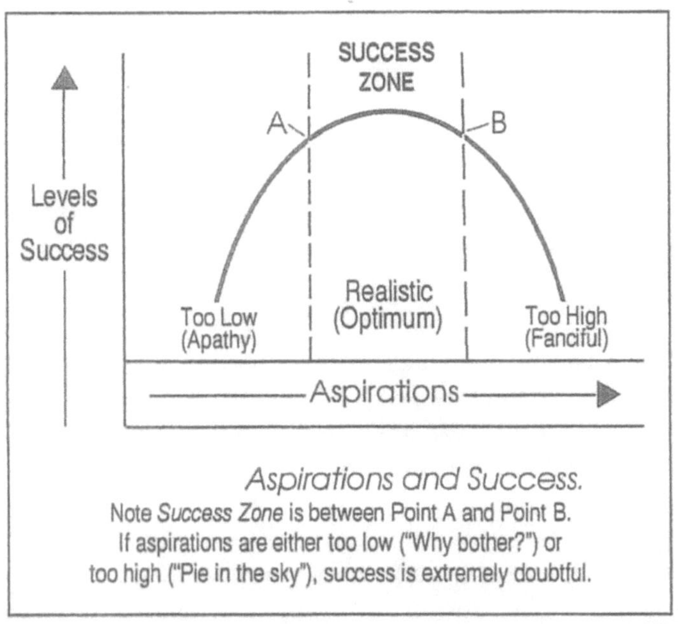

Aspirations and Success.
Note *Success Zone* is between Point A and Point B.
If aspirations are either too low ("Why bother?") or
too high ("Pie in the sky"), success is extremely doubtful.

You may have lost a job; a relationship may have gone sour; may have suffered a debilitating illness, or a financial reversal. In life, it can be anything that throws us off stride. Experience the *psychological moment* to the fullest before moving on. It will pay dividends.

In the process, you will uncover a new sense of self, along with a new humbleness. Out of this, support may materialize from unexpected sources to go with your new sense of balance and maturity.

But perhaps the most important lesson that comes out of failure is a new sense of self-direction. People you once trusted or counted on may have vanished. That is okay. It happens! Don't waste your time plotting revenge. Call it a lesson learned in more wisely choosing your friends.

Once you have had time to heal and gotten through the bitterness, you will have a new sense of autonomy, self-awareness, self-acceptance and confidence that you didn't know you possessed.

You are stronger and a better person for having gotten through this episode of failure.

TEACHING SMART PEOPLE HOW TO LEARN

In our culture, we avoid failure at all costs. Little learning takes place if one is afraid to make mistakes, try difficult tasks, or step away from the familiar.

- The first mistake smart people make is that learning is "problem solving." Solving problems is important, but it is a mechanistic process while learning involves thinking outside the box or beyond cognitive reasoning.

Mechanistic learning involves linear logic and cause and effect analysis. It is the learning we pursue in academia to acquire credentials. This one-dimensional conditioning severely handicaps the learner as not everything can be quantified.

- Scholastic knowledge increases awareness of the environment but it is no substitute for experience. Smart people cannot expect others to take them at their word because they have book knowledge. They must demonstrate knowledge in ways congruent with those with whom they work.

Failure to do so is the first mistake of smart people. The problem may be as simple as a lack of understanding of what is being proposed.

- Another mistake is to consider learning to be a matter of motivation. Learning does not automatically translate into readiness to do or be because the learner has a good attitude. It requires a change of mindset, of looking at problems differently. It requires an open mind to new ideas.

Defensiveness can become a reflective routine so that the same tired arguments are repeated whatever the situation. This paradox rises from the human tendency to act so as:

- To remain in unilateral control.
- To maximize winning and minimize losing.
- To suppress negative feelings.
- To remain as rational as possible in the most irrational of situations.

This value construct is designed to avoid embarrassment or the suggestion of incompetence, which of course makes it only more apparent. Brittle personalities fall apart when suddenly faced with situations that penetrate this patina.

This vicious circle can be broken only by developing self-acceptance. This leads to greater tolerance of others as they are. Then learning is possible through self-awareness:

- You can be taught to recognize the kind of reasoning you use.
- You can begin to see the inconsistencies between your intended and actual behavior and the reason for the inconsistency.
- You can learn to identify what you do well individually as compared to in groups and calculate its relative merits.
- You can learn to accept your shortcomings as part of your persona with no need to be defensive about them.

Once smart people get past the self-justification; once they get past the impediment of their biases, they can make us all a little wiser.

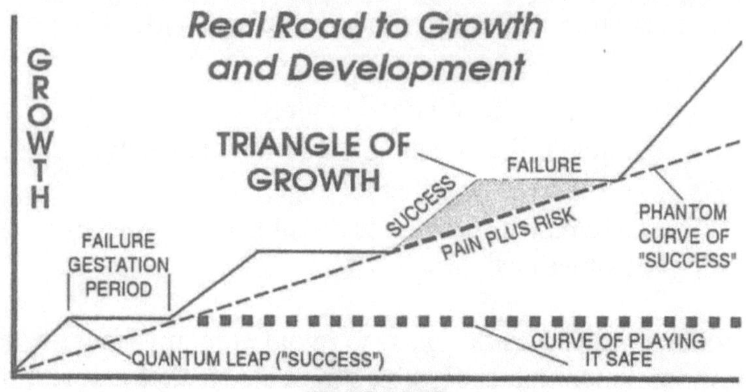

* Growth is not in linear increments, but in strategic leaps
* Gestation period is period of real learning
* Gestation period is time of trauma, retrenchment,
  assimilation of failure; a time when the learner
    Please Self Mentality:
        ✓ Is not concerned about letting the group down
        ✓ Does not have to appear smart
        ✓ Is open to taking risks and enduring pain
* Quantum leaps are periods of success,
  but of little real learning

THE POWER OF AN OPEN MIND

The *"plateau of failure"* is common to all of us but familiar to too few of us. We don't like to admit when we are stuck and seemingly can't get beyond where we are. When it happens, we find ourselves in a job with little or no prospects for advancement, or in a relationship that is going nowhere. It can also be experienced when flunking out of school, being fired from a job, losing best friends, or just feeling very much alone. Paradoxically, we think we can avoid it by languishing on the *"curve of playing it safe"* when we are actually on the *"plateau of failure."* Forgotten is how we got to where we are now, which is more than likely to involve this formula:

PAIN + RISK = GROWTH

This is *"The Triangle of Growth."* Everyone experiences it. We have a spurt of success, then we coast when we reach this plateau. This is where most people spend their lives. If this sounds cruel, more than fifty years of observing people at all levels in the complex organization is my source. It is easier to complain than contribute. The cartoon *"Dilbert"* repeats this often. It is easier to say, *"I had no good teachers"* than to be the best teacher you ever knew.

We in the West have misconstrued *"failure."* It is a plateau that everyone encounters on his or her way to success. Those willing to keep growing encounter it many times over a career, but they don't take up residence. They move on. It is on the *"plateau of failure"* that learning takes place.

You may not be fans of Supreme Court Justice Sonia Sotomayor or former President Barak Obama, but I suspect they have had many plateaus and endured much pain and taken many risks on their way to their respective eminence. Moreover, chances are they are still not satisfied as they continue to grow and to contribute meaningfully.

Notes

1. Maxwell Gladwell has built three intriguing books around three rather common terms: *blink, outlier and tipping point.*

   - *Blink* is about thin-slicing as a psychology or philosophy term describing the ability to find patterns or even track events based on *"thin-slices"* of narrow windows of experience;

- *Outlier* refers to a person or situation or thing that is markedly different than that expected in the normal range of perceptions or experiences;
- *Tipping point* is that magic moment when everything changes; when an idea breaks through the mundane; when an unrecognizable trend suddenly asserts itself; or when social behavior crosses the threshold and literally tips and then spreads like wild fire across the culture.

TEN

SECRET LANGUAGE OF RELATIONSHIPS

"Thinking cannot be clear till it has had expression. We must write, or speak, or act our thoughts, or they will remain in a half torrid form. Our feelings must have expression, or they will be as clouds, which, till they descend in rain, will never bring up fruit or flowers. So, it is with all the inward feelings; expression gives them development. Thought is the blessing; language, the opening bud, action the fruit behind it."

Henry Ward Beecher (1813-1837), American clergyman.

"Unhappy are they who struggle, to be persons, not machines, to whom the Universe is not a warehouse, or at best a fancy bazaar, but a mystic temple and hall of doom."

Thomas Carlyle (1795 -1881), English essayist and philosopher

BEING AUTHENTIC IN A ROBOTIC AGE

Carlyle captures the mood if not the essence of the modern dilemma of relationships. Nowhere is struggle more apparent than in what is known as married love. Such love has become self-incarcerating for many role players. Even advice columnists have seen the mystical temple of love given way to something resembling a chamber of doom.

We shall revisit some who operate in life consistent with the curious logic of such advisers. One adviser confessed recently that her own husband of 36 years had given her the boot. Married love has taken a frontal hit from advice columnists who monitor the distress signals, but provide little solace to those experiencing the spontaneous irrational disruption.

Language may play surrogate to reality but it cannot become its substitute. The word, "love," unfortunately, has too often been estranged from the operative action of being "loving."

In this modern age of science, some of us have developed a silver-tongued lexicon of love only to avoid its commitment. A client once told me in perfect *Master & Johnson speak* that he was sensitive to the needs of his wife, and committed to her sexual desires, but was unable to engage her in conversation.

They continued to have sex but she claimed he was obsessive compulsive in his demands that she repeatedly tell him she loved him. She loved him, she said, but was suffocating from his need for constant reassurance. *"I married him, an older man, because he was a good lover as am I, and I thought that was enough."*

But clearly it was not. He in turn didn't find her especially interesting. When asked why, he said, *"She's as sophisticated as a doormat,"* then realizing how harsh this sounded, added, *"of course she finds my special interests totally boring."*

If this sounds as if two fourth graders are quarrelling, it is actually not too wide off the mark that I have found as to the maturity level of many married adults.

What she needed most, and hadn't found with him, was a friend, a confidante, someone she could trust. To this he bellowed defensively, *"How can I be a friend when I've never had one in my life?"*

To have a friend you must be a friend, starting with yourself!

Friendship starts by accepting ourselves as we are before venturing beyond that to seeking others as friends. Too often we look at this in reverse of this order.

The key to accepting others as we find them is first discovering the capacity to accept ourselves as we are. As many reading this know, it is easier said than done. Yet, self-tolerance is conditional to extending the olive branch of tolerance to others.

Frustrating this process, we think we are expected to be perfect, to be blemish free. Although that is impossible, we can't seem to help ourselves from looking disapprovingly for imperfections in others that we ourselves possess, but most likely deny having.

Know this, *there is no one a hater hates more than the self-hatred that he has buried in his own soul.*

Conversely, self-worth is the gauge by which we measure the worth of others. Words cannot replace deeds. Just as you cannot eat the word "apple," love is not a word but an action. Knowledge of self is not simply being yourself. It involves the behavior being useful. Good intentions are no substitute for doing.

WATER AS METAPHOR

The Buddha has an expression: *You cannot push the water.* On the other hand, water confined creates pressure. The trapped water leads to heat. This heat ultimately seeks release, which leads to disruption.

Human emotions are like this water. If emotions are accepted, embraced and allowed to flow they seek a natural state and level. But alas, we have trouble allowing things to flow and more of a tendency to see them mount in pressure, ignoring the building destabilizing situation as if everything is, as it appears on the surface, to be just fine.

Instead, we tinker with irrelevancies until the pressure gives way beyond our capacity for containment, as our gates are flooded with emotions. We not only lose our cool, but our self-control when terrible things can happen to us and others.

As I was preparing this book for publication, Darrin Campbell, 50, a corporate executive, renting the Avila mansion of tennis star, James Blake, in Tampa, Florida, killed his wife Kimberly, 51, and his son, Colin, 19, and daughter Megan, 15, then torched the house before killing himself.

If this were an isolated case, there would be no point in mentioning it, but it has happened again and again in this Tampa Bay area, and across these United States.

There is no situation or predicament, no embarrassing contretemps or terrible disruptive circumstances that can metaphorically be the equivalent of taking the water off the hot burner, and allowing that water to cool to room temperature.

In this chronological age, where time is money and stress and upward mobility is the norm, our mentality leaves little room for humanistic levity and therefore emotional balance.

Even so, we like to espouse humanistic verities and plug them into our mechanistic system where *progress is our most important product*, and where *no one can rest on their laurels,* therefore no one is expected to be content with who they are and where they are even if that is where they should be.

Consequently, this constant social pressure to *become* (what we are not) dispensing with *being* (who we are) leads to discontinuity, disruption and ultimately the insanity of homicide, suicide, and genocide.

Have we relinquished our personal responsibility to the sobriety of sensible collective norms?
Have we conceded to experts the role of charting our destiny while we remain passively inert? Experts can intellectualize our

worst moments into simplistic solutions with *"the paralysis of analysis,"* while nothing changes.

We can nod with approval as a Dr. Phil on television frames the problem of a guest seeing the sense in his nonsense because what he knows of the individual under review is only a hint at what that individual is. It resonates with us, protected as we are, from being the subject at hand.
Marriage and relationships have become mind games, distractions that we welcome. The last place husbands and wives look for answers are their relationships with each other. Small wonder problems are seldom resolved.

This is not the fault of experts. We have created experts as "fall guys" for those things we don't want to think about, but have no problem treating as entertainments. The Dr. Phil's of the world provide comic relief while we tell ourselves we are being very serious about such matters.

Experts have evolved in the popular media as gurus with the narcotic of simplistic reinforcement of scapegoat answers to disenchanted couples. These couples expect experts to solve problems that demand change, and change is not part of their relational language. They are looking for self-justification. They see love as a commodity like everything else in their lives which can be suitably packaged, purchased and consumed or discarded if the product doesn't produce instant happiness.

Family, society and civilization find married love as the first card in the tumbling house of cards in modern society approaching the need for an umbrella of life support measures. It doesn't help that married love has never quite lived up to its alleged billing of romantic ecstasy. Romance has a limited staying power.

Married love is a struggle for equity and fulfillment of two disparate individuals, which are as much at war with themselves as with each other during the long struggle to reach what diplomats call reconciliation.

The case study that follows, deals with sex role identity and the clash of values that can lead to role confusion.

BETTY AND BOB

Betty has attempted suicide three times. Each time she has come closer to this final solution. Her doctor insists each time was a genuine attempt to do herself in, not a call for help.

Prior to my working with her, she had been in group therapy for five years. The group became a family substitute for love and affection and understanding not found at home. She went through the usual emotional changes common to such therapy, falling in love with her doctor, propositioning him, being propositioned by other members of the group, finally involving herself in guilt-ridden petting, and later remorse for her conduct.

When she talks about the group, her face lights up. That is not true when she talks about her own husband and family.

She has two children, 21 and 25, the oldest, a son, and honor student at university who suddenly became disoriented and was diagnosed schizophrenic. He had been institutionalized, but has now been remanded to his parents.

Betty is a small woman in her late forties with a petite body and a dark, sultry appearance. Her lips are pencil thin that gives her a cruel look in contrast to her eyes that sparkle with warmth and intelligence. Her appearance goes from unattractive to beautiful when she smiles, an incongruity that appears consistent with her personality. She can be petty and cruel one moment, when referring to her husband or children, or warm and vivacious when referring to her past doctors or college professors.

This is how she sees herself:

I was a good Catholic girl. I never did anything wrong. I went to Mass and Communion every day, said my prayers, helped the nuns, helped my mother, helped my father, I was always giving, giving, giving.

My father never once held me. He didn't like that sort of thing, didn't think it was manly. My mother wasn't very warm either. She constantly waited on my father. I think he wished I had been a boy. I'm sorry I disappointed him.

Bob came along when I was sixteen. He was 22 and going off to war. I didn't think much of him. He was too short, too stocky, and just not my type at all, don't know what my type is though. Never dated, can you believe that? My father wouldn't let me, when Bob came along. I quit school and married him, just like that.

God! It was terrific, really fantastic, sex, God! Do I love sex! I couldn't get enough. I didn't know what was going on. I had never once touched my own body, or anything like that.

Well, he went to war, and I moved into an apartment, but I wasn't able to make it, and had to move back home, play the little girl's role again. It was awful, still went to church a lot. But that incredible sexuality of mine, it was there all the time. But what it did to me, him going off like that leaving me behind to suffer was maddening. Anything I would do, I knew, would cheapen me. God! But how I wanted a man, a boy, anything, anybody.

Of course, I wouldn't do anything, but did I think about it? Well, let me tell you, it was awful!

Once he came home, he got this stupid little job as an insurance salesman, never could do anything right, wasn't even a very good salesman, still isn't.

Now, after all these years, he doesn't want sex any more than once a month, imagine that? Once a month! After making me suffer all those years while he was gone, while he was probably fucking some foreigner. I've got the screaming ninnies, I tell you, just thinking about it now. Sometimes I have had to literally rape him to have sex.

But he did give me two damn nice kids. I'll say that for him, even if he beats me sometimes. Do you know he has beaten me so badly that I landed in the hospital, not once but several times?

I hate him but I still need him for economic reasons. If it wasn't for that check he brings home every two weeks like a big dope, I would have left him long ago. But the kids, well, they are a drain on me, too, always taking, taking, and taking some more.

I probably should have been a nun instead of a mother. I am just not the sympathetic type, you know what I mean, I like to be left alone. They have been very demanding of me in their very selfish ways.

Take Ted now, he thinks of no one but himself, his precious mind having run amuck. What about my mind? What about me? But I have to keep him happy. There is no time for me.

Every time Helen comes home from school she eats everything in the house (Helen is in medical school), telling me I don't appreciate her and what she has accomplished.

Bob only gives me so much money to run things. I'm not a magician. My aunt left me a few dollars. Bob doesn't know how much. I'm going to buy myself a new Buick, some new clothes, and some sexy under things, and have myself a ball. I deserve it. I am so happy I am able to go to school (she is in junior college) to develop my intellect. I love intellectuals. They are so sexy. I know I'm jumping around but I'm so happy talking to someone who understands, someone who is not so, well, common, you know what I mean...."

*　　*　　*

Bob, for all I can gather, is a carbon copy of Betty's father, not only physically, but also in attitude and philosophy. Betty's father sold insurance, and Bob, like her father, played things close to the vest. He doesn't trust anything that has to do with an "ology," such as psychology or theology or any other "ology."

He came to therapy sessions with Betty but never commented about anything that happened in the five years they attended the group. He was even put into a different group and still refused to open up. He would sit there and wait for the session to end to drive his wife home. He saw the whole process as a con game.

Now, in a session with me, he was unwilling to discuss his son, except to say he is a little feminine, then adding, *"thanks to his mother. He's not willing to act like a man,"* implying there is an obvious definition of what that is. When it was suggested he might have a gentle personality, his face reddened and he got up to go to the bathroom.

When he returned, the suggestion was repeated making reference to the fact that man came from woman, that most of a child's adolescent life is spent with or around a mother, so why the surprise that a child's personality or gestures might suggest behavior mirroring that fact? He replied, *"You shrinks are all alike."*

He became more defensive when asked why he went to group therapy sessions with his wife in the first place. He replied he didn't like *"the wife out on her own at night."*

He was then asked how he felt about his wife's growing independence. He looked at me curiously. *"What about it?"* I mentioned that she seemed to be happy going to college. "So?" He said looking at me defiantly. It was clear she hadn't told him anything about her sudden inheritance or the new car and new clothes she was planning to buy. I waited in silence.

Rather than getting angry, he became nervous. Finally, he confessed he had an urgent appointment with a client, and left without another word. He never returned.

*　　*　　*

Betty and Bob display conflicting attitudes toward their status role obligations; roles with which they have been programmed. This is not usual in these times as carefully defined roles and relationships are no longer apparent.

Role-playing in marriage is no longer a linear function with the man as the head of the house, and the women as his obliging and loyal partner. Nor is the sexual act any longer locked safely away as primarily the domain of procreation, but as much for pleasure as therapeutic bonding.

It has been said that love was locked out of Roman Catholicism with the church's failure to acknowledge and then deal with the changing psychosexual demands of a *Post-Industrial Society.* *"Mortal Sin"* no longer had the impact that it once enjoyed becoming something of an aberration.

There was no place for sexual love in the Catholic *Baltimore Catechism* that was our impressionistic monitor for prepubescent Catholic lads and lasses of the *Great Depression* era. The baby boomer generation that followed, however, lacked even this roadmap. Carnal lust and Catholic guilt lost its relevance and purchase by then as sensual permissiveness had reached an open season.

Today, a more accommodating society has evolved in which sins of the flesh have taken on a peculiar character and identity for Catholics barely out of puberty. The conflict now is between the

158

ways it was and the way it is today, which finds women tired of being treated as one-dimensional persons.

Bob is unsympathetic to this disposition partly out of ignorance and partly out of malice. He wants things to be the way they were, like Betty's father. The irony is that he was a convert to Roman Catholicism as was Betty's father. Neither of them understands nor are they interested in knowing the anguishing nuances Catholic morality can cause. Betty does. Her anxiety demonstrates the difficulty of gaining traction when guilt and lust bombard the conscience with no off ramp to relief.

Betty had a great sexual awakening at 16 only to find nuptial love was devoid of romance and courtship. She sought to recover this fantasy in group therapy. At sixteen, her body was ready to be a woman but not her mind and heart.

Now, a middle-aged women, she is trying to regain this lost enchantment while remaining prisoner to a morality that no longer exists.
Bob uses her conflicting dilemma against her. Betty believes she stays with him for financial reasons when she is more prisoner of her Roman Catholicism. Like a little girl, she says, *"Bob has no idea what time I came in last night, or what I was doing. He thinks I'm such a frivolous girl, don't you know, so shameless and impulsive."*

Of course, quite the converse is true. Bob knows she has a horrible fear of dying with mortal sin on her soul, that she doesn't believe in divorce, that his best watchdog is her conscience. He knows she desires other men, how could he not, as often as she is reminding him? In his quiet, and imprisoning way, he has her under control.

The last two times she has gone to the hospital due to an overdose, a neighbor has had to bring her home, as he refused to do so with the twisted logic, *"She won't kill herself because that is a mortal sin and against her religion."*

Meanwhile, Betty continues to seek a happiness pill that does not exist. She blames everyone for her pain but herself. Since she has received some reinforcement from her doctors, "being sick" has become a favorite role.

The family is held together by mental illness and little else. Helen, the sane one, is aware of this irony. She does not date, has little patience with her family, much less with anyone else. She hides in her medical studies.

Last summer, Helen went to Ireland totally on her own with little money, worked her way across the country, and loved it. She is cheerful but guarded, intelligent but suspicious, delightful but manipulative. She finds older men more appealing than younger men, seems not to be restrained by religious morality, or the values of her parents. She takes pride in being her own person, and being unlike any member of her family. Affection is her weakest expression, and as intelligent as she seems to be, she is unaware that she is damaged.

Ted has found a role for himself in his mental illness. He did not want to come home from the sanitarium. When he told his mother this, she promptly took an overdose of sleeping pills. He takes peculiar pride in that his doctor sees him as suicidal, which to him means he has escaped the dogmatic trap of his religion.

It is all a game to him. His personality test data indicate he lacks internal integrity. While showing no initiative, no active I.Q., and very limited attention span, Ted managed in the *"Draw-a-Person"* exercise to display a classical appreciation of the schizophrenic personality. He produced a picture of his father in a business suit, which was actually a drawing of himself.

It would appear that in the psychological shrinking of American society, where nearly one in every three adults of some means is in therapy, the nation has become a pill factory bazaar with the mystical template, previously religion, now catering to fantasy needs to accommodate the *Lost Soul of the Machine.*

ELEVEN

A COUNTERINTUITIVE IDEA: "PLEASING- SELF" IN A CULTURE OF SELF-DEPRECATION!

THE "PLEASING-SELF MENTALITY" EXPLAINED

Is the *please-self mentality* the ultimate in selfishness? Not necessarily. Unselfishness at root is a cultural condition. A counterintuitive case could be made that the ultimate in selfishness is found in the unselfish.

The unselfish allows himself to be exploited by being taken for granted, taken advantage of, given faint praise, and treated as a gopher.

When a person permits others to bankrupt him emotionally, physically, and spiritually, he does himself no favor, or anybody else. The unselfish redistributes his pain, agony, and self-pity where it is least deserved, on family members and loved ones. This causes deep unhappiness everywhere. In a zero-sum game, those who are the takers are the unhappiest of all.

Takers never get enough, always demanding more—more attention, more sympathy, and more time, more of everything, always more. Worse yet, takers have little respect for givers. There is only one way to be truly unselfish, and that is by being totally selfish.

Look at the evidence. If we first meet our own personal needs before we meet the needs of others, we do so with a generous spirit and a sense of freedom. Yet it is considered virtuous to meet the needs of others at the expense of our own needs. That is how we have been conditioned. It fails to work in the chemistry of being because it is dishonest and self-abusing.

More virtuous is to assert ourselves by meeting our own needs, then meeting the needs of others with a light heart. To submit to social conformity at the expense of one's own free choice does not engender a kind heart.

Sainthood defies the human condition, placing itself above the vanities while reinforcing cultural vagaries. Sainthood is perhaps the most narcissistic of postures.

Albert Schweitzer (1875–1965) may not be considered a saint, but many consider him the noblest figure of the twentieth century for his altruism. He lost patience with what he called a *"Jackass society"* – the bourgeoisie society of Europe, which included his own intellectual community – leaving a brilliant career as a theologian, musicologist, and organist to study medicine. Upon the completion of his medical studies, he abandoned Europe for Africa, where he undertook the task there of building African hospitals and clinics.

There is no question that Schweitzer was a gentle and deeply religious man. Only 31, he set up his paternalistic services to Africans in a deserted mission at Lambarene in French Equatorial Africa. He did this in a spirit *"not of benevolence, but atonement"* to fight leprosy and sleeping sickness. Even his ethical principle, *"Reverence for Life,"* was fully worked out in relation to the defects of European civilization.

Schweitzer's selflessness has always been troubling to me. He turned his back on a *"jackass society,"* but brought European arrogance to Africa. Africans managed to live for centuries without European progress. Moreover, his *reverence for life* was confusing to the natives, for he couldn't kill the smallest of insects. His hospitals, as a consequence, would never receive the *Good Housekeeping Seal of Approval.*

Conceivably, Schweitzer went to Africa to find himself and to expiate his guilt for being European. Characteristic of the Christian-Judaic culture is for the individual to identify with society, not with nature. The religious animism of Africans is to yield to nature, not control it. Schweitzer had the arrogance of the European intellectual with the predisposition of that elitist community to know what was best for Africans, a totally Western man perspective.

Perhaps a sense of life's futility drove him there to pay a humanistic debt to atone for these misgivings. By sacrificing his life to the natives, perhaps he felt he could realize his salvation. Western man is consumed with the idea of debt and repayment, in contrast to the Eastern man who prefers moving from ignorance to illumination. Whatever the motivation, European society, far from being incensed at his rebuke, celebrated him as an altruist.

Was Africa improved? Is it better now? It is impossible to say. What is more remarkable about this man is not what he did, but that he had the courage to do it. He had the courage to *please-self* by serving others. In that sense, he escaped European society and its shackling culture.

The most significant characteristic of the *please-self mentality* is the need to be purposeful. The world outside may be in disarray, which provides the motivation to restore some order to that chaos, first *with-in* and then manifested *with-out*. The payoff is to experience more internal order. It is the *Manichaeism duality* of seeing things in terms of good and evil; black and white; order and chaos.

St. Augustine was first a Manichean before he was a Christian and some of that dualistic philosophy followed him into his Christian theology as it did into Albert Schweitzer's

"Reverence for Life." One does wonder, however, what Schweitzer could have done if he had stayed in Europe and applied that same altruistic zeal to his own society, obviously that would have been a more monumental task.

In the corporate world, managers and workers are trying to please customers, bosses, stockholders, suppliers, subordinates, peers, community leaders, even confessors, ending up pleasing no one. They are all at wit's end and still manage to smile through clenched teeth.

So, what do they do? Do they say, *"Damn it? Time out! Enough already!"* No, they open up another pack of cigarettes, have a couple of double martinis at lunch, go on a health kick, giving up one narcotic for another, punishing themselves into a condition they never had when they were half that age.

They acquire younger significant others, while carrying a pack of Rolaids in their briefcase, alongside a deluxe container of *Extra Strength Excedrin*. They drink gallons of coffee, concealing the forlorn and perplexed look with false bravado, then they have a cerebral hemorrhage, myocardial infarction, or peptic ulcer. If not that, they take on a washed-out jaundice look with live complaint, develop colon cancer, kidney failure, or prostatitis, or they simply retire on the job. Were these same people inclined to *please self*, the outcome would be different as would their persona, but they are not into that, and that is the problem. Albert Schweitzer deserted Europe for Africa and lived to be 90. Think about it.

THE PRICE OF *"PLEASING-SELF"*

Not everyone has their Lambarene (Albert Schweitzer's hospital in West Africa) in which to escape. Like Desiderius Erasmus (*Catholic leader of the Counter Reformation*), most people with a *please-self* inclination seek their destiny inside the system, rather than outside its confinement as did Martin Luther (*leader of the Protestant Reformation*).

The clash of cultures between feudalism and capitalism, which was first religious and then economic is still with us today. We are in the postmodern, post-capitalistic period, and what is evolving with this dynamic is the *please-self mentality*. It is evident with millennials who are not into the common good (of society) but into personhood. This is neither particularly economic nor religious, yet its chaos and dysfunction was quite evident when I wrote *Work Without Managers,* a quarter century ago. We are now in *Nowhere Land* of *Nowhere Man.*

SHIFTING AMERICAN VALUES

	Common Good	Personhood
Authority	Position Power	Popularity/knowledge
Loyalty	To the organization	To self/peers
Discipline	Reward/punishment	Caring/respect
Motivation	Fear	Challenge/contribution

It is a time for personhood. The *please-self mentality* in today's society stands out like a sore thumb. People of the *please-self orientation* might agree with naturalist Stephen Jay Gould's message in *"An Urchin in the Storm"* (1987) that all organic life is programmed to survive only when it is threatened with extinction. Otherwise, there is no instinctual mechanism that preserves a species. Only the sense of danger precedes activation of the survival behavior.

Likewise, with people, if there is no sense of danger, or if the danger is felt exaggerated, it will be ignored. The human species has a herd mentality that necessitates being frightened to death to act. Biologist Richard Dawkins relates in his book *"The Selfish Gene"* (1976) that selfishness is indigenous to survival.

Dawkins studies single-cell organisms and sees an interesting correlation between biology and social theory. He suggests that selfishness is neither good nor bad, but is simply inherently robotic. Evolution, he claims, has always been selfish, and all organic life acting as if a survival machine, on both a molecular (genetic) and mechanistic (human) scale. So, why are we so afraid to be selfish when it is so critical to our well-being?

TWELVE

THE DISSEMBLING NATURE OF IDENTITY AND ITS COSTS

Strangers are likely to ask young students when they first meet:

- Where they come from,

- Where they go to school,

- What is their major, or if they have already graduated,

- What is their profession,

- Where do they work?

Variations of these questions follow when they are older:

- Are you married,

- How did you meet,

- Have you any children, how many,

- What are their names,

- Where do you live,

- What do you do,

- Do you play golf,

- What club do you belong to,

- What church do you go to?

Hobbies take on increased significance when we reach the age of retirement, which is likely to include variations of these other questions.

Strangers like to get a fix on us so that they can put us into a stereotypical box. It is a form of breaking the ice, and deciding if we want to get to know someone a little better or not. When I first moved into my new home in Johannesburg, South Africa – I was there on assignment from my American company – an anthropology professor living in the neighborhood who taught at the University of Witwatersrand, an English speaking white institution, asked me a bevy of such questions. Apparently, my responses or nonresponses, as the case might have been, were sufficient that I never saw him again.

Strangers distill this code with their eyes studying the way we dress, the manner of our responses, our ethnicity reflected in the lilt of our voices, the way we carry ourselves, our educational level demonstrated in our semantics and diction, and how we express ourselves in words.

I was an American executive who didn't warm up easily or quickly to strangers. Compounding this I dressed somewhat formally even at leisure – it was my Irish uniform! Moreover, I was neither given to small talk nor corporate speak, but more of a listener than talker. I was not expansive, didn't put strangers at ease with humor, but I made them feel as if specimens under glass.

No, I didn't play golf. No, I wasn't forthcoming with a biographical synopsis that might explain how someone so young was assigned to this estate, and this "big" assignment, and no I didn't belong to anything fraternal, social or academic association that might give a further clue as to my persona.

The irony is that even when I was quite young, strangers mistook me for an academic. True, once back from South Africa, having resigned my position, I did subsequently go back to school to acquire a Ph.D. and to teach as an adjunct professor at a number of universities. This identity quest by strangers is somewhat unsettling as a former nurse, who was working at the checkout at a Wal-Mart asked me as she sacked my groceries if I was a psychiatrist. *"No, no!"* I protested, which she took to confirm her guess with a smile.

When I explained that I was a psychologist, she beamed with satisfaction at her discernment, but the smile faded when I added, industrial to psychologist. Clearly, the juxtaposition of "industrial" with "psychologist" was confusing.

I've also been taken to be an aging actor of one name or another which in turn confuses me as I'm not that familiar with most actors' names. Most everyone is taken to be someone else at some point in their lives by the way they look, talk, walk, the manner of their dress, or simply reminding them of someone they know or have seen somewhere before.

The temptation is there to please strangers with answers fitting their conjectures about us. This finds men often asked how tall they are, and women how slim they are. Men add a couple inches, and women shed a few pounds in their answers to bring smiles of envy.

Author James T. Farrell once wrote a delightful story about a middle age couple returning home on the train after a shopping trip to Chicago. Asked where they lived, the man told the stranger in a suburb where they owned a block of apartments and lived in one of them.

The woman turned her head aside. They rented one of the apartments and didn't even own an automobile. Asked what he did for a living, the man said he owned an engineering company, when he was actually a plumber's assistant for a licensed plumbing company. When asked where he went to school, having only finished grammar school, he mentioned an upscale high school he never attended. Finally, the man asked the stranger what he did. The stranger answered he was unemployed and wonder if the man could spare him a fiver or two. The comeuppance worked with the man putting a ten-dollar bill into the stranger's hands.

WHO ARE YOU, RIGHT NOW?

In meeting a new person, there is a strong need to please, to make an impression. Should that impression be negative, it is immediately discernible on the other person's face long before that person realizes he has assumed the posture of withdrawal.

To combat this, we feel we have no other option than to lie. We justify the lie saying it is not a lie but just a harmless exaggeration, besides, what damage does it do?

My da often corrected strangers we met while traveling across the length and breadth of the country on two-week summer passes from his employer, *The Chicago & North Western Railway*. Strangers would ask him where he worked, and he would tell them. *"You're a conductor, are you?"* *"No,"* my da would answer, *"I'm a brakeman; I work for conductors."*

"Oh," they would say, looking at him askance. Then before they could take this totally in, he would add, *"I'm not even a regular brakeman, but on the extra board which I've been on for more than ten years, as there is a waiting list for regular brakeman jobs."*

On that trip from Clinton, Iowa to Los Angeles, California, I asked him at a rest stop in Nevada, *"Why did you say that? Why couldn't you say you were a conductor? You took the exam. Why all that about the extra board?"*

He looked me in the eye and said, *"Jimmy, what I am is an extra board brakeman. Yes, I took the conductor's examination, but I didn't pass it. Did you want me to tell the stranger that?"*

"No!" I said emphatically.

"Jimmy, I love working on the railroad. It is the best job I've ever had. I am proud of what I am, and comfortable with what I do. You are the son of an Irish Roman Catholic brakeman on the railroad. That is who you are. The day you deny that, you won't know who you are, and everyone else will own you.

"Your father completed the seven grade at St. Patrick's, the same school you attended. That's who your father is. Your mother graduated from St. Mary's high school, but she has a tendency to exaggerate who she is, and about you kids, especially about you.

"She has filled your head so full of BS that it is a wonder your feet ever touch the ground."

Angered, I asked, *"What's that supposed to mean?"* I was twelve years old at the time.

"It means you're full of malarkey, Jimmy," adding, *"thanks to your mother."*

I went to sit in an empty seat a few rows away. I was so mad at him that tears rolled down my cheeks, clouding my vision of the passing beauty of the countryside. How could he be so cruel? I never had a follow up conversation with him on the subject.

*   *   *

A couple of years later, I was complaining to my mother about a coach in high school. He rose out of his chair in the living room where he was reading *The Clinton Herald*, and looked at us in the kitchen. *"Jimmy, got a minute?"* I then followed him into the living room and sat down on the sofa facing him in his favorite lounge chair.

"Have you told the coach how you feel?"

"Of course not."

"You think he's an asshole, right?"

"Yes."

"Well, he won't know how big an asshole he is if you don't tell him to his face."

"But .."

"But what? Are you afraid he won't play you, kick you off the team, what?"

I pushed my chest out, and smiled, *"He won't do that. I'm too good. He needs me,"* then less confidently, *"he doesn't need to know how I feel."*

"Jimmy, he already does."

"He does?"

"Of course he does. You are as obvious as a naked man at Mass. That's not the point. The point is to take responsibility for the way you feel."

"How?"

"Always imagine the person you're talking about is standing right behind your shoulder. If you do, you won't say anything or think anything you wouldn't say to his face."

He wasn't through. *"If you don't like the man, fine. Show him the respect that you're a person of sincerity, have the courage not to be two faced. It doesn't mean you're wrong about him. He's in charge and your job is to play for him or get off the team. You don't want to become a sniveling cry baby, do you?"*

At first, I pondered what he said. The long term result of that advice has been for me to be direct to the extreme. It has gotten me into more than a little trouble. It is even apparent in my prose. People ask me how I feel about something, and I tell them, which is not often what they expect or want to hear.

In my defense, I asked finally, *"What about when guys spread gossip about me that is not true, what about that, what am I supposed to do about that?"*

"Nothing."

"Nothing? Shouldn't I confront them?"

"What good would that do? They are likely to lie and deny it. Guys on the road talk about you, some of it gets back to me."

"About me? Why?"

"Oh, for a lot of reasons, because coaches play you rather than their kid, because you're always getting your name in the paper for this or that. I suppose because you're a cocky SOB."

"Thanks for that. What do you do when they talk about me?"

"Nothing. I just listen, which gets their dander up more than if I did something."

"Da, why do people do that?"

"You'd have to ask them." He lit a cigarette on the end of his butt. *"Men are far worse gossipers than women. You know this when they start talking about whoever isn't there. Sure as the Pope is a Catholic, they'll be talking about me when I'm not there."*

"That's sick."

"No, sick is when they try to knock you to your face using humor to hide their true colors. That is not only cowardly it shows you have an advantage over them you never understood you had." *"Guys do that to me,"* I said, *"they mock me."*

"I'm sure they do."

"But why? What do they get out of it?"

"They think they're being funny. Don't react to it; let them think they have you where they want you. It is their way to think they have you where they want you when they don't at all."

"I totally disagree. When somebody does that to me, I want to knock their lights out, but I don't, so I'm in their face."

He shakes his head. *"Jimmy, Jimmy! Does it make you feel any better?"*

"Yes, as a matter of fact it does."

"Then they've won."

With that, I started to moon over what he had said. *"Mom doesn't gossip."*

"No, but she doesn't hear very well. She dominates the conversation talking about you kids, always with exaggeration."

"Have you told her that?"

"Oh, Jimmy, if you only knew how often."

"Does it do any good?"

"Of course, not. You are the light of her eyes. You justify her life. You are her calling and she's determined you'll be somebody."

"How is she going to do that?"

"Beats the hell out of me."

"Da, how do you feel about that?"

"No opinion."

A few years later, we had another conversation. I was near graduation from college and was feeling especially giddy.

"Remember, da, when I was a sophomore in high school, and you wanted me to quit school to take a job on the railroad?"

"So?"

"Then a couple of years ago when a professor wanted me drop out of chemistry, and take a position in the Humanities Honors Program, you asked me if I was a fag."

"Where is this going?"

"Da, why have you never believed in me?"

"You ask why I have never believed in you. That is not how I see it. I know all the hurt and backstabbing you will encounter in your attempt to rise above your father."

"You don't think I'm equal to that?"

"I don't think any of us are. No, I don't think you are. Now, your mother has an unbelievable capacity for risk, for putting you into her fantasy world and standing tall. She is bound and determined for you to reach her brother's level since you were a little boy."

My uncle earned two Ph.D.'s at the University of Iowa in psychology and economics, was head of the Department of Commerce at the University of Detroit, and an international consultant, rising out of South Clinton, which was on the wrong side of the railroad tracks.

"Well, she wasn't wrong!" I said with finality.

He didn't say anything.

*   *   *

The next episode was when I came home on emergency leave from the navy. I was a Hospital Corpsman on the USS Salem (CA-139), the flagship of the Sixth Fleet, which was operating in the Mediterranean Sea. My da was dying of multiple myeloma, a form of leukemia, a few weeks from his fiftieth birthday.

From his hospital bed in our home, still able to talk, he said, *"Remember when you asked me how I felt about all this pressure your mother put on you."*

"Yes."

"I want to tell you something now. I talked to your brother and two sisters. I'm going to die soon." He would die three weeks later, January 3, 1958, three days after his fiftieth birthday. *"Your mother says you want to be a writer. That is hard for me to see as you don't even write a good letter."*

"Why then did a professor want me to be in the Humanities Honors Program at Iowa, an internationally recognized program?"

"No idea."

"That's when you asked me if I was a fag."

"Yes, do you know why?" I waited. *"You and reality have always had a mixed relationship, and you didn't even have a girlfriend, what was I to think? You were always with your head in a book. There is a big word to describe how I felt."*

"Ambivalent. You felt ambivalent about me."

"Whatever. I have no idea what that word means. Anyway, you played this game with yourself, and so did your mother.

Somebody had to show some sense. That's what I'm talking about. Of you four kids, I'm most worried about you. You've got your head so far in the clouds you can't even see the ground. That's dangerous, Jimmy. It's a cruel world out there. It's a world that likes to cut people like us up and have them for breakfast, people too big for their own britches."

I started to cry, me a grown man in my twenties being hurt when this man, my da, was dying and unconcerned about his slipping mortality. How absurd that looks now. How narcissistic it painted me to be. I immediately retreated into self-justification. I had seen a good bit of the world, I had a wife and son, I had a professional job to return to, I had had one success after another, and my dying da saw me as a loser. I was into "I" "I" "I" and couldn't see how pathetic I was, but that is how I was, and I have to live with that.

"Tears aren't going to change anything, Jimmy." My crying turned to sobs, shaking with emotions. *"Here, take this."* He gave me a tissue from a box beside his bed. He was dying and he was tending to me. He weighed only about sixty pounds at the time on his five-seven frame normally weighing about one-fifty.

He had bed soars on his back so bad that I had to medicate them twice daily. Since I was a Hospital Corpsman, the doctor allowed me to give him morphine shots for pain whenever he needed them. I cannot exaggerate how brave a man he was in the face of death, although he could not mask the pain in his eyes. *"Blow your nose!"* he said to me, as mucous covered my lips. *"You look disgusting."*

Then he said something that hit me hard. *"Keep your tears in a vault. If you don't, people will have you for lunch."* It only made me sob harder. Then he closed his eyes and went to sleep. Sitting on a chair reside his bed, I cried myself to sleep leaning my head against his cold clammy hand. *You're pathetic,*

Fisher! I whispered to myself. My da was dying and I was acting as if it was all about me!

The rest of the story is that on January 3, 1958 my mother sent me to the store for some groceries. We took turns monitoring him on a twenty-four hour basis. When I returned, my mother was crying. *"What is going on, Jimmy, what is happening?"*

My da was in his death rattle. He looked at me raised his head off his pillow, and then the rattle stopped with his eyes still staring at me. My mother was hysterical, clinging to me to do something. I held her until she became limp with emotions, went over and closed my da's eyes, and rested his head on the pillow, and called Dr. Joseph O'Donnell.

He was so right about me. My mother was a disaster. We were in our little house alone and I had dry eyes, thinking someday I'd write about this. I promised myself I would live the life that he did not have. I was angry with God, but totally functional. I organized his funeral with *The Johnny Dalton Funeral Parlor*, Johnny a boyhood friend, and called Dr. Ed Carey, another boyhood friend. The Irish stuck together no matter their station in life.

Mass donations poured in from his railroad buddies and others. I gave Father McInerny half of them, and the other half to my mother to live on.

The good padres suspected there was something not right about this as far more mass donations were anticipated. I found I could take his insinuations with composure and without comment. My mother never knew she was living for months off Catholic Mass money.

I checked the *Chicago & North Western Railway* survivor's benefits for my mother, and learned for the first time how little money my da had made over the years, and therefor how modest my mother's benefits.

Railroaders didn't contribute to the *Social Security System* and therefore derived no benefits from that money source. She was forty-four years old. My da only made a fraction of what I made as a chemist in R&D at Standard Brands, Inc. It wasn't fair. It wasn't right.

Life is always a collection of what ifs. In my case, my da's early death spurred me on to harness my anger to some purpose using lessons he taught me along the way. My children, even my grandchildren don't like to think that their roots are so common, but that is their legacy and their greatest strength. They don't need to dissemble, don't need to pretend, don't need to look life in the eye and turn away. They are real. They have the freedom to see what they are right now, right this minute, and not apologize to anyone about for being seed of an extra board brakeman dignity of being something real. It is who they are. There is no point in trying to be anyone else. They have the

THIRTEEN

THE PALLIATIVE TO ANXIETY!

Palliative: *to reduce the violence of a disease; to moderate or reduce the intensity of anxiety; to sooth.*

The evidence is overwhelming that we live in an "Age of Anxiety." If one penetrates below the surface of political, economic, business, professional, or domestic crises to discover their psychological causes, or if one seeks to understand modern art, poetry or philosophy or religion, one runs athwart the problem of anxiety at almost every turn. The ordinary stresses and strains of life in the changing world of today are such that few if any escape the need to confront anxiety and to deal with it in some manner.

Rollo May, American psychoanalyst, *The Meaning of Anxiety* (1977)

Stress is the spice of life. Without it you would be a vegetable, or dead. Stress is not something to avoid. It is the extreme of stress or distress that causes so many ailments of modern society.

Hans Selye, American born Canadian physician, *Stress Without Distress* (1974)

Anxiety is a luxury of a self-indulgent culture. It is a culture which has time on its hands. Instead of focusing on living to experience the pleasures that cost nothing, the anxious take themselves too seriously and life not seriously enough.

James R. Fisher, Jr., *Meet Your New Best Friend* (2014)

Someone must have been telling lies about Joseph K., for without having done anything wrong he was arrested one fine morning.

Franz Kafka, *The Trial* (1925)

A CHILD'S VIEW OF ANXIETY

It is no accident this is called an "anxious age." As we have moved away from the comfort of faith in God and the cultivation of a spiritual life, we have moved towards melancholy and a moral ambivalence.

We have come to expect the other shoe to fall at any moment, throwing our lives into ultimate turmoil. From our exodus of trust in God, we have departed from trust in ourselves. We don't talk about it. We don't have to. It is revealed in our sense of helplessness dangling with no certain attachments in sight. Nothing stays the same not even for an hour.

At the same time, men are slow to give up their boyhood when they never had a childhood. Now as adults, they surrounded themselves with toys that blunt their curiosity, and with games designed for that lost childhood.

Girls rush their biological clock to prance about as mothers when the insouciance of youth is not even a memory.

Anxiety has become the poison parent of most sins; the misery that haunts the child man and the child woman. In a world where doubt is magnified and disappointment denied, there is a restless stir of commotion as the homeless mind for certainty, which doesn't exist, and thus the dilemma.

Albert Camus (1913-1960) wrote:

I shall tell you a great secret, friend. Do not wait for the last judgment, it takes place every day.

These words of the 1957 Nobel Laureate for Literature proved prophetic as Camus was cut down from life in an auto accident at the height of his fame at age 47.

All any of us has is this moment, not tomorrow, not even the rest of this day. So, it doesn't make sense to be anxious about tomorrow, or about things we cannot change. My granddaughter, Rachel, six years old, asked me about anxiety.

"Where did you hear that word?" I asked.

"Mommy's always saying daddy is full of anxiety."

Her father is an attorney, entrepreneur, and sportsman, sleeps four hours a night, and is always on the go. Although successful, he continues to put himself in jeopardy by carrying others and allowing them advantages they haven't earned and don't deserve, thus the anxiety.

Obviously, money is not the cure for anxiety. If anything, money is the curse of anxiety masking a palliative role.

"Anxiety, Rachel," I said, *"is worrying about something that hasn't happened, and is not likely to occur."*

American reformer William Jay (1789-1858) stated it well:

One of the most useless of all things is to take a deal of trouble in providing against dangers that never come. How many toil to lay up riches which they never enjoy; to provide for exigencies that never happen; to prevent troubles that never come;

sacrificing present comfort and enjoyment in guarding against the wants of a period they may never live to see.

The word "anxiety," like "stress" means different things to different people.

Defining anxiety is difficult although it has become part of our daily vocabulary. Is anxiety merely synonymous with stress? Obviously, it involves effort, fatigue, pain, fear, and therefore stress if not distress.

Anxiety is apparent with changes in the vital signs of our body such as sweating, a bump in our temperature, or our blood pressure rising. But is it only these things? Or could it be losing touch with ourselves and feeling self-estranged? Think about it! When are we most anxious?   It is when we no longer trust ourselves, trust our experience, or our history to cope with the situation.

It would seem anxiety is a frantic desire to know outcomes before they occur, which is impossible. As Hans Selye points out, *stress is the spice of life, and without it we would be a vegetable.* It is distress that is the culprit to our anxiety, and it is fed by that mania for certainty in an uncertain existence. Just as it is impossible to have a stress free existence, it is equally impossible to have an anxiety free conscience.

Venturing outside ourselves inevitably produces stress and anxiety, which can lead to distress. It is a common fear that people will see us as the fraud we believe ourselves to be. Actor Leonardo DiCaprio puts it poignantly: *"I want an authentic life. Once I achieved fame, I realized I don't value it at all."*

The hardest thing to face is that we are forever a contradiction. There will always be a contrast between our *projected ideal self* and *actual real self*; between our imagined reality and the reality of experience.   Our culture programs us from birth to be inauthentic, to be pretenders, to take on the guise of what others tell us we are, and to value the persona of others as our idols.

Those most attentive to this idolatry achieve a successful phoniness. Actors such as DiCaprio know this best. They epitomize the quintessential counterfeit self. Those infatuated with these celluloid identities on television and in film can become as inauthentic in life as their counterfeit heroes. A rash of shootings in movie complexes bears this out. Item:

On July 20, 2012, a mass shooting occurred inside of a Century 16 movie theater in Aurora, Colorado, during a midnight screening of the film *The Dark Knight Rises*. A gunman, dressed in tactical clothing as if a character in the film, set off tear gas grenades and shot into the audience with multiple firearms. 12 people were killed and 70 others were injured, the largest number of casualties in a shooting in the United States. The sole assailant, James Eagan Holmes, was arrested in his car parked outside the cinema minutes later. It was the deadliest shooting in Colorado since the Columbine High School massacre in 1999. Prior to the shooting, Holmes rigged his apartment with homemade explosives, which were defused by a bomb squad one day after the shooting.

These psychotic episodes go well beyond anxiety, but the question still has to be asked: when did the neuroses of anxiety escalate into psychoses?

Psychiatrist Karen Horney in *The Neurotic Personality of Our Time* (1937) writes:

"Anxiety is the dynamic center of neuroses and thus we shall have to deal with it all the time."

As we see here, a six-year-old child wonders about the meaning of the word, anxiety, when she observes it first hand in the psychodrama of her home.

"That sounds stupid," she replied.

"Yes," I answered. *"It is stupid."*

A child in the womb of the family doesn't feel her security threatened. Horney holds that anxiety is derived from compulsive drives that are born of feelings of isolation, helplessness, fear, and hostility.

Anxiety, then, represents a way of coping with the world despite these feelings. The aim is always safety, never satisfaction. The compulsive quality of this is due to anxiety lurking behind repressed feelings. Rachel, up to this point, has had no sense of this. Innocence never leaves the womb, while her parents seem unaware of the impact of their behavior on her delicate psyche.

"Then why do people do it?"

"Because sometimes we act stupid as adults."

People make the complex simple to cope, and the simple complex to problem solve. The clarity of vision escapes us once life takes on age and history. Sociologist Lewis Mumford writes in *The Condition of Man* (1944):

"People whose course of life has reached a crisis must confront their collective past as fully as a neurotic patient must unbury his personal life; long-forgotten traumas in history may have a disastrous effect upon millions who remain unaware of them."

*   *   *

"Do you do it, papa?" she asked.

"Ah yes, many times," I confessed.

The truth is I have learned over time that all my history is important because it is forever contemporary. Nothing is more important than those hidden parts that still survive in me without my being aware of them or their importance. They drive me from, rather than towards my contradictions. I ride my anxiety like a surfboard in stormy waters.

"Then you must be stupid, too," she laughed, then paused and studied me a moment. *"But you're not stupid. So you must not have to be stupid to have anxiety."*

How could I convey that stupidity is that neurotic distortion between expectations and reality experienced without confusing her?

Fear of failing a test in school found me studying hard and earning an "A." Fear of being discovered a coward found me racing down the field to make the opening tackle on the kickoff in a high school football game. For this play, I was touted as a hard-nosed player. Fear of botching an assignment on the job and getting fired resulted in a succession of promotions.

Confronting my anxiety, and accepting the responsibility and guilt associated with it resulted in increased self-awareness and enlarged my sphere of creativity. Anxiety is home to the writer, or any person not comfortable in his own skin. Where would art be without anxiety?

On the other hand, anxiety displaced found me critical of my da when his paycheck never stretched from payday to payday. My anxiety was also manifested in being accident-prone. This grew into an aversion to doctors and instant headaches when my parents argued.

Later, migraine headaches would plague me the moment I experienced any pressure. Driven by my anxieties, it was paramount that I be focused and disciplined to the point that I was no fun at all.

How could I explain this to my granddaughter? Competitive success was my dominant drive and the pervasive cause of my anxiety. This would in no way compute with my granddaughter who saw me only as "successful." Seeing me as I am for her is yet to come.

"You're right," I said, always surprised, when I shouldn't be. *"Smart people are known to sometimes do things that make no sense."*

She folded her little arms over her chest, and said, *"Papa, anxiety doesn't make any sense to me at all."*

Indeed, when you worry about things you can't change you experience anxiety. Someone once said, *"Never trouble trouble till trouble troubles you."* Yet, it is so easy to worry about what never happens, which of course makes no sense. Life's misfortunes hardest to bear are those that never come. There is much more to anxiety, however, then confused self-identity and irrational behavior.

DOWNSIDE OF LUCK!

People think that if they won the lottery all their anxieties would vanish. A series of lotto winners have complained that it was the worst thing that ever happened to them.

On Christmas Day 2002, Jack Whittaker of Charleston, West Virginia won the largest lottery jackpot in U.S. history to that date, $314.9 million in the Powerball jackpot.

Previously, he was already a wealthy contractor. He took his winnings in a lump sum of $113 million after taxes, and held an immediate news conference to appear as a jolly saint.

Without hesitation, he split $7 million among three churches, gave money to improve a Little League park, bought playground equipment for children, and set up a charitable foundation.

Eight months later, his life and fortune started to unravel. A briefcase was stolen with $545,000 in cash and cashier checks from his SUV. It was parked at a strip club. He not only became a well-known strip club devotee, but also confessed to now being a high-stakes gambler, which is why he was carrying so much cash. Several thefts to his home, office and other vehicles followed.

At one of the thefts, in September, 2003, an 18-year-old friend of his granddaughter's was found dead. The boy died from overdosing on a combination of oxycodone, methadone, meperidine, and cocaine.

Next, his 17-year-old granddaughter came up missing. In December, 2004, Whitaker's granddaughter was found dead on the property of a male friend. Her body was wrapped in a plastic tarpaulin and dumped behind a junked van. The death was ruled an overdose.

In July, 2009, Whitaker's daughter, the mother of his dead granddaughter was found dead. Foul play was not ruled out.

He got in a fight at a nightclub, and two men sued him for assault. Other similar suits followed from related brawls. A judge fined him and assigned him to attend weekly *Alcoholics Anonymous* meetings.

In less than a year, he had gone from saint to sinner to profligate in his community. One person quipped, *"This clown is not capable of handling a $10 bill much less all those millions."* His charitable foundation is now closed; his business is in jeopardy; his own health is on the fence. One of Whittaker's friends remarked, *"I think it's pretty sad, really. It just goes to show money can't always buy happiness."*

UPSIDE OF PLUCK!

Rachel is an extraordinary little girl as many young people are. I am convinced that young people like Rachel will redirect our society into a less anxious configuration. The irony of our times is that despite the hyped-up technological explosion there is a drab sameness to everything and nearly everybody.

The herd mentality has extended to technology with everyone using an iPhone, laptop or some other mobile device. In a way, texting and tweeting have acted like our "worry beads," providing connection with others if only electronically. It would seem we dread being alone and are intimidated with silence.

Anxiety doesn't happen "out there." Anxiety is part of our make-up. It is the friction of ourselves rubbing against ourselves that produces what we call "art." Art brings out our buried demons that wreak havoc with our soul. Art is talking to us with creative verve and is a palliative to anxiety. Nothing is as bad as it seems when it is neutralized by the light of day. Art brings out the sun.

Rachel is already writing stories. She loves everyone, finds school exciting, and loves to teach her friends the things she has learned.

Will society kill that spirit? Will it put her in its cage? Will it blow out her flame of curiosity and egoistic joy, and turn it into sorrow and self-contempt? Will she look to what she doesn't have and isn't rather than what she is and has? Will she balance optimism with doubt and pessimism with reason? Will she wrap her life in confusion and fill her shoes with fretting anxiety, or will she embrace her fears and soar to new insights? I don't know. I can only hope and pray.

She asked me the other day, as I was taking her to ice skating practice, *"who is more creative, papa, you or me?"*

I answered, *"Is this important to you?"*

"Yes, why else would I ask?"

Refusing to talk down to her, I explained that comparing and competing is a form of imitation and subject to anxiety.

"You see, Rachel, you cannot be another person or experience what that person experiences. You will see others more fortunate, perhaps happier, but that is okay. Feel good about them and their good fortune. You will feel better about yourself. Likewise," I continued, *"you will see others less fortunate and not as happy you are. Be kind to them but don't think you know what is best for them. They will have to find that out for themselves."*

Then I added, *"To your question of who is more creative, your creative powers are now at their highest. One day when you are as old as your papa you will appreciate that creative powers fade with age. Then you will rely more on your learning, experience and history.*

"You can never take your creativity for granted. It is a gift from God. You must feed it and breathe life into it. Otherwise, it will shrivel up and die. That means you must use it. You must read, wonder, observe and ask questions like you are doing now, and

never be afraid to challenge anything that makes no sense to you."

"I do that all the time now, papa."

"Yes, you do."

She left a message on my machine yesterday. *"I scored four goals in soccer, papa. Just wanted you to know."* Then a short pause. *"Papa, I don't think you're old. I think you're handsome."* Thank God for little girls who are blind as well as gifted.[1]

WHEN A CHILD TAKES ON THE ROLE OF THE ADULT

During the Thanksgiving weekend of 2004, when Rachel was eight, her family went on holiday to their Michigan lakefront cottage. Rachel's parents made arrangements for a charitable organization to deliver a twelve-foot Christmas tree, fully decorated, in their absence.

It was the responsibility of the groundskeeper to see that the tree was properly placed in the living room. Unfortunately, once the family had departed, he took off. Consequently, the volunteers delivering the tree were unable to place it in the home, deciding instead to leave it at the front door.

As fortune would have it, a violent thunderstorm erupted soon after. Tree limbs and ornaments were spread in a thousand pieces over the expansive manicured lawn, a $1,200 disaster. So, when the family returned from holiday, the sight, leastwise for Rachel's mother, was first incredulous, then shocking, finally disrupting into vociferous despair.

To put it mildly, Rachel's mother lost it. She was reduced to hysteria with damning epithets. This greatly upset Rachel. She had never seen her mother so distraught. Meanwhile, Rachel's father, a former police officer who was familiar with domestic disputes, took off to avoid his wife's fury and the object of her rage, her husband's trusting the unreliable groundskeeper.

He would later explain to his daughter that once anger reached the level of rage the person's appetite for continuing the hysteria was impossible to subdue as long as the cause for it was there. It was he who had made the arrangements for the tree's delivery entrusting the assignment to his hopeless groundskeeper. This eight-year-old saw the situation in the most drastic terms and imagined her parents divorcing.

A sense of being abandoned, security jeopardized, and peace shattered are conditional to spontaneous anxiety, especially for a child who is likely to retreat into tearful self-pity. Not Rachel. She took charge.

She instructed her mother to sit down. *"Mother,"* she said, *"get hold of yourself! It's only a tree!"* Then to put an exclamation point on the situation, she added, *"Daddy's left. He may never come back!"* She then informed her mother that the tree was something that could be replaced, but not her father.

Her mother listened, whereas earlier she had exploded when her husband dismissively said, *"It's no big deal, only a business expense."* This response triggered a reminder of his spendthrift ways. On the other hand, Rachel was appealing to her mother's self-interests as well as her own.

When a child fears the breakup of her family, it creates the sense of abandonment, isolation, separation, and helplessness. Consequently, the expected behavior is weeping, not taking charge. Rachel had the presence of mind to appeal to her mother's reason and apprehension. She created a climate in which her mother calmed down; recognizing it was only a tree, while finally realizing what was actually at stake.

Within the hour, Rachel's father returned. Peace was tacitly restored in an aftermath of emotional catharsis and apologies. Rachel stepped off stage and allowed her parents to bond again. But it had been she who acted like the adult in the situation, not her parents, and she was eight-years-old.

A child became the parent, the interventionist, the therapist, but who will be this child's therapist when emotional trauma surfaces at some inopportune time in her future? This is part of this little girl's history, a fissure of vulnerability in her innocence, but at the same time, placed anxiety in perspective.

A FATHER'S TAKE ON ANXIETY

My da was a wise man albeit life's Job from the Bible. His mother died in Cook County Hospital in Chicago when he was born; his father took off for points unknown never to be seen again.

Reared by his Irish relatives in Iowa, he grew up into young manhood during the *"Roaring Twenties,"* and had difficulty settling down even after he met my mother. She was patient and would in time be his anchor and lighthouse. The 1930s were the years of *The Great Depression*, and then came *World War Two*, rearing four children on a railroad brakeman's income.

He was proud of his work and loved the railroad. During the war, he carried wounded soldiers from the battlefields of the South Pacific from Boone, Iowa to Clinton, Iowa on his Chicago & North Western Railway trains heading to *Schick Army General Hospital* in Clinton, Iowa. Often, he was so troubled seeing these wounded young men that he could not talk to my mother or anyone of us after completing his trip. When the war was over, and life slowed down and became more manageable, he contracted multiple myeloma, bone cancer, a form of leukemia, and died at the age of 50.

It was impossible to miss my da's physical courage, which was on display to the end. He never complained although in great pain, and reduced to less than sixty pounds before he expired. His cage was mental anxiety. Little as he feared death, he seemed terrified of life, afraid to push the envelope. He would give others the benefit of the doubt and not himself; cower to authority figures even when he knew they were wrong. To him, everyone was more gifted than he was. I often asked him why.

The incongruity of his humility with my arrogance gave me the courage to venture into the world of work believing no one more talented, only to drop out myself at the pinnacle of my career to enter the less certain world of words as a writer. Here are a few of his boilerplate observations that have become etched on my soul:

- A man needs only three square meals a day, the roof over his head, and the clothes on his back. Everyone, no matter how high they fly, share this in common. Yet society can take away your table, the roof over your head, and the clothes off your back, but it must kill you to take what you put between your ears.

- You are the son of an Irish Roman Catholic brakeman on the railroad. The day you deny that is the day you won't know who the hell you are. That's the only thing you have that is yours. I see college students boarding my trains leaving their parents at the station pretending they don't know them. You cannot run from who you are, but you can lose who that is.

- Don't be too impressed with high flyers. Chances are they have connections you'll never know. You have no choice but to find your own way with hard work. Don't envy them; don't copy them; and by all means, don't pretend to be like them.

- Money is not the root of all evil. It is what people make of money. Everyone likes money. Some will lie to get it; cheat to get it; betray their friends to get it; or steal it. But most people are content to have little of it. What separates us from the rich is that we are only capable of venial sins when it comes to money, while the rich have a great talent for committing mortal sins in pursuit of it. Don't ever be impressed with the rich. Most fortunes are built on selling your soul for money.

- Your mother expects you to be a big deal. That will never happen. What your mother refuses to understand is that our classless society has a caste system even in this dingy little town of ours. The haves decide who belongs and who doesn't; and have nots better know where they belong or they won't belong anywhere.

- Whenever someone badmouths someone not there, be weary. Rest assured that when you're not present you're fair game.

His good counsel simplified his anxiety instead of giving him reason to venture beyond his self-imposed doubt. He was an honest man who stayed in his Irish Catholic conclave. We had an Irish grocer, two Irish doctors, an Irish dentist and Irish insurance man, two Irish pubs in the neighborhood, lived in an Irish parish, had Irish friends, and even an Irish undertaker. This was something considering the community was more than eighty percent Protestant.

ANXIETY & LIFE CHANGING EXPERIENCE

There is a saying when the student is ready the teacher will arrive. This seems less true today. Students appear disinclined to seek pedagogic direction. Likewise, mentors, coaches and counselors in everyday life are prominent as justifiers, not changers or improvers. We are in the impersonal electronic age glued to a cell phone or a modem.

With so much information available, curiosity has faded by frequent solo flying on the Internet. Active life has been relegated to the back burner. Most experience is second hand or play station reality.

If humanity is anything, it is a social group, and social dynamics at every level are critical to developing social skills. The irony is that as we are pushed closer together by the heterogeneity of the population, while further apart by our conditional xenophobia. As a consequence, as the distance between us continues to vanish, we become more insular and secluded, not less so, and more guided by inappropriate stereotypes than enlightening interpersonal relations.

Self-awareness only occurs when we confront life's obstacles and move through them to new understanding. To confront anxiety, it requires departing from the familiar to embracing the unfamiliar, from reassuring safety to challenging freedom, from the context of meaning to the subtext of identity. Each life is loaded with possibilities. This was one of mine.

A CASE STUDY

Only in my mid-thirties, after completing an assignment in South Africa, I resigned, retiring from the world of work and moving to the hedonistic leisure and sunshine of Florida.

My executive assignment in South Africa had been to facilitate the formation of a new modest conglomerate of an American subsidiary, a British affiliate, and a South African chemical division of a major chemical company.

There were a number of reasons for my early retirement for what, on the surface, might seem a hasty if not impulsive decision. To wit:

- There was the cultural shock of British colonialism clashing with my modest lower middleclass upbringing in a working class family in Iowa, coupled with

- The observation of blatant human rights violations of the Afrikaner government of the Bantu peoples, the black majority population, which essentially had few rights.

- Then there was the passivity of my Irish Roman Catholic Church in the midst of these draconian practices.

- Add to this a cavalier disregard of basic ethics by company executives. [2]

This threw my value and belief system into cultural shock and chaos. It didn't help that my wife and four preadolescent children didn't take to life in Johannesburg, exacerbated by the fact that I traveled extensively leaving them to deal, alone, with a very strange society.

At every turn, there was the matter of South African apartheid, or separate development of the races. This reminded me of the Tama Indian Reservation near my home in Iowa. My work was demanding, but that was not the problem. The problem was I couldn't get my mind around the ambience of what I had been thrown into with absolutely no orientation as to what I might face.

In fairness, this was 1968 and less than a quarter century since WWII. The United States was still basking in unchallenged supremacy in the world marketplace giving little attention to the emotional stability of its minions.

My intuition told me the only rational escape from my free-floating anxiety was a full-fledged retreat. I needed a "time out" to regroup and refocus. My life made no sense to me anymore. I resigned and relocated to Florida.

After doing little more than reading and writing for two years, I entered a doctoral program at a local university seeking answers. I was in the program only a short time when a member of my group approached me after an evening seminar. He was a decade younger than I was, and we had never spoken to each other before.

Straightforwardly, he asked, *"Do you plan to graduate in this program?"* It was 9 p.m. and we would talk to nearly 1 a.m. The gist of the conversation was my obvious disdain for academics or professors who weren't better read than I was, and whose ignorance of the real world beyond academia was insulting to me.

"What is obvious to me," he continued, *"is that with your attitude you are doomed to fail."* He now had my rapt attention. *"If failure is in your plans, you are working the strategy to perfection. But if you plan on earning a Ph.D., you're doing everything wrong by intimidating and demeaning your professors.*

"As little as you may think of them, they have the power of the grade. As petty as their internal squabbling may offend you, they are masters of this arena. Believe me, they can be as treacherous as I suspect you were in your previous work, perhaps more so. They have to grovel for petty raises and petty perks. Pettiness is their battlefield.

"If you were to measure their antipathy for you against your contempt for them, it would not be a contest. It would be like a hot draft from hell compared to a summer breeze. They don't like you, and don't plan on trying.

"You either step more lightly or make humble, or they'll squash you like a bug.

"They've never known power, real power as you have. They've never had people part the waters for them when they approach; and they've never made the kind of money you've made. You're the enemy on their turf, and you are showing no respect."

Driving home across Tampa Bay, I reflected on his words and my previous career. He was right. I was being an ass. Even though I was quite young in South Africa, I had authority, respect, a generous budget, ample human resources, and total freedom to implement my "intuitive strategy," as my minders called it. No one could explain my success so I was given *carte blanche*.

It was the major reason I returned to the university: to find answers in psychology and sociology to the conundrum of why I had been so successful yet so unconventional in my approach.[3]

Unknown to my young counselor in the university parking lot that night, I was surprised and frustrated, even angered, to find the university a veritable factory of reification and regurgitation with a haunting resemblance to the world that I had recently left.

The corporation had no answers for me. Now I found the university a *de facto* corporation. I was like the child looking for the pony in the haystack, only to find I had been duped by false expectations.

Instead of being consoled by my success, I was troubled by it. I had expected, perhaps naively, that there was something beyond making money. I was not a spender so money had little meaning to me. This discovery was maddening. I had passed the turnstile where making money was the ticket to the future to being very confused as to what might lay beyond.

It was on that basis that I resigned, telling my superior, a wise and decent man, that if I wasn't doing my job, the company would fire me; the company was not meeting my needs, so I was firing the company. All he could say was that he predicted the road ahead would be rocky, and of course, he was right.

EDUCATION'S PALLIATIVE TO ANXIETY ALONG THE WAY!

Retiring young was a life wrenching experience, but there were many mentors, coaches and counselors along the way, some of whom were not at first heeded, people who pointed the most reliable direction they saw for me. In disclosing this now, I would like readers to reflect on their own lives in similar terms and how life has spoken through interested parties to them in their own life's journey.

My mother was my first coach and I write about her in some detail in my memoir as a novel. [4] You have already been introduced to my da and the student in the parking lot. Complementing them were the Sisters of St. Francis in grammar school. They made me aware that I had a terrible temper, and that I must curb it or be in constant trouble. They taught me discipline and introduced me to a way with words. To this day, I have a love of books and ideas that they first sponsored.

At our courthouse playground, older boys introduced me to baseball and taught me the game, while a high school athlete, and former student of St. Patrick's grade school taught me the love of basketball. Were it not for the introduction of sports into my early life, I would imagine I would have been more withdrawn than I naturally am. The Sisters of St. Francis encouraged sports for me as a calming influence to my temperament.

In high school, I had an exceptional math teacher in third and fourth year mathematics. But that is not why he is included here. We took a national test at mid-term of the first semester of my senior year, and I did poorly.

Unbeknown to me, this had troubled him, as he considered me one of his good students. The same test was given again in the middle of my final semester. I was unaware that it was the same test. I did well on it. Afterwards, he explained what he had done, and why, reminding me that I was high strung. *"When you become anxious your brain seems to fog up and shut down,"* he observed. His insight has proven useful to me throughout my life.

At university, taking a required core course in literature my sophomore year, I contracted infectious mononucleosis and missed the mid-term, which was on James Joyce's *Portrait of the Artist as a Young Man* (1915).

Everyone in the class was much better read than I was, and so I was mainly quiet. My professor chose to have me complete the mid-term on the book as an oral examination. When I concluded it, he asked how I knew this work of Joyce's so well. I said, matter-of-factly, *"I am Joyce!"*

My life paralleled much of what was in the book. He asked me my major. I told him it was chemistry. *"You belong in literature, not science,"* he said. It would take me thirty-five years to heed his words.

WELCOME TO HELL! OUR NEXT STOP HEAVEN!

There is no time in which anxiety, free floating and otherwise, is at greater intensity than those halcyon days of college. Rollo May devotes a good deal of his book *The Meaning of Anxiety* (1977) to academic anxiety and the development of the self. College, compressed into a short number of years, isolated from the real world, and confined to the regurgitating of ideas, theories, truths, facts, myths and biases is a time of much anxiety and agitation.

Uncertainty, depression, stress, distress, confusion, and angst compete for attention most of a student's waking hours. If that were not enough, these same demons play havoc with his dreams while he's asleep.

When in such a state, I have a variation of two dreams even now in my advanced age. One, I am afraid to get my grades for fear I am flunking out. Mind you, I graduated from university more than half a century ago. The second dream I have forgotten my class schedule, and where and what time my next class is scheduled. I find myself lost on campus. I encounter students rushing to class, but am too embarrassed to ask them where my class might be. I wake up in a cold sweat, and go to my study to write, unable to sleep the rest of the night.

Someone might look at my accomplishments, then at my comfortable existence, and say, *"How is that possible?"* Soren Kierkegaard had the answer:

To venture causes anxiety, but not to venture is to lose oneself. So it is too that in the eyes of the world it is dangerous to venture. And why? Because one may lose. But not to venture is shrewd. And yet, by not venturing, it is so dreadfully easy to lose that which it would be difficult to lose in even the most venturesome venture, and in any case never so easily, so completely as if it were nothing – one's self. For if I have ventured amiss – very well, then life helps me by its punishment. But if I have not ventured at all – who then helps me? And, moreover, if by not venturing at all in the highest sense (and to venture in the highest sense is precisely to become conscious of oneself) I have gained all earthly advantages . . . and lose my self! What of that? [5]

Long before I knew Kierkegaard's words, I was stumbling and bumbling along, and ineptly but diligently embracing my resistance to anxiety. I found it true that the creative imagination is stimulated by accepting anxiety with its lessons as teacher; that it is important to resist the urge to seek safe haven in some cage.

Each of us has a role in life to play involving the positive aspects of our selfhood. We develop as individuals as we confront, move through and overcome anxiety, creating experiences. There have been many people along my long life that have opened the door of my cage, which I have not always heeded. When I have, the road ahead became easier.

IS KAFKA'S TRIAL OUR OWN?

How often I have heard variations of Kafka's lament in his book *The Trial* (1925):

Someone must have been telling lies about Joseph K., for without having done anything wrong he was arrested one fine morning.

The Trial is a novel of vast symbolism as well as a psychological study of a system whose leaders are convinced of their own righteousness. To some the judicious court of the novel is a symbol of the Church as an imperfect bridge between the individual and God. Today, it appears as a faulty symbolic bridge between corporate culture and its promise of economic security and spiritual need for meaning in a secular universe.

It is a challenge to trust the "system" to produce the leadership necessary when individual freedom is treated mockingly as a societal collective. Leadership out of such a system is crass, of course, because it implies that the burden leadership is just a few individuals to bridge the gap between the ideal and the real in a world enamored of the surreal. What happened to Joseph K happens every day because the passive majority expects social justice to materialize without any effort on their part.

Plants close, jobs disappear, industries evaporate, communities become lifeless, values change, as well as sacred beliefs, skills become anachronistic, positions atavistic, neighborhoods deteriorate, and trust as a value becomes as lost as everything else. What is a person to do when he has done nothing wrong? But is this true?

We can't change the world to fit us but we can change ourselves to fit the world. Managing anxiety involves the self-development of the self to an ever-changing world. W. H. Auden captures this in *The Age of Anxiety* (1947):

. . . . it is silly
To refuse the tasks of time
And, overlooking our lives,
Cry – "Miserable wicked me,
How interesting I am."
We would rather be ruined than changed,
We
would
rather
die in
our
dread
Than
climb
the
cross
of the
mome
nt
And
let
our
illusio
ns
die.

We remain architects of our demise no matter how much we would prefer to project that role to others. In the end as in the beginning, we get better one person at a time, and if we don't, we have no one else to blame.

Notes:

1. Granddaughter Rachel graduated with honors from a top prep high school in Tampa, Florida. With advanced courses already completed in high school, she will register as a second semester sophomore as she enters college in the fall of 2014.
2. This tense experience is given a novelist treatment in *DEVLIN, a psychological novel.* This biographical novel takes place in 1968 during South Africa's troubling apartheid policy for the Bantu and those of Color.
3. See James R. Fisher, Jr.'s unconventional approach in *Confident Selling*, TATE Publishing, 2014.
4. The memoir is *In the Shadow of the Courthouse: A Memoir of the 1940s Written as a Novel*, 2014.
5. Soren Kierkegaard, *Sickness unto Death*, Princeton University Press, 1941, p. 52.

FOURTEEN

HOW LOSERS BECOME WINNERS!
THEY NEVER QUIT!

Ralph Waldo Emerson (1803-1882) in *"Self-Reliance"* (1841) insists that society's view of failure and success was skewed:

"If our young men miscarry in their first enterprise. They lose all heart. If the young merchant fails, men say he is ruined."

Today, college graduates are considered failures if they are not connected in their chosen profession within a year. Emerson argues:

(The flexible person who) *"tries all the professions, who teams it, farms it, peddles it, keeps a school, and so forth, in successive years, and always like a cat, falls on his feet, is worth a hundred of these city dolls."*

Emerson was making allowances for his friend, Henry David Thoreau (1817-1862), who seemed to fail at everything. So, he bankrolled Thoreau, let him set out on his land, and contemplate nature, which produced *Walden* (1854).

The book would influence many, including Tolstoy, Mahatma Gandhi, Walt Whitman, John Steinbeck, B. F. Skinner, President John F. Kennedy, Dr. Martin Luther King, Jr., E. O. Wilson, Marcel Proust, Ernest Hemingway, W. B. Yeats, and many more. They would make him immortal although he would live only to the age of forty-four.

Today, we are fond of quoting him, such as:

- *The mass of men lead lives of quiet desperation.*

- *If you have built castles in the air, your work need not be lost; that is where they should be. Now put the foundations under them.*

- *I love to be alone. I never found the companion that was as companionable as solitude.*

In *"Walden,"* he writes: *"I tried the trade of my father* (pencil making) *but found that it would take ten years to get underway in that, and that then it should probably be on my way to the devil."*

He was convinced that, *"The way you get money almost without exception leads downward."*

So, he abandoned business and pursued art, using other people's money (mainly Emerson's) to pave his way to his pondering.

If Thoreau's lackadaisical waywardness seems incompressible in today's hectic hyper purposefulness, consider John Brown's unconventional exploits in the same era. In 1859, abolitionist Brown would attack Harper's Ferry with an impossible plan to liberate blacks while killing many whites with the aim to start a revolution, only to fail and to be hanged.

"Self-Reliance" was written sixteen years before Emerson met John Brown, but the abolitionist lived the transcendental philosopher's message that he espoused to the letter.

At the time, there were cells of abolitionists across the United States, but they were essentially pacifists who hoped that slavery would eventually end of its own accord through non-violence. Not John Brown. For him, it called for the bloody scourge at Pottawatomie and Harper's Ferry, where white slaveholders were cut down mercilessly. Brown and his men, and the freed slaves then fled to the mountains where they were eventually caught.

These impulsive acts would be made into legend in song, theatre, film and books as if Brown were a messiah, as Emerson clearly saw him suggesting he was Christ-like.

Abraham Lincoln spent a good part of his early life as the failures Emerson describes in this work. Whereas Brown was a man of action, Lincoln was essentially a prudent man of reflection. He was never an abolitionist, but read of the exploits of Brown and not unkindly. David S. Reynolds writes in *"John Brown: Abolitionist"* (2005):

"Though John Brown did not live to see the Civil War, he embodied its spirit in advance. What Abraham Lincoln became by the end of the conflict – an antislavery warrior who resorted to extreme violence and who humbled himself before what he called 'the providence of God' and 'the judgment of the Lord -- is a heightened version of what John Brown, the God directed fighter against slavery, had been when he died on the scaffold six years earlier."

Harriet Beecher Stowe wrote *"Uncle Tom's Cabin"* (1852). The story, she acknowledged, was inspired by the memoirs of Reverend Josiah Henson.

Henson, a Negro and abolitionist, was recognized for his work in the *Underground Railroad* from his home in Canada. His courageous struggle for freedom, and to free others was captured in his memoirs.

It was quite a find for Stowe, as she wasn't taken seriously as a writer. *"Uncle Tom"* is modeled after Reverend Henson. More than one hundred and fifty years later, children of all ages read *Uncle Tom* as the book captures the mind of the time.

Harriet Beecher was one of thirteen siblings of the famous abolitionist preacher Lyman Beecher, and sister of Henry Ward Beecher who was equally famous as a preacher. H. W. Beecher was accused of adultery and put on trial in 1875. This trial was called the "scandal of the century."

*   *   *

Mark Twain is considered to be our greatest American writer. He wrote many books, but one great book, *"Huckleberry Finn"* (1885). It is great because it is well written, bold, and written in the vernacular. Again, it was a reflection of the mind of the times.

Like John Brown, Henry David Thoreau, and Abraham Lincoln, Mark Twain evolved. He encountered more than his share of failures or miscalculations along the way.

Twain was something of a gambler and speculator. He managed to invest in schemes going nowhere, while failing to see the possibilities of Alexander Graham Bell's telephone, passing up the opportunity to invest in it by Bell.

He was, however, the publisher of the autobiography of Ulysses S. Grant, which I suspect he edited himself, as it is considered the greatest biography of any American president, and is compared with *Caesar's Commentaries of the Gallic Wars* (58 B.C.).

The Personal Memoirs of Ulysses S. Grant (1885) was published shortly after the death of the 18th President of the United States. The book focused mainly on Grant's military career during the *Mexican-American War* and the *American Civil War*. Written as

210

Grant was dying of cancer, the two-volume set has become a classic.

Twain created a unique marketing system for Grant's book designed to reach millions of veterans with a patriotic appeal just as Grant's death was being mourned. Ten thousand agents canvassed the North, following a script Mark Twain devised.

Many of these agents were themselves veterans who dressed in their old uniforms. They sold 350,000 two-volume sets at prices from $3.50 to $12 (depending on the binding). Each copy contained what looked like a handwritten note from Grant himself. In the end, Grant's widow, Julia, who the general felt might be destitute if he didn't complete this work before he died, received about $450,000, suggesting a gross royalty before expenses of about 30 percent.

Here we have Grant, an alleged drunk as a soldier, being picked by Lincoln to salvage the Civil War, taking that war from the jaws of defeat to total victory, ultimately becoming President of the United States, an administration laced with scandal, only to leave office, then upon his death an immortal work of monumental significance.

WHAT DO LOSERS & WINNERS HAVE IN COMMON?

Most remarkably, first they are unlikely to think of themselves in terms of being winners or losers, or taking themselves too seriously in any regard; secondly, they are as unlikely to be conscious of being either special or gifted in any extraordinary way.

Developing anger might be a more appropriate metaphor as if a slowly gathering storm, welling up in them before it cascades into some kind of expressed action. Their motivation is not likely to be readily apparent at first as that is not the focus of their attention. They find themselves in a situation not of their making trapped in escalating hysteria that requires some kind of action.

Ralph Waldo Emerson was not of that temperament. He was a man of reflection and contemplation, a poet who behaved much as the discreet observer does today as an OD psychologist, some one hundred seventy five years later.

Emerson processed and interpreted the actions of others careful to maintain a certain unobtrusive sobriety. He was just provocative enough to be in demand as a speaker and writer.

He could see American society was moving from an agrarian to an industrial society, and he wasn't happy about that. In a sense, he was totally a man of his times. He could see society going from a subsistence economy of need to a progressive capitalistic economy of want, from the handyman to the specialist. He wrote:

"Functions are parceled out to individuals, each of whom aims to do his stint of the joint work, while each other performs his. This reduces man to a thing, into many things. The food gathering man on the farm becomes the mere farmer, the businessman a moneymaker, the attorney a statute book, the mechanic, a machine, man thinking the bookworm, and so forth."

Emerson was describing how our occupations can marginalized us as human beings. He resists the notion of being seen as the equivalent of a machine by writing his eloquent defense of people as persons.

Certain individuals in this transitory and ambivalent age make their mark by departing from the norm. We read about them and celebrate their courage, when it is not courage at all. It is an attempt to make the content and context of their character iconic while ignoring their authentic self that resides in their subtext.

These losers as winners were in effect unconscious outsiders with a passion to right wrongs that they could not stomach.

For John Brown, Harriet Beecher Stowe and Abraham Lincoln it was slavery. For Mark Twain it was chaos, corruption and the dysfunction of *"The Gilded Age."* The irony is that his best friend, Ulysses S. Grant, was one of the unwitting architects of this age by his quiet complicity.

Twain, through his own misguided proclivities, was forced to go on the road in his white suit with his gift of sarcasm and humor to delight audiences because he couldn't pay the bills back home with his writing.

One hundred years later, Hal Holbrook would revive his own declining career by training himself to emulate and imitate the Hannibal, Missouri native on stage to approving audiences across the continent.

The first volume of Mark Twain's autobiography is now on sale, one hundred years after his death titled *Autobiography of Mark Twain Volume I, Reader's Edition* (2012). This first volume of 760 pages (hard cover edition) provides insight into the past, the events of Twain's personal life and further demonstrates his role as an eyewitness to history.

During his lifetime, Samuel Clemens watched a young United States evolve from a nation torn apart by internal conflicts to one of international power. He experienced America's vast growth and change - from westward expansion to industrialization, the end of slavery, advancements in technology, big government, big business and foreign wars.

And along the way, Clemens as Twain often had something to say about the changes happening in his country and in his own topsy-turvy life. I suspect readers are not going to be too pleased with how closely he resembles the characterization here of losers as winners. We like to romanticize our heroes into stick figures.

Winners who were once losers are always individuals. They manage to touch a cord in the heart of everyman by their ability to break free.

Already in the second quarter of the nineteenth century, factories were replacing guilds, machines were replacing manpower, corporations were replacing family businesses, commercial farms were replacing family farms and other accessories of capitalism were ushering in the age of depersonalization, the age that has steamrolled into our times.

Emerson, as an OD psychologist consistent with my training, could see this and was moved to not only write about it but to interpret it as well. He blamed it on Christianity, mainly Calvinism, and organized what would come to be called the *"Transcendental Movement,"* which was something of a hybrid of Christianity and Eastern religions. It never took.

Losers that become winners do not have the temperament much less the patience to compare and compete with each other. The reader may use the sports analogy to defend his belief that competition in sports makes winners. It does not.

Competition in sports as elsewhere makes a bland confection of what is perceived as perfection but in actuality is a tired standard of conformity to a prescribed ideal type.

Competition has made society so bland, so common that everyone looks, dresses, acts and thinks alike down to the same body tattoos, which were once the province of mainly outsiders. Now, the quality and character of tattoos no longer differentiates. Tattoos personify the herd mentality, which has taken over. This mentality has come home as the common brand that nobody notices.

There are many other attributes of losers and winners but never before was this disposition a
"Stop sign," as it is now. Formerly, whatever our temperament, we would pause to take inventory before moving on when we hit a bump in the road. Now, we all have the same roadmap and ignore the pot holes if experts say they are of no concern. Before, that would never have happened; before we were individuals. Now, we are all part of the herd.

WHY DO WE NOT EMBRACE WHAT IS GOOD FOR US?

Losers who become winners have no problem with this question because "good" and "bad" are not relevant. Emerson, I suspect, would gladly return to his grave once exposed to our times. He would see the prevalent mediocrity in practically every aspect of our existence wondering how everything could have gone so terribly wrong in one hundred years. In his most nightmarish reflections, it would be impossible for him to believe:

- That commercial television represents entertainment,

- That more than 95 percent of working people are wage slaves, and act as if they are satisfied with their lot while one-tenth of one-percent of the population controls the wealth,

- That everyone is talking into some handheld device or pounding on another one impervious to their surroundings,

- That the "seven deadly sins" have reached capitalistic splendor as wealth creators,

- That religious zeal, which he thought was insane in his time, has become a patricide phenomenon in our time,

- That what masquerades as art in music, literature, painting, architecture and philosophy has taken on a blandness that doesn't reach above our lower quadrant of our biological anatomy, and

- That science, which he thought was the rational answer in the *Age of Enlightenment*, now contains the spark of mankind's possible total destruction.

Alas, we don't have a poet or philosopher like Emerson, and suffer mightily for the absence.

FIFTEEN

LIFE IS WHAT WE MAKE OF IT, NOT WHAT OTHERS MAKE OF US!

Contentment is natural wealth, luxury is artificial poverty.

Socrates

CONTENTMENT IS NOT A MATTER OF CHANCE, BUT A MATTER OF CHOICE

Currently, I am proofreading the second edition of *Work Without Managers*. First published a quarter century ago, it remains relevant as our transitional and transformational society continues to resist this unescapable evolution.

While technology engulfs our lives with little resistance, our institutions, indeed, our places of employment hold desperately to tradition and unfiltered power. So it has been since the beginning of time. Apropos to this is an excerpt from *Work Without Managers*;

Fairness is an interesting issue, largely because there is no such thing. Whether we are winners or victors, losers or victims is to a considerable degree a function of how we see ourselves, not how others see us. Workers who are obsessed with finding fairness, consistently find instead the lack of it. What they fail to see is that they allow unfairness to happen... not always, of course, but most of the time. It's the true 'bad break,' however that they cling to— labeling it unfairness.

When destiny is tied to someone else's rainbow, life is forever a disappointment. Management consultant Peter Drucker is emphatic: *"To predict the future, one must create it."*

William Jennings Bryan adds, *"Destiny is not a matter of chance, it is a matter of choice; it is not a thing to be waited for, it is a thing to be achieved."*

In that same connection, Percy Shelley adds, *"As to us — we are uncertain people, who are chased by the spirits of our destiny from purpose to purpose, like clouds by the wind."*

And, finally, Robert Louis Stevenson submits, *"Wherever we are, it is but a stage on the way to somewhere else, and whatever we do, however we do it, it is only a preparation to do something else that shall be different."*

These are voices like our own who have had to deal with the pain of disappointment, surprise and false expectations, and have seen fit to take measure of the situation with the distillate of a few words. Many, however, simply agonize in anxiety, and wonder why this is happening to them.

Incidentally, the *Fairness Issue* is generally viewed in terms of deprivation, rather than excess. Yet how often we read of the children of celebrities who fail to cope with the excess of privilege, from Dianne Barrymore (*Too Much Too Soon*, 1961) to Lindsay Crosby (*Parade Magazine*, February 25, 1990). Death came to both of them at an early age because of alcohol, depression, debauchery, and failure to make suitable choices and take control.

Once the support system of family is removed, a sense of worthlessness can intervene and an inability to cope without the celebrity money, and so they either commit suicide slowly by drugs and alcohol or more quickly with the gun.

Read biographies of Peter Drucker, William Jennings Bryan, Percy Shelley, and Robert Lewis Stevenson and you will see how they dealt with adversity, riding it like a mad bull to achievement.

Life and work for them was not always fair, but their focus was on making the most of the circumstances by taking charge of respective destinies. They looked for opportunity rather than solace in complaint. They made things happen rather than wait for their luck to change. There is no room for steel in the spine when it is first filled with Teflon.

Yet, having said that, Human Resources has been successful in making the *Fairness Issue* a predominant factor in its quest to bring passive professionals and tradespeople up to speed with the daunting challenges of new technology. Unwittingly, this strategy has been doomed to failure because the emphasis is what is "owed" not on what might be contributed.

As a dominant issue, fairness confirms the thesis of the worker's counter dependence on the organization for the worker's total well-being. Thus, the organization has become straddled with the debility of carrying workers as dependence, which has led to workers being suspended in terminal adolescence reactive as if twelve-year-olds in fifty-year-old bodies.

Employers and employees have been complicit in this dependency as management was more willing to concede generous pay and benefit concessions than relax the screws of control as little as one turn. Workers have come too late to realize they have enslaved their will to the caprice of management and have no back story of justification.

DUPLICITY HAS A NAME CALLED "RENT!"

Nobel Laureate for Economics Joseph Stiglitz in *The Great Divide* (2014) sees CEOs of Fortune 500 companies treating themselves as the indispensable "1% to the "99%" dispensable American workforce. He writes:

(CEOs) get paid much more for their work than they once did, while everyone else gets paid about the same, or less. Corporate CEOs, for instance, are paid for more today than they were in the 1970s, while assembly line workers aren't. And while incomes at the top have risen in countries around the world, nowhere have they risen faster than in the US.

To be more specific, CEOs' pay has risen 876 percent between 1978 and 2012 as most of CEOs control their Boards of Directors, which was unheard of forty years ago. Stiglitz doesn't buy into the rationale that the critical value of CEOs today drives this incredible pay rise. He blames it on a phenomenon known as "rent-seeking."

Most of us think of rent as the payment a landlord gets in exchange for the use of his property. Economists use the term in a broader sense, that is, any excess payment a company or individual receives because something is keeping competitive forces in check and from driving returns down. So the extra profit a monopolist earns because he faces no competition is a rent.

Consider this: the extra profits that big banks earn because they have the implicit backing of the
Federal Government, which will bail them out – "being too big to fail" – if things go wrong. This is another example of a rent.

Here it is 2015 and we cannot seem to put WWII behind us, but must pay tribute and homage and coin to management and labor unions for their contributions to that total victory. Yet, in the interim, the workforce has gone from 90 percent blue-collar to

90 percent professional, and power and control has gone from position power to knowledge power, and management – all the way up to the CEOs – is not privy to most of this knowledge, but the humble professional workforce that continues to take it on the chin as if nothing of merit or moment has changed in seventy years.

Worthy of note, a full 34 percent of millennials are college graduates in this new century.

Workers, rather than taking charge of their power, have been exposed to the ruse of human resources "Employee Empowerment Programs," which have little to do with either power or control as these interventions are mainly cosmetic.

Still, with the economy teetering on the verge of recession and jobs being scarce, many workers, professionals and blue-collar alike, find comforting solace in whining about how unfairly they are being treated among themselves, playing the "victim of the system" card, which insulates and isolates them from the *Culture of Contribution* where risk and managed conflict are required. Lost in this preoccupation with fairness is recognition of worker power.

In the *Information Age,* where knowledge holds most of the trump cards in this game of bridge that links the past with the future, workers hold a finesse hand, while continuing to play the dummy hand. It would be comedic if it weren't so tragic.

It is an endless battle of control with those exercising control (management) not having it, and those having control (workers) not exercising it. Productive work falls between the chairs. In praise of fairness, it is reduced to a praise of folly. Who orchestrates this scenario? No one has clean hands.

To be fair, an oblique explanation of this development can be traced to the rise of college educated blue-collar workers. Many of these college graduates went into the "helping professions," which included Human Resources. These first and second generation professionals came from families used to taking orders, not giving them; to maintaining the agenda of management, not contributing to its design; being influenced by management, not influencing management; following, not leading.

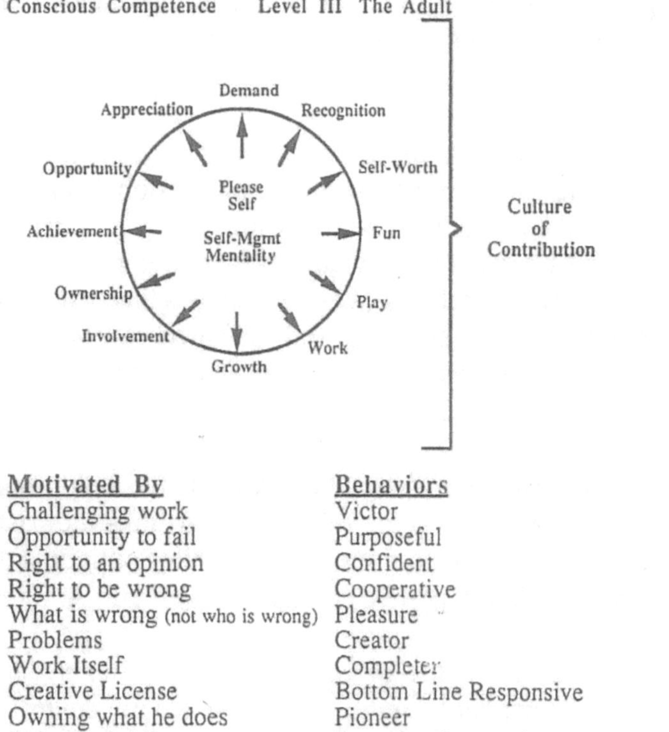

Motivated By	Behaviors
Challenging work	Victor
Opportunity to fail	Purposeful
Right to an opinion	Confident
Right to be wrong	Cooperative
What is wrong (not who is wrong)	Pleasure
Problems	Creator
Work Itself	Completer
Creative License	Bottom Line Responsive
Owning what he does	Pioneer
Calculated risks	Proactive Responsive
Doing	Positive
	"Selfish"

As a consequence, Human Resources has unwittingly become *management's union* instead of workers' advocate, selectively creating cosmetic changes that were no threat to either management's power or its control.

SIXTEEN

ARE YOU TRYING TOO HARD?

It has been the glory of the great masters in all arts to confront and to overcome; and when they had overcome the first difficulty, to turn it into an instrument for new conquests over new difficulties; thus to enable them to extend the empire of science. Difficulty is a severe instructor, set over us by the Supreme guardian and legislator, who knows us better than we know ourselves, and loves us better too. He that wrestles with us strengthens our nerves and sharpens our skill. Our antagonist is our helper.

Edmund Burke (1729-1797), Irish statesman and philosopher

THE TANGLED WEB WE HAVE ALL CREATED

The challenges we face are never as great as we think they are, never as difficult to overcome as we present them to be, never as critical to our success as they might imply. This is as true on a personal basis as it is on at the national level.

An individual, or indeed, a nation can take itself too seriously and become traumatized at the effort to maintain the pace required of events. The fear of success can paralyze as much as that of failure. So agitated, it is difficult to act with prudence much less wisdom.

We see this in students who fall apart when their academic careers suddenly crash, in young people when their romances abruptly crumble, in athletes who blow out a knee, in career workers who fail to win an expected promotion, in families who are visited with misfortune.

Given these circumstances, a tranquil nature can suddenly become aggressive, a temperate individual assertive, a failing student depressed, a loving couple conflicted, the athlete embittered, the career worker passive aggressive, and the family self-destructive. To wit:

Darrin Campbell, an executive who was staying at a mansion owned by ex-tennis star James Blake, killed his whole family before killing himself.

Campbell, who lived in the affluent area of Tampa Bay (Florida), executed his family "systemically," officials reported in The Tampa Bay Times. He killed his wife, 51-year-old Kimberly Campbell, then his two children, 15-year-old Megan Campbell and 18-year-old Colin Campbell, before killing himself.

"This has been determined to be a murder-suicide," Hillsborough County sheriff's Col. Donna Lusczynski told The Tampa Bay Times.

"It's unclear why he killed his wife and children, she said, but he "systematically shot his son, his daughter and his wife in the head. He then placed fireworks throughout the residence, used an accelerant to assist in lighting the fire, lit the fire, and then shot himself," she added.

Campbell, 51, was leasing a five-bedroom home in the exclusive gated community of Avila. He had been a top executive with several companies and was said by neighbors to be a calm and cordial resident of the community.[1]

Hard times are actually endemic to our thinking. They can be real or imagined, but the sense in any case is that there is no way out.

We are programmed in our society to have a stiff upper lip and blast our way through our troubles without a second thought. We celebrate toughness and give kudos to those who bear up well under pressure and stay the course. Seldom do we give kudos to those who take a *time out* and ask for help when something has gone terribly wrong. We shutter at weakness for it may remind us of our own. This is especially true for those who gravitate to leadership positions in corporations, the government and other institutions.

Dropping out or retreating from the fray is discouraged. It is deemed unacceptable. Weakness, indeed, vulnerability must be hidden. Yet disclosure might be the best therapy. So, many try to make the impossible possible and never seem to notice when all passion is spent, when there is no longer energy for a fallback position.

Be wary of someone who comes to feel he has nothing to lose.

History tells us that no international problems have ever been resolved militarily yet leaders from prehistoric times to the present pursue that pusillanimous course. Prudent politics and pragmatic diplomacy invariably gets short shrift. Military solutions are first on the table driven by fear and paranoia and the last to be taken off that table. Despite the expense of *"Arms Races"* and the motivation to reduce tension between rivals, it is the failure to address socioeconomic problems that ultimately leads to national distress.

A nation is never destroyed from the outside. A nation is always destroyed from the inside. That lesson is clear back to the Roman Empire, but the eminence of the bellicose mindset never changes.

It is no accident that people of such persuasion frequently rise to leadership roles and are called "hard liners." This has been personified in recent history by Vice President Dick Cheney and Secretary of Defense Donald Rumsfeld in President George W. Bush's administration with the preemptive wars in Iraq and Afghanistan that followed, which proved iatrogenic. What emanates from within trickles down to below and affects the mindset of a nation.

This should give pause as it echoes the vitriolic sentiment, *"I don't get mad I get even."*

Sometimes we forget that the individual and the nation are cut from the same cloth. Perhaps that is why we cannot see our personal life contributing to our collective life as a nation.

Politicians on the stump vying for elected office like to say we are an exceptional people. In truth, we are one people among many other exceptional peoples if you want to continue that line of thought in this tangled web of circumstances that we have all created.

Perhaps the *"American Century,"* the 20th Century, ended a little early because we as a nation tried too hard to be everything to everyone globally and were begrudged for doing so.

Lance Morrow in *Time* magazine (January 11, 1988) claims that *"the year 1968 was like a knife severing the past from the future."*[2]

The year was the "theatre of rage" as no one in America seemed to see it coming. American society was still working hard as ever while the rest of the world was increasingly working smart. Most

Americans still did not take all their allotted vacations because most Americans had never learned how to relax. Leisure was as foreign to the American temperament as it was natural to Europeans.

Nineteen sixty-eight (1968) was the year of constant surprise fueling this rage:

- On January 23, the U.S.S. Pueblo was captured by North Korea.
- On January 30, North Vietnam launched the Tet Offensive.
- On March 31, President Lyndon Baines Johnson said he would not run for reelection.
- On April 4, Civil Rights Leader Dr. Martin Luther King, Jr. was assassinated.
- On April 23, Columbia University students seize the university buildings.
- On May, 3, were injured in Paris in student riots.
- On June 6, presidential candidate Robert Kennedy was assassinated.
- On June 19, *The Poor People's March* on Washington, DC.
- On August 20, Soviet tanks rolled into Czechoslovakia ending the Prague Spring.
- October 1-27, Gold medalist Tommie Smith and Bronze medalist John Carlos give black glove salutes to Black Power as the National Anthem is played and the American flag is raised.

Bob Kirkpatrick suggests in *"1969 – The Year Everything Changed"* (2009)," that in the twelve months that followed 1968, it was a time unparalleled in American history.[3]

It was as if the American psyche had a frontal lobotomy and was going in several directions at once without a clue as to the grand scheme of things. Another way of putting it might be that our complacent past and our natural inclination to move away from ourselves met in a collision course.

You could see it everywhere:

- Rebellious youths camped out in Haight Asbury State Park in San Francisco.
- Abandoned American factories across the land as Europe and South East Asia were eating our lunch flooding the American market with high quality cheap manufacturing goods.
- The Sexual Revolution was in full swing with the mantra "make love not war," which was supposed to free naturally uptight Americans from being so.
- The Feminine Movement was coming out of the closet, while men were coming out as well in another form.
- The Civil Rights Movement sponsored nonviolence but would become increasingly so in its aftermath.
- Political correctness became the litany on campus and in the political arena.
- Americans had lost their confidence and identity in the rush into the future.

Suddenly, nothing seemed authentic anymore. The evidence was everywhere as people now had to try so hard to seem natural and spontaneous, and most important of all, not to offend. Nearly a half century later, 2014, some schools were labeled "failed factories" because the majority of third graders were unable to read, write or do simple mathematical problems expected at that grade level. 4

MILLENNIALS vs. BOOMERS

We have had two rather serious disruptions, or some might say, transitions brought about by the changing value system that accompanied the end of World War Two (1945), under which a new generation was born:

- *Baby Boomers* were born between 1946 and 1964 or during the post-war climate when the USA became the manufacturing center of the world, as nations across the globe had been decimated by the war and were in full recovery mode.

Jobs were plentiful and pay and benefits to the working middle class were generous. It was a prosperity never known before for average Americans. A good percentage of baby boomers became the first members of their families to go to college.

But America got a wake-up call in 1958 when the Soviet Union successfully launched Sputnik into space. This was accompanied by an industrial boom in Europe and South East Asia threatening American markets and the job security of blue-collar workers. On the horizon was the controversial Vietnam War.

- *Millennials* were born of baby boomer parents between 1981 and 1997 coming into the world during a booming economy with both parents likely to be working hard leaving millennials pretty much to themselves. Millennials took note of how their parents were enslaved to the job, made redundant or forced to relocate on the job. The Soviet Union and the Cold War ended in 1989 during their developmental years. As teenagers, they found themselves ready to embrace the new electronic technology of the *Information Age*, but not the culture that spawned its development.

- *Baby boomers* witnessed the first landing on the moon, and the progression from black & white TV to digital television with huge pixel colored flat screened televisions. Popular culture changed along with social sexual mores. Commercial films became more explicit and pornography became a stable multibillion dollar industry.

Suddenly, everyone wanted to be eternally young with the pharmaceutical and the plastic surgery industries booming to meet demand.

Rebellion became popular in nonfiction and fiction books with the cry, "never trust anyone over thirty."

Traditional religion took a backseat to the new civil religion of secular materialism.

Optimism and idealism prevailed in the face of growing corporate tyranny, cavalierly sending good paying jobs to India and China, as well as entire manufacturing industries. Meanwhile, wages and benefits were frozen or fast declining for American workers.

- *Millennials* saw how their parents were treated, how the government said one thing and did another, how prices went up but not wages and benefits for their parents, how their parents rationalized their disappointment, and decided that was not for them.

They were part of the new digital age and found escape in its electronic wonders.

- They didn't resent authority; they ignored it;
- They had no taste for rebellion as they couldn't see the point;
- They were not anti-culture, they simply ignored culture;
- They embraced the spiritual without being churchgoers;
- They are the best educated generation in American history with a full 34 percent college graduates;

- They have an unexpected almost primitive tribal identity in that they have legitimized tattoos to make the practice mainstream.

It remains to be seen if millennials will control events or fall in line with their parents in having events control them.

Baby boomers are embarrassed by *millennials'* disregard for what they see as tradition, such as love of work and an aversion for leisure, which they find intimidating.
Baby boomers are obliging connoisseurs for fads that promise to keep them eternally young. The result is that *baby boomers* are in fact living longer, the majority well past traditional retirement age of 62 to 65.

Most *baby boomers* are expected to live 24 years past retirement, which will be 150 percent longer than any previous generation.

Baby boomers are also learners rather than knowers and technology savvy with a full 85 percent comfortable with iPhones and other mobiles texting and tweeting on a daily basis.

- *Millennials* are not in a hurry to do anything or be anywhere;
- They are confident and optimistic without being idealistic or realistic;
- They have observed their parents and have decided not to be like them;
- They are not embarrassed living at home treating the family dwelling as a motel, restaurant, and grocery store with full laundry and maid services;
- They are biding their time postponing marriage or permanent hook-ups;
- They want more than a job, more than a career, more than money;
- They like the idea of working but not having work to define them;

- They would prefer a job that paid $40,000 that they loved than a job that paid $100,000 that they didn't;
- They are programmed learners as their grammar school, high school and college indicates;
- They don't consume the educational menu without question;
- They are free thinkers proving this with more than 30 percent unaffiliated with any political party, church denomination, or social organization.

Time will tell whether this mindset will serve or handicap them, as their optimism is in the face of a changing global dynamic. Many other advanced societies are superior to them in terms of educational pursuits in mathematical, literacy and technical skills, but despite this they remain optimistic.5

Given this assessment, my sense is that millennials will be just fine. They will take charge and peak at the right time, absorbing the lessons of life, and bringing order to the age. They are not in a hurry to do so which is to their benefit. Moreover, they are not likely to work hard for the sake of pleasing others, but to find the rhythm of life that best suits them. Their approach is personal, intimate and situational. This sees them quietly rejecting the cultural pressures of cultural programming, something their parents, despite vigorous protests, continue to be enslaved. Rejection of these pressures is proven a millstone.

FROM MY OWN FILES

To give the reader a sense of *baby boomers*, as the jury is still out on *millennials*, here are two lifted from my files.

- This person was the first member of his family to be a college graduate with a manic desire to succeed. It didn't start out that way. The red flag came early as he had to repeat his first year of studies having failed every course. It proved a blessing in disguise. It told him he was resilient, something he had previously ignored.

- A successful executive failed medical school, only to realize years later he never wanted to be a doctor.

- An internationally recognized choreographer on Broadway admitted he failed to earn his Ph.D., although he submitted his dissertation several times, being always rejected. Scholarly work required writing skills he did not possess. What was his talent? Choreographic set design. This came easy to him with his spatial and mathematical acumen for the engineering and architectural requirements of set design. These skills were picked up along the way, and taken for granted. He thought he wanted to be a fine arts professor and *"Not a backstage jockey."* What came easy and for which he was celebrated failed to ease the pain of his early academic failure.

One of the great differentiators of generations is romantic love. *Boomers* believed in it; *millennials* do not.

Boomers believed the myth of romance can sustain a relationship. *Millennials* do not. They see romantic love like a dying swan expected to rise again as the Bird of Paradise; in other words, not very likely.

Romantic love was perpetuated by such Great Depression authors such as Nathaniel Brandon (1930-2014) with his *The Psychology of Romantic Love* (1980).

Baby boomers were into romantic love, shame and guilt. *Millennials* are into none of this.

Millennials are amused but not scandalized by the seamy sex of *Generation X* bestselling author E. L. James (born in 1963) in her *"Fifty Shades of Grey Trilogy"* (2012). They are equally glib about the acerbic political commentaries of Jon Stewart (born in

1962) of Comedy Central, as they fail to take politics or politicians too seriously.

Millennials might be the first American generation not so self-regarding that they can't have a sense of humor about the indulgences that embrace their times.

LIFE, WORK, RELATIONSHIPS

If you have to work hard at a relationship, chances are there is no relationship with which to work. What you are actually doing is working hard towards tolerating an intolerable situation. You have failed to recognize and accept the intrinsic different between you and another. So, when a romance goes sour, and acceptance does not fill the void, it is best both parties move on.

- That same premise is valid for one's life work.

Arthur Ashe, the great American tennis player and first black male American to win at Wimbledon, once said that the odds of a black athlete making it to the top ranks in professional sport were 1 in 500,000, whereas the chances to become a doctor of medicine dropped the odds down to 1 in 500. Despite this, he said, where do we find our young black men? We find them on the playgrounds, in the neighborhood recreation centers or outdoor basketball courts, not in libraries. They punish themselves playing against the odds rather than having the odds made to work for them.

- Then there is the tangled web of untenable circumstances being difficult to put to rest.

A family can experience misfortune with the aftershock being felt for generations. President Richard Milhous Nixon suffered a consuming paranoia for his family's early misfortune. The Nixon family was near destitute. Nixon's father was forced to sell the family farm for little during the Great Depression. Later, oil was discovered on the land that would have made the Nixon family millionaires.

Perhaps because of this, Nixon became something of the quintessential grind, the person who used football imagery to illustrate his "try harder" toughness. This surfaced in law school at Duke University. He was called *"iron butt"* because he did little else but sit on his behind and study. His pervading paranoia showed up when he broke into the Dean's office to check his grades and was caught. He couldn't wait for them to be posted; yet he would finish third in his law graduating class.

Once president, leading in the polls for a second term, there was the Watergate break in, and the subsequent cover-up. Reelected with a comfortable margin, he was forced to resign the presidency to avoid being impeached. The seeds of this debilitating behavior were planted early.

We never overcome who and what we are. This is as true of heads of state or like my da, a brakemen on the railroad. If we never invite our real self to our conscious mind, the harder we try to escape our reality the more we are likely to become lost to our potential.

THE FOLLY OF COMPETITION

The irony is that the obstacle to success and happiness is seldom the object of our attention but rather our obsessive attention to the object. Goethe puts it this way:

Whatever liberates our spirit without giving us mastery over ourselves is destructive.

We can become great mythmakers in the scheme of things, inventing slogans to justify our inanities, chief of which is the one claiming that without pain there is no gain. The problem with this myth is that pain becomes the operational word and not the action.

Marathon runners talk of running into a wall of resistance. Only the hardy prevail in blasting through what is actually a psychological barricade. So compelling is this myth that all runners talk of confronting the wall when the wall is a case of the conscious mind anticipating that inevitable barrier which awaits them. The impediment is a combination of stamina and pain.

For thousands of years, men of science claimed that a human being was incapable of running a four-minute mile, or four 60-second quarter miles in succession. Roger Bannister, a medical doctor, destroyed that myth on May 6, 1954 in Oxford, England running the mile in 3 minutes 59.4 seconds. He used science to understand the physiological demands and the staying power requirements in his methodical study of the challenge.

Today, sixty years later, hundreds of milers have broken the four-minute barrier. After his success, Bannister admitted his knowledge of physiology was important in his training, but concluded, "I still had to overcome my doubt that I could do it." Doubt is the operational word in nearly every case of failure to reach one's potential.

Another great American myth is that competition is good for the soul and the high ground to greatness. Nothing could be further from the truth.

Yet Americans assume competition is the reason for personal greatness. Alas, the belief persists that competition is as inherent to an American's nature as is breathing. Consequently, Americans wear competition as a badge and swagger with a sense of having the spirited edge.

Economist Walt Whitman Rostow sees this as part of our damaged psyche stating that before America can compete it must learn how to cooperate -- something that has been missing more often than not in the national psyche.

The United States prefers to go it alone. For this preference, Rostow fears the US may go the way of Great Britain for its lack of tribal capacity for communal action on an international scale. Between 1870 and 1971, as a reference point, he reminds us that Great Britain went from 32 percent of the world's industrial production to generating less than four percent.

Competition measures differences and attacks them as if the enemy. Cooperation assesses commonalities and builds bridges across them. Psychiatrists Willard and Marguerite Beecher writing in *Beyond Success and Failure: Ways to Self-reliance and Maturity* (1966) observe:

Competition enslaves and degrades the mind. It is one of the most prevalent and certainly the most destructive of all the many forms of psychological dependence. Eventually, if not overcome, it produces a dull, imitative, insensitive, mediocre, burned-out, stereotyped individual who is devoid of initiative, imagination, originality and spontaneity. He is humanly dead. Competition produces zombies! Nonentities!

Think about it. Competition imitates initiative.

We see this as those in competitive athletic drills train hard to outperform each other doing the same thing. In the era of visual media from television to the Internet, our little toddlers as athletes dress and display the uniforms and logos of professional sports mimicking the mannerisms and peccadilloes of Major League professionals in Pee Wee Football and Little League Baseball. Worse yet, no one seems to see this as absurd.

Next, we will have eight-year-olds with body tattoos in iconic imitation of their millennial cousins. Imagine if fifteen or twenty years from now, when reactionary styles have changed, as change they will, what then?

This trickle down nonsense continues through society from competitive companies to universities, from artists to writers. An incredible sameness pervades the current universe where comparing and competing is the mantra of that mania.

Deifying competition has saddled the times with a repetitive dullness that is on display in professional athletics, television series, novels, alas, in all of modern life, and to what end?

Watch a Major League Baseball game on television and you see the same car commercial four to fourteen times over the course of a game, and even then it is probably more interesting than the game televised. Our collective boredom delights advertisers. With apologies to Marshall McLulan, the media isn't the message, the subliminal bombardment is.

When someone breaks through this banal monopoly, do we celebrate them? Hardly, we disparage the audacity to impinge on the sacred turf of our sacrosanct accord. But should they be successful, all is forgiven, and then we copy them, again and again and again. Take religion and the newest genre of fiction for example.

Dan Brown's novel *The Da Vinci Code* (2003) inspired an industry of imitators. Tom Clancy's *The Search for Red October* (1984) spawned the techno-thriller market.

Academics are masters at sullying the reputation of those who successfully break through our collective boredom with original ideas. *The New York Review* had this to say about a professor's book on Dan Brown's theme:

For the last few years, the dramas of scholarship have attracted a striking number of readers. This unexpected and welcome development, a rare moment of sun in publishing's Ice Age, resulted in part from the extraordinary stylistic gifts of writers.

Then with faint praise to Brown:

*It helps to explain the vogue of novels like "The Da Vinci Code"
– a sillier book, and far worse written (than the academic's book
being reviewed).   At no point does he (the academic)
acknowledge the debt owed Brown for appealing to an audience
beyond academics and students. "The Da Vinci Code" caught
the imagination of the general reader. He admits his student's
book is mainly a "campus book" and that says a lot.*

My wonder is why academics are so petty. When they review
books outside their discipline, they can border on the pathetic.
As a person who has lived most of his life in the real world, but
spent nine years matriculating in academia, I have met precious
few professors who could write.

Dr. Bannister broke the four-minute mile barrier, not by being
more competitive, but being more creative. He didn't imitate the
training ordeal of great former middle distant runners, but
applied his knowledge of physiology. He trained against his own
standards, erasing from his mind the psychological limitations
imposed since the age of the Ancient Greek Olympiads.

It is easy to confuse being competitive with being competent.
Imitators are the pyramid climbers up the organizational ladder
to executive status. They eventually become our leaders in all
walks of life. They mirror the values, beliefs, interests and
behaviors of their superiors.

Put another way, while magnifying their superiors' strengths in
imitation, they also magnify their weaknesses. Where success
requires initiative and creative engagement to deal with
ambiguities, they are out of touch and out to lunch. Evidence
suggests this is a global syndrome.

No one is questioning the fact that leaders work hard in all
endeavors. Take coaches in the National Football League (NFL).

The majority are known to spend as many as 80 hours a week working: reviewing film, conducting strategy sessions, studying the team's playbook, which is as detailed as the Encyclopedia Britannica.

These grown men put their lives and families on hold in quest of the Holy Grail, which is the Super Bowl. Only a handful of them will ever reach that pinnacle. No one seems to see the futility in this. Imagine putting all this mind power and energy to life changing creative pursuits.

It doesn't stop there. The same behavior is repeated at the college, high school, and even the Pee Wee Football League level where eight and nine-year olds prefer this crushing sport to academics.

The mania goes well beyond NFL coaches and players. Hordes crowd into $ billion stadiums, while millions watch games on television, just as the Roman hordes watched gladiators in coliseums fifteen hundred years ago. The NFL is the popular palliative of the moment to dull and boring collective conscience that is the temper of the times.

Eric Hoffer registers concern for this uninhibited self-indulgence. He writes:

When people are free to do as they please, they usually imitate each other. Originality is deliberate and forced, and partakers of the nature of a protest. A society, which gives unlimited freedom to the individual, more often than not attains a disconcerting sameness. On the other hand, where communal discipline is strict but not ruthless – an annoyance, which irritates, but not a heavy yoke which crushes – originality is likely to thrive. It is true that when imitation runs its course in a wholly free society, it results in uniformity, which is not unlike a mild tyranny. Thus the fully standardized free society has perhaps enough compulsion to challenge originality.

TENSION AND NOISE

Tension should not be misconstrued as something to avoid when it is suggested you are working too hard. Hans Selye reminds us in *Stress Without Distress* (1974) that tension reminds us we are alive. Tension that is embraced produces music. Tension that is avoided produces edginess, and then noise.

Tension is as natural to the American spirit as joy is foreign to it. It is captured in the mantra: *I work hard and play hard.* You might think the word "hard" was part of our DNA. Notice we don't say, *I work creatively and play creatively.*

"Hard" is the operational word. We describe a task in terms of how hard it is to do, and equate performance in terms of this difficulty in how many hours are spent in the doing, seldom in terms of results realized.

We associate education in terms of contact hours spent in the classroom, not on what has been learned. We treat learning as if something to endure, not something to cherish. We pursue degrees, rewards, bonuses, accolades, and payoffs, finding little exhilaration in the experience at hand. We live for the future that never comes.

No surprise, we see life an end instead of a happy journey; earning a degree as the ticket to the good life, a good job and a comfortable retirement instead of an enlightening experience.

There are exceptions.

- Years ago, I had a colleague in my doctorate program who was well into his 60s. Another student was curious and asked, "What do you plan to do with your Ph.D.? You're already past social security age?" The elderly gentleman smiled, "Oh, I hope to enjoy it of course."

The questioner shook his head and wandered off in confusion, saying under his breath, "Enjoy it? What's there to enjoy?"

We Americans are tense and intense and find it difficult to deal with things going well. If something is easy, or we are not struggling to achieve it, something is wrong.

It never occurs to us to go with the flow, to discover the rhythm of Henry David Thoreau's drum. We are waiting, always anxiously for the other shoe to fall. A common expression is, *Shit happens, then you die!* Perhaps that is why being happy is hard work, leisure is intimidating, and life is a grind.

On holidays, we have to go somewhere, do something strenuous, and be with someone. We can never be alone. If caught reading a book, we apologize for doing nothing. We might be found lazy if we were to admit we were reading simply for pleasure.

Students associate reading with having some instrumental value, that is, to be done to attain something else. How often I have heard: *"I never took a book home in high school,"* or *"I haven't read a book since high school?"* This is always said with absurd pride. We must be constantly on, motivated to do better, so what would be the point in reading a novel, right?
Incredibly, we don't see texting, tweeting, and checking our e-mail forty times a day wasting time. We see reading for pleasure vegetating but not this electronic absorption.

- A quite successful man confessed to me that he kept getting married and divorced because "I've got to keep my nose to the grindstone, otherwise I'd shrink into a flabby old man. My obligations keep me focused." He apparently thinks to look old and flabby is un-American yet the United States is the world's "fast food nation."

For this businessman, working hard was an artificial construct fed by a need to be married to insolvency. Such people buy automobiles and houses they can't afford, join upscale country clubs they never visit, send their children to prestigious private schools that finds them chronically delinquent in the fees required, or divorced paying alimony and child support. Such providers typically enjoy six figure incomes, but are in constant debt continuously robbing Peter to pay Paul. There is a lot of tension and, indeed, noise in such providers but very little music.

FOOT ON GAS & BRAKE AT ONCE

Alan W. Watts in *The Wisdom of Insecurity* (1951) describes trying too hard in the most metaphorical terms. He writes:

Man in modern society has his foot to the floor on the accelerator and brake at once, burning up rubber and going nowhere.

William F. Buckley, Jr. has described this same predilection as *"forward inertia."* Both expressions are quite apt for revealing the probable cause of employee and executive *"burnout."* We are blighted with *"progress fatigue."*

Gregg Easterbrook has an intriguing theory about the contradictions of modern life in *The Progress Paradox: How Life Gets Better While People Feel Worse* (2003). Research shows that most people judge their well-being not by where they are, but where they expect to be when their income improves in the coming years.

This is the *"compare and compete" syndrome* on display. Not content with who, what and where they are, they see on television or read in the newspaper or find out at their church or temple or club that an acquaintance is doing better than they are, and they go ballistic.

Easterbrook calls this *"catalog-induced anxiety."* People look to what they don't have, not what they have. They fear it can be taken away from them, leaving no time for gratitude.

Progress, like greed, is never satisfied. There must be more. This means the pursuit of progress must be intensified to be sustained. With no time to let up or let go, progress has become synonymous with greed. It will eventually lead to the death of capitalism.

I once wrote a piece titled, *"Learn to Let Go!"* It failed to generate a reaction. The piece suggested that people spend more time working smart and less time working hard, more time focusing on the "right things" that make 80 percent of the difference, and less time "doing everything right the first time" that makes only 20 percent of the difference in outcomes.

This was not what readers wanted to hear. They wanted to be reassured that what they were doing and the way they were doing it was not only right, but the proper way to do things. They saw my piece as lecturing them as if giving a sermon, which turned them off. They simply wanted a thumbnail guide to a better quality of life without changing. One reader wrote, *"Don't lecture me on the shoulds and should-nots. I've heard enough of that from my parents."*

To my suggestion that they pray for guidance, which was another way of saying that they reflect for insight, made them noticeably uncomfortable. Praying is but a form of reflection. One reader wrote that he was an atheist. I responded, *"What has atheism got to do with reflecting on what troubles you?"* I never heard back from him. Clearly, the piece made readers uneasy.

The aim was for readers to get in touch with their center, with their primordial guidance system. Praying with beads, feeling the wind in the hair on a summer's stroll, kicking water with bare feet at the edge of a dock, pealing an orange and smelling its fragrance are all forms of prayer.

Jogging or walking *without* headphones is yet another. The mind grows quiet and all sorts of wonderful thoughts come up from the soul. Life is experienced on another plane.

Hence, you could say, I haven't departed too far from letting go and going with the flow. We can step out of our cage at any time and experience the wonders beyond. Easterbrook writes:

Surveys show the majority of Americans think only the very rich are well-off; that no matter how much they make, most Americans believe twice as much income is required to "live well."

SO WHAT?

If people don't believe they are working too hard and feel they are working smart, then the rest is academic, isn't it?

Likewise, if that is the case, it would imply they are happily in harness doing what they are doing and being where they are.

Chances are they have been content in every job they have ever had, from being a student, which was their first job, to that with a company, and then as a husband or wife, mother or father, and all the associations those endeavors entail. They have discovered that happiness is a state of mind, not a condition, or a designation.

- Happiness is not without pain or sorrow, disappointment or surprise, tragedy or fear, longing or regret. Happiness recognizes the cage, and on occasion has visited its confinement, but has never sought the cage as a permanent residence.
- Happiness is not a serene state of uninterrupted euphoria, but the human experience that oscillates with the rhythm of the heartbeat.

If the reader is ambivalent about trying too hard, this frustration can become a cage. There is no definitive assessment of this status. Nor is there a recipe for escape from such confinement that fits all.

Poet John Donne notwithstanding, *"Every man is an island unto himself."* We are inclined to be mesmerized by the cage seeing it as a refuge rather than a prison. Only listening to the rhythm of our own hearts can we hope to find the peace that suits us. There is no other way.

Notes:

1. Josh Rojas, *Tampa Bay Times*, November 5, 2014. It was later revealed that Darrin Campbell was implicated in a securities fraud scandal, which may have influenced his decision to kill his wife, son and daughter, and himself.

2. Lance Morrow, "1968: Like a knife blade, the year severed the past from future, *Time*, January 11, 1988, pp. 12-21.

3. Bob Patrick, *1969: The Year Everything Changed*, Skyhorse Publishing, New York. Patrick opens with: *Prologue: Revolution, Apocalypse and the Birth of Modern America.* He quotes Barry Miles here from his book *Hippie* (2004): *"It was a year of extremes, of violence and madness as well as achievement and success."*

4. Cara Fitzpatrick, Lisa Gartner and Michael LaForgia, *Failure Factories: Five "F" Schools in South Pinellas County* (Florida), *Tampa Bay Times*, August 14, 2015.

5. *Millennials* are the hot topic at the moment for media writers and observers of the baby boomer generation such as David Brooks (*New York Times*), Abby Elliott (*Parade* magazine) and Joel Stein (*Time* magazine), which must amuse *millennials* for all the unsolicited attention.

SEVENTEEN

THE IMPORTANCE OF EVERYONE! PLUMBER, ELECTRICIAN & DR. STEINMETZ!

"He who would really benefit mankind must reach them through their work."

Henry Ford (1863-1947), Detroit Automaker

"Man must work. That is as certain as the sun. But he may work grudgingly or he may work gratefully; he may work as a man, or he make work as a machine. There is not work so rude, that he may not exalt it; no work so impassive, that he may not breathe a soul into it; no work so dull that he may not enliven it."

Henry Giles (1809-1882), British Unitarian minister and writer

WORK IS OUR CONNECTION TO EACH OTHER

Over the weekend, our electrical heating and air conditioning system went out. At the same time, our hot water heater went on the blink. We were experiencing a mild cold wave in Florida and were not used to being unable to take a shower, use our electrical dishwasher or even to wash our hands in hot water.

Not being handy, we have what is called *"American Home Shield,"* which provides such services at a hefty quarterly cost, which we have been paying for nearly twenty years, or since we returned from Europe and made this our home.

There are two things I have learned:

- There are things that I can do well, and

- There are things that I cannot do well at all and need help.

In my long life, I've never denied that reality, but have acknowledged it and acted accordingly. So, I have saved myself the embarrassment of having to pay for the damages I might have caused because I tried to do something myself of which I lacked both the competence and expertise.

Today I had an electrician and a plumber come to my house, sort out my problems and with due diligence dispatched the problem. I must confess I enjoyed watching them work with quiet confidence and ease.

The electrician had only to check the reset button in the air conditioner, and voila, heat and cool air were restored.

The plumber had only to drain the water pan and heater and replace the heating coil, and voila, hot water returned.

The speed, agility and modesty with which these men did their tasks reminded me of a story of a personal favorite of mine, the irascible and cocky German-American mathematician and electrical engineer, Charles Proteus Steinmetz (1865 - 1923). Steinmetz, a little man with a giant ego, one day found himself making a consulting call on a General Electric facility. The electrical generators were down and GE was losing money, and so they quickly brought Dr. Steinmetz in to solve the problem.

He examined the machines, checked them with his instruments, and then asked for a rubber hammer. He gently ran his hand over the steel skin of the cylinder, marked it with chalk, and then gave it a single blow at that spot. The system came alive the generators kicked in and operations resumed.

Later, the Director of Operations received a consulting fee from Dr. Steinmetz for $10,000. The director called the consultant on the phone and said, *"Your fee of $10,000 seems a bit exorbitant. Five people have to sign off on this type of request. I will need an itemized bill to describe the nature of your services."*

Dr. Steinmetz said, *"No problem, glad to oblige."* Here was the itemized statement for the fee:

- $1.00 for hitting the system with a hammer.

- $9,999.00 for knowing where to place the blow.

This was reported a number of years ago in *The Reader's Digest*. Steinmetz, who had more than 200 patents to his name, suffered the discomfiture of dwarfism and being a hunchback. He made his mind as one of a super cerebral athlete. Indeed, much of General Electric's rise to prominence is accredited to Dr. Steinmetz's inventions in the area of artificial lighting.

I told this story to the electrician and the plumber citing how important they were in the scheme of things with their special knowledge, as Steinmetz was with his. We need electrical engineers, but we also need plumbers and electricians as well, and none more than the other, but all equally the same.

EIGHTEEN

GENIUS REALIZED: GETTING FIRST PUBLISHED AT AGE 96

"Genius is only the power of making continuous effort. The line between failure and success is so fine that we scarcely know when we pass it, so fine that we are often on the line and do not know it. How many a man has thrown up his hands at a time when a little more effort, a little more patience, would have achieved success. As the tide goes clear out, so it comes clear in. In business, sometimes prospects may seem darkest when really they are on the turn. A little more persistence, a little more effort, and what seemed hopeless failure may turn to glorious success. There is no defeat except from within; there is no failure except in no longer trying, no really insurmountable barrier save our own inherent weakness of purpose."

Elbert Hubbard (1856-1915), American pragmatic philosopher

IT IS NEVER TOO LATE!

Harry Louis Bernstein (May 30, 1910 – June 3, 2011) was a British-born American writer with his first published book, *The Invisible Wall: A Love Story That Broke Barriers* (2007) at the age of ninety-six.

This novel dealt with Bernstein's long suffering mother Ada's struggles to feed her six children while putting up with Yankel, her abusive and alcoholic husband.

It is also the story about the anti-Semitism that Bernstein and his family experienced growing up in a Jewish neighborhood in a Cheshire mill town called "Stockport" (now part of Greater Manchester) in northwest England.

Stockport was a community of Jews and Christians many of whom were lost in World War I. Bernstein shapes his story around the Romeo and Juliet-like romance that his sister Lily experienced with her Christian boyfriend.

The Invisible Wall tells the story of his older sister doing the unthinkable. She falls in love with a Christian boy. But they are separated culturally by an *"invisible wall"* that divides the Jewish families on one side of the cobble stone street from the Christian families on the other.

When the young Harry Bernstein discovers the secret affair quite by accident, he has to choose between the strict morals that he has been taught all his life, his loyalty to his religious and selfless mother, and what he knows is right in his own mind.

The book was started when Bernstein was 93 and was published in 2007, three years later. The loneliness he encountered following the death of his wife, Ruby, 91, in 2002, after 67 years of marriage, was the catalyst for him to begin working on his book.

His second book, *The Dream*, published in 2008, centered on his family's move to the West Side of Chicago in 1922 when he was twelve.

In 2009, Bernstein published his third book, *The Golden Willow*, which chronicled his married life and later years. A fourth book, *What Happened to Rose*, was published posthumously in 2012. Bernstein lived in Brick Township, New Jersey. He died four days past his 101st birthday.

Before his retirement at age 62, Bernstein worked for various movie production companies, reading scripts and working as a magazine editor for trade magazines. He also wrote freelance articles for such publications as *Popular Mechanics*, *Family Circle* and *Newsweek*.

THE PATIENCE OF GENIUS

From Harry Bernstein's earliest recollections, as early as when he was four-years-old and started to read words on a page, he felt an urge to write. Through grammar school and high school, composition was his favorite subject.

As a young man out of high school, he attempted to publish, but received only rejection slips. He persisted, finding work where he could edit other writers, but the passion to be an author in his own right never left him.

He met his wife, Ruby, at a dance, and it was love at first sight. He loved her to pieces and took a job reading movie scripts of authors' books, but changed his focus from his writing obsession to enjoying her completely.

They had two children, and a happy home, but he was put into a total funk when she died, and found the only way to fill his loneliness was writing, which he had always done throughout his life, publishing an article here and there, but never able to capture enough attention to make a living at it.

The Invisible Wall at first experienced a fate of which he was quite familiar – constant rejections.

He attempted to write a novel after a short piece generated enough interest that an editor asked him to give the novel idea a try, which he did, but without success.

After Ruby died, he decided to go back to the beginnings of his life, nearly ninety years in the past, and found that he had a retentive memory of those early days as if they were only yesterday.

Instead of being discouraged at the rejections *The Invisible Wall* generated, he admits in the afterward of this book that he's never lacked confidence in himself or his ability to write. In an amusing aside, he admits to being a rather cocky soul.

In any case, an editor from Random House called, and said she had read his manuscript and that Random House would like to publish it in a small printing. He was so elated he couldn't believe his good fortune.

Random House published the book, and the book reviews were unanimously positive, while *The New York Times* put his picture on the front page of the newspaper celebrating his being a published author for the first time at the age of 96.

Columnists from across the Western World called or visited him for interviews. He was in demand on radio, television and in magazines. He satisfied all these demands willingly and enthusiastically.

Other publishers wanted to publish his works. So, at 96, he wrote a sequel to *The Invisible Wall* and followed it with another published during his lifetime, with one published posthumously.

Were Elbert Hubbard alive, he would have joined the celebration as he believed with all his heart that genius was not rare, but common. The problem, he argued, was that people pay too much attention to those who say *"you're wasting your time"* and not enough time listening to that inner voice that says, *success is right around the corner!*

NINETEEN

Understanding Others!

No one knows what strength of parts he has 'til he has tried them, and of the understanding one may most truly say, that its force is generally greater than it thinks till it is put to it. Therefore the proper remedy is, to set the mind to work, and apply the thoughts vigorously to the business, for it holds in the struggles of the mind, as in those of war, that to think we shall conquer is to conquer.

John Locke (1632-1704) *An Essay on Human Understanding* (1671)

UNDERSTANDING, NOT AN EASY TASK

John Locke, an English philosopher and physician, is considered one of the first of the British empiricists following the tradition of Sir Francis Bacon. He is equally esteemed for his *"Social Contract Theory,"* influencing many other thinkers including Voltaire and Rousseau, as well as the American revolutionaries Madison, Hamilton, Jefferson and Franklin. Accordingly, his ideas are reflected in the United States Declaration of Independence.

Locke's theory of mind is often cited as the origin of modern conceptions of *identity* and *the self*, figuring prominently in the work of later philosophers such as Hume, Rousseau and Kant. He was the first to define *the self* through a *continuity of consciousness*, postulating that at birth the mind was a blank slate or *tabula rasa* to which experience is added. He insisted that we are born without innate ideas, and that knowledge is instead determined only by experience derived from sense perception. Each of us, then, is a depositor of experience as Emerson has written from which *self-reliance* is developed.

That said John Locke followed the custom of his time by explaining the path of human reason and its obstacles. In that sense, he was a practical philosopher and believed philosophy ought to be built upon reasoning and common sense rather than metaphysical speculation with the mind the equivalent of a blank sheet of paper, upon which experience is imprinted.

Understanding is not based on something innate in our perception, which causes us to know and understand a situation when it confronts us. Understanding is only acquired through our experience in the material world. Our minds act as filters processing ideas that are encountered and weighing them in light of how they compute with our experience.

In other words, the mind is a filtering system that acts as a coping mechanism. Based upon the quality of that experience and how perceptively and supportively that filtering system is engaged has much to do with our confidence, health and happiness in life. Locke insisted that ideas were not absolute representations of our knowledge because our biases are part of the filters through which our senses color our knowledge.

Viewing the world only through our impure ideas may be too limited for contemporary philosophers, but Locke's philosophy did become the first comprehensive exposition of empiricism and the foundation of modern social science. A broader view is that of Julian Johnson in *Path of the Master* (1939) which states:

No one can gain even an intellectual understanding of his own interests, until he has some comprehension of the universe of which he is an integral part, and with every part of which he is in some manner related.

LOVE AND UNDERSTANDING

The basis of empathetic understanding in any case is love. Without love, the possession of all knowledge is for naught. St. Paul describes the nature of love:

Love suffereth long, and is kind; love envieth not; love vaunteth not itself, is not puffed up, doth not behave itself unseemly, seeketh not her own, is not easily provoked, thinketh no evil; rejoiceth not in iniquity, but rejoiceth in the truth; beareth all things, believeth all things, hopeth all things, endureth all things; love never faileth; and now abideth faith, hope, love, these three; and the greatest of these is love (1 Corinthians 13: 4-8, 13).

We are in the scientific age, the age of empirical knowledge, where the secular authority of things has supplanted the spiritual authority of things as once was understood. Yet, the secular and spiritual remain interrelated and interdependent.

Locke was part of *"The Enlightenment,"* the European intellectual movement of the late 17th and 18th centuries. It was distinguished for being accessible to ordinary people as it emphasized reason and individualism rather than tradition. Besides Locke, it was heavily influenced by 17thcentury philosophers such as Descartes and Newton, and its prominent exponents came to include Kant, Goethe, Voltaire, Rousseau, and Adam Smith.

Contrast this with analytical philosophy that has been practiced for more than a century in English speaking academia, which is only accessible to fellow academics. It is far too technical, too mathematical, generating vocabularies and theories far removed from problems *The Enlightenment* would have considered philosophical.

Once philosophical questions concerned humanity and were within reach of that humanity with concepts of love and understanding. This is not the territorial imperative of analytical philosophy, which has accompanied the scientific age and secularizing of modern society.

It would appear our spiritual side (social systems) has been separated from our material side (technical systems), as if the soul had no body. Since the soul cannot be quantified, isolated and studied as a discrete phenomenon, it does not exist in the realm of science or analytical philosophy. The irony is that this is as troublesome as past times when superstition, the miraculous, the occult, the mystical and mythological were in vogue.

If one is by nature spiritually inclined today, he is likely to be seen as unworldly, whereas were he obsessively of a material inclination, it is likely he would be considered worldly if not also informed.

For a person to be fully human both the spiritual and material realms come into play as we, alone are a conscious being while part of as well as separate from nature. Only through wholeness can we truly understand and love each other.

That said conscious man has wondered from the beginning:

- *If this is all there is;*
- *If we are alone in the universe;*
- *If there is not some higher power beyond our consciousness that is dictating our existence;*
- *If there is a puppet master beyond us with which we must reckon or perish.*

We humans are by nature a simple animal, but with a conscience with an incredible capacity for making the simple complex while constantly jeopardizing our existence by the folly of ways. We wage wars, create weapons of mass destruction, burn the candle at both ends working and playing hard, and not taking the time to enjoy the wonder and beauty and splendor of this paradise in which we have come to find ourselves.

Other animals without a conscience do not propagate beyond their food supply because they instinctively know they will perish. Humans with a conscience do it to an unconscionable excess. Paradoxically, the richest countries about the globe have the lowest birth rates while the poorest countries the highest.

The world population is some seven billion souls half of which are below the poverty line without adequate food, clothing, shelter or hope for a better life, while ten percent of the world population controls the planet's wealth and lives in luxury.

Among this privileged population, there are many philanthropists who attempt to meet the needs of the impoverished but fail dolefully. It is impossible because the need can never be filled by attempting to feed the poor fish, but showing them how to fish. This is the intent of many philanthropists such as the *"Bill and Melinda Gates Foundation."* But others simply throw money at problem, which invariably is siphoned off by corrupters, .and so the heartbreak continues.

Wealthy nations demonstrate similar intentions, but also fall prey to these exploiters. Human society has a long way to go to first understand and then effectively support the disadvantage throughout the world. Thankfully, we do have *The Peace Corps* and *Doctors Without Borders*, along with many religious missionaries of various church, temple and mosque affiliations providing humanitarian services.

While this is not the focus here, it is offered to show how difficult it is to relate to others in the general as well as the particular with love and understanding. Too frequently society has off-loaded this problem to religious institutions when it is humanity's challenge.

LOVE IS THE KEY

Empathetic understanding involves reason as well as feelings. It is not a mechanistic or mathematical construct that determines *quid pro quo,* or what constitutes the getting and giving involved in understanding.

It is rather a "letting go" of the self in free flowing trust with significant others and listening at the *thinking level* to what they are saying where understanding registers. Everyone talks in code, and what complicates the matter is that everyone's code is unique to that individual or group even when the expressions are in common words.

We are not a listening but a talking society.

Watch commentators on television interviewing people in the news. They constantly interrupt and destroy the continuity of the person's words and therefore what they are trying to communicate. Television commentators are slaves to ratings and therefore looking for crisp sound bites, not ideas. We at home as listeners can see the folly of these exchanges, but we still stay glued to the television screen when it is a mockery of good sense.

Alas, we are like the commentators in our private exchanges with others. We don't listen; we constantly interrupt when a word expressed triggers an automatic response from us. Actually, we're not interested in what the person has to say, but only interested in hearing our own voice expressed to an audience of one. It is not totally our fault. It is how we have been schooled. Education has no time for a curriculum that involves learning to be an astute active listener. We are taught instead to be good talkers in expressing our ideas.

Complicating the matter further, people do not behave the way they talk. If someone says, he likes you but belies that fact in his actions, be aware. Study behavior and compare that to what people say. This process will never let you down, but it will surprise you. Behavior doesn't lie. People do. Rest assured behavior speaks loudly, as Emerson puts it, *so loudly, I cannot hear you!*

A professor friend of mine wondered why I didn't want to do anything socially with him and his wife. How could I tell him his wife constantly demeaned him when he wasn't present?

People do not behave the way they appear in conversation with gurus on television, as portrayed in television dramas, or projected to be in films, the theatre, or novels. Nor do people behave as depicted in graphic comic strips. These are carefully orchestrated fragments designed to bombard our senses with stereotypes to grasp quickly our narrow attention span.

Alas, people never behave as we would expect or would have them behave.

Even so, there is an overwhelming desire to categorize people into definable types to fit comfortably into a comprehensive mental picture. This is our quest for control to confirm our cognitive dissonance.

It makes it easier to convince ourselves why someone is successful, *"He's not what he seems; he didn't get it on his own. Besides, he's not smart at all but an opinionated bastard."* This translates, *"I envy the hell out of his success and wish it had been mine."*

Years after I left my home state of Iowa, and had the career that I've enjoyed, I learned it was *common knowledge* that a prominent doctor put me through school. Not a single syllable of this was true. I worked summers in a chemical plant while attending university and was on an academic scholarship for my tuition. Still, there was no point in trying to dissuade hometown folks to think otherwise.

Remember, envy is seeing someone being or having what you want, and don't possess, while jealousy is the fear of losing something that you already have.

To get through life with something approaching equanimity, it behooves us to understand ourselves as much as possible in order to understand others. That, of course, is not easy.

This requires that we accept ourselves as we are, warts and all. That we love and respect ourselves not as we should be but as we actually are, right now!

Love gives us the patience to embrace self-awareness rather than deny it or run from it. So much of our conditioning from the home to the school and beyond is designed to be self-critical rather than self-accepting.

We are expected to be loving of others before we are loving or appreciative of ourselves. Can you understand how absurd this is?

Loving and respecting ourselves is not narcissistic. Nor is it self-absorption or self-indulgence. It is as impossible to be loving of others without first loving ourselves. In *Meet Your New Best Friend* (2014), it states:

To have a friend you must be a friend starting with yourself.

- So much of our programming is maddeningly self-critical. Consequently, it becomes something of a major mountain to climb to have a decent appreciation of ourselves as persons.
- Before one is angry with someone else one is first angry with oneself.
- Before one is violent, the violence fist rages within seeking an outlet with little understanding of why.
- We worry more about what others think of us and much less what we think of ourselves.

- An authentic person is a product of self-regard who embraces his fears and deals rationally with his shortcomings in a loving, patient and thoughtful way.
- If we allow ourselves to listen with our whole body, not only with our minds, we will gain an understanding of ourselves that will contribute mightily to understanding others.
- Our moral compass will be engaged and our internal guidance system activated, which will show us the way. It requires that we trust ourselves, which is perhaps the last person we have learned to trust.
- Try to feel your way beyond the words to what you are trying to communicate.
- Remember, we are all complex contradictory systems that require separating the self-critical noise from the self-accepting music.
- That same contradictory system is operating with whomever we are talking. It is why we get defensive in conversation and say one thing and mean another, why we exaggerate and demean in an effort to impress, and why it is difficult to take us at our word.

My brother was fond of saying that when my mother spoke of me, *"Divide what she says by four and believe half of that."* He had a point. She wanted me to be all that I could be and had an inclination to exaggerate my achievements and to minimize my failures, simply defending her treatment of me, saying, *"Jimmy, it is a work in progress."*

The result is that I developed a self-confidence I might otherwise not have had, and when I have stumbled in life, her words reverberate in my consciousness, *Jimmy is a work in progress.*

THE IMPORTANCE OF OUR REPTILIAN BRAINS

Decoding the elements of frustration in speech requires active listening, which is displayed nonverbally in our posture and attentiveness. Sometimes a person needs an audience simply to quiet the mind.

Sigmund Freud was the first to identify psychosomatic disturbances as real illnesses. He did so in World War One having success with his "talking cures" (i.e., psychoanalysis) with "shell shocked" soldiers. Before he intervened, the French and British saw such soldiers as "slackers" and considered executing them before military firing squads.

People are dissemblers. They cannot help it. From the earliest moments of our existence we are trained to behave as if postgraduates in verbal inventions (boldface lying), histrionics (playacting to cover faux pas), defensiveness (playing the victim) and manipulation (turning accusers into defendants).

Dissembling is the way we get through the day. The average person from breakfast on lies at least 634 times before dinner, starting with saying "Good morning."

Daily life is a psychodrama played out in a dramaturgic style to win friends and influence others, to collect sympathy for our point of view, to justify unjustifiable behavior, and to appear on top of things when nothing could be further from the truth.

What we do in this *"Theatre of the Absurd"* is not always pretty and sometimes even morally repugnant if our behavior were exposed to the light of day. It is how many of us restore a facsimile of equilibrium to the madness that has become the tempo of our daily lives.

We can't help ourselves from comparing and competing, always trying to get an edge without realizing it is a losing proposition. Like it or not, we are stuck with ourselves. There is no point in competing with anyone other than ourselves. To do otherwise is simply imitations after the fact. No cage is more confining than the cage of self-contempt and envy for not being or having or accomplishing what someone else is, has or has accomplished.

People with empathetic understanding process information with uncanny alacrity as if they were intuitively defining a noun: *The name of a person, place or thing.*

A person has a Personality Sphere (sense of worth), Geography Sphere (sense of place) and Demography Sphere (sense of self). These are profiled in *The Fisher Paradigm*©™ as:

Personality; Geography; and Demographic Profiles

This designation is essentially a graphic reference to our reptilian brain. It is still active and utilized some 12,000 years after it was primarily engaged for human survival.

We sense danger before we know fear. We don't know why, but the sense is real. The problem is that we don't listen; don't take seriously the warning. Thousands of years ago it was imperative that primitive man listen to his rushing heart as wild beast, were larger, stronger and more vicious than his capacity to confront and best them.

To ignore reptilian warnings is to do so at our peril. Messages are pulsating at our temples telling us *"this is not good"* -- *"this is not right"* – *"this does not compute."* But too often we ignore the warnings claiming we are over reacting or being paranoid. Paranoia has its place in man's survival kit contrary to the popular notion.

Recently a man came to me, a man who works very hard for a living, a man who is frugal to a fault, a man who prides himself in his cognitive skills, a man who was duped out of $27,000 of his hard earned money by a con artist.

A big man, he was in tears before me, trying desperately to justify giving the money to a man to invest for him because *"he had this huge yacht with a lavish clientele of celebrities and high rollers on board. He had made a fortune himself, why shouldn't I have trusted him to guarantee a 10-20 percent return on my investment?"* Why not, indeed!

The "why not" was that everything was too perfect. His reptilian brain should have alerted him to the fact that the man was too slick; the situation too orchestrated. A reptilian cliché should have kicked in:

When something looks too good to be true, it probably is.

The yacht, he learned later, was rented, the high rollers were part of the con, and the man's fortune was a fantasy to which this investor was blindsided because the con played on his greed, which put his reptilian brain to sleep.

The man was not listening to the warnings pulsating through his heart. It takes listening with the *third ear*, the thinking level, before a message registers the naked truth to our minds.

- The *first ear* is the hearing level, the muddled noise we call "talking."
- The *second ear* is the listening level. We hear what the person is saying, but fail to register its underlying message.

The con knows this. It allows him to manufacture the moment to his purposes, creating the theatre of affluence in a rented yacht with the possibility of instant wealth in the company of actors playing their parts.

Were our reptilian brains not to have come into play thousands of years ago, we would not have survived as a species. The danger is still real, only today it has moved from threatening man killing wild beasts to the psycho-physical danger of men in Armani suits with the killing instincts of primitive savages.

One of the great myths is that we think before we feel. Our reptilian brain would suggest otherwise (see Antonio Damasio's "Descartes' Error," 1994).[1]

FOUR KEYS TO UNDERSTANDING

Confidence comes from interaction. You cannot expect to have confidence without working hard to understand others, because in understanding others you better understand yourself.

It takes time and experience to comprehend the implicit messages behind all the verbal noise of conversation. Typically, conversation is taken at face value instead of being decoded to understand what the other person is actually saying.

Rarely, if ever, do we say precisely what we mean. In this electronic age, we flippantly send out sound bites to friends that can go viral to hundreds if not thousands of others. Then it is too late to redact, deny or retract what has been said and sent.

Young people have been known to commit suicide for being inundated with deprecating messages sent to them by mean spirited peers. These senders had little sense of how damaging their hateful comments might be to someone trying desperately to find his way through this most vulnerable period called *"adolescence."* Incendiary comments can be magnified to throw the situation into instant tragedy as text messages burn like branding irons into a vulnerable psyche.

Television soap operas play on this vicarious appetite of love and hate, revenge and betrayal, lust and envy, jealousy and hurt. It can get quite dicey when reality imitates art. Once the contretemps becomes public, misadventure and misunderstanding saddle the same horse and ride it wildly into our living rooms. Where would cable television without this?

Take Donald Sterling, 80, the billionaire owner of the National Basketball Association (NBA) Los Angeles Clippers. He had a private conversation with his girlfriend, V. Stiviano, 30, in which he made disparaging remarks about NBA Hall of Famer Irvin "Magic" Johnson, now retired, and about African American basketball players in general. His girlfriend recorded this conversation and then made it available to the media.

The octogenarian was obviously jealous of his girlfriend's association with black athletes, having her picture taken with Johnson and others, bringing them to the owner's games, and hanging out with them. He wanted her to cease and desist. The video of this conversation made him sound like a plantation owner of the antebellum South. Millions viewed the video and million more followed Sterling's marital spats with his wife over control of the Clippers. You would think people had nothing better to do with their lives than follow this soap opera.

Sterling had provided his girlfriend, fifty years his junior, with a $1.8 million home, expensive cars and clothes, including select seats at the Clippers' NBA home games. He cancelled these tickets, Ms. Stiviano being miffed at this action, got her revenge with this secret recording.

During the recording, Sterling not only expressed his prejudices against black athletes specifically and blacks in general, but left little doubt that he was a racist.

The irony is the NBA would not have its sound financial success were it not for black athletes. Eighty percent of NBA players are of color. These athletes are instant millionaires for their athleticism and have demonstrated their athletic superiority. So, it wasn't a surprise when the new NBA commissioner, Adam Silver, fined Sterling $2.5 million and banned him from the NBA for life.

Mark Cuban, 55, NBA owner of the Dallas Mavericks, in an attempt to tone down the conversation to a more rational level, unwittingly added fuel to the fire by first saying the banishing of

Sterling from ownership of the LA Clippers was "a slippery slope," then compounding this by saying:

"If I see a black kid in a hoodie and it's late at night, I'm walking to the other side of the street. And if on that side of the street, there's a guy that has tattoos all over his face - white guy, bald head, tattoos everywhere - I'm walking back to the other side of the street."

Should this be seen as evidence of the reptilian brain in action, it clearly is not. Instead, it is a register of personal bias. Moreover, the inanity of these remarks indicates that someone who rose to great wealth as has Mark Cuban is no guarantee of getting beyond early impressionistic cultural biases.

What was heard, magnified, and characterized as the essence of Cuban's message was the reference to *"hoodie"* in the wake of the Trayvon Martin case.

On the night of February 26, 2012, in Sanford, Florida, George Zimmerman fatally shot Trayvon Martin, a 17-year-old African American high school student. George Zimmerman, a 28-year-old mixed-race Hispanic, was the neighborhood watch coordinator for the gated community where Martin was temporarily staying and where the shooting took place.

Nearly three years later, the nation has not made its peace with this unfortunate tragedy, especially as Zimmerman was acquitted on the grounds of the Florida law, *"stand your ground."*

Reduced to its essentials, overlooking the precipitous draconian finality of the NBA's judgment on Donald Sterling, and the court of public opinion, we find a lonely old man jealous of the companionship of a beautiful young lady in a lover's quarrel that would never appear on a television soap opera.

As a comical Macbeth, Sterling expected the same control over her as he exercised over everything else in his life, and was willing to pay for it, but as we see, his misogynistic disposition overestimated the control of his girlfriend.

Is Donald Sterling a racist? Probably. Is he a despicable human being? Probably not, perhaps closer to pathetic. Is he an isolated case? Absolutely not, especially in these declining days of white supremacy in virtually all avenues of twenty-first century society. Will the self-made billionaire go peacefully into the night? Not on a bet.

This incident reveals how little variation exists between the high and low brow, the affluent and impoverished when it comes to emotions as both are capable of behaving equally juvenile and wretched.

Being understanding and understandable, pivotal to interpersonal success, can be explained in four simple keys:

- *We are all self-centered.*

We are born egotists, and since our egos are fragile, we will do just about anything to protect them. This makes meaningful exchange difficult and bizarre behavior common if not always predictable.

- *We are all more interested in ourselves than anyone else in the world.*

We invariably attempt to turn any conversation around to what we think, feel and value. Failing that we become bored, stop listening, or excuse ourselves from the conversation.

Some of us hate small talk with a vengeance. If it is important to the other person, then it should be important to us as an obliging listener. On the other hand, if the person hates small talk, and you understand that, it would be best to honor that tendency.

- *Every person you meet wants to feel important.*

Treat people with respect, whatever their station in life. Respect is returned tenfold. Be condescending in manner and you create an adversary. Show you care and the balance will fall in your favor.

- *We crave the approval of others so that we may in turn approve of ourselves.*

Self-hating is a cultural condition elevated to a chronic disease. Essayist Murray Kempton asks the rhetorical question: *"And why, America, did you, in your arrogance, teach so many of your children to hate themselves?"* Why, indeed.

The hardest person to win our approval, and make friends with is ourselves. To escape this handicap, you must rebel against false modesty and self-recrimination to establish a healthy sense of self.

When our interaction with others is not motivated by love, when it is not a result of self-acceptance, it is likely to be driven by manipulation. Enabling others to be themselves is a function of accepting them as they are, not as we would wish them to be.

Billionaire NBA owner Mark Cuban considered himself sincere, I'm sure, when he offered his conciliatory remarks regarding the NBA's case against another billionaire owner, Donald Sterling, who also happens to be a friend. But as we have seen, his use of the fear analogy to illustrate his point only complicated the issue, as fear is personal, ambivalent and has no anchor in the storm when *"hoodie"* is the only word that registers.

It takes a healthy ego to see past our limitations. Those who fail to display empathetic understanding have had an incomplete education no matter how much money they have. But for those who have healthy egos, they find consistency with this passage:

I shall light a candle of understanding in thine heart, which shall not be put out.

2 Ezra XIV, 25

Notes:

[1] Antonio Damasio in *Descartes' Error*, Vintage Books, 1994 challenges the ideas about the connection between emotions and rationality. He claims that concentrating only on the cognitive aspects of brain function and disregarding emotions is in error. He takes the reader through a series of case studies to show emotions are not a luxury but essential to rational thinking and normal social behavior.

TWENTY

IS IT MORE IMPORTANT TO BE LOVED OR RESPECTED?

"Accept yourself as you are, warts and all, and you cannot help but accept others as you find them. Self-acceptance is the hardest hurdle in life to negotiate. It is key to a success that otherwise could not but be imagined. Nothing is more important than to like or accept what one is and isn't. Once achieved, you can read others as if an open book while others cannot take advantage of you. For a con artist to succeed he must have a willing accomplice, a fool who is a stranger to himself, and a perfect patsy for exploitation."

James R. Fisher, Jr., *"Confident Selling for the 90s"* (1992).

DIFFICULTY OF BEING AT HOME WITH ONESELF

Although self-acceptance may sound as if self-evident, it is something of a challenge. Love and respect of self are not prominent in our programming. A case could be made that we are conditioned to be self-haters. Without a foundation of self-acceptance, there is little chance for self-respect.

Self-acceptance is knowing oneself and not denying the *"other self"* that is denied or hidden from our nature. Self-acceptance indicates you like yourself. It does not mean you are narcissistic or see yourself as perfect. It means you accept the fact that you are human, far from perfect, but a work in progress, and that you like yourself blemishes and all.

You recognize you are fallible, vulnerable, fragile and dying a little bit every day. There is no time to be wasted on pettiness, revenge or hatred. Having this perspective gives you a sense of balance, and a measure of reality. It clarifies what you say and think from what you do and are.

It means you will not knowingly associate with people who are toxic to your nature. You will guard yourself from harmful self-indulgence so that you may thrive in health, happiness and well-being. You will behave as a mature adult.

You will be alert to impulses towards and away from what is decent. Kindness and maliciousness, generosity and jealousy, happiness and misery, joy and despair, love and hate, vie for our constant attention. It is why Nietzsche referred to us as *all too human.*

When I came back from South Africa in 1969, after experiencing apartheid, I was disillusioned, confused, and close to a nervous breakdown. As an American executive, I had been treated to British colonial splendor. Seeing the way the majority Bantu (black) population was treated, it was too much. Back home my sanctuary became the west coast of Florida. There I vegetated for two years reading, writing, swimming, playing tennis, and basketball with my son and his friends after school.

Like a sailor on sojourn, I drove about the Tampa Bay area finding refuge in bookstores and out of the way restaurants, bus stations and a railroad depot where I would observe busy people and write.

On occasion, I would park by the Tampa Bay seaport where freighters would line up to deliver their produce from South and Central America, imagining myself climbing aboard a freighter and disappearing from my former self, wandering the world as Herman Melville once did. What saved me from this escape was words and ideas out of books.

It was during this respite that I came to realize I had allowed my life to play a game on me, a game in which I had little control. For the first time, now in my mid-thirties, I realized how robotic my life had become, how much I was on automatic pilot. I had been a rising executive with Nalco Chemical Company with a future, but felt as if I was living life in a straitjacket.

Clearly, I had bought into my cultural programming losing touch with "my subtext."

My life was controlled by the content and context of winning -- awards, promotions, perks and power – which had become increasingly meaningless to me. Even so, my mind was bombarded ceaselessly with the refrain, *"James, you're a lucky man! Enjoy it! Don't think about it! Go with the flow!"*

Going with the flow had been my modus operandi before South Africa. I was an idealist who was full of himself. Then I found myself in South Africa in 1968 assigned to facilitate the formation of a new company, while wearing my narrow-minded Irish American Catholicism on my sleeve.

Somehow I had assumed *"that all Men are created equal, that they are endowed by their Creator with certain unalienable Rights, that among these are Life, Liberty, and the Pursuit of Happiness,"* never stopping to reflect that it wasn't true in my own country much less South Africa.

Surely, I thought, my Roman Catholicism saw apartheid as it appeared to me, but that proved not the case. Then, too, since my rise in the company was so trouble free, I thought the values of senior management were consistent with my own. Instead, I learned economics and politics revolved around gamesmanship with little attention to issues of fairness and equity.

It was profits that mattered. I expected to find peace and fulfillment in marriage and that too proved to be a lie. My carefully constructed life suddenly made no sense to me. I was in a cage of my own making that I had entered willingly and then thrown away the key.

To escape this cage, I resigned from my position in the company and essentially from my church as well. I stayed in my marriage with four young children to rear.

In the 1960s, this was called "dropping out," which was still quite rare. But I was in agony and not functioning. In stepping off the merry-go-round, the vertigo I experienced differed little with the vertigo that had been my life.

This abrupt change now in retrospect seems like serendipity. I wrote a book I called *"Let's Take the Worry Out of Selling"* and sent it to Prentice-Hall, Inc. It was accepted two weeks later, but with the new title *"Confident Selling"* (Prentice-Hall 1971).

The book was written in six weeks by an author with no publishing credentials, and published without editing. It was in print for twenty years. I thought I was a real author, but soon learned that I was simply lucky. The window of opportunity was right in 1970 as confidence was a concern, and I was writing as much to restore mine as that of the reader.

While in New York City in 1970 to be interviewed by Prentice-Hall, I stumbled on a book at a newsstand by Alan W. Watts: *"The Book: On the Taboo against Knowing Who You Are"* (1966).

Watts created a philosophy of Zen and Christianity into a psychotherapy blending cultures of the East and West tapping into the collective anxiety a quarter century after World War

Two. The 1970s was an ambivalent era that in many ways mirrors that of today.

It is now sixty-four years since World War Two (1945-2009). Whereas then, young people in the 1970s left home to join communes in California, slip into Canada to avoid the Selective Service Draft during the Vietnam War, or decided to hang out and do drugs to levitate in a psychedelic haze. Today escape is much more mundane.

People of all ages escape into some electronic widget to avoid thinking about the ambivalence of a chaotic world. We are now in the wake of the 9/11 terrorist attack destroying the Twin Towers of New York City and nearly 3,000 innocent lives, the great economic meltdown of 2008, which nearly led to another Great Depression, and the ubiquitous nightmare of terrorist cells possibly anywhere and everywhere.

Watts was the darling of the Hippies and the counterculture, so it is strange that he had impact on me as I couldn't be more conventional. Living and working abroad during the 1960s, I missed the tie-dye generation and the commune brigade. But in 1964, I had a speaking engagement for Nalco in San Francisco and visited *Height-Asbury* where *Flower Children* were out in force. Seeing them, men and women in long multi-colored dressing gown; young women with hair to their waists; young men with equally long hair and full beards, I thought I had stumbled into another galaxy.
If you can imagine, I felt lost and out of place in South Africa, only to come home and feel equally lost and out of place in America. I searched desperately for tether.

Alas, it was early in 1972 that I came across another author, J. Krishnamurti, at Haslam's bookstore in St. Petersburg, Florida. Owner Charles Haslam had earlier interviewed me on his PBS television show, *"Book Beat"* to discuss my book. He operated the largest independent bookstore in Florida at the time, which became a regular haunt for me.

Like Watts's title before, a Krishnamurti title caught my eye: *"You Are The World"* (1972). Krishnamurti insists:

"In oneself lies the whole world, and if you know how to look and learn, then the door is there and the key is in your hand. Nobody on earth can give you either the key or the door to open, except yourself." (p. 158)

It was the perfect bromide for my troubled soul after South Africa's apartheid. Krishnamurti speaks here of the power of a quiet mind, of the importance of letting go of thought where evil and dissipation reside.

His metaphor of walking blind over the cliff of despair when obsessively Life he insists is real not surreal. You must look to your feet to see what is under you and ahead of you, and go forward in the world with purpose.

Krishnamurti's meditation lifted me out of myself. It carried me into that Eastern calm of Zen that has now become so familiar to the West. Like Watts, he made sense to me. I found I couldn't rest until I read everything Haslam's had on him in stock, which was more than a score of books. I thought I had discovered a great man and wandered into a gold mind.

Then much later I read, *"Lives in the Shadow with J. Krishnamurti"* (1991) written by Radha Rajagopal Sloss, the daughter of his mistress, and the wife of Krishnamurti's most trusted friend. The cuckolded husband chose for twenty years to ignore the affair, as they all lived together in a California Ojai retreat.

The Indian teacher promoted the idea of spirituality, being above lust, and having a morality of mind that transformed the individual above the mundane. Yet his mistress had more than one abortion to keep his celibacy intact.

You get the impression that Krishnamurti was misogynistic for keeping his mistress as a sex slave available on demand for his pleasure. It wasn't a shock to discover that he was only a man. It was however devastating to learn that he valued women so little, while preaching one thing and living another.

You could say that I have been naïve during my formative years, and you would be correct.
There is a real danger of putting certain individuals on pedestals only to find them all too human. Still, that would be missing the point.
To be authentic doesn't necessitate being foolproof. It means being real in the life that you live. My problem is with him preaching and teaching one thing and living the exception.

Krishnamurti reminds me of the importance of a healthy subtext. His benefactor and his idolater wanted to make him a god and build a religion around him, but he refused. Thereafter, he was called *"the reluctant messiah."* His subtext didn't fail him in that instance.

Resisting that pressure was a major achievement of his life. The fact that was found to have clay feet only makes him more engaging. He was, after all, a manifestation of the Greeks four types of love: *Eros* (sexual love or lust); *Narcissism* (self-love); *Agape* (unconditional love); and *Altruism* (humanistic love).

And so it is with all of us. Whatever your age whatever your circumstances, it is time to get in touch with yourself. You are unlikely to be as good as you would like to think or as bad as you fear you might be. You're simply a human being, coping, often on automatic pilot without a clear sense of what you're about. So, welcome to the family of man which is all too human, and be kind to yourself. That is what I am still trying to do, and the reason for my sharing an outline of my own personal struggle in that regard.

TWENTY ONE

CONFLUENCE OF ESSENCE & PERSONALITY

From the big dawn until now, every single advance in civilization was made by an individual acting outside of the influence of the social controls of the tribe.

William L. Livingston IV, American author and inventor

PROBING THE GHOST OF IDENTITY

Everything starts with the individual. The science of people in general and the individual in particular has not made equivalent progress to that made in the material world dealing with things.

Man remains essentially lost in description, yet an object analyzed, categorized, labeled, and identified, subject to conjecture, bias and paranoia, but not understood.

The idea of man varies according to metaphysical belief systems. A physical scientist and theologian accept the same definition of a crystal of sodium chloride. They do not agree on the same definition of man. The sociologist, psychologist, anthropologist, ethnologist and etiologist have their definitions as well.

We are late to make man understood and understandable so that when we speak of man we have a common perspective. Astronomy was already far advanced at a time when man's physiology was relatively primitive. Copernicus, Galileo and Kepler reduced the earth from the center of the universe to a humble satellite of the sun, while their contemporaries had little idea of the elementary structure or function of the brain. Even earlier, the study of spiritual life and philosophy attracted greater men than the study of science and medicine.

Our mind is designed to contemplate simple facts and solve simple problems.

There is a reluctance to unravel the contradictions and aberrant behaviors of man. French philosopher and Nobel Laureate Henri Bergson (1859-1941) stated flatly:

"The intellect is characterized by a natural inability to comprehend life."

He claimed we love to discover in the cosmos the geometrical forms that exist in the depths of our consciousness. *"You can see it,"* he said, *"in the exactness of our monuments, the precision of our machines, and the purity of our algorithms, all a fundamental character of our minds. Yet, geometry doesn't exist in nature. It originates in us."*

We extract from complexity simple systems that bear certain relationships to one another and reduce them to pure mathematics.

Alexis Carrel (1873-1944), Nobel Laureate for Medicine (1912) writes in *"Man, The Unknown"* (1935):

"The knowledge of ourselves will never attain the elegant simplicity, the abstractness, and the beauty of physics."

Three-quarters of a century later, little has changed. Carrel's point was that while our universe is exclusively mechanical; man is not. He claimed in this 1935 treatise that with each technological advancement in society that man was threatened with greater mental deterioration than any infectious disease.

Carrel goes on to say:

"Modern civilization seems to be incapable of producing people endowed with imagination, intelligence, and courage."

Is this salient grounds for concern? Perhaps a better question might be: has man's development kept pace with his technological advancement?

Science and technology have sprung from man's brain, but what is the status of man's moral compass?

Imagine if Galileo, Newton and Einstein had applied their intellectual gifts to the study of man, would our world be the same? Men of science do not know where they are going. They are guided by chance, curiosity, craving to explore the unknown, but always outside themselves as men.

Each is in his own world governed by his own laws.

From time to time, obscurity is penetrated with some meaningful discovery without prevision to its consequences. Einstein admitted as much:

"I made one great mistake in my life when I signed the letter to President Roosevelt recommending that atom bombs be made; but there was some justification – the danger that the Germans would make them."

We are now in a postindustrial postmodern society moving further from the idea of man. Our *factory programming and mentality* continues to dog us. We are structured to behave and operate like well-oiled machines. Our academic institutions have become manufacturing centers complete with the hardware and software to turn us out to behave consistent with the widgets we hold in our hands to text and tweet to our heart's content. No one seems to notice that our mental landscape is in shambles.

Modern industry has been based on the idea of progress:

- Progress in school, in health care, wealth and happiness.
- We measure happiness and usefulness by the benchmarks of progress in our careers,
- Our employers measure progress in terms of our productivity at the lowest unit cost,
- We have accepted the rationale of progress because that is how we have been programmed.

With progress, more is always the goal. There is never enough progress as there is never enough greed. Progress and greed have become synonyms.

The individual who runs the machines gives little thought to the long-term costs to his health and happiness. He embraces the concept of the machine because he personifies and emulates the machine.

Education today is essentially job training as man is packaged and produced as a manageable commodity to meet the demands of this *Information Age*.

Man has taken a leap backward as an all-embracing passive receptor. Should man resist this passive role, a series of palliatives have been devised to keep him content including nurturing his obsession with electronic games of virtual reality, his mania for professional spectator sports, and his fixation on celebrity watching,

At one time, he was reduced to the status of a television and video game couch potato. Now, he cannot exist without his mobile constantly at his side.

As the microchip has been reduced to little more than a grain of sand, videophones, video watches, and lapel pin sensing devices are on the horizon as common condiments to man's psyche as McDonald hamburgers have become to his obesity.

Inert science of matter has come to be matched by man's physical inertness. The power to clone animals has resulted in our cloning ourselves without having to be involved in the DNA and stem cell differentiation.

THE MORE THINGS CHANGE THE MORE THEY REMAIN THE SAME

Protagoras (born c. 420 B.C.), who created the philosophy of sophistry, was confident that *"Man is the measure of all things."*

Sophism is a method of teaching. In ancient Greece, sophists were a category of teachers who specialized in using the techniques of philosophy and rhetoric for the purpose of teaching excellence and virtue primarily to young statesmen and nobility.

That was the intent, but actually sophism evolved to a specious argument for displaying ingenuity in reasoning while deceiving someone with a false argument.

Today, sophism is defined as an argument correct in form but invalid in its conclusion. For example, *man is capable of organizing this world for himself, but not himself for this world.*

Sophistry, or deceptively subtle argument has become an art form to which politicians and pundits are devoted. We may conclude from this that man does not possess the practical knowledge of his own nature. This may explain why his solutions invariably create new problems for him.

Meanwhile, technology soars on the great advancements in the sciences of nature while nature through tsunamis, earthquakes, typhoons, hurricanes, mud slides, avalanches and floods become increasingly hostile to man.

"Man has lost the capacity to foresee and forestall," observes Einstein, *"He will end by destroying the earth."*

The science of matter has taken precedence to the science of man. Science has opted for the less challenging conundrum.

That said we shouldn't wait for science to create a definitive mind map to guide us. We should instead develop confluence between our essence and personality on our own. There are certain facts we know:

- Everything in Nature is connected to everything else.

- Everything in Nature has to go somewhere.

- Nature knows best.

- We can't change Nature.

- There are no free lunches in Nature.

This is as true of matter as it is of man. Self-confidence is not rocket science. It is a practical consideration to realize the better understanding of ourselves and to give us more leverage to experience more satisfying lives.

While neurophysiologists dig into the neurons of our brains, theologians into our souls, psychologists into our subconscious, and sociologists and anthropologists into our work and play dispositions, we have the important business at hand of living and saving our planet from ourselves.

Society gets better one person at a time. To be useful to others we must first be useful to ourselves. To be comfortable with others we first must be comfortable with ourselves. This means we must know, understand and accept ourselves as best we can, in order to accept others as we find them.

We are all more alike than different. We are all products of our experience. We are inclined to see others as reflections of what we see and understand in ourselves.

A society is an organism as real as the individual. If a society can only see other societies in its own image, then it is a blind society.

Whatever society's plans, without a comparable consideration of how those plans impact other societies, it will quicken our mutual doom and ultimate demise. We as individuals must recognize this connection. We must plan our work and work our plan to connect rather than to divide us.

Nothing is ever wasted. Curiosity is a blind impulse that obeys no rule. We may go down many false roads before we find the right one.

- Our minds are as naturally given to exploration as that of lower animals.
- We are intrigued with machines but forget we mirror the same complexity in our human anatomy, physiology and psyche.
- Our curiosity extends quite naturally to outer space but not so naturally to inner space.
- We are drawn to the terrain of the unknown, but it seems to stall when the curiosity turns to human behavior.
- We remain a puzzle to ourselves. Cartoonist Walt Kelley's Pogo states the obvious, *"I have seen the enemy, and he is us."*

We hear variation of this, *"We are our own worst enemy!"* No matter how many false turns we make we are picking up valuable material along the way.

No one escapes the morality of his time. It surrounds each of us and bombards our senses with its stimuli while we think we are exercising free will. Therefore, we should give pause before we make choices recognizing that this ambient influence is always present. There is a natural confluence between our essence and personality, which is our failsafe protection to sanity and survival.

TWENTY TWO

JUST SAY, "NO!" THE HARDEST WORD IN THE ENGLISH LANGUAGE TO SAY

CHECKOUT CLERK WHO COULD NOT SAY "NO!"

Depositing purchases made by my wife, Betty, into the shopping cart, the spinning plastic bags rotating on the turnstile, listening to the cashier at the checkout as she expertly pressed the electronic key to the barcodes, then deposited the purchases in bags, sometimes double bagging should the purchases be too heavy for a single bag, all the time talking. Her nervous staccato jarred my senses to reflect on the hardest word in the English language to ever utter, "No!"

This nice lady with an Irish lilt to her lovely voice, plump, cherubic, middle aged, a woman with tired eyes but a stalwart chin, was working at Walmart as a cashier, a job she desperately needed, and was not afraid to admit it. But that was not what I found unsettling. It was the content of her chatter.

She was telling my wife, *"My son and his girlfriend moved into my apartment, a tiny one bedroom place, and I'm beside myself on what to do. They asked me if they could stay. How could I not say 'yes'?"*

She looked to my wife for support, was met only with rapt attention.

"We got our bonus check for the year. Mine was for $114. It is usually $200 or more. I had to use it all for groceries to feed them, what else could I do? They have to eat.

"You see my son doesn't have a job."

She turned to me bagging away imploring my eyes for understanding. I gave her a noncommittal look. She continued.

"What if the girlfriend gets pregnant," pushing her hand through her hair as if the gesture might get rid of that possibility, *"then what?"*

She glanced at me again perhaps thinking I was reading her mind and had an answer. I turned away.

"My place is not big enough for me much less company."

All the time, she never lost the rhythm of her barcode clicking, or filling the bags, rotating the turnstile or losing her place in the story.

"It is my own fault, isn't it?" she confessed without conviction. *"I could have said, 'no,' now couldn't I?"* Then declaring rather effusively, *"There is no way I can make my bills and afford to feed them. I have no place for me, no privacy, no chance to unwind at day's end, now do I?"*

At this point, I had to walk away, and Betty got out her credit card to pay. I couldn't let her or the checkout clerk see my anger. I felt a deep sadness as I wheeled the steel cart out to the car. How many relatives have I had who were like this good woman? How many of my cousins and friends were sandwiched into houses or households where they no longer belonged? How many parents or parents' of parents were given a guilt trip by their wayward dysfunctional progeny if they didn't take them in?

How often this was an Irish ritual I observed in my growing up years that became so common no one talked about it, thought about it, or did much about it except cave in to the pressure and guilt.

The first five-years of my life I knew of such a ritual personally, and have hated it all these many years later, a ritual when my whole family as I knew it was only my little sister, Patsy Ann.

We would be with relatives or foster parents. I remember an Aunt Sadie, or other people who, like her, weren't our relatives. Then, we were split up and I went to my grand Aunt and Uncle, lovely people who already had seven grandchildren of their own living with them of various sons and daughters at the time.

I never heard my Aunt or Uncle complain. It had to be hard on them. For me, it made an indelible impression on my psyche. I promised this would never happen to me. It never has, although many times it could have.

BEYOND IQ

Early on, I made it clear to my children that once they left the nest they were on their own as we of *The Great Depression Generation* had been forced to be on our own, and it didn't hurt us, but made us dig deep into our souls and find what we were made of, and not *compare and compete* to explain away how we were disadvantaged coming of age in such desperate circumstances. The consequence was that many developed self-reliance and discovered a backbone.

My generation was obsessed with IQ or the Intelligent Quotient, which is determined by dividing the person's *Mental Age* by the *Chronological Age* and multiplying this by 100. *The Stanford Binet IQ test* was prominent in my day.

The Stanford–Binet Intelligence Test was from the original *Binet - Simon scale* by Lewis M. Terman, a psychologist at Stanford University. It is a cognitive ability and intelligence test that is used to diagnose developmental or intellectual deficiencies in young children. The test measures five weighted factors and consists of both verbal and nonverbal subtests. The five factors being tested are knowledge, quantitative reasoning, visual-spatial processing, working memory, and fluid reasoning.

It is still used while many myths associated with it continue unabated although proven unreliable, such as that intelligence is fixed for life, that the higher the IQ the more likely the individual is to be successful, that if you don't have a high IQ you should not dream of being rich and famous, brilliant in some field, or rise to a position of leadership.

IQ has warped many of my generation because the IQ index was treated with the infallible authority as if it were an encyclical from the Holy Father, the Pope of Rome as if dogma.

Yet, someone like James Dewey Watson (born April 6, 1928), of *The Great Depression Generation*, who admits to having an average IQ (110 range), managed to become an American molecular biologist, geneticist and zoologist.

Not stopping with those achievements, he became the co-discoverer of the structure of DNA in 1953 with Francis Crick. Watson, Crick, and Maurice Wilkins were awarded the 1962 Nobel Prize in Physiology or Medicine.

To say he was diligent and curious to the extreme doesn't even cover it. He believed in himself and had the confidence in that belief to be all that he could be. He earned degrees at the University of Chicago (B.S., 1947) and Indiana University (Ph.D., 1950) following that with a post-doctoral year at Copenhagen University with Herman Kalckar and Ole Maaloe. He then worked at the University of Cambridge's Cavendish Laboratory in England, where he first met his future collaborator and friend Francis Crick.[1] The rest is history.

                    *   *   *

Columnist David Brooks of the *New York Times* sometimes varies off his day job of reporting on politics to go deeply into the social self in *The Social Animal* (2011). Here he exposes the biases in modern culture that overemphasize rationalism, individualism, and the I.Q. He does this not as an expert but as a person learning from the pain and memory of his own youth, which obviously was his greatest teacher, along with what he has learned along the way with his research. He writes in *The Social Animal*:

Once a person crosses the IQ threshold of 120, there is little relationship between more intelligence and better performance. A person with a 150 IQ is in theory much smarter than a person with a 120 IQ, but those additional 30 points produce little measurable benefit when it comes to lifetime success.[2]

No question, the ability to do well on IQ tests is significantly influenced by heredity. The single strongest predictor of IQ is the IQ of the mother. People with high IQs do better in school and in school-like settings. Yet, in life, what compounds if not contradicts this is people with reasonable rather than outstanding IQs, but their superior work ethics have been defying experts for more than a century.

Another factor that needs much more attention to explain success and failure vis-à-vis IQ is the character, composition and nurturing capacity of the environment. Minorities and inner city children are unlikely to have the climate to grow intellectually that is available in the suburbs. Then there is the business of parental involvement, psychological encouragement and readiness to be there when their children need mentoring. In a word, self-confidence and success go well beyond an IQ index.

As to those aspiring to great wealth, a study of 7,403 Americans who participated in the National Longitudinal Survey of Youth, conducted by Jay Zagorsky of Ohio State, found no correlation between accumulating great wealth and high IQ.3

NO ANSWERS IN THE DEEP HOLES IN THE SOUL

David Brooks writes about the conscious and unconscious layers to our personality and makeup. This is quite a challenge as the deep self is alien territory to most of us, as we don't allow our minds to have that conversation with ourselves. We go along to get along buying into the popular notions of what we can't do, can't be, and best not think about. We see ourselves as quite average and practically everyone else we see or read about as exceptional. So, why bother, right?

The basic problem is having low expectations for and of ourselves.

We don't think we have a right to a center independent of the demands of others, including family. This is necessary for our own self-preservation. Being able to say "No" is a basic requirement for being able to function as a healthy and engaged individuals.

The irony is that the more you do for others the less they do for themselves and therefore you penalize their development, independence, self-reliance and happiness.

Meanwhile, a voice deep within us, a voice we often ignore is likely to be constantly gnawing away at our conscience from deep within us that tells us we are much more than we are letting ourselves know or be. The pain of this gnawing sensation can act as an inducement to do something, to be something that lifts us out of our malaise, or it can drive us deeper into depression as if we have a hole in our soul. That hole is likely a product of never standing our ground, pleasing others at the expense of pleasing self, not wanting to hurt someone else feelings, but having no trouble hurting one's own. It is masochism to the extreme.

That pain echoed in my mind from memory of my Irish clan as I listened to that checkout clerk at Walmart. She feels trapped and her son has exploited her self-imprisoning mindset to his advantage and that of his girlfriend. Why does this feel so strange?

The checkout clerk's dilemma is rooted in her hapless efforts to escape family and to function apart from its continuing demands. She is the product of a culture where the family never stops being central.

As you read these pages, you will observe I ask the reader to think outside that box, to look outward to the oppressive world of collapsing corporate power in on the individual. That power includes government policy, science, economics and our collective history.

Our cultural history is treated as if a religion. As such, we are obeisant to corporate power while corporate power is not obliged to play by the same rules. Consequently, the checkout clerk feels she has no choice but to jeopardize her health and economic stability by taking in her son and his girlfriend. It is morality as an invisible hand that is not designed to serve but to question that individual's self-interests. Consequently, behavior has yielded to a preoccupation with what other people think, and not what is best for us.

We are heaped in the rational, the cognitive and the linear, in the quantitative grab bag of popular culture, in that which is approved by society at large. Now this is compounded with the Internet that has competing platforms that are united in their ambition to define every term of our existence. No religion ever enjoyed such power and this is undisguised corporate power.

We are mainly instinctive animals operating at an evolutionary level with that *"outer layer"* (in Brooks' words), instead of paying much attention to that buried *"inner layer"* of the unconscious. Most of the drivers that control our behavior reside in the *"inner layer."* This finds most of us self-estranged operating 24/7 compulsively on the *"outer layer,"* or mainly on automatic pilot. This was the case with this matronly well-meaning checkout clerk at Walmart.

Theologian Paul Tillich would have a slightly different take on this. He would say this women cannot say "no" to her son because as much as she thinks she has suffered she has not suffered enough to know herself.

He would claim that if she had suffered enough she would realize that if her son became hostile to her for saying "no," she would have no problem with it. On the other hand, if her friends and family were equally unsympathetic to her, this might cause her great distress. Should that occur, then it would be clear what they thought about her was more important than what she thought about herself.

Tillich would insist that only when people have moments of intense suffering, which is psychological suffering, and not physical suffering, then and only then do they finally discover that they are not the person they thought themselves to be. It is then that the mask melts away and they experience being one with themselves, alone, self-accepting and self-aware, and have no trouble whatsoever saying "no."

Should you think this is a hypothetical proposition, you only have to ask my children, who are now in their mature years to find out that I am a legendary practitioner of "no." They are all doing just fine knowing that when push comes to shove they had better lift themselves off the turf rather than look elsewhere for aid. Self-reliance as with self-acceptance is key. Ralph Waldo Emerson in his essay *Self-Reliance* (1841) suggests:

"What I must do is all that concerns me, not what the people think. This rule, equally arduous in actual and in intellectual life, may serve for the whole distinction between greatness and

meanness. It is the harder, because you will always find those who think they know what your duty is better than you know it. It is easy in the world to live after the world's opinion; it is easy in solitude to live after our own; but the great man is he who in the midst of the crowd keeps with perfect sweetness the independence of solitude."

If we could, we would like to see this nice lady be blessed with this ability to say "no" when it suits her, but each of us has to find this out for ourselves on our own, and of course, most of us never do. So, we have the pampered society of sons and daughters like this couple that has thoughtlessly destroyed the integrity of this woman's home and life as if it were their right.

Notes:

1. James D. Watson, *"DNA: The Secret of Life,"* Alfred A. Knopf, New York, 2003*; "The Double Helix: The Classic Account of the Discovery of the Structure of DNA,"* Weidenfeld & Nicolson, London, 1997, *"The Double Helix: A Personal Account of the Discovery of the Structure of DNA,"* New American Library, New York, 1968; Sigmund Brouwer, *"Double Helix"* (a novel), Word Publishing, Dallas, 1995; Brenda Maddox, *"Rosalind Franklin: The Dark Lady of DNA,"* HarperCollins, New York, 2002.

2. David Brooks, *"The Social Animal: The Hidden Sources of Love, Character, and Achievement,"* Random House, New York, 2011, p. 165.

3. Ibid. pp. 165-166

TWENTY THREE

WHEN MEN WON'T WORK & THE WOMEN WHO CARRY THEM!

"Man is a worker. If he is not, then he is nothing."

Joseph Conrad (1857-1924), Polish-British novelist, author of *The Heart of Darkness*

WHAT NOW SEEMS LIKE ANCIENT HISTORY

A generation ago, when the *Feminist Movement* was in full swing, women came to view life through the *Feminist Prism*. They campaigned for an *Office of Gender Equity*, insisting there was a gender bias favoring men, especially with regard to education. What now seems like ancient history, in 1970, it was then observed:

While boys get higher scores in mathematics, girls get higher scores in reading and writing; boys in eighth grade are 50 percent more likely to repeat a grade, while boys in high school constitute 68 percent of the special education population; two thirds of female high school graduates go on to college, compared to 58 percent of male high school graduates; women were only 41 percent of all college graduates.

Regarding graduate education, in 1970:

Women receive 40 percent of all master's degrees; today, two thirds of all master's degree candidates and more than half of all master's degree holders are women; women earned only 6 percent of all first professional degrees; by 1991 that figure had increased to 39 percent, and now hovers around 50 percent; then only 14 percent of all doctoral degrees went to women; by 1991 that figure was up to 39 percent, while today it is pressing 50 percent; medical degree earned by women between 1970 and 1991 jumped from 8 percent to 36 percent. By 1993, 42 percent of first-year medical students were women; today more than half of all medical students are women.

In 1970, 5 percent of women earned law degrees; by 1991, that figure was up to 40 percent, and today it is around 50 percent; in 1970, women earned 1 percent of dental degrees compared with 32 percent in 1991, and today more than half first year dental students are women, and more than 40 percent have earned dental degrees; women today earn the majority of doctoral degrees in pharmacy and veterinary medicine.

The gender imbalance is even more pronounced for African American and Hispanic women. In 1990, fully 62 percent of all bachelor's degrees to African Americans went to women, while 55 percent of Hispanic students receiving bachelor's degrees were women. In 1990, the white student imbalance was 53 percent to 47 percent in favor of women. It is even more pronounced today.

BACKGROUND

On April 4, 2011, I wrote an article in longhand on my observations on men who refused to work and the women who support them. This was written while waiting for my daughter at the eye clinic where she was being operated on for a detached retina.

On May 11, 2011, David Brooks, New York Times columnist, wrote a piece on the same subject, not speaking from empirical data but economic statistics. Brooks insisted in his piece that energy defines us, and that we are becoming less energetic insofar as American males are concerned.

- In 1954, 96 percent of American men between the ages of 25 and 54 were actively engaged in some kind of regular work. Today, that number has slipped to 80 percent, whereas women, once only allowed to enter the workforce in small numbers in menial tasks have steadily increased in the last half-century.

According to the *Organization for Economic Cooperation and Development*, the United States now lags behind all other G-7 nations in prime age men in the workforce. Brooks says,

- "More American men lack the emotional and professional skills they would need to contribute."

Most startlingly, however, according to the *Bureau of Labor Statistics*, 35 percent of American males are without high school diplomas whereas only 10 percent of men with college degrees are out of work.

Brooks becomes something of an apologist for structural changes in the economy, which although relevant, fail to get inside the fact that there are more idle men walking the streets of the United States than at any time since the Great Depression.

Brooks sees the problem in terms of economics when it seems clear to me it has been a natural progression of the *Feminist Movement* as many American males feel emasculated by the soaring prominence of women who have "forgotten their place." James Burke and Robert Ornstein present an intriguing conceptual framework for this phenomenon in *"The Axemaker's Gift: A Double-Edged History of Human Culture"* (1995).

They argue that with each cultural change something is gained at the expense of something lost never to be experienced again. Men never felt challenged before by women, and assumed, because that was the popular nuance of the culture, that men were superior to women in many if not most occupations when clearly women have demonstrated that is not the case.

Half the world's population is women. Yet, prior to WWII, they had been given secondary and subjugated roles. It was evident ten-years after WWII that American society wanted to put the genie back in the bottle, meaning working women, as displayed sixty years ago in *Good Housekeeping Monthly* (May 13, 1955):

"THE GOOD WIFE GUIDE!"

Has dinner ready, plans ahead, even the night before to have a delicious meal on time for her husband's return. This is a way of letting him know that you have been thinking of him and are concerned about his needs.

Prepare yourself. Take 15 minutes to rest so you'll be refreshed when he comes home. Touch up your make up, put a ribbon in your hair and be fresh looking.

Be a little gay and a little more interesting for him.

Clear away the clutter. Make one last trip around the house before he arrives.

Gather up schoolbooks, toys and papers and run a dust cloth over the furniture.

Over the cooler months of the year light a fire for him to unwind by.

Prepare the children. See that they are clean, are not noisy, and eliminate all noise from vacuum cleaners to dryers.

Be happy to see him.

Greet him with a warm smile and show sincerity in your desire to please him.

Listen to him. You may have dozens of important things to tell him, but this is not the moment. Remember, his topics of interest are more important than yours.

Make the evening his. Never complain if he comes home late, or goes out to dinner, or other places of entertainment without you. Try to understand his stress.

Your goal is to make your home a place of peace, order and tranquility.

Don't greet him with complaints and problems.
Don't complain if he's late or stays out all night.

Make him comfortable. Have a cool or warm drink ready for him.

Arrange his pillows and offer to take his shoes off.

Don't ask him about his actions or question his judgments or integrity.

A good wife always knows her place.

If this sounds incredible, given the fact that women are in virtually every occupation today, including combat in the military, read this article on the Internet. This was, indeed, the actual proposed wifely social menu for the happy home after WWII.

Good Housekeeping Monthly presented this itemized list with attractive smiling housewives decked out in stunning colors doing the cooking, baking, housecleaning, washing and drying, and ironing as if this was the ultimate joy to feminine fulfillment. Women, however, didn't buy into it from the get go.

One of my aunts was a certified welder in a defense plant during the war, another worked as a tool and die lathe operator, and still another was a machinist. They didn't leave the workforce after WWII, but worked in their important jobs until retirement. Incidentally, they all had better jobs than their husbands and brought more money home to the family. You can imagine who ruled the roost literally as well as figuratively.

Seventy years later after the end of WWII in 1945, this fantasy retinue of selfless devotion is still the obsession of some men, as 20 percent of them, ages 25 to 54, aren't working, or if working, not working full time, or not in work they have been trained. I know:

- An attorney with several degrees including a doctor in jurisprudence who refuses to practice law full time, or when he does, gives free services to friends. His family suffers for this indulgence, forcing his wife to work as a freelance insurance agent driving fifty, sixty or more miles for appointments while still being mother, housekeeper, cook, baker, and taxi service for her children's after school activities. She is even expected to pick up her husband's dry cleaning.
- A father of two children sits at home strumming his guitar when he is able bodied except for suffering the carpal tunnel syndrome, a disorder acquired from overworking his hands performing the repetitive task of strumming the guitar all day long. His wife cheerfully, by default, has become the family breadwinner.
- A number of college graduates who have given up the effort to find work while living with their parents at home, the wife or girlfriend out busing tables in some restaurant or club.

Then there are women who would like to be home spending time with their children when their husbands are making a comfortable living for the family. But that is not good enough. These husbands feel their wives should be bringing in money, too, forgetting that being a wife and mother and housekeeper and family taxi service is a full time non-paying job.

- Another couple has four preteen children in which the husband is a high school graduate and the wife a college graduate. She is a dedicated mother feeling she cannot afford to take on a full time teaching position at this time in her children's lives. So, besides being a full-time mother, she substitute teaches and cleans houses to make ends meet, while her husband refuses to leave a job that is, at best, only a part-time position and never brings in much income.

Women described here are treated in the manner of this 1955 *Good Housekeeping Guide* although none of them were yet born. These husbands subscribe to the 1955 dictum, "a good wife knows her place."

What is not stated here, but every reader familiar with men of this ilk knows, is that these men, simply stated, are financial liabilities to their families. They bury their sorrows in the neighborhood bar and smoke two or three packs of cigarettes a day. Then they wonder why the family can never meet its financial obligations at the end of the week.

THE WALTER MITTY SYNDROME!

Humorist James Thurber wrote a short story in 1939, *"The Secret Life of Walter Mitty,"* which touched the collective American psyche denoting the ineffectual male who spends his time in heroic daydreams paying little attention to the real world.

Many of the men described above fit into the *Walter Mitty Syndrome* as they live in the world of "what if":

- I had gotten the breaks I would have made something of myself.

- I had been born into a better situated family I would be better off now.
- I had gotten the breaks writing a song I might have had a career.
- I had married the right woman I would not have been dragged down to this. ☐ I not had had children then I would not have had to struggle.
- I had gone into the military or the government I'd be retired by now with a great pension. Men who don't work are great daydreamers. This is consistent with Thurber's short story. Walter Mitty would spend his day in a deep state of daydreaming imagining himself a fighter pilot during WWII, a world-class doctor, always someone far removed from what he was.

It was why in that eye clinic waiting for my daughter that I wrote this missive, which follows.

WHEN MEN WON'T WORK & THE WOMEN WHO SUPPORT THEM

People in the 1970's watched their families disintegrate as women increasingly carried the economic and emotional load. Since then, women as wives and mothers not only do most of the work, but are on call for the demands of the family. They carry their children to and fro, run errands for their husbands, and suffer the aggravations as well as the joys of their children.

They are the silent partners in the marital relationship, never in the know, until their husbands need a signature on a second or third mortgage. Husbands make deals and then tell their wives after the fact. It would never occur to these men that they needed wifely counseling. They believe they are always in the know, see no reason to consult their wives and share the risks they have taken, and therefore often drive the family to ruin.

Husbands scheme and daydream and find no need to consult their wives as they believe themselves to be more efficient problem solvers; to possess superior minds and information needed to the problem solving. They may have the information and good enough minds, but it is very doubtful that they possess superior intelligence.

In the 1950s, 80 percent of the top 10 percent high school graduates were women. This was reversed during the same period for college. Now, it is being reversed again as 80 percent of the top 10 percent college graduates in this new century are women.

The nostalgia for the way it was, hangs on.

"Men have sight," observed Victor Hugo, *"women have insight."*

Yet, women are often reduced to and treated as if maids, housekeepers, nannies, chefs, waiters, dishwashers, launderers and supervisors of the children, keeping order and avoiding chaos with little allocated down time or special economic or moral compensation.

Again, in the 1950s, the situation was essentially independent of socioeconomic status, education, or social standing. Families with the advantage of affluence, education, cultural enhancement, travel and social engagement were as likely as not to display male dominating attributes.

The only time attention was brought to this matter was when women were coming apart, or in failing health, and therefore were forced to slow down or stop their demanding schedule altogether. Women persevered, for the most part, in the most trying circumstances.

How say you of this matter in the 21st century?

PRIDE ON THE LINE

Cultural bias would imply that I am addressing the dregs of society. Not true. Men who won't work can be physicians in their forties who won't practice medicine, attorneys who won't practice law, and carpenters who won't apply their craft, and yes, poorly educated men who have lost their safe jobs in automobile manufacturing, chemical processing, oil refineries, or other safe jobs for the unskilled and under educated. These workers refuse to suffer the embarrassment of going back to night school or junior college to learn 21st century skills.
These men could also be:

- Active teachers who refuse to acknowledge or engage students who challenge their authority or the relevance of the curriculum being taught;
- Engineers who are unwilling to adjust to the digital demands of the new engineering; and
- Managers who refuse to concede and adapt to the power shift from position power to knowledge power that is now mainly in the possession of professional workers.

These men are caught in a time warp in which their authority was once infallible whether they were doctors, teachers, or managers. Seventy years ago, few had the gumption to challenge the views of authority. Now, these men bask in nostalgic pride and lace together excuses for why they have given up and given out.

Men across society at every socioeconomic level have been dropping off and dropping out of the workforce, many while being employed, because work has changed and they cannot cope with or adjust to that change. What do they do?

Many become couch potatoes. These men love to follow violent sports vicariously such as professional wrestling, football and ice hockey. It gives them a buzz to exercise their *Walter Mitty fixation.* They identify with these combative warriors who sacrifice mind, body and sense for their entertainment.

These same men spend a small fortune for season tickets and sports paraphernalia often while not having a budget to make ends meet on the home front. Still others spend the little money they have gambling on professional sport teams they watch on television.

The problem is that men in general like to soar like birds and identify with those who successfully break free of the herd by demonstrable athletic prowess while they themselves have trouble seeing over their belt buckles for the protrusion of their stomachs.

The gender differences are inescapable:

- Women like to feel the soft earth under their feet and deal pragmatically and practically with the possible and probable more often than not without complaint.
- Men applaud physical courage, and have since the times of ancient Greece.
- Women respect moral courage and those who confront life stoically with humility and without false pride.

That is why the educated housewife can find her way to cleaning houses while the under educated husband mopes about like a spoiled child complaining about everything while doing nothing.

To be fair, some with initiative read self-help books, attend self-help workshops and self-help seminars and think they are engaged and doing something about their situation. They are not. They are fooling themselves and mainly wasting time and money.

Self-help publishing is a post-WWII invention and $ billion industry. It has become something of a panacea. Self-help books have less to do with changing circumstances, and more to do with excusing failure to make satisfactory progress in work and life. Self-help authors get rich while they spin their hypnotic rhapsody on readers' delicate psyches.

Such readers are daydreaming their way through life writing music, strumming guitars, or doing anything that doesn't give off the scent of work.

They are *Walter Mittys* to the tee, fantasizing for the quick score, the perfect franchise, standing on acres of diamonds without a care in the world, while their inherent disability receives scant attention. They subconsciously spend their lives looking for answers in all the wrong places.

Those who don't read such books may be eating and drinking themselves into a state of amnesia and permanent inertia or find themselves retreating into some psychosomatic illness. They deplete the limited energy they possess to the point that they couldn't look for work if they wanted to.

These men are casualties of Western civilization's deification of men and denigration of women over the centuries. The irony and paradox is that this all starts with the nurturing practices of mothers.

Men born after the *Good Housekeeping 1955 Guide* for the "good wife" are the spoiled brats of our culture and their sponsors are their mothers. In a counter dependent way, mothers continue to enslave their daughters to accountability and liberate their sons from responsibility.

Yet, these same women that are nursemaids to their husbands and children are often ridiculed rather than appreciated. This is especially true when these women use their limited free time to go back to school to better themselves while their men are not so inclined. In my career, I've counseled hundreds of women who suffered this enigmatic dilemma.

DOUBLE EDGED SWORD, OR WHAT HAS BEEN LOST

The *Great Depression* generation entered maturity in the 1950s and survived because they were small in number with unlimited opportunity in a post-World War II climate.

They had been schooled in scarcity, and learned to live with little. When they came to maturity, they failed to teach these same lessons to their children. Not only were these parents guilty of this, but teachers, the religious, managers, and leaders all were as well.

An insouciant society, such as ours, develops without a guidance system or directional roadmap, and therefore without wisdom.

The irony is that children of the 1950s had more freedom, more creative license, less parental involvement, less organized activities, less artificial symbols of achievement and recognition, and more opportunity to decide on their own what to do when they failed, as they had no safety net, no one to turn to but to themselves when depressed or lost or confused, as their parents were too busy just surviving. Children of the *Great Depression* era were well acquainted with the Darwinian cliché of "survival of the fittest." They understood that struggle could be reduced to a simple equation:

PAIN + RISK = GROWTH

Therefore, the era was a microclimate conducive to the development of leaders through pain and struggle, a fluid environment with nothing written in concrete. Adults and children alike were familiar with experimentation as they had no other choice.

The generation of the 1950s, essentially the pre-television era, lived within their means, didn't buy expensive houses, or drive fancy cars, nor did they dress or attempt to mimic the rich and famous, but lived within themselves, and they prospered.

The societal train, however, went off the tracks in the 1960s.

Parents attempted to save their children from the pain and struggle they had experienced, pampering them to excess. One of the casualties was that school became a failed factory and a combat war zone with little opportunity for real education.

Young men of the 1960s burned their draft cards, refused to serve their country, fled to Canada, created chaos on college campuses, or retreated to *Haight Asbury* at *Golden Gate State Park* in California to drift into a psychedelic high and hedonistic lifestyle in defiance of the Protestant Work Ethic and the American establishment.

This hippie generation felt sexually repressed and looked for liberation in free love, but instead gave birth to the *United States of Anxiety*. This spawned the psychotherapy industry that is still with us. Instead of being a palliative, psychotherapy has become iatrogenic, the cure being worse than the disease.

THE POWER OF DENIAL

People who came to maturity in the 1950s, now parents, were not prepared for a world that had caught up with the United States economically and technologically.

1950 style parents were drunk with success, and had little time for child rearing. Their children were allowed to be pretty much on their own. As a consequence, they became essentially their own parents as their parents were seldom home both working to keep up with the Jones.

Children forever have invented their own play, but the world of the 1960s was a very different world than the 1930s, something most parents refused to acknowledge. It was a much more dangerous place.

At the same time, the inchoate power shift to women was underway. Men were being pushed aside in leadership, scholarship and professional acumen, as women climbed the ladder to be the majority in college, whatever their ethnicity or profession.
Women have not been deterred by the fact they make only 75 percent as much as men doing the same work.

Nor are women allowing the fact that they are still being treated as baby factories to delay their upward mobility. Indeed, they are working their way up the corporate pyramid to the boardrooms and into the highest offices of government and corporate society. This is happening because the way women think is now important to the survival of society.

RIGHT BRAIN, LEFT BRAIN

In this digital age, we are finding the right brain, the so-called "feminine brain" is a powerful and necessary complement to the left-brain, the so-called "masculine brain."

The key to the problem solving is not primarily aggressive action, but a more tactful and perceptive response to chronic problems. Likewise, the key to economic health is no longer the competitive verve, but the spirit of cooperation.

LEFT BRAIN	RIGHT BRAIN
Masculine	Feminine
Demanding	Contracting
Aggressive	Responsive
Competitive	Cooperative
Rational and Cognitive	Intuitive and Affective
Analytical	Synthesizing
Concrete Orientation	Conceptual Orientation

Although rational cognitive thinking is still important, intuitive wisdom and the use of the affect have come into prominence (see David Brook's *"The Social Animal,"* 2011), as the affect and intuitive is an important match to the cognitive and rational. In that same vein, analysis need not lead to paralysis if suitable attention is given to synthesis.

No one has been more energetic in exposing the limits to pure Socratic thinking, or linear logic than Edward de Bono in such books as *"Lateral Thinking"* (1977) and *"Parallel Thinking"* (1994).

Women are inclined to problem solve conditionally when dealing with contradictory situations, which are common to daily experience in this new century.

Aware of their biological clock, delayed gratification is programmed into the female psyche as well as the genes. The necessary investment of time, patience and care are familiar feminine territory. Stated another way, women have their feet solidly on the ground while men prefer to soar to avoid the detritus of normal everyday life.
The decline and fall of men has been accelerated by making excuses in perpetuity for why men won't work, won't study, won't get off their behinds and do something useful. Unfortunately, exacerbating the problem, women still attempt to carry their men as if they were dependent children at the age of twenty, thirty, forty, fifty, or older.

Ergo, women can be accused of complicating the picture by carrying their men who refuse to work. They do this by absorbing physical, mental, and emotional abuse, and acting as if the punishment is deserved.

It doesn't take a crystal ball to imagine if the situation were reversed how men would act: many of them would walk out. That is still something that seldom happens with women.

WHAT CAN BE DONE WHEN MEN WON'T WORK?

The short answer is for women to tell their men to get off their behinds and look for work or get lost!

If this sound like tough love, so be it. Everyone has interests, even those currently stuck. One of the problems is that few men follow their bliss. They instead chase the buck. That finds them taking jobs outside their interests and being miserable for the attention.

Meanwhile, women have been locked into a comparable prison for centuries, but continue to thrive despite circumstances due in a large measure to their patience.

What am I saying? I am inferring that men are not made of such firm substance as women. I know a number of men in their fifties who have the maturity of a ten-year-old. How many women do you know of a similar temperament?

Men may find, as women have found, that their interests may be kindled in volunteering at school, church or in a community project, or around some favorite activity such as music, sports, or some other social pastime. In this age, men could find a way of making a living at home surfing the Internet.

EXPECTATIONS OF MEN	EXPECTATIONS OF WOMEN
Active and Productive	Passive and Receptive
Rational and Cognitive	Irrational and Intuitive
Aggressive, Competitive, even Ruthless	Responsive, Cooperative, and Consolidating
Conscious of Themselves	Conscious of Environment
'Thinkers'	'Feelers'
Inclined toward Science	Inclined toward Mysticism

It would be helpful, too, if men would give up cigarettes and booze or tickets to sporting events especially when they can't afford these pacifiers.

At the very least, men could become house husbands. They could be cleaning the house, painting, doing the grocery shopping, going to the cleaners, doing the laundry, taking the kids to and from school, and to youth events. The shoe is now on the other foot, and remember, the person who has the coin has the power.

These men often keep their women out of the loop as to how they spend their money. Now, they can experience a little of their own medicine.

Here is the rub. I've talked to countless women who never had a clue as to how their husbands spent the family income, never understood why they had to sign papers without prior conversations on the investment, never were asked if they would like to go to this or that event, but assumed they would go to satisfy their husband's commitment without question or protest.

Now, these men who won't work and are not bringing in the bacon still have wives who feel obliged to get permission from their husbands to do this or that with their hard earned money, something they never experienced when their husbands were making the majority of the coin.

Moreover, women are reluctant to take legal action against deadbeat husbands and fathers, blaming themselves for the anxiety in the family. Deadbeat dads are good at being abusive of their wives, the mothers of their children.

Eventually, given the stress and strain of carrying these men, given the unlikely chance anything will ever change, these women have to decide whether they would be better off without these men altogether.

There are many families who have gone through more than one generation of deadbeat dads, men who would work only for premium wages or not at all, men who were alcoholics and abused their wives and children psychologically if not physically, and women who were willing to put up with this nonsense because they knew no other.

In the last quarter century, the plush jobs in the automotive and steel industry have evaporated. Generation after generation of workers with high school diplomas or less were conditioned to making $50,000 to $75,000 a year in unskilled jobs, and to retire with pensions of $40,000 with full medical benefits. The boilerplate for this workforce still exists but the jobs do not.

Then there are men who soared during the booming 1990s, and have suffered major setbacks, finding themselves in deep financial trouble, unable to cope much less work. They need help but they are unwilling to seek counseling. Many are educated in law, medicine, engineering and education. They are the walking wounded that are part of this problem and need help not criticism. The world of the *Big Easy*, be it Detroit, Gary, Seattle, or New Orleans is gone. We are a declining nation in a world that has not only caught up with us but is passing us. We cannot complain our way back to prominence by denying this reality.

I've known engineers making six-figure incomes who were let go when high tech companies downsized. Some started new businesses using their skills, many waited for the upturn to return. They are still waiting.

I know of one engineer who was given a quarter million dollar separation package from IBM, and went through it in two years. He has never had a stable income since. I would like to think this an isolated case, but I don't think so.

Men who won't work are not a mirage. It is indicative of our times and a profile all too familiar. We are aghast that unemployment hovers around 9 percent, when I think it is closer to 18 percent, when you take in part-time workers, and workers no longer looking for work.

Economists write books with economic solutions when I see the problem basically a behavioral and psychological one.

These are not bad men who won't work. These are men who need help. I'm not sure we have the tools to do that job. The psychological and psychiatric professions are mainly explanatory factories. They present an interesting vocabulary to identity maladies and an equally interesting vocabulary of remedies. Nothing changes. The solution will evade discovery if the problem is not definitively identified in useful operational terms.

I would also suggest the problem is a spiritual issue as well. In other words, a problem that has little to do with mechanistic algorithms and paradigms. It is the soul of society that is sick.

We have lost our moral compass and our way. We need help to crawl out of the ditch of despair and take quiet inventory of where we are, how we got here, and where we want to go. This involves men and women as collaborators.

TWENTY FOUR

MEN LIKE TO SOAR, WOMEN LIKE TO STAY ROOTED!

WHY THE POSTMODERN WORLD BELONGS TO WOMEN!

THE QUIET SURFACING OF THE FEMININE PARADIGM

Work and workers have changed dramatically, while management and the measurement of work has lagged behind. This cannot be blamed on management, alone, for many workers would rather work hard than take risks and work smart.

Being culturally conditioned to results, they want personal guarantees, to know what they are going to get for what they give. Nor are they likely to be inclined to take an apprenticeship in electronics, computers, or some other program for technicians, which pays less than they would be making on their old now redundant jobs. They are also unlikely to bid on jobs that test their mettle.

As medicine has become a high-risk profession due to the rising tide of lawsuits, women are replacing men in medical schools. In 1970, only 14 percent of medical school graduates were women. Today, half of all medical students are women. They are more willing to take risks and work the process than men.

Women have always preferred to work smarter than harder. Women, as a rule, don't have the physical strength for labor intensive jobs. Their powers are more subtle and insightful.

Women are less prone to shame as pride is more indigenous to men.

An upper level female executive was demoted and given a non-functioning job where I worked. She maintained an office, but no longer had a secretary or a private parking space. Otherwise, she continued to draw her salary and benefits. I would pass her office and see her doing her nails, smiling broadly, reading the newspaper or talking on the telephone. She continued to dress to the nines and displayed all the aplomb as if she was still a fully engaged power broker.

In contrast, a male colleague of mine, once revered as a chief engineer, was demoted because of a drinking problem. He suffered a similar fate to this women, but a different reaction. He was given an office, kept his parking space, but no longer had engineering duties. He took on the role of organizing the engineers into a union, which failed. Picking himself up from that embarrassment, he campaigned throughout the facility as a political activist, which also fell on deaf ears.

After his engineering colleagues were exposed to these two fiascos, they commenced to avoid him as if he had the plague. This made him despondent. He considered going back on the sauce, but to his credit, resisted. The fall out was nevertheless devastating. He lost his sense of humor, desire to mingle, seldom spoke to anyone about anything, moped about, and went home from work early. Then one day he had a heart attack at the age of 50 and died.

The female executive spent seven happy years in limbo, giving no indication that she felt any remorse at her demotion, or psychological trauma retiring at age 65. Today, she is still going strong ever the striking lady.

It is no mere coincidence that women are adjusting more philosophically to the violent shift in role relationships at work with its concomitant new cultural demands than men. Women are used to being in charge without authority, not on mahogany row, not in command and control positions, but as mothers and wives on the home front. They have had to roll with the punches since time immemorial.

Women, without titles or portfolios, have had to be the family problem-solvers with limited resources and have learned to make the most of what little they have had to work.

Limits, and not being taken seriously, are new experiences for men.

Women have been saddled with this assumed role of subservience for centuries. From the age of four or five, men learn the game of bullying choosing their leaders on that basis. Physical prowess until age 18 commands respect and attention, especially in athletics. Gradually, leadership takes on a more cerebral aspect as men in such roles adopt the psychological façade of doers, decision-makers, talkers, spin doctors, movers and shakers.

With women:

- The cerebral has always been more enchanting.

Women are used to men taking the credit when solving problems with their ideas. Women have been obliged to listen to men acting like spoiled children when matters fail to go their way, women then assume the role of comforting angel.

- Women watch their ideas take root knowing the source of the idea has long been forgotten.
- Women have had no other choice but to be passive, until now. The male brand and bias was that of society's. Now they have access to the same toolkit and are making their presence known and their mark apparent.

Men like to soar like birds. Women prefer to feel the earth firmly under their feet. Women have kept the culture extant by practicing the tenets of being grounded for centuries.

- Men fall back on the culture when in dire straits.

- Women personify the culture as they carry its collective soul with them wherever they go, out of which come society's sons and daughters.

- Men argue the metaphysics of soullessness with pious impunity.

Yet men and women are more alike than different as they are equally programmed to please others than to please themselves.

- With women, the drive is to please men.

- With men, the drive is please power, which usually resides in men.

This handicaps women, who remain more man-conscious. What handicaps men is that they remain more power conscious.

Now we have the unisex gender with such advocates as Bruce Jenner, former 1972 *Olympian Decathlon Gold Medal* winner. He has assumed a new identity as a transgender woman.

Sex role identity, in any case, is learned behavior and not biological.

The scales appear to be turning toward a more relaxed balance between male and female attributes. We all have, after all, male and female proclivities. Then there is the bicameral mind with a left cognitive brain heretofore related to men and a right intuitive brain usually linked to women.

Stated another way, the complementary attributes of brain functioning translated into behavior are becoming more clearly essential to the effective creation of a mutually serving organizational life for each of us. This includes:

- Listening skills
- Acceptance of limits
- Dealing with reality
- Using our whole brain
- Being comfortable equally in the abstract as the concrete
- Not needing to promote "action for action's sake, and
- Not being afraid to respect and play intuitive hunches

There is something else going on as well and that is more cooperation between men and women. Being recognized is the unity in our collective identity.

Collective identity is a mockery with others unless we relate honestly with ourselves. This expands our consciousness and our predisposition to cooperate. This is new for men and women who have spent their lives pleasing others. Previously:

- It was more acceptable to be mediocre than to step out of the crowd and be great.

- Only "geeks" were believed to love work without regard to pay.

- Audacity was discouraged, as was conflict, not realizing that managed conflict is what generates cohesive pursuit.

- A person who was willing to admit that he valued his own opinions more than others was considered arrogant. The mask of humility was encouraged.

Those full of pleasing-self above pleasing others were put on notice that this was not acceptable. Yet the mindset of pleasing others at the expense of pleasing self comes out of the cultural landscape of comfort and complacency, not contribution.

The *Culture of Contribution* is a very different place. It is the land of giant achievers, giant pains-in-the-ass, of giant contradictions and giant misconceptions. It is the land where inconsistencies collide with consistencies, where the status quo has no place, and where breakthroughs are as common as the name.

Psychiatrist Karen Horney anticipated this emergence:

"Like all sciences and all valuations, the psychology of women has hitherto been considered only from the point of view of men ... The question then is how far analytical psychology also, when in its researches have women for their object, is under the spell of this way of thinking, insofar as it has not yet wholly left behind the stage in which frankly and as a matter of course masculine development only was considered. In other words, how far has the evolution of women, as depicted to us today by analysis, been measured by masculine standards and how far therefore does this picture fail to present quite accurately the real nature of women." (*Feminine Psychology*, 1967, pp. 56-57).

Now, all we have to be is intelligent and mature enough to appreciate what wonderful opportunities postmodern life promises to be for all men and women.

TWENTY FIVE

SOUL OF ENABLERS VERSUS CHAMELEONS

"I will buy with you, sell with you, talk with you, walk with you and so following; but I will not eat with you, drink with you, nor pray with you. What's news on the Rialto?"

William Shakespeare, *The Merchant of Venice*

He said, 'I hunt for haddocks' eyes among the heather bright, and work them into waistcoat-buttons in the silent night. And these I do not sell for gold or coin of silvery shine, But for a copper halfpenny and that will purchase nine.

Lewis Carroll, *Through the Looking-Glass*

Everyone lives by selling something.

Robert Louis Stevenson, *The Lantern-Bearers*

THE CULTURAL CAGE WE ALL SHARE

Conceivably, we all share the common cage of denial. Not only in a general sense, but in a specific sense as well. After all, we are promoting our individual and collective legitimacy.

Our integrity is always for sale but not always to the highest bidder. Sometimes we step back and ask ourselves, *"Is this all there is to life?"* Sometimes love intervenes and we self-forget ourselves and escape the confinement of the ego. In a capitalistic society, everyone is in sales barring none, everyone is in one sense or another aspiring to "make it." .

We are selling our tastes and talents from the moment we wake in the morning until we put our heads down on our pillows at night. While we engage our talents, our tastes dominate our every action.

These tastes are essentially synthetic commodities manufactured for us through cultural programming and subliminal advertisement from the ubiquitous noise that emanates from ghetto boxes to blaring car radios, from the cacophony of the screeching sounds of city streets to the noiseless pressing of fingers to the Plexiglas surface of mobiles that accompany, everywhere.

Few are aware of these automatic transactions as they innocently enter our subconscious, take residence, and then play havoc with our conscious behavior. The picture fails to change from region to region, city to city, as we are lock stepping to this clandestine master puppeteer.

We think we have free will and are in charge when clearly we are not. Quite absurdly, these blatant hawkers are allowed to enter our sanctuary unopposed, then become like family translating our wants into needs while literally placing our very existence at risk.

We purchase cars we cannot afford, houses and other amenities, too, creating a façade meant to impress others when they couldn't care less. These people are too busy playing the same game pursuing the same artificial agenda where wants become needs. Together, we all become slaves to our creditors while feeling we have done nothing wrong.

Isn't it strange that we want to rub elbows with people with whom we have nothing in common? We are obsessed with celebrity failing to appreciate the empty lives many of them lead needing a throng of admirers to justify their existence. As profligate spenders, we see ourselves as patriots pursuing the free enterprise debit system of eternally robbing Peter to pay Paul.

When I was at the University of Iowa, Bob Hope came with a large entourage to put on a show in the Iowa Fieldhouse. Few showed up. This was in 1956. So incensed was he that he took his show off stage, and performed at the Veterans Administration nearby to surprised and adoring fans shackled to their hospital confinement.

Arthur Marx in *"The Secret Life of Bob Hope"* (1993) shows the entertainer was obsessed with fans and idolaters, while being calloused and a bully to staff members and those close to him. Richard Zoglin's biography "Hope" (2014) claims in his book on Bob Hope that the comedian took a minor talent and marketed himself, managed his celebrity, cultivated his brand and converted his business acumen into show business fame. He was not what he seemed and few remember him today.

Those who do package and market themselves irrespective of talent are legion. What separates one brand from another is a function of deception. One thinks of a magician's sleight of hand tricks to a vulnerable public that desperately want to believe. Paradoxically, it has become the consensus identity of the masses.

This finds parents sending their children to prep schools and prestige universities. Deficiencies in *the owned self* or essence can be effectively camouflaged with *the acquired self* or personality with the proper pedigree.

You don't find such people as regular shoppers at K-Mart or Wal-Mart, but you do find them lined up at dawn to purchase the new Michael Jordan basketball shoes for upwards of $150 even if their children couldn't compete one-on-one with the typical African American youth. They want connection to what is "in" and what is admired.

Teenagers and young adults pay staggering prices to attend celebrity concerts, such as U-2, when you can't hear the words of Bono over the noise of the band or the yelling of the crowd. If you could, it would sound more like shouting than singing.

The man or woman who eventually becomes CEO of a company is likely to have more in common than you might think with Goethe's "Faust." My da, a railroad brakeman and part-time bartender, once asked a minor league baseball player in a Class B league, how much difference there was between him a "Class B" player and a major leaguer. He put his thumb and fore finger a smidgeon apart and said, "This much!" Talent matters, but apparently in baseball as other more mundane pursuits, you have to sell your soul to make it to the top.

What is perhaps surprising, especially in these times of soaring science and exploding technology, is that there is a sameness that approaches an incomprehensible mediocrity. Consequently, no matter how high the flyer or how many zeroes he has after the dollar sign in his coffers he cannot seem to escape this common cage.

Just as we all receive a report card every day of our lives, we differ much less with each other than we might like to think no matter where we are in the food chain. Technology has created a common appetite that no one escapes.

THE KALEIDOSCOPIC MAJESTY OF SELLING

Despite this, many in the selling profession would prefer to be seen as *"buying consultants."* Being a salesperson, or only a salesperson, is not very elevating in the common parlance. There is denial that as buyers we are not sellers as well. In truth, the buyer and seller are not adversaries but part of the same whole.

What is ironic is that the buyer is often the seller and the seller often the buyer in believing there is no role for him in the exchange.1

Few want to be seen as merchants on the make, but rather as "entrepreneurs." Obviously, Shakespeare's *The Merchant of Venice"* is not how they would like to be seen. Yet, the most important job of a college president is not to demonstrate academic brilliance, but to have a knack for grant writing and fund raising to increase the endowment status of the university. College presidents are consummate salespersons. They are also selling when recruiting top academics and students, along with needing a flair to entice philanthropists to sponsor university chairs, colleges or fund new building projects.

There isn't a job in capitalistic society that doesn't involve selling. Denial of this is not only a cage, but seriously handicaps the individual from making a difference.

Nothing happens until someone sells something. Still, there are few quotes from writers over the centuries about selling.2 It is unfortunate because the poetry of life is uncovering what touches our soul. Steven Jobs did that by designing a mobile of splashing colors in compact beauty that could fit in one's hand and perform its magic.

Selling is not duping someone to purchase what they don't need and cannot afford. Selling is translating wants into what is needed by providing the platform of ideas where wants are translated into affordable products and services.

The selling situation is a great teacher, greater than any academic course, or any book read because it is the basic arena of relational exchange. It is experience on steroids.

In sales, you find people as they are, not as they would like to appear. They have the power, you do not. You are interested in impressing them; they feel no need to impress you. They have the authority, you do not. They have control of the situation, you do not. What could be more ideal for seeing people as they really are?

So, if customers are bullies, you are an apt candidate to be bullied. If they are malicious, they will play you as their ploy. They will make promises they won't keep, laughing at you behind your back, lying through their teeth with a snicker, having fun with you at your expense. It will be the high point of their day because, true or not, they feel in charge.

Equally threatening, there are those who cannot say no to anyone about anything. You think you have made a sale, but no sooner are you out the door and someone else has the account. Selling is human nature on display in all its kaleidoscopic majesty. What could be better training for the budding novelist, or social scientist?

Television and the Internet have turned the selling situation into a circus with high and low wire performers. You don't need a lion and a trainer in the cage, you have the buyer and seller acting out the drama of predator and prey, the hunter and hunted, only the seller doesn't have a whip but his sales tools and his moxie to control the drama like the trainer does the lion in the cage.

No longer does caveat emptor, or *buyer beware* hold true. Instead, *"The Hidden Persuaders"* (1957) as Vance Packard put it, or conspicuous consumers as Christopher Lasch has inferred in *"The Culture of Narcissism"* (1979). We have *Craig's List* and *eBay* on the Internet as the marketplace has turned into compulsive theatre. Most products sold on *The Home Shopping Network* on television or the Internet are soon-to-be junk.

Eighty percent of the products available on *eBay* or *Craig's List* are discarded whimsical wants of a maddened crowd.[3]

No longer is an automobile merely transportation. Now, to satisfy tastes of the affluent and the want-to-be's, a new vehicle can costs as much as a middleclass house.

The buyer as prey has been deluded into believing he has taken on the role of the predator, as he hunts for "bargains" while the seller rakes in the cash. Vance Packard saw this coming and wrote a series of books on the subject, incidentally, long before the Internet.[4]

Now, it is difficult to keep up with the demand as a *Universe of Junk* has become the normal clutter of most homes of all socioeconomic classes. We are at the crossroads of a throwaway society with two discernible types of people in the headlights. They both have always been with us, but now one seems to have emerged dominant at the expense of the other.

CHAMELEONS AND ENABLERS

There are two behavioral types that have found a home in the new marketplace and the new millennium, *chameleons and enablers*.

- *Chameleons* are like the people we meet as strangers in the street, people who change colors to suit the situation, and are not burdened with a conscience. They are "quick in" and "quick out" satisfiers.

When chameleons encounter disingenuous people equal to their own pretense, they act vulnerable and use this to exploit the deceit to their advantage. Thus they overwhelm the unaware with the sincerity of smoke and mirrors.

- *Chameleons* have no sense of moral restrain. They operate with reckless abandon dumbing down to cultural tastes on television, engage in senseless texting on iPhones and other mobiles when it serves them. As parents, they are likely to spawn hyperactive children reduced to catatonic zombies at school controlled by numbing Ritalin.

Unburdened with any clear identity or moral quandary, chameleons can change color codes on demand looking at the situation from the standpoint of what is in it for them. This reduces commerce to whatever the traffic will bear.

- *Chameleons* cannot be reduced to conformity by rejection, accusation, criticism or complaint. They are inured to offense as the focus is always on the next conquest.

Then, there are the *enablers*. These are people with a conscience, well aware of the moral dilemma between what is wanted and what is needed. As a consequence, enablers are sensitive to people as persons. They are intuitively aware of what and why people behave so often in contradiction to their own best interests.

- *Enablers* translate this dynamic into definable needs, which are seldom understood at first by the benefactor. *Enablers* use their sensitivity to tap intuitively into what seems to drive others. They do this by studying their behavior. *Enablers* see themselves as agents serving the interests of others by demonstrating trust in meaningful exchange.

- *Enablers* look at every situation as much as possible from the others' points of view. Listening is critical in gaining this understanding from that perspective. *Enablers* go beyond making connection to developing common understanding. They see their role as assisting others in defining their problems while leaving the problem solving up to them.

It is certainly less demanding to be a *chameleon*, to simply imitate the mood and play it back to advantage. *Chameleons* play on sympathy; enablers develop empathy.

- *Chameleons* give legitimate needs a bad name, while *enablers* expose wants while promoting genuine needs.

- *Enablers* consequently feel the sting of wrath left over from *chameleons* and must move past it. Criticism fails to disturb the *chameleon*, while it reaches the soul of *enablers*.

- *Chameleons* know people are more interested in wants than needs, therefore they champion wants while enablers do not.

- *Chameleons* appear clever but not wise.

- *Enablers* recognize the journey to a solution has many false steps, whereas *chameleons* champion the cosmetic or the quick fix.

- *Chameleons* are emphatic and look for quick solutions.

- *Enablers* are tentative weighing several options promising no definitive answers.

- *Chameleons* rely on making an impression; *enablers* rely on effective performance.

- *Chameleons* concentrate on the part; *enablers* on the whole.

- *Chameleons* are convinced that others are as devious as are always looking for a bargain with no downside.

- *Enablers* believe people can be persuaded to take the long view with some risks and pain if shown the possibility of real and sustainable benefits.

Chameleons see selling as a mechanistic process of overcoming resistance (objections) with enticing benefits using an assumptive close and penalty of delay.

Enablers see selling as a systemic process and believe once need has been established the problem solving becomes a joint affair between seller and buyer as they are now both on the same side of the table.

By "sale" enablers mean the first-step in the problem solving. They picture each sale as a short-term trial to justify a long-term solution (commitment).

Chameleons believe the sale is the final step in the strategy. *Enablers* use mechanics as well, but believe trust takes time and goes far beyond charismatic posturing. Enablers know convincing words do not necessarily lead to concrete results. The order is not the end but the beginning of the process.

Because of this difference in approach, *chameleons* desperately need a convincing presentation, whereas *enablers* see themselves as competent problem definers. This involves asking the right questions. *Enablers* believe asking open-ended questions, questions that cannot be answered with a "yes" or "no," and then listening with the third ear, or the understanding level, which is key to the problem solving. Then, it is a matter of matching those needs to the appropriate intervention. Often, *chameleons* are poor listeners and dominate the sales conversation as talkers, not listeners.

Several years ago, I was selling chemical water treatment to large utility cooling systems and high-pressure boilers to prevent scaling and corrosion. One manufacturer had the best positive displacement pump for incremental chemical feeding on the market. Each account I sold, I recommended that these chemical pumps be purchased, and they were.

One day I got a call from the chemical pump salesman in my area. *"You've sold one hundred of my pumps to your customers, do you know that?"* I didn't. *"What I'm wondering is what commission do you expect?"* I didn't expect any. I was amazed that he would make such an offer, which I declined. It would be years before I realized he was a *chameleon* and not an *enabler*, a seller of products, not a systemic problem solver. How sad that he didn't realize what he had going for him.

ENABLERS HAVE HEARTS AS WELL AS HEADS!

In a world that continues to grow more complex, the basic instrument of that world is the individual, an individual who is increasingly cut and quartered into ever more discrete parts until he doesn't know whether he's coming or going, or who or what he is.

He has been dissected into synthetic appetites so that he can be manipulated into satisfying a consumers' marketplace with few limits. Indeed, the individual has been disembodied into a mass marketed and consuming commodity. It finds him motoring in an atmosphere of haste.

As long as we are on the move, chances are we'll be running into ourselves as a *chameleon*. Noise has become the conduit to self-negation, sameness its counterpoint. It is a cognitive world that feels anesthetized and digitized. The machine seems more "in" than ever. It rules the head of a misplaced heart. *Chameleons* are winning! *Enablers* are disappearing!

Obviously, a head without a heart is akin to separating the body from the soul, love from work, dreams from thought. Love once was said to make the world go around, but now it is business. Trust links the head to the heart. It is a world of *chameleon,* where the obsession is with getting not giving.

Love has been reduced to Viagra. It is not the world of the *enabler*.

The organization of enterprise has considered itself rational, orderly, and predictable. As a consequence, in its frenetic attempt to make it so, today it is instead pervasively chaotic. It is the world of the head absent of the heart. The heart has a rhythm, a melodic symphony of tonality that beats to the rhythm of the universe.5 It is the rhythm of the *enabler*.

Awareness provides the *enabler* with intuitive insight that might otherwise be lacking if challenges were lumped into impersonal categories. Each individual is unique and treated as such. *Enablers* refute the idea that enterprise is simply a "head trip."

This is not to suggest that *enablers* are empathetic without qualified conditions. Selling, like life in general, is the complement of irrational forces and self-imposed restrictions. This finds *enablers* using their heads to the advantage of others, but not at the expense of their hearts.

Enablers know they cannot succeed if they are in denial. They know that the first sale they must make is to sell themselves on themselves. Confidence is not bravado, not strutting your stuff, not pulling the wool down over yours or other people's eyes. Confidence is self-acceptance and appreciating that you are working within your capabilities to do your best.

Nor are *enablers* threatened if the situation doesn't listen well. Seeing the situation clearly may make it more challenging. What is said may be inconsistent with what is observed. This does not deter the *enabler*. Contradiction has been exposed in his own nature and that of others. He accepts this inconsistency as a given and works through it without becoming defensive.

The largest barrier to confidence is attitude. The predisposition to act in a certain way is programmed into us. In sales, this is demonstrated in the belief that straightforward engagement is bound to encounter rejection; that trust must be built in a circuitous route through guile rather than sincerity. *Chameleons* promote guile; *enablers* sincerity. For *chameleons*, selling is finessing to overcome objections, with *enablers* it is finding out what is needed.

One reason this discussion on *chameleons* and *enablers* is apropos is that most products and services of companies today are nearly indistinguishable from each other. The problem is matching and matchmaking. This is the imperative of *enablers*, whereas *chameleons* hawk their brands as if truly unique.

Enablers match needs to budget and what is needed and available. Knowing what my company lacked, which was a highly efficient positive displacement pump mentioned earlier, enabled me to design a system with that pump in mind instead of ours in the chemical feeding system recommended.

A few decades ago, that was not common, but it is increasingly a standard practice in servicing complex systems today. *Chameleons* may blast competitors, but enablers do not because they are likely to use them mixing and matching to satisfy customers' requirements.

Unfortunately, our ambivalent world stubbornly holds to ambiguous practices that serve no one.

Enablers may be tempted to resort to "no holds barred" aggression when empathy seems to be failing in the problem solving. That is to be expected. Nothing is ever either or. This is a way of saying there is likely to be some *chameleon* in every *enabler*. But equally so, *chameleons* can become enablers with a capacity to think outside the box. With the *enabler*, instinct uses insight to evaluate the situation. *Chameleons* would have to give the "male brain" a rest and to use the
"Feminine brain" a bit.

*   *   *

The cage we all encounter in an interpersonal sense is self-imposed. It is the cage we construct between ourselves and others. The wall of this cage dissolves if we can get past our biases, deceits, lies and false assumptions and become one with our subject.

To illustrate, once a painter was observed going to a certain hill overlooking the bay, setting up his easel and tripod chair, looking at the mountains and forests beyond for a good hour or more, then collapsing his equipment without painting a stroke. This went on for several days confounding an observer. So, one day, the observer asked the painter what he was doing. The artist told him he was painting the landscape. "But I've seen you now for several days and you haven't lifted your brush to the canvas once." The artist nodded his head. "That is true. My problem, you see, is I cannot paint until the landscape and I become one, and unfortunately, that has not yet occurred."

It is the same when we meet others and decide instantly who they are, what they are about, and what they need. We see them through our eyes and the eyes often lie, but seeing them through the heart, through our feelings, chances are, we get another sense of them. Some call this a "gut feeling," and such a feeling often guides us to the truth about another. Otherwise, we talk to each other through our respective cages that not only prevent connection and communication, but derail the building of trust. Enablers aren't looking for ways to outwit each other but to resolve issues of mutual concern.

Notes:

1. Partnership has been a central theme in *Confident Selling* and *Purposeful Selling*, now in its second editions, 2014.
2. You'll be hard pressed to find more than one or two quotations on selling in any book of quotations.

3. Granddaughter Rachel purchased a musical instrument for elementary school on eBay. The price was modest, but the shipping and handling was not.
4. Vance Packard was one of the first social critics to bring sociological conditions to the general reader. He did this with such books as *The Hidden Persuaders* (1957), *The Status Seekers* (1959), *The Waste Makers* (1960), *The Pyramid Climbers* (1962), *The Naked Society* (1964) and *A Nation of Strangers* (1972).
5. Joseph Campbell, *The Myth Makers*, MFJ Books, 1974, pp. 141-142.

TWENTY SIX

ENABLERS & THE FISHER PARADIGM©™

Confidence and empowerment are cousins in my opinion. Empowerment comes from within and typically it's stemmed and fostered by self-assurance. To feel empowered is to feel free and that's when people do their best work. You can't fake confidence or empowerment.

Amy Jo Martin, American author

TAPPING THE RELATIONAL SPHERE OF INFLUENCE

Enablers empower individuals to harness their intellectual capital to their specific purposes. The Fisher Paradigm©™ is a vehicle through which that can be achieved. Information is processed relative to three spheres of influence:

- Personality (Sense of Worth)
- Geography (Sense of Place)
- Demographics (Sense of Self)

Most of this is done in a split second or as an intuitive appraisal, as people as persons come in contact with each other. Enablers do this by processing this information, which in turn leads them to decide what action to take, now.

Personality Sphere (Sense of Worth)

A person's personality, his expressed values, sense of identity, appearance, and actions with you as well as with the people around him are evident. An organization has a personality. In a business climate, this is apparent from the reception on.

Geographic Sphere (Sense of Place)

A person carries his geography with him wherever he goes. This is his personal baggage. His comfort and conflict level are demonstrated in self-demands (expressions of pride) and role demands (approaches to work). These clues reveal the relationship between his *"Real Self"* (actual behavior) and *"Ideal Self"* (expected behavior). From this, it can be determined if he defines his situation accurately or inaccurately. If poorly defined, the work of enablers is more difficult.

Demographic Sphere (Sense of Self)

The person's age, gender, role, ethnicity, job, history, experience, relationship to others, along with maturity, mindset and thinking are reflected in his cultural DNA.

His *"Real Self"* or essence represents his intrinsic qualities with which he was born, while his personality or acquired self reflects his *"Ideal Self."* Given this, how he processes information (visually, verbally, spatially, and cognitively) are indicators of value and meaning to him. We advertise ourselves without knowing it by the way we talk, walk, relate, and do things. We are veritable billboards advertising what we are and who we think we are.

How this is done provides the bridge between the real and the ideal as perceived by the individual. This allows the enabler to use information to create trust and understanding in the problem solving.

Enablers take in the entire environment. Should this be a workplace, it includes the office, personnel and particulars of operation as a novelist might stage a scene or a painter might consider his canvas before placing brush to the surface.

Enablers note the person's control of control (*Personality Sphere*) and whether it is a congenial or hostile climate (*Geographic Sphere*), functional or chaotic (*Demographic Sphere*).

The distinction between chameleons and enablers is that chameleons will look past these obvious indicators and go blindly forward, whereas enablers will use this information to design their approach.

SEVEN VIRTUES OF ENABLERS

The first thing we think of when it comes to being successful is confidence. Confident selling does, indeed, require confident thinking, but confidence is not only a mindset but also a process for action. Enablers don't empower others, they facilitate their self-empowerment. They do this by engaging them in a meaningful and productive ways. People often have to be reminded of their power to put that power to work for them. This involves the seven virtues of enablers:

- *Enablers practice humility*: Enablers take their assets and limitations seriously, but not themselves. They use their assets with humility. They don't compare and compete, don't imitate or mirror colleagues or competitors, but develop their own style and approach. Enablers use their understanding of diversity in individuals and groups to tailor their approach accordingly to the demands of the situation. This involves bridging differences with understanding, and deficiencies with empathy.

Chameleons practice arrogance: Chameleons take themselves too seriously and see their role as telling the prospect what he wants to hear rather what he needs to know.

- *Enablers practice generosity*: Generosity is not limited to reliable service. Competitors are often partners in bringing the best value to a functional need with complementary products. Working with competitors in the interest of the customer is an act of prudence as well as generosity. Enablers are pushovers. Material success is important to them as well, but they know what you sow you reap. Generosity always comes back tenfold.

Chameleons practice greed: They sell whatever the traffic will bear. Since avarice is their guiding light, they believe it motivates everyone. Greed, of course, can never be satisfied.

- *Enablers practice restrain*: Human spontaneous combustion is always a possibility. The veil of suspicion always lurks in the shadows, which can trigger impulsive disruption. This cannot always be anticipated. Therefore, suspicions should be allowed to be expressed to reduce that possibility. On the other hand, enablers should be prepared to deal with stonewalling. *"It is clear you have had a bad experience before with our people. What exactly happened?"* Enablers don't resort to argument, but to clarification through open ended discussion. They show restrain by allowing suspicions and angst to be vented. By listening, this allows the person to take control of the interview. Enablers demonstrate control without needing to be in control.

Chameleons resort to bluster: They dispute the person's criticisms with argument, often choosing to take control by overwhelming the criticism with bombast, which finds them losing control. From this point forward, nothing they say is heard.

- *Enablers are moderate*: Everyone has a bad day; everyone sometimes says what they don't mean and regret. Everyone at one time or another is in a defensive posture. Guided by moderation, enablers maintain a sense of balance, a sense of humor during the circumstances. One enabler took such a blast from a prospect that it led him to say:

"Wow! It must be my day to be in the lion's cage!" The prospect laughed, relaxed, and apologized. The hostile atmosphere was cut with humor. Moderation is a requirement of life: eating, sleeping, walking, talking, working, exercising, loving, and living. Enablers know this. They don't subscribe to the 80-hour week for chronology's sake. They work smart rather than hard. They have a moral center and compass to hold them on course.

Chameleons are excessive living on the edge, working, playing hard, driving themselves to the brink of disaster, and then compensating with periodic sabbaticals from drying out to exercising to the extreme, along with following a crash diet. Moderation is a framework of control. Enablers respect the demands of control. Chameleons take short cuts to cheat control.

- *Enablers are kind*: They may be bullied, abused, humiliated, compromised, or their competence questioned. Instead of taking umbrage, they ask themselves "why" and face down with their accusers with the same question. There has to be a reason. Even cruelty needs to be rectified. Enablers absorb this outburst in silence waiting for it to dissipate before exploring its origin. They may say: "Perhaps it would be better that I come another time." Once the catharsis is complete usually there is a mood swing back to the rational often with an apology. Enablers allow emotions to peak then deflate with the kindness of understanding silence.

Chameleons are heartless. No one is going to bully them! Who do they think they're talking to? Pride (*self-demands*) overcomes the job at hand (*role demands*). A chameleon was reported to have reacted in this manner: *"Sir, speaking person to person, forgetting that you are the general manager here and I am simply a salesman, you have no right to address me in those terms! No right at all!"* This resulted in a series of misfortunes for the salesman and his company, eventually resulting in the loss of a national account that amounted to millions.

The man he addressed so caustically never forgot this affront. In due course, he became the CEO of this multi-national corporation. What is sad to report is that the customer was right to be incensed. The chemical sales engineer had applied the wrong chemicals to the customer's system shutting down operations for several hours. Confession and contrition might have saved the day, but the chameleon was not of such a mind.

- *Enablers are loving*: Work is love made visible. Work as such cannot be prostituted by envy, greed, hate, fear, or evil. Love makes life worth living. Mature love in work is expressed in meaningful contribution. We also see it expressed in times of natural disasters, or when people are suffering. Enablers see loving as a way to bring out the best in others by understanding and accepting them as they are, not as they would like them to be. It is helping others to help themselves by making their situation better.

Chameleons are skeptical of feelings, incredulous of this business of loving: They would be horrified to suggest they should "love" their work and customers. They see them as marks. This loving business to them is being namby-pamby, weak and phony. Chameleons deplore weakness because they have never made peace with their own vulnerability. They abhor phoniness because they have never admitted to themselves that they are insincere and deceptive. How could they be loving when they have failed to be loving of themselves?

- *Enablers are diligent*: What we do is what we become. The purpose of life is what we do, not what we think of doing or plan on doing, but what we are doing, right now! The most important thing in life is to be needed; to be needed we must be useful; to be useful we must develop some kind of skill, which involves doing. The popular notion today is personal development, which in its present form is narcissistic. There is nothing wrong with personal development if it is a process of improved usefulness. Where it gets dicey is when it becomes an end in itself or totally self-aggrandizement. To enablers being diligent is manifold usefulness.

Enablers know to acquire value added skills involves taking risks and encountering the pain of failure. Without risks or pain, there is no growth, only stasis. Enablers are diligent and therefore experience success, but they do not rest on their laurels. They are dedicated to self-learning, and pushing the envelope to new experiences and challenges. Enablers read people without putting them into boxes. They are enriched by learning from them, and developing new ways of serving them. The happiest people are busy people, and the happiest busy people are those who have learned to let go of self and to embrace the world of service to others.

Chameleons are diligent for a discrete period, and then coast on their laurels, or what they have learned. They are knowers rather than learners, tellers rather than listeners, complainers rather than doers. When they sink into dismay, they feel a need to bring others down to their level. They look at enablers with contempt not realizing they are looking at the sunny side of themselves.

- *Enablers* and chameleons are part of the landscape. They are part of each other. Together, they represent the conflicts and contradictions, the consistencies and constructions that make up the way things get done or fail to get done.

Enablers and chameleons relate to the way we see ourselves.

Enablers learn to trust themselves with confidence that comes with letting go of self, allowing answers to surface. They know their success is not due to genius, but to a higher power that they have been able to tap.

Some calls this diligence, others God, others love, and still others simply letting go. In any case, it starts with not being afraid to love what you do, to appreciate who you are, and to accept where you are and have been, which is your history, and then showing the boldness of spirit to chart your course to where you want to go.

It is allowing your soul to touch everything you do and are. Like magic, it can transform a chameleon into enabler. When it does, life is a little easier for everyone.

TWENTY SEVEN

AN EXCHANGE:

WHEN MEN WON'T WORK & THE WOMEN WHO CARRY THEM!

Since creating a blog (peripateticphilosopher.blogspot.com), this missive has generated responses across the Western world. It seems I have let the genie out of the bottle.

Women, who have embraced continual change, have hunkered down making the most of sometimes difficult if not abusive situations. They write in unison, "I hear you."

Some have suggested I write a book on the subject. Others have asked what they should do about the situation, and I have made some comments about that.

For every hundred responses only one has been from a man. Surprisingly, men don't challenge my premise, or appear bitter. They simply feel lost as to what to do about this societal transition to a gender neutral situation as to roles and relationships of the two sexes. I will attempt to address that here.

I know this is April first, but this is not an "April Fools" missive. These are difficult times for everyone.

A READER WRITES (born and bred in the American Midwest):

Dr. Fisher,

Thank you for your missive. I don't think all women are the enablers for the men who don't work. Some men, like many women I know, are just plain lazy.

I guess I should never write things at 2 A.M. in the morning when I can't sleep, but felt I needed to add my 2 cents worth at that time in the morning I guess. I do enjoy your missives but have to look up many words you use sometimes. Reading you is a continuing learning experience for me. Hope you are well also.

Mary

DR. FISHER RESPONDS:

Dear Mary:

A fine two cents it is.

My inclination is to go for the jugular, exploring the weaknesses of men as they are shared with me from many women contributors. That landscape is not however gender specific as men can be just as abused and taken advantage by women.

Yes, there are lazy men and lazy women in our society, but they are a very small segment of the general public. Work is the essence of life for most Americans. We take pride in some kind of work.

Should we meet a stranger, we are inclined to ask what he or she does for a living. It is how we identify ourselves and get to know each other as persons.

We don't say, where did you go to school, what was your major, but how do you like to spend your time. We don't become billboards for institutions, elite schools or otherwise, or ask what fraternity or sorority to which you belong. Nor do we use the more subtle approach to calibrate the other person's pedigree by asking what prep school your children attend. To put it succinctly, we are just folks when we first meet, usually.

The late Joe Moldt was a classmate of mine at St. Patrick's grade school, but we went to different high schools. He was at my high school's fiftieth class reunion, and someone asked him where he worked. *"I work at Mercy hospital,"* Joe said. Then the classmate, asked, *"Are you a doctor?"* Without hesitation, Joe answered, *"No, I work in maintenance."*

That is identity. That is integrity. That reflects a man with a center proud of what he does and who he is.

America won World War Two with men of Joe's ilk and built itself into the lone superpower of the world over the last sixty-five years.

During that period, the world was changing. Thanks to the *Marshall Plan* and the *Truman Doctrine*, Europe got its feet back under it and rose to self-sustaining autonomy. The same can be said for Japan, South Korea, Israel and such countries as Iran, Egypt, Turkey and Saudi Arabia. America did the same in South East Asia for such countries as Singapore.

America built the post-World War Two world into a fine competitor.

Indigenous to America, it has always been most purposeful when it has had a viable enemy such as Germany and Japan in World War Two, and the Soviet Union in the post-World War Two "Cold War."
In 1989, when the Berlin Wall came down, and East and West Germany unified, America fed aid and technology into the renewed Republic of Germany, as it did to Japan and South Korea and other redeveloping countries after 1945.

Something happened to America, though, when the Berlin Wall came down. It was as if America no longer had to operate on all its cylinders, and could retreat back to the safety of its isolation between two giant oceans, the Atlantic and Pacific, with tranquil neighbors to the North and South in Canada and Mexico, and coast for the foreseeable future.

This was apparent to me as an American sailor on the flagship of the Sixth Fleet operating in the Mediterranean in the late 1950s, later as a consultant working across the United States, South America in the 1960s, then living and working in South Africa in 1968 and Europe in 1986.

It was apparent from those various venues that America was no longer feeling a menacing challenge from abroad, but was becoming increasingly and unapologetically comfortable by leading from behind. This was the equivalent of resting on its laurels gingerly slipping into complacency while disregarding an explosively changing and increasingly combative world.

Unwittingly, a suspect system, "*corpocracy*," evolved across industry and commerce, Wall Street and government, academia and the religious. These traditional institutions of society came to operate with infallible authority with business as usual practices whatever the challenges from abroad or within at home.

It was comparable to the "divine right of the anointed," those in charge as if by papal decree. No one complained as employment was booming, jobs were aplenty with generous pay and benefits that in Freudian parlance "kept a lid on the Id."

Despite colossal charades, blatant failures, and scandalous revelations, these institutions continued to operate with impunity whatever the circumstances.

This led to the real estate meltdown of 2008 and the insolvency of Wall Street and financial collapse of *"The Big Two"* (General Motors and Chrysler) of the automotive industry in 2009. These key chess pieces were deemed "too big to fail," requiring the federal government and taxpayers to save their bacon.

When I came back from Europe in 1990, I wrote a book describing precisely what I had experienced in Europe and over the course of my career to that date. I bought a house in the Tampa Bay area of Florida and settled down to write books and articles and give speeches at professional conferences on the new persona of American workers in the late 20th and early 21st century.

If truth be known, we Americans have always been suckers for optimism and avoid the idea much less the reality behind pessimism as if it were the plague. This was clearly apparent when
President Jimmy Carter gave his speech about America's "crisis in confidence."
On the evening of July 15, 1979, millions of Americans tuned in to hear President Jimmy Carter give the most important speech of his presidency. After sharing some of the criticism he had heard at talks at Camp David regarding energy, Egypt and Israel, Carter put his own spin on this. *"The solution of our energy crisis can also help us to conquer the crisis of the spirit in our country,"* the president said, asking Americans to join him in adapting to a new age of limits.

But he also admonished them, *"In a nation that was proud of hard work, strong families, close-knit communities and our faith in God, too many of us now tend to worship self-indulgence and consumption. Human identity is no longer defined by what one does but by what one owns."*

It was clearly a sermon from the bully pulpit. It had the themes of confession, redemption, and sacrifice. He was bringing the American people into this spiritual process that he had been through, and was presenting them with an opportunity for redemption as well as redeeming himself. It became his *"crisis in confidence"* speech, and the American people would have none of it.

They wanted a call for optimism, reassurance that despite the stormy clouds on the horizon that the future looked bright, that Americans were exceptional and would triumph in the end, not that Americans had become complacent and were in crisis. He never recovered from that candid delivery.

We were used to booms, but we liked to forget about the busts. In 2008, my house was valued at three times what I paid for it, only to slip after 2009 closer to the original price. Not planning to move, the value of my house has been an indicator of the health of the American economy. We have lived in this house twenty-three years and counting watching its value go up and down as if it were a yoyo.

A neighbor of mine bought essentially the same house on another street for that inflated value in 2006. Were he to sell today, chances are he would be underwater with his mortgage greater than what he could get if he sold the house. Purchasing a house has become as speculative as playing the stock market. This situation is likely to continue for at least the next few years. Therefore:

- It is not wise to attempt to keep up with the Joneses;
- It is good counsel to be a little pessimistic if not a little paranoid when making big purchases.

Author William L. Livingston IV has written perceptively on the subject and concludes that despite what we experience, optimism is endemic to the American character. Authors have to tread cautiously when pessimism is mentioned. Readers want to be reassured, not informed of the way it is. They want to be entertained, not advised to be alert and prudent.

ARE WE ABOARD "THE SHIP OF FOOLS?"

The *"ship of fools"* is an allegory that originated with Plato, and has been something of a fixture in Western literature. The allegory depicts a vessel without a pilot, populated by human inhabitants who are deranged, frivolous, and oblivious to the nature of the danger and ignorance and unconcerned of the ship's course.

The concept was outlined in the 15th century book *Ship of Fools* (1494) by Sebastian Brant. It also inspired Hieronymous Bosch with his famous painting, *Ship of Fools*.

Brant's novel has an entire fleet of ships setting sail from Basel, bound for the *Paradise of Fools*. In literary motif of the 15th and 16th centuries, the *ship of fools* served as parody to the *"ark of salvation"* of the Roman Catholic Church, which was in style at the time.

In 1962, American writer, Katherine Anne Porter, published her novel, *Ship of Fools*, which was set in the autumn of 1931. It was a frontal attack on a world that allowed the Second World War to happen. The novel was later the basis of a 1965 film.

Ship of Fools is also the title of a 2002 science fiction novel by Richard Paul Russo where the *Ship of Fools* is, not surprisingly, a space ship on which no one knows the destination.

In addition, *Ship of Fools* was the title of a book by the Irish journalist Fintan O'Toole on the causes of the financial crisis in Ireland, the metaphor being used to describe the Irish political establishment and their self-deception regarding the economic situation in the country. The Irish apparently are also not enamored of pessimism.

Theodore Kaczynski, more commonly known as *'The Unabomber'*, wrote a play *Ship of Fools* while in prison, which uses the allegory of the profligate state. In his novel, he advocates violent revolution on environmentalist grounds.

The alternate history novel *The Years of Rice and Salt* by Kim Stanley Robinson portrays a *"caravan of fools"* composed of outcasts, criminals and liberals, whose clashes with Muslim ideologues prompt them to abandon their lives in newly recolonized Al-Andalus and form new settlements in modern-day France.

If you are still with me, what I'm trying to point out is that the United States is in a state of flux and the rest of the world with her.

Not to be too disparaging, but we are all on this same *Ship of Fools* with seemingly nobody in charge. Too much too many too soon has happened in this mad rush into the future and has proven telling on us.

We have no choice but to build our lives one person at a time as sensibly and prudently as we have the wits to do so.

Women, perhaps because they carry our future survival in their womb, seem to deal with these mind boggling traumatic times better than their men.

Identity is still derived from what we do for a living. The problem is that change is moving so fast in that regard that what we have done and are used to doing may not exist anymore.

Millions of jobs have been lost because new skills are required and workers and managers have not been equal to facing this fact. Instead, fingers are pointed or promises are made by politicians and nothing changes. We are in a leadership funk across the board with those appointed to that role trying to do the impossible, as we go forward on our *Ship of Fools*.

- *Men Who Won't Work* have watched their normal livelihoods dry up because of obsolescent skills or because jobs were exported to other countries where the labor was cheaper. When a man does not have work;

when a man does not have pride in having a viable role in society, all bets are off.

- *Men Who Won't Work* never saw continuing education as part of their job, and so have failed to make that investment, waiting for the company to make it for them or for the situation to change to the way it was, which will never happen.

One of the great tragedies is our collective preoccupation with *content and context* as it relates to the idea that everyone needs a college education. Academic study is as much a vocation as the priesthood. College graduates now see academia as job training, and so universities have departed from the medieval mindset of the Renaissance to no longer be institutions of enlightenment but the more prosaic role of job training centers.

- *Men Who Won't Work* are not bad people. Chances are they are depressed people, people who have been marginalized because they have no faith in the system, find no reason to hope, and no place to put their love of doing.
- *Men Who Won't Work* see work has been taken from them, and they have done nothing wrong. These are the assembly workers, tool and die makers, and steel workers who are no longer needed. But there is a scarcity of carpenters, bricklayers, plumbers, pipe fitters, electricians, and computer technicians, appliance repairers, on and on and on. These are jobs that the *Men Who Won't Work* could be motivated to work and to find joy in the exercise. Invest in them!
- *Men Who Won't Work* have been left in the lurch. We take pride in being the schoolhouse of the world with our great universities. But while our heads are in the clouds about this, we have not made it easy for ordinary Americans to find their way to a decent living, decent lifestyle and decent return on their individual investment. Shame on us!

A century ago, when the American population was 100 million, eighty percent of Americans worked on farms or worked in industries that supported farming. Today, with the population 320 million, only two percent of Americans are involved in farming. Quietly and efficiently, the science of agriculture continues to educate farmers so that farmers not only feed the nation but the world.

When I worked as a chemist for Standard Brands, Inc. in Clinton, Iowa, I once found myself in Dewitt, a small town in Clinton County. Four farmers were drinking coffee and having breakfast at this family coffee shop, and I got to talking to them. All four farmers were graduates of Iowa State University in agriculture. They found my surprise a bit disconcerting. I apologized. One said, *"How else do you think we'd get these crop yields?"* Point taken.
The shift in jobs and the requirements of work is not the only thing that is changing drastically. The world is moving toward a collection of *City States* reminiscent of Athens, Rome and Baghdad.

One hundred years ago, two out of every ten people lived in an urban area. In 1990, it was four in ten. By the time a child entering primary school today turns forty, seven out of ten across the globe will reside in metropolitan areas.

Influence will shift gradually away from national governments to *City States*, especially in countries chronically suffering bureaucratic paralysis and political gridlock.

This should give us pause. From a century ago and the dominance of American farming to what is on the horizon, it is necessary to find something equivalent to the farmer's paradigm, which is a learning and adjusting template and not the knowing and resisting mindset that seems to still plague American workers and society's institutions.

TWENTY EIGHT

SELF-CONFIDENCE, COPING AND CULPABILITY

"Human spirit is the ability to face the uncertainty of the future with curiosity and optimism. It is the belief that problems can be solved, differences resolved. It is a type of confidence. And it is fragile. It can be blackened by fear and superstition."

Bernard Beckett, New Zealand author

STUFF HAPPENS AND THEN WE DIE!

The question of confidence, who has it and who doesn't, is revealed by an intricate complex of subtly interconnected emotional states forming a singular framework and approach to daily life.

Self-confidence has taken a hit in recent times due in no small measure to an emerging climate of doubt and uncertainty. Nothing is certain anymore if it ever was, but there once existed that imagined confidence.

That has vanished with economic fluctuations, chronic national and international crises, unreliability of what we call our gender, collapsing belief systems, while nobody seems to be in charge anywhere. This has led to the cynical suggesting, "Stuff happens and then you die."

Misplaced is an appreciation for the richness and diversity of human experience with its endless variety of people, places and things as increasingly these have become cross currents with false expectations spiraling individuals and societies into a torrent of despair:

- Terrorists took control of two commercial airliners and flew them into the Twin Towers in New York City on September 11, 2001, killing nearly 3,000 innocent people and reducing these magnificent structures to rubble.

- In 2003, President George W. Bush launched a preemptive invasion of Iraq claiming Saddam Hussein had weapons of mass destruction, which proved completely false.

- In 2008, there was an economic meltdown on Wall Street with collapsing banks and brokerage houses, and a wave of bank failures across the globe threatening another *Great Depression* even worse than that of 1929. The US Federal Government felt compelled to bailout businesses too "big to fail" with taxpayers' money such as General Motors, Chrysler and Wall Street, an approach that was also taken to that crisis by European and Asian governments.

- In 2011, the Tahoka (Japan) earthquake and tsunami took nearly 16,000 lives destroying more than 120,000 building, and collapsing another 300,000. The Japanese Prime Minister Naoto Kan said, *"In the 65 years after the end of World War II, this is the toughest and the most difficult crisis for Japan."* Around 4.4 million households in northeastern Japan were left without electricity and 1.5 million without water.

The tsunami caused nuclear accidents, a level 7 meltdown at three reactors in the Fukushima Daiichi Nuclear Power Plant. This necessitated the evacuation of hundreds of thousands of residents with chances of them ever returning to their homes between unlikely to none.

At least three nuclear reactors suffered explosions due to hydrogen gas that had built up within their outer containment buildings after cooling system failure resulting from the loss of electrical power. Residents within a 12 mile radius of the Fukushima Daiichi Nuclear Power Plant were evacuated. The area today is little more than a death zone, uninhabited with questions of why it was allowed to happen.

- The American withdrawal from Iraq in 2013 led to a civil war in that country. That spun over into Syria and Turkey with ISSI, an al Qaeda like terrorist group, declaring itself a new nation state. ISSI commenced to take hostages, beheading scores of people further destabilizing the Middle East. Millions of Syrian refugees have fled to Lebanon and Jordan to avoid the carnage.

These and other unexpected or unanticipated developments have followed the withdrawal of American forces from war torn Iraq and Afghanistan with tribal and ethnic hostilities filling the vacuum.

Equally wrenching, these events continue unabated across the globe with citizens preferring to act as if unconscious of them. Yet that is impossible. Stress related diseases are palpably evident. Society's collective anxiety is on display with the flagrant use of illegal recreational drugs accompanied by the soaring crime rate in murder, rape, domestic violence, suicide, homicide, genocide and riots.

We are in the *Information Age* and there are no secrets anymore. Billions of souls across the globe have instant knowledge of any untoward or disruptive event. Sometimes the social media are the last to know as citizens on the spot have already recorded the relevant data. Seemingly everyone is at the ready to download pictures on their mobiles as these devices have become the worry beads of the postmodern secular world.

LONGING FOR STABILITY IN AN UNSTABLE WORLD

Self-regard and confusion of aims reside beneath the patina of public life, often to a chaotic degree concealing presumed motivation and authentic experience.

We long for some unitary truth that will transcend our problems, but are dogged by distractions that hinder that routine. In the course of a century, we have departed from our spiritual anchors of family and church to scientism and material secularism blurring our boundaries and blunting our progress to a consoling peace. We have created an alien of self-estrangement having forgotten how fundamental a spiritual life governs human existence. In the process, we have left ourselves behind, homeless minds bereft of self-confidence and self-control.

Laws now divide us between science and Utopia, effectiveness and vanity. In every realm of our lives, we have relegated our existence to reason and science having forgotten the contentment of the unknown and unknowable.

We are governed by an expected protocol that has no roadmap, charting a course that has no certain destination, moving in synchrony without a moral compass wondering why we are lost when the past is treated as the future. We cannot seem to extrapolate ourselves from the detritus of the 20th century carnage and chaos.

We have limped into the 21st century bruised and beaten with misplaced optimism expecting to survive in this climate of doubt on the ingenuity of man, alone. Given this predicate, we have yet to decide whether our creative or destructive capacities are to prevail.

We as human beings can be radically altered, re-educated, reconditioned and turned topsy-turvy into something other than what we are or what we thought we were.

Daniel Yankelovich writes in *New Rules: Search for Self-Fulfillment in a World Upside Down* (1981) that traditional ethics of self-denial and self-reliance are being replaced by self-indulgence in an effort to seek narcissistic self-fulfillment. In other words, not only is there no longer a roadmap, there no longer are rules to point the way.

Yankelovich is writing in the tradition of such cultural pique of David Riesman's *"The Lonely Crowd"* (1950) and William H. Whyte's *"The Organization Man"* (1950). These observers were sharing their annoyances of the much more quiet norms of the 1950's. The current age, in contrast, is much more muddled and upside down.

The traditional American credo:

"I will work hard, defer my gratification, swallow my frustrations, love my spouse and family, and, in return, I will receive a steady and increasing income, a house in the suburbs, have a loving family, and the respect of my community."

This myth is now committed to history.

That post-WWII cliché was displayed with much confidence between 1945 (the triumphant end of that war) and 1975, when Japan and South East Asia quietly stole the manufacturing base away from the United States.

Wages since the 1980s have failed to appreciate, tens of thousands of manufacturing jobs have been lost forever, and the American dream and with it the formerly sacrosanct views of marriage and family, women's roles, work, and leisure time, money, and security have faded away. We are truly in a new day.

That cultural shift came at a time when the United States was on route to double digit inflation and double digit unemployment. At the present moment, forty years later, the American economy is relatively stagnant. Meanwhile, politicians, pundits and gurus continue to promote self-assertive psychologies insisting the future is in our hands.

The future is actually hostage to failing schools, high illiteracy rates, worthless high school diplomas and college degrees when it comes to the new skill required on the job of a digital economy. In addition, we have a crumbling infrastructure while commercial, industrial, academic and religious institutions have failed to take inventory of their deficiencies, or to anticipate and be in the ready to engage the material and spiritual needs of a changing society.

Aldous Huxley attempted to stimulate our collective unconscious with the shock of *Brave New World* (1932) as he anticipated the impact on society of cloning, robotics and pharmaceuticals used to alter states of consciousness.

George Orwell followed with *Nineteen Eighty-Four* (1949) to alert us to the dangers of a closed spiritually vapid totalitarian state of omnipotent authority and ubiquitous intrusion with the metaphor of "Big Brother" watching us 24/7, as he is today. Three quarters of a century later, Orwell's dearth of privacy and freedom and Huxley's prescription for disaster are now common fare everywhere.

We have become an obliging parody of ourselves as if a patch quilt of synthetic pieces grafted onto our collective conscience and free floating anxiety have come to represent our totality. Our fixed habits and uncritical assumptions have come to leave us in the void, supported only by the frivolous language of psychological psychobabble, corporate speak, the hubris of science and the annoying cacophony of the media catchall cable television 24/7.

We think in words, as I am doing here, but fail to realize language is suffused with irrelevance and clashing metaphors, and therefore a disingenuous retreat from reality to an elaborate hoax that we embrace with surreal delight.

It is only when our nerves touch other nerves deep within us that we feel what we are feeling, think what we are thinking, and are conscious of the electric shock of what is genuine and germane to us. Then, we are in touch with our spiritual side. Otherwise, we go through life robotically with nothing touching our essential self. We become discarded furniture of the world.

TOWARDS A MORE CONSCIOUS SELF

Self-confidence requires self-awareness, self-acceptance, and self-actualization. Each requirement synergistically supports the other. Together they put us in charge, in control. It allows us to pulsate with energy, passion, meaning and joy, a satisfying medium to life's endeavors.

In a pragmatic sense, confidence evolves from the problem solving, as problem solving is central to our sense of self. Americans pride themselves in taking on and successfully dispatching challenges, that is, when problems are external to themselves.

Do not confuse defining the problem with the problem-solving. We have an appetite for seeking solutions and giving a polite pass to the hard work of problem defining. As a consequence, we are adept at generating solutions looking for problems to attach to these, and for this obsession we have the world that we have created.

*You cannot effectively **seek** solutions to problems. You can only effectively **create** solutions out of the problem solving.* That is as true in the personal as it is in the occupational sphere. The effective problem solver is well acquainted with his subconscious or spiritual side where most answers reside, and therefore seldom surface. Problem solvers are not comfortable with this meditative process for it sounds too much like philosophy. That said it is nonetheless the location of the creative well.

The aim of science is to note the similarities in the behavior of objects and to construct propositions of generality from which the largest number of such uniformities can be logically deduced.

For the novelist and philosopher it is just the opposite. Feelings and introspections do not lend themselves to the rigors of mathematics, yet science separated from that most real world of the intuition can result in unintended negative consequences. Does anyone know where cloning, the use of drones, the forgiveness of self-indulgence with pharmaceutical palliatives, or the building of nuclear reactors will lead? Of course not, this is not the purview of science, but it is the purview of the novelist and the philosopher.

The novelist sets forth subconsciously a somewhat biased way of looking at people, places and things. He does this to exercise control over the landscape with which he intends to develop his story.

Journalist Malcolm Muggeridge claims he can identify every one of Tolstoy's characters in his novels as people in the Great Russian's life. This lifting of the subconscious into a bevy of classical figures has found our conscious minds celebrating his works, and using his insights to chiaroscuro of character as guidance for our own. This is what it *"to understand"* is largely about.

Literary language describing ordinary experience is employed in an opposite manner to that of scientific language. Feelings and impressions are treated as facts and are integral to the story, but not so in science. Massive amounts of data are reduced to verifiable facts, and proved to be true in a discrete scientific process.

Literary language, so used, is not meant to develop unassailable principles but to communicate relatively stable characteristics of an external world, which forms the frontiers of our common experience in a life largely consisting of external controls.

It is good that we have science but sensible self-adjusting, self-adapting methods as well. Obviously, this methodology cannot be measured precisely or weighed exactly or fully described at all. It is necessary that the reader plug into it with the relevance of the story to his own life beyond being simply entertainment.

What I am saying here has only value if it has value to you, the reader. Otherwise, it has no value and can be ignored. Like Muggeridge's comment about Tolstoy, my writing rises out of empirical experience and is as much a part of me, as I hope it will find connection with you.

Confidence is metaphor for fluctuations in experience that are our teachers, and which become the basis of our understanding of what works for us and what does not. No one can teach or tell us this. We must find it out for ourselves.

Unfortunately, we live in the age of the professional, where knowledge is power, and *'power'* often gets lost in what can and cannot be done. We trust experts more than we trust our own experience.

Since education is constructed on the basis of what has worked before, there is a rigid dependence and loyalty to the past. We are asked to trust what we are taught. When experience proves inconsistent with that learning, we are expected to adjust to that teaching.
That has proven a fatal flaw to the educational system as education has been reduced to an infallible construct rather than a malleable learning tool. Students leave with diplomas and degrees in miseducation. They enter the workforce as educated but not necessarily educable.

Confidence is the practical genius that differentiates learners from knowers, and listeners from tellers. It is the difference between people having a conscious self with a trusted center that governs their behavior, or a rationalization repertoire that apologizes for its dysfunction.

When we are on top of things, we behave confidently because we are confident. We may not be able to explain why we are so. We just are. We need not worry. It is like being able to ride a bike. As soon as you learn, you may not be able to explain how it is done, but you know the skill is part of you.

IS THERE A CRISIS IN CONFIDENCE?

President Jimmy Carter got into trouble, as pointed out earlier, giving a "crisis in confidence" speech. The nation was in an economic slump and he turned to the political scientist James MacGregor Burns to write his speech with such a compelling phrase. This was meant to be in the style reminiscent of the fireside chats of President Franklin Delano Roosevelt during WWII, but it had quite the opposite impact.

The president was dressed casually in a cardigan sweater to suggest intimacy. Unfortunately, the "crisis in confidence" speech found the president's popularity tumbling, and the nation didn't want someone like themselves but someone they could look up to with authority and presence displaying the symbolic persona of leadership, but instead were greeted like themselves in casual attire.

Recently, *The New York Times* columnist David Brooks wrote a column on how Americans' self-confidence had also pummeled in this new century. Brooks asked readers to respond to the question of their self-confidence.

- A mother wrote that she might as well have her vocal cords cut because her children want her to stay calm, talk nice to the point of not wasting their time.
- A military man claimed women shut down women who are confident more than men do.
- Another woman, a business owner, claimed that workers don't want her to interfere with their dress or manners, much less their work, and prefer her to act as if invisible, blending into the woodwork as passively as wallpaper.
- Another person pronounced that all men and women suffer equally from "under confidence." Men bluff their way through while women choose to be skeptical and to look for advice or simply remain passive.

In each of these instances, the projection of spineless confidence is centered on the need to please others at the expense of pleasing 'self,' preferring the role of victim to that of victor.

Syndicated columnist Leonard Pitts shows what happens when our confidence deserts us.

Pitts writes of Brenda Heist who showed up at the police station in Key West, Florida stating she was a missing person. Eleven years ago, when the bottom fell out of her marriage, and she was turned down for housing assistance, three strangers found her crying in a park and asked her to hitch a ride with them. From that moment forward, her existence went into a tailspin of false alliances, petty crimes, panhandling, trailer parks, and common law marriages, sleeping under bridges, and working as a housekeeper. This lifestyle was mirrored on her recent mug shot, measured against her old driver's license photograph. She looked at least a decade older than her actual age.

Pitts believes everyone thinks at one time or another of running from life, but it is just that, the thought and not the act. Yet, tens of thousands of people do it every year.

Brenda Heist's daughter says her mother can rot in hell, her husband doesn't want her back, and the saddest part of all, she is so damaged that she doesn't want herself either. With confidence, we embrace our resistance to life's challenges and soar over them, but with despair, we run away from life and ourselves until life catches up with us.

New York Times columnist Maureen Dowd, while not engaging this subject of confidence directly, implies its relevance by default.

Dowd's subject is sexual harassment citing a Pentagon study estimating that 26,000 men and women in the military were sexually assaulted in 2012. Only 3,374 incidents were reported, as the majority of victims were afraid to lose a paycheck, while only 238 assailants were convicted.

The columnist profiled United States Air Force Colonel Jeffrey Krusinski who was accused of sexual battery. Krusinski, it so happens, is in charge of the sexual assault prevention programs for the U.S. Air Force.

Dowd bolstered her column against Krusinski by reminding us of the Thomas-Hill hearings, in which Supreme Court Justice Clarence Thomas was Anita Hill's boss, and was accused by her of vulgar and insinuating behavior while in his employ. Thomas at the time was the nation's top enforcer of laws against workplace sexual harassment.

The angels and demons of our nature are often revealed by what we claim to be vehemently against rather than for. Our angels take on the hue of our demons revealing our buried secrets, and personal obsessions, while presenting the persona of the high-minded person.

Ergo, be skeptical of the person who protests too much. That person may be revealing more naked truths than he would care for you to know.

Confidence is an enabling disposition, and exposes culpable behavior for what it is, how it takes hold, and why those who seem the most in control and confident, are more likely out of control and victim to their own personal demons.

TWENTY NINE

WHO ARE YOU, WHERE ARE YOU, RIGHT NOW?

"To thine own self be true" – with what a promise that phrase sings in our ears!

Lionel Trilling, *Sincerity and Authenticity* (1980)

In the social jungle of human existence there is no feeling of being alive without a sense of identity.

Erik H. Erikson, *Identity, Youth, and Crisis* (1968)

In healthy people (motivation) usually is autonomous of its origins. Its function is to animate and steer a life toward goals that are in keeping with present structure, present aspirations, and present conditions.

Gordon W. Allport, *Personality and Social Encounter* (1955)

To see ourselves as others see us can be eye-opening. To see others as sharing a nature with ourselves is the merest of decency. But it is a far more difficult achievement to see ourselves amongst others, as a local example of the forms human life has locally taken, a case among cases, a world among worlds.

Clifford Geertz, *Local Knowledge* (1985)

This is a society in which the individual can only rarely and with difficulty understand himself and his activities as interrelated in morally meaningful ways with those of other, different Americans.

Robert Bellah, et. al., *Habits of the Heart* (1985)

ASKED BUT NOT NECESSARILY ANSWERED

You can see from these various quotations that none of us knows, really, who we are not even those who claim to be students of the question or scholars whose beat is to provide such answers.
We are pretty much an anomaly to ourselves, but we do try to make sense even if it is only with nonsense.

It would be so easy to be overwhelmed with this question. Man throughout the ages has been asking himself this question, invariably coming up with an answer not terribly different from his predecessors. This should not be surprising as we are all working with the same machine, our brain. But is that true? What of the body's role? We shall explore this. But first, let us put this in perspective of how serious an issue it is to self-knowing.

THE SHRINKING OF OUR HORIZONS

On Friday the 13th, December 13, 2013, a young lady wrote:

I was a well-adjusted mostly happy 20-year-old. And then I wasn't. I've never been superstitious, but it was an unlucky day, I woke up at 6 a.m. after a week filled with intense panic attacks. I was sleeping in my parent's bedroom, something I hadn't done since I was a child. I wanted to die. I was a star student at the University of Florida, home for winter break. I'd dealt with anxiety in the past, but never like this. Things were getting worse, and I was desperate to feel better. Don't worry, my mom told me. We're going to get you help. It turns out, it's very expensive to be mentally ill in America.[1]

This confession is unfortunate, but far too common. Many of us allow the pressures of modern life, and the constant need to progress, to get better, to be high achievers, to set the curve, and then we fall on our own sword and wonder why, or what has happened as this young lady has.

Then instead of dialing down our nervous rush to the future, instead of taking quiet inventory of where we are, as well as who we are, and how we got to be in this mess, we turn to professionals to bail us out with psychobabble along with some life soothing, life comforting pharmaceutical elixir.

Seldom do we stop to wonder if these psychiatrists, these psychologists, these psychotherapists are not on the same merry-go-round that is going faster and faster at breakneck speed. By some absurd logic we don't see them governed by the same insanities that are common to our culture. Somehow we see them in a cerebral rhythm dancing slowly and confidently to life's challenges that however consume us but of which they are protected. We can't imagine their horizons shrinking, and that one day they might also find themselves out-of-control, but alas, it happens.

Professionals in all walks of life, from medicine to psychiatry to academia to command and control positions in commerce, industry, government and education, many are falling on their swords as well for failure to step back, take a "time out," and examine where they are, how they got there, as well as who they are, right now.

We have fancy names for these maladies including the most popular of all, being bi-polar, which means in common parlance that you are running into and away from yourself at once, and therefore are incapable of deciding whether you are coming or going. In other words, you are incapable of functioning without a menu of mood altering medication.

It becomes a problem of identity, and we have come to accept someone else's assessment of this personal conundrum, usually a paid professional, then our own sense of the situation. Our rationale for doing so is that these experts devote their lives to such questions so, who are we to doubt their evaluations? The answer is an unequivocal "we don't!" So, the question is moot.

It never occurs to us that they could be hucksters with credentials from Harvard Medical School or Johns Hopkins Psychiatric Center. Surely they know what is best for us; surely they have our best interests at heart; surely it never crosses their minds that we may be worth $50,000 - $100,000 to them as a client.

Moreover, it is unlikely that we consider they are exposed to the same vicissitudes in life as we are: they marry, divorce, have affairs, drinking problems, spouse abuse, child neglect, and bouts of depression, anxiety, and such trauma that they lose control. Yet, it happens. We read about it in newspapers, books and magazines all the time. *No one is immune to the vagaries and verities of modern life.* Doubt and contradiction are endemic to everyone.

Just as you cannot separate me, the person, from what I write here, the same holds true of what you read on the question of identity.

We process information from "experts" as self-evident and accept it without questioning as to its actual merits to our situation and self-understanding. We assume "they" know because they are in the business of knowing.

It is as if we think philosophers and theologians, psychiatrists and psychologists, priests and nuns, educators and pundits, gurus and mystics hold the keys to the source material unfathomable to us in our self-confessed confusion. It never occurs to us that they may have been attracted to the said discipline to escape their own personal demons.

Sociologist Billy G. Gunter has studied this propensity, and has identified it as "ambient deficiency motivation," that is, we are attracted to what we lack or believe will save us. For example:

- The criminal to become a police officer,
- The profligate sinner, a priest,
- The prostitute, a nun,
- The mentally troubled, the psychologist,
- The dull student, an academic.

It is therefore unlikely to occur to us that they may be exploring this source material to penetrate their own perplexities to establish some sense of confidence in their own identity and purpose in life.

We have a propensity to look outside of our cage for answers to personal conundrums instead of inside our hearts to the indelible impression of experience. Scholars are no different than the rest of us. They are on the same journey as we are only sometimes more maniacal about the exercise.
Whenever we get beyond skin deep issues, we find we behave as a common species.

The irony is that many of those we elevate to such authority status are lost men looking for an audience for authentication. Nigel Dennis writes in *Cards of Identity* (1984):

"On all matters of fact I am perfectly honest: I can state dates, acts of reason with absolute veracity. But once I start confessing the why-and-wherefore of my behavior (as one is expected to do in a book), I become so entertained by the personal drama of it all that everything I put down has a wonderful ring of truth: I feel myself growing from a particular person into a universal design."

Now, before we congratulate Nigel Dennis for the sincerity of this revelation, take a pause.

As candid as this remark may seem, have no doubt it is meant to capture the reader's attention to relax suspicion and approach what is to follow with an open mind.

The shadow play of self-help books has a wide market and mass appeal. German psychotherapist Erik Erikson latched on to the hunger of the American conscience for ego identity and self-improvement. He did this with such tantalizing titles as *Childhood and Society* (1961), *Insight and Responsibility* (1964) and *Identity, Youth and Crisis* (1968).

Erikson understood the anxious American temperament for belief in progress and happy endings. He developed a clear formula to satisfy that need. What's more, it was a need that invited the expert with the certainty that someone else possessed that key. We are quick to claim genius for these people with answers while seldom wondering at the relevance of the proposed remedies for us. Incredibly, we are disinclined to ask them to take off their masks, but willingly remove our own.

Irish author James Joyce took his mentally troubled daughter, Lucia Joyce to the celebrated Swiss psychotherapist, Carl Jung. She only got worse for the attention. Carol Loeb Shloss writes perceptively about this episode in *"Lucia Joyce"* (2003).

The Swiss medical man suffered his own demons, which he was fond to write about, while suffering something akin to delusion of grandeur, revealed in the controversial study, "The Aryan Christ: The Secret Life of Carl Jung" by Richard Noll (1997). Noll reveals Jung as the all too human man, a genius, who believed he was a spiritual prophet. In the process, the author shows Jung came from a family troubled with madness and religious obsessions.

DONNING THE MASK

Erik H. Erikson's soothing counsel on matters of conflicting identity was not there for his daughter when she was going through a mind wrenching divorce. She had to turn to her mother for her sanity who had no credentials at all. *The Atlantic Monthly ("Fame: The Power and Cost of a Fantasy,"* November 1999) gave her an opportunity to explain her pain in terms of her celebrated father's public and private self:

How was I to reconcile my experience of that emotionally fragile man (who understood so little about his feelings or mine and was terrified by both) with the public image of the intellectual pioneer who had challenged the authority of the great Sigmund Freud, daring to revise some of Freud's basic assumptions about human nature? How was I to reconcile the picture of the father I knew at home with the image of him as he appeared in public, where he radiated a humble but confident sense of his own ability to understand human behavior and to help others -- and where he demonstrated (both in his writing and in his personal style) an exceptional level of comfort in exploring the most intimate human emotions?

In the public sphere he was the authority on feelings, and his audience received emotional nourishment and reassurance from him. In my lifelong effort to reconcile the two seemingly disparate facets of my father's personality, I feel I have come to understand something general about the nature of fame.

In the relationship between the public image of a famous person and the private human being there is inherently something profoundly paradoxical. The public image is the reverse of the private person as experienced by him or herself and by intimate others. It might be accurate to say that the public image reflects what the private person most longs to be. It represents an ideal self.

It gets even murkier. Erikson, the identity architect, wasn't Erikson at all, but rather Erik Homburger. In his youth, he was as uncertain about his religion as about his parentage. His observant Jewish family was jarred when he formally broke off relations with the rabbi at the local synagogue. He began to study the Christian Gospels and was electrified one morning when he heard the Lord's Prayer spoken in Luther's German.

Without any formal training or credentials, a Freudian group hired him on the basis of his way with children. What is ironic is that Anna Freud, Sigmund Freud's daughter, found him personally appealing and professionally useful. She was happy to welcome a tall handsome, talented young man of Gentile appearance who was attracted to their revolutionary enterprise.

Erikson's genius lay in his extraordinary clinical insights, not in academia. A clinical artist if anything, he kept journals since a young boy. These are full of insights that reflect his troubled childhood. With Anna Freud's blessing, in any case, he came to America and assumed clinical positions at Harvard, Yale, and the University of California at Berkeley. In 1939, he became an American citizen, changed his name to Erik H. Erikson and launched a most successful literary and academic career (see Lawrence J. Friedman, *Identity's Architect: A Biography of Erik H. Erikson*, 1999).

Then there is the case of Bruno Bettelheim, who for more than four decades, was regarded by the public-at-large as one of the world's most important and influential psychotherapists, a Viennese intellectual who stood as "one of Freud's few genuine heirs of our time."

In fact, Bettelheim was a lumber dealer who grandly invented himself with a faked set of academic credentials after immigrating to the United States in 1939. In the years that followed, deception followed deception as Bettelheim claimed that he had traveled in Freud's circle, had treated autistic children in Vienna, had interviewed 1,500 fellow prisoners for his famous psychological study of concentration camp behavior, and had been freed from Buchenwald through the intervention of Eleanor Roosevelt.

A gifted writer if also fabricator, he headed the *Orthogenic School for Emotionally Disturbed Children* at the *University of Chicago* for three decades. There he continued his fabrications, maintaining that he had treated "hundreds" of schizophrenic children who feared for their lives at the hands of their parents, shaping pseudonymous case histories to enhance his reputation, and claiming, with concocted statistics, that he was returning 85 percent of his young patients to normal lives.

Popularly known as "Dr. B," he often spun angrily out of control and abused the children both physically and emotionally, all the while insisting in his books and from the lectern that such punishment was absolutely verboten.

Autism, he insisted in such books as *The Uses of Enchantment* (1977), could be treated successfully with psychotherapy has proven wrong as well as ill advised. Autism has proven to have a physiological origin in the brain.

Bettelheim won the *National Book Award* for this book that dealt with the psychological meaning of fairy tales. Later, parts of this work were discovered to have been plagiarized. In 1990 he died by his own hand, by asphyxiation, his head covered in a plastic bag.

Biographers relate that Bruno Bettelheim was a boy who grew up in a home darkened for years by his father's struggle with syphilis, a son who felt ugly, loathed his poor eyesight, and resented having to drop out of the *University of Vienna* at age twenty-three to take over the lumber business after his father died. He was plagued with depression all his life and felt constantly the outsider, a self-hating Jew who compensated by noisily blaming the Jews of Europe for walking into the ovens of the *Holocaust* without a fight (see Richard Pollak, *The Creation of Dr. B: A Biography of Bruno Bettelheim,* 1997).

Then there is Werner Hans Erhard, the founder of *est* (*Erhard Seminar Training*), the most popular guru style system of self-discovery of the 1970s. He left a wife and four children and his original name, John Paul Rosenburg in Ohio, slipped off to California, and created a new identity and persona. He advertised himself as a critical thinker with transformational models for people to rebuild their lives. He and *est* became the rage of Hollywood's tinsel town set, which in turn spread across the United States and Western Europe.

Erhard created a mixed bag of disciplines, consciousness techniques, and religious systems to wow his devotees. His story is the equivalent of an American soap opera. He enticed the American will with Oriental mysticism directing them to journey inward in a smorgasbord of half-baked intellectual appetizers. This is also the story of a rogue genius who struggled mightily for self-mastery and self-fulfillment from an early age. With mesmerizing efficiency, he made his devotees feel that their struggle matched his own (see W. W. Bartley, III, *Werner Erhard: The Transformation of a Man,* 1978).

Identity and authenticity at root spring from the loneliness and anxiety our secular society has produced. We feel untethered, free floating in consuming angst. Before, it had been comforting when there was God to turn to because turning to God was, in fact, turning to one's inner self for peace, solace, and renewed hope.

The men profiled here recognized the vacuum and rushed to fill it as God's replacement. They came into being because modern society willed it to be so. They took on a role we gladly surrendered as it meant we could abandon self-responsibility. We are at the ready for self-escape.

SEARCH FOR IDENTITY

In achieving personal identity, most of us must start back at the beginning and rediscover our feelings. The tendency, when looking back, often is one of self-pity blaming parents, peers, circumstances, teachers, preachers, coaches, or partners for our lot in life. Even then the inventions are often wide of the mark as Freud shows in his many studies.

There may be precedence in our histories of real or imagined abuse. There can also be confusion. My middle aged daughter was recently retelling me of a favorite vacation of her childhood, and in the retelling involved the juxtaposing of different times, places and happenings incongruous with the actual vacation she was remembering. This happens.

Likewise, it is surprising how many of us have only a general sense of what we feel. We say I feel "fine" or "lousy" or "okay," as if we have no actual idea. It is just a mechanical response. In T.S. Eliot's *"Hollow Men,"* we experience ourselves as

Shape without form, shade without colour,

Paralyzed force, gesture without motion.

For many of us, it is hard work to feel. We have little intuitive sense of who we are, where we are or what we are because of this seemingly sensory deficit. However, if we would "listen to the body," we would know when to work, when to rest, when and with whom to engage in relationships, and with whom not to trust or go near. We would also feel what situations create the premonition of danger and the ones that give us the reassurance of safety.

- *The body knows and is ever alert if we would but listen to it.* So, the first step is to welcome the body back into union with the self. It means experiencing the body from the pleasure of eating and resting to a sense of when to withdraw and regroup, indeed, when to call "a time out!"

- *Awareness of one's feelings lays the groundwork for the second step: knowing what you need and want.* Again, most people cannot identify needs or separate them from wants. Life can so easily fall into the cage of routine in which they are treated as synonymous.

You need a job to provide for yourself and family, but what do you want? A career? A college education? The luxury and freedom to be able to write a book? What? The adolescent disposition, which can grab hold of a person in his youth and hold on for a lifetime, represents a failure to understand and realize the difference between need and want.

An obsessive-compulsive person, or even a person who is primarily of an impulsive nature, is unlikely to have a firm grasp of his feelings. Feelings are his master.

A popular limerick of Freud's fits this dilemma: *The ego is the lid on the id.*

Stated another way, reason has no control over our impulsive nature. In transactional analytical (T/A) terms, it would suggest the child, which is the "id," has control over the adult, which is the
"ego," and there is no parent around (see Eric Berne, *Games People Play: The Psychology of Human Relationships*, 1964, and John M. Dusay, *Egograms: How I See You and You See Me*, 1977).

- *The third step in this process of rediscovering our feelings and their relationship to our needs and wants is to recover our relations with the subconscious.* This has been deemed an alien force in modern man. We are programmed to think, not feel; to be objective, not subjective; to be "value free" in our observations, not conscious of the unconscious side of our personality.

Consequently, most of us are skin-deep personalities. We suppress the irrational as if it does not exist. We insist on being fully conscious of ourselves as rational beings in a rational ordering society where there is a place for everything and everything has its place.

You only have to look around you at the chaos of contemporary life to see how absurd and counterproductive this is. It is one of the reasons we have been attracted to Eastern thought, and why people such as Werner Erhard hit upon transformational models for *est*. Eastern religions, including Buddhism, Shintoism, and the ethics of Confucius, leave room for dreams, myths, fairy tales, and unhurried insights:

There is no place to seek the mind. It is like the footprints of the birds in the sky. Above, not a piece of tile to cover the head; Beneath, not an inch of earth to put one's foot on. Sitting quietly, doing nothing, spring comes, and the grass grows by itself. The water before, and the water after, Now and forever flowing, follow each other. One word determines the whole world. One sword pacifies heaven and earth. If you do not get it from yourself. Where will you go for it?

Robert Sohl, **Audrey Carr**, *The Gospel According to Zen* (1970)

We look for authorities to interpret our life so we will understand its meaning. Erich Fromm insists in *The Forgotten Language* (1957) that no such expertise is needed, that we are part of a universal language shared by all mankind. It is the language of the subconscious that we have forgotten, but have the ability to relearn if so moved.

To do this we must get beyond our passive state, the part of us that allows the deterministic forces in experience to take the place of self-awareness insights. Equally damaging is *activism,* the part of us that uses activity as a substitute for awareness.

Aliveness often means the capacity not to act, but to be creatively idle. This is more difficult than to do something. Doing something wins approval in our times, while doing nothing raises eyebrows.

Robert Louis Stevenson puts it this way, *"To be idle requires a strong sense of personal identity."* Self-awareness brings into focus a quiet kind of aliveness where contemplation and prayer bring a new appreciation of being something rather than merely doing something.

WHO ARE YOU, RIGHT NOW?

It is hoped that this discussion proves helpful. Obviously no one else can drive you to your destiny other than yourself. It is a solitary journey and made more difficult without a reliable center of values with an equally reliable moral compass. You can ask yourself some questions that might prove useful:

- Did you throw away your career as a musician because accounting was more practical?

- Do you pay close attention to fashion trends to see what you should wear?

- Are you obsessed with being "in"?

- How important are other people's opinions to you? More than your own?

- Do you follow celebrity activities more than you pay attention to your own?

- Do you have a true, trusted, loyal friend? Is it you? If not, why not?

- Are you caught up in other people's lives and worried about what is best for them?

- Are you lonely when alone?

- Are you anxious when there is no distracting noise?

- Are you uncomfortable in your own skin?

Many of us need to get in touch with whom we are and not what our parents, teachers, preachers, friends and bosses tell us we are, or worse yet, how they tell us we should be.

We grow from the outside in, not the inside out, subject to all of the influences during our impressionistic years. A time arrives when we must set our own agenda, when we need to find a way to accept who we are and where we are, and to understand how we got to this place and these circumstances rather than somewhere else.

If we can manage that, if we can be kind, caring and accepting of ourselves as we are, it is an easy move to accept others as we find them. We can then enable others to be what they would be by listening to them empathetically. We cannot, however, rescue them from their self-deceit, self-indulgence or self-destruction any more than they can rescue us from ours.

There is one person we need to satisfy in order for everything else to fall into place, and that is ourselves.

The more we try to be everything to everyone else, the more we fail to learn to say "no" when we should, the further we retreat from self-contentment and control of our situation.

That proverbial "no" also extends to our saying "no" to self-indulgence. Generosity of spirit is derived from a self-satisfied heart that understands the wisdom of self-restrain.

If the way you behave fails to serve you and is inconsistent with what you say you value, you are out-of-step with yourself. You are an accident waiting to happen. You are vulnerable to the inexplicable blind spot in your nature that prevents you from knowing who you are and seeing clearly where you are going. You are poised to be unhinged, disappointed, embarrassed, and likely at some point to spin out of control.

No one can do for you what you refuse to do for yourself. If your life is out of sync, only you can restore the balance to its desirable rhythm. In the end, we are all left with ourselves.

Rollo May in *Man's Search for Himself* (1953) writes:

Man must make his choices as an individual, for individuality is one side of one's consciousness of one's self. We can see this point clearly when we realize that consciousness of one's self is always a unique act – I can never know exactly how you see yourself and you never can exactly know how I relate to myself. This is the inner sanctum where each man must stand alone. This fact makes for much of the tragedy and inescapable isolation in human life, but it also indicates again that we must find the strength in ourselves to stand in our own inner sanctum as individuals. And this fact means that, since we are not automatically merged with our fellows, we must through our own affirmation learn to love each other.

To that end, I wish you well.

Notes:

1. Avana Stewart, "I was a well-adjusted mostly happy 20-year-old. And then I wasn't," Tampa Bay Times, "Perspective," Sunday. October 4, 2015.

THIRTY

TAKING CHARGE!

BEST EXPERT IS ONE'S OWN EXPERIENCE!

SUNDAY NEWSPAPER BLUES

Today, reading the Sunday newspaper I am reminded how inauthentic existence has become, how dependent we all are, from our national leaders to what we do as ordinary individuals every day to what our leaders or their spin doctors promulgate for our consumption. It is as if we wait with baited breath as to what is real and what is not, what is important and what may be dismissed as unimportant or trivial.

David Brooks writes *"How leaders get to 'yes,' 'no' and 'maybe'."* He cites the ambivalence of "experts" and "consultants" with regard to critical issues from the President of the United States, to CEOs, to leaders in academia, to the religious. He finds a fading difference in the President of the United States between campaigning and governing, in corporate leadership between rhetoric and promoting the brand, while in academia and religious institutions a 180-degree pivot from the mission to submission to special interests.

Leonard Pitts, a syndicated columnist who happens to be African American, takes Attorney General Eric Holder to task, who also happens to be black, on the rhetoric that comes out of the Attorney General's office, rhetoric Pitts claims *"we have swallowed whole."* For example, the *"War on Drugs"* was launched in 1971, but has not seen a decrease in drug use since that war began. Instead, it has experienced a spike in drug crime of 2,800 percent, and Pitts adds, *"This is not a typo."*

Elsewhere I read in the Sunday newspaper that people are afraid to state their views based on experience if those views clash with those of science. Religion has never had the dogmatic impact of science, not even in the 12th and 13th century when the fear was that of *The Inquisition* in Spain.

There is a Sunday review of the young French economist Thomas Piketty's book, *"Capital in the 21st Century"* (2014). Piketty excoriates Adam Smith's capitalism and Karl Marx's communism in equal measure, while his critics excoriate him for being "naïve." Bully for him following his inter-disciplinarian research wherever it takes him.

Piketty has a problem with American economists whom he sees having tunnel vision, being too quantitatively and economically pedantic, while he peruses histories and novels to gain an intuitive sense as well as cognitive fix on the inequality in the distribution of income.

He sees the rate of return on capital could go on forever while Marx claimed the rate of return on capital would eventually fall to near zero, spawning revolution. Likewise, he punches holes in Adam Smith's laisser-faire capitalism with the idea that "wealth raises all boats." Piketty, not surprisingly, falls off the grid to some economists.

Then there is a review of *"John Wayne: The Life and Legend"* (2014) by Scott Eyman. Wayne, a fellow Iowan, born Marion Morrison, 1907, crafted his brand in Hollywood before brand consciousness was apparent. I had read previously Garry Wills biography of the actor *("John Wayne's America,"* 1997).

Wills subtitle was *"The Politics of Celebrity."* John Wayne managed to become the prototype of the American as the *"lone ranger"* of individualism, dispensing his brand of justice, but apparently without a moral compass or center. Unfortunately, too many Americans found John Wayne epitomized their own quintessential American, and so they imitated his swagger and bravado although they only knew him as a celluloid image on the screen.

Reading these stories in the Sunday newspaper is why I have the Sunday morning blues. Robert Frost, an engineer and instructor at NASA, says reading this Sunday's edition is like *"learning by connecting new information with old information already there."* I would substitute "experience" for information.

Given these diatribes, Americans like to think they are in charge, that they are contributing, that they are making a difference. Life to Americans has always been more than a paycheck.

TAKING CHARGE
CULTURE OF CONTRIBUTION

Proof of this is that the workplace culture supports contribution. Obviously, this is not straightforward but nonetheless evident in a myriad of behavioral indicators, among which are:

- *Workers have a sense of purpose with a short-term minor goal and a long-term major goal.* They are natural planners without portfolio. Once they have a clear objective, they don't return to confirm and report every little iota of progress made. They have a plan, a schedule, benchmarks to monitor their progress, and a target date to complete. As long as they are working within time constraints and "on plan," they stick to their work. No one develops this schedule for them. It is of their own design and construction and serves their peculiar style of operation.

- *Workers move with confidence, but not cockiness.* They don't hesitate to seek help and assistance when they have questions or problems. They are available to help others who have the need of their expertise. The work they turn out is user-friendly and shows evidence of understanding the needs of colleagues in that connection.

- *Workers are learners, not knowers.* When someone asks them a question, they don't punish the person with their knowledge, nor are they afraid to say, *"I don't know."* If they know an alternative source, they add, *"but you might check with so and so."*

Where we want to be - Interdependent Management

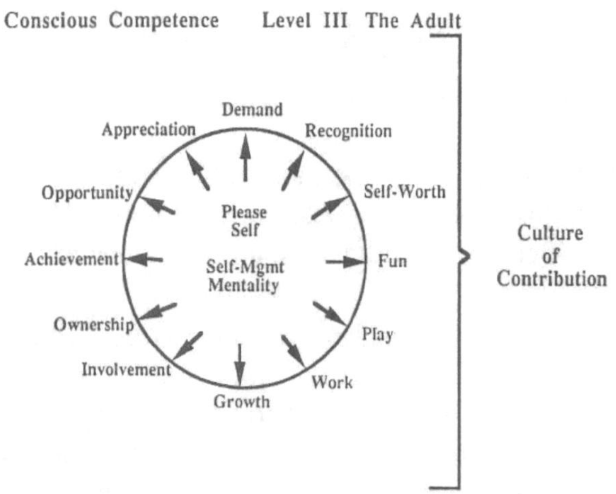

Motivated By	Behaviors
Challenging work	Victor
Opportunity to fail	Purposeful
Right to an opinion	Confident
Right to be wrong	Cooperative
What is wrong (not who is wrong)	Pleasure
Problems	Creator
Work Itself	Completer
Creative License	Bottom Line Responsive
Owning what he does	Pioneer
Calculated risks	Proactive Responsive
Doing	Positive
	"Selfish"

- *Workers have opinions and are not afraid to express them.* If they disagree with someone, they tell them. They express their disagreement directly and politely and focus on the subject, not on the person.

There are no secrets. Trust is the foundation of all relationships in this culture. There is no claptrap of "on a need to know basis." Information is up front and available.

The focus is on designing and building concepts that lace together the important ideas necessary to get the job done. Out of this comes mature practices that are flexible, relevant, and changeable. Nothing is written in concrete.

The frame of reference is broad, deep, and diverse. Conventional problem-solving is passé, where the emphasis previously was on cause and effect analysis, linear logic and linear curves, and quantitative analysis. Creative thinking is in vogue, which looks beyond what is known and what has been done before, whereas critical thinking relies exclusively on proven methods and expected results.

There are no adversarial relationships anymore, no winners and losers. Work and results is not a zero sum game, but the complement of creative and critical thinking.

Parallel thinking is in, which explores the problem at several levels and perspectives and creates a solution. It does not *"search for and discover"* a solution.

Change is a natural phenomenon, not an artificial construct with workers in collegial engagement without being pretentious. Cooperation is not the attention-getter, but the product of joint exploration in the problem solving.

- *Workers are self-organized and are no longer externally controlled. The fire is within, not under them.* They understand that their perceptions are constantly in a state of flux, self-organizing, and changing, as they work and experience new things.

- Workers are free to personalize their work, founded on the trust that they will do a good job. They are in control. Should they fall short of the mark, however, they seek help and correct their errors accordingly.

In the *Culture of Contribution*, you sense that it is fun to be at work. Problems occur, but there is no panic.

What is conspicuously absent is the too controlling manager, who in his effort to motivate kills the worker's spirit by getting in the way. In the *Culture of Contribution,* the focus is on creating a performance climate that reinforces values of contribution:

- Providing the training and tools necessary;
- Presenting workers with an objective and the time constraints to do the job properly;
- Providing back up and support to allow workers to achieve the objective on their own.

What is unfortunate in many instances is that the first two requirements are commonly provided. Only the third is commonly missing, which is the support and trust issue.

Trust is basic to the *Culture of Contribution.* This means there is no time or inclination to finger pointing. The focus is on what is wrong, not who is wrong. Humility is more common than arrogance. *"We accomplished"* rather than "I accomplished." Wisdom is much more appreciated than cleverness, so workers don't waste time making an impression, or being crafty.

To an outsider immersed in the flow of this casual chaos, it might seem people are goofing off, but this could not be further from the truth.

Work is fluid and dynamic, with action evident by the rate of completion of tasks, with no one standing around waiting to be told what to do next. They know their complementary roles and move to fill them. There is a lot of give-and-take humor but little evidence of complaining. Workers pride themselves in anticipating and dealing with problems.

Crisis management is an anathema to the *Culture of Contribution*. Managers and workers hold each other accountable while equally esteeming and supporting each other.

The most subtle characteristic of the *Culture of Contribution* is confidence.

It is that unspoken quality that you feel more than you see. You have the sense that people wouldn't be here doing this work if they didn't want to and that they have a high personal regard for themselves and feel no need to assert that dignity.

Workers are selfish in the sense that they have a high need to please themselves, but not at the expense of co-workers.

If they didn't enjoy the work or like their co-workers, they would clear out and not become a nuisance. They are far less self-centered than those of the please-other mentality. Those with an obsessive need to please derive their satisfaction by complaining and drawing attention to themselves. Those of a please-self mentality are more inclined to be guided by enlightened self-interest. This is displayed in their enthusiasm for work, which is catching, and is directed toward the service of others, not because it is the thing to do but because it is how they feel.

Workers in the *Culture of Contribution* see managers and workers there to serve each other as first customers.

They feel traditional management fails to see workers and managers in complementary roles. Some have attempted to educate management into understanding this new relationship.

No organization, within my experience, has been completely successful in this regard. Most successful in establishing the *Culture of Contribution* are ad hoc groups demonstrated by the famous "Skunk Works™" of Lockheed Martin.

Skunk Works™ is an official alias for Lockheed Martin's Advanced Development Programs in the realm of informal group activity. Yet cultural change of this nature is not likely to be accidental. Without the direct involvement of senior management, the full benefits of this culture will continue to linger. Meanwhile, conventional wisdom still holds most organizations captive to conventional practices.

It is helpful to see the workplace, in any case, as a system. In this system, there are at least three levels of consciousness. This is especially true of the traditional organization:

Level I -- *The Culture of Comfort* or *Unconscious Incompetence*;

Level II -- *The Culture of Complacency* or *Conscious Incompetence.*

Level III – The *Culture of Contribution,* or *Conscious Competence.*

Conscious competence compels the organization to make a supreme effort and, yes, a radical departure from the conventional approach to doing business. This is true of Skunk Works™. It is also true of any organization that espouses to be a *Culture of Contribution.*

What we have, at Level III, is *mature adult workers*, not sniveling workers in suspended adolescence, nor do we have codependent bonds between employers and employees. Obviously, the *Culture of Contribution* threatens the status quo.

With this culture, control shifts from a select few to a network of managers and workers throughout the workplace.

The technology is already here begging for this cultural development, but the social dynamics lag, as one might expect, because workers and managers are not ready, nor are they mature enough to fathom its implications.

THIRTY ONE

PRISONER OF THE MIND

"Psychological manipulation pervades all areas of society, not only through the use of skills and techniques, but through the conveyance of oppressive behavior to the oppressed themselves, and through the use of psychology as an ideology for the defense of the status quo."

Phil Brown, *Radical Psychology* (1973)

IS SOCIETY SICK?

There is a reluctance to focus on the question: is society sick? This is not only a problem for professional thinkers but also for laymen. There is a kind of normalcy to the idea that society is sick and people are sick in society. So what? When has society not been sick?

The frenetic pace of society, the compulsive waste making, the robbing Peter to pay Paul, the planning for planning sake, the living without consequences, the lifestyle diseases, the looking for miraculous drugs to cure addictions, hey, what's all the fuss about? It's the way it is, Mac! But is it? And if so, why?

- We are told we are a nation of believers in God but that doesn't include going to church.

- We are told we are religious and a caring nation, but that doesn't include knowing and fraternizing with our neighbors next door.
- We are told we are a melting pot of nations, but that doesn't include socializing with other ethnic groups.
- We have had our national character freeze framed into our collective identity, when this has little to do with our shared reality.

The religion of the West is imbued with the idea of God and the individual as infinitely precious and irreducibly real for his having an immortal soul. Yet, the history of carnage in the West, and violent crime in the United States, contradicts this perception.

Thinking and behaving are worlds apart. Churches are constructed as houses of worship, but have become increasingly empty of worshipers. Modern society has moved away from religious doctrine to secular dogma and the civil religion of money.

In Freudian speak, religion once kept the *"Lid on the Id,"* or society's impulsive child, but no longer. That impudent child is now in charge. The evidence is pervasive as the moral highway has no speed limits, no consensus on *"rules of the road,"* and so crashes have become the symphonic thunder of the times. We lost 55,000 Americans in the Viet Nam War. We lose that many every year on American highways, a large number from drunken driving.

The *Id* (our compulsive self) is running amuck, as there is little *Superego* (moral self) on display. We have lost our moral compass and thus our way.

The paradox is that everything is set on the rational when it is the emotional needle that commands the moment. Incest and murder, corruption and malfeasance, and coveting the neighbor's wife and property have become banner headlines, not only in supermarket rags, but in venerated newspapers. With the loss of a sense of proportion, even being nice has been replaced by being with it.

The idea of the immortal soul has been superseded by the idea of the individual personality, which is not immortal, but is considered all the more precious for not being so.

Identity and role relationships have become the new psychology. The irony is that psychology rose out of philosophy and has never since found its own identity much less its role. So, rather than create that role, it continues to search for identity by inventing a new discipline for every unforeseen behavioral disruption.

The evidence is palpable. Psychology develops a new discipline every time a perplexing issue surfaces. This is not surprising as we are a solution driven culture always looking for problems rather than the reverse of this. Problem defining takes too much time. Moreover, once defined, problems typically call for a radical cultural change of the status quo. Society is never interested in change, per se, except cosmetically. So, nothing changes.

Currently, we have existential psychology, which rises out of the philosophy of the absurd, and humanism, which attempts to be everything and to please everybody suggesting the philosophy of Pollyanna, having a blindly optimistic view of the future. The clergy, desperate for survival, have championed this psychology as if a long lost relative, becoming the premise of their sermons as if pure wisdom.

Then there is psychiatrist Eric Berne's reducing Freudian psychology to the level of a parlor game with his *quid pro quo* implications in the *"Games People Play"* (1964). Here Freudianism is simplified to *"transactional analysis"* by creating the *"Adult" (Ego), "Parent" (Superego")* and *"Child" (Id)* ego states. These were then used to illustrate the dynamics of interpersonal relationships.

Thomas Harris then came along shortly thereafter, turning Berne's transactional analysis into a practical guide with his *"I'm OK—You're OK"* (1967).

A decade later, John Dusay translated these ego states into *"Ego grams"* (1977), solidifying the role of the *"Adult" (Ego),* but further differentiating the *"Parent" (Superego)* into the *"Nurturing Parent"* and *"Critical Parent,"* and the *"Child" (Id)* into the *"Free Child"* and *"Adaptive Child."*

Parents, teachers, and preachers, as well as gurus latched onto this new nomenclature seeing children, as well as people in general in these schematic terms.

In this new age of the idea of the individual, we measure a person's worth not by his bond, or what he has done, but by what he can become. *Becoming*, not *being*, is the philosophy of instant celebrity consistent with instant everything.

THE PRESIDENCY AND PHANTOM LEADERSHIP

Syndicated columnist and practicing psychiatrist Charles Krauthammer saw this trend apparent in national politics in 2013. *"President Barak Obama is perhaps our greatest president as campaigner,"* he reflects, *"but this excellence doesn't appear to extend to governance."* The columnist was referring to the procession of *"fiscal cliffs"* that had stalled monetary policy between the President and Congress from 2011 on.

Then in the fall of 2013, while promising everyone could keep their health insurance if they wanted to, which proved not to be true, the president delegated the problem solving to the bureaucracy on the *Affordable Healthcare Act*. Instead of rolling up his sleeves and taking charge of the enrollment computer glitch, he went on a national whistle stop campaign across the country to sell the program.

Barak Obama, the first African American President of the United States, not only shocked the nation by winning the presidency in 2008, but also confirmed the power of his personality and charismatic presence by being reelected in 2012.

That said President Barak Obama has unwittingly personified phantom leadership or leaderless leadership, which allows events to dictate circumstances rather than initiatives to command events.

It is not the color of the president's skin that is significant. It is the quality of his mindset that is troubling. Unwittingly, he personifies an outlook consistent with our pusillanimous times. Looking good is more important than leading; making an impression more important than performing, appeasing our adversaries rather than pursuing our vital interests; waxing political in crisis when the presidency is where the buck stops, forgetting America speaks softly but carries a big international stick.

Everything has been reduced to show business and President Barak Obama has assumed the role of the consummate actor. In this 24/7 media age with electronics capturing every scintilla of action, nothing seems real as everything is compressed into the moment. It would appear he has lost the will and the way to lead. How could it be seen otherwise as he has constantly wavered?

Like the flawless actor he has chosen to be, Obama has the widest appeal where substance is reduced to shadows of the mind, where intentions are written in ambiguities. The only problem is you cannot eat shadows and ambiguities provide little security.

Should the reader think I am being unfair, the state of the presidency and the nation, at the moment, demonstrate collectively that Americans are unconscious of being *"prisoners of the mind"* when seemingly nobody is in charge.

You need go no further back than the American Civil War to understand the consequences of this mindset. George Brinton McClellan (1826 - 1885) was President Abraham Lincoln's General of the Army of the Potomac briefly (November 1861 - March 1862).

Lincoln relieved him precipitously of that command because he would not fight.

Although McClellan was celebrated as a cerebral general, meticulous in his planning and preparations, a skillful organizer of combat readiness, these characteristics hampered his ability to challenge the aggressive Army of the Confederacy in a fast-moving battlefield environment.

He chronically overestimated the strength of enemy units and was therefore reluctant to apply principles of mass engagement. As the enemy pressed forward, large portions of the Army of the Potomac never moved out of camp. Meanwhile, the Army of the Confederacy, led by General Robert E. Lee, was winning one decisive battle after another as Lee marched towards the nation's capital planning to make short order of this war.

The president had to do something, fast! First, he had to assume military command of the army and press the nation's troops into battle to defend the nation's capital, or all would be lost. He looked frantically for a replacement of McClellan, and found a retired general, a reputed drunk with a spotty record, but who had been known for his courage in battle in the Mexican War. That man was General Ulysses S. Grant.

Lincoln saw the same passion in Grant that he saw in himself, the same resolute determination to engage the enemy whatever the odds, whatever the costs. Grant wore his uniform like a sack, hardly looked like a soldier much less a general, whereas McClellan was the picture of rectitude. Nor did Grant display the social amenities or intellectual range that McClellan prided himself to have. The contrast even went beyond this, as

McClellan felt himself the superior of the President of the United States in every sense. He would demonstrate this aplomb by running against Lincoln in the national election of 1864 that Lincoln, of course, won.

Grant was pivotal to the unconditional surrender of the Confederacy by General Lee at the Appomattox Court House in Virginia on April 9, 1865. It was a long and bloody road for Grant and his troops. At first, he had a series of crushing defeats and heavy causalities, but pressed on until the tide turned. Grant was joined by other commanders, including General Tecumseh Sherman, who, like Grant, was relentless in quest for ultimate victory.

Eric Hoffer could have been thinking of General McClellan when he wrote, *"Give intellectuals anything, but power."* This suggests an interesting comparison between President Barak Obama and General George McClellan:

- Both commonly considered the smartest man in the room,
- Both tentative, indecisive, overestimating opposition and therefore unable to make high risk decisions in a timely fashion,
- Both gifted at articulating their case for inaction with aplomb and grace,
- Both tacticians but poor strategic thinkers,
- Both far more comfortable in the theoretical than operational,
- Both with high cognitive acumen but suspect spiritual depth.

Leadership throughout the ages has demonstrated that unbounded high risk, high intervention passion is protocol to lifting victory out of the jaws of defeat. God only knows where the West would be today were it not for the indomitable spirit of Sir Winston Churchill in 1939-1945.

EXIT, VOICE, LOYALTY

Political economist <u>Albert O. Hirschman</u>'s treatise, *Exit, Voice, and Loyalty* (1970), is a work that hinges on the organization, its people and its leadership in modern everyday life.

When it comes to the individual, Hirschman argues a person has essentially two possible responses when the organization is about to leave the rails.

- He can *exit* (withdraw or leave), or
- He can *voice his concerns* by confronting the leadership in an attempt to repair or improve the relationship through his complaint, grievance, and concern or he can propose some change to ameliorate the situation.

If the environment is not conducive to his values and well-being, he can elect to quit the unpleasant job, or express his concerns in an effort to improve the situation.

This can allow for a new perspective on daily social interaction. *Exit* and *voice* represent a union between polite confrontation and managed conflict.

Voice is self-interested and therefore political. While *exit* and *voice* can be used to measure organizational dysfunction and decline, *voice* is more informative in that it also provides reasons for the decline.

Exit, taken alone, only provides the warning signs of decline. *Exit* and *voice* also interact in unique and sometimes unexpected ways: that is, by providing feedback and criticism. *Exit* is a distinct possibility when dissent or criticism is stifled. This leads to increased pressure to use the only other means available to express discontent, that is, departure.

The greater the availability of *exit* the less likely *voice* will be used. Even when *exit* is used, it has negligible impact, as I can attest personally.[1]

This brings forward the third component, which is *loyalty*. It is the most emotionally wrenching and conflicting of the three.

- *Exit* means to quit the job, the association, and the organization.
- *Voice* means to stay on the job but speak out publicly for change in direction. For *voice* to correct gross errors and inequalities, it must be fearless and fierce, and loud enough to be heard, always at some risk to its security.
- *Loyalty* means to stay on the job or in the association whatever the climate, the ethics, the morality, or the effectiveness of the operation. Support of the leadership and the organization is constant whatever the policies, competencies and practices.

Author Hirschman observes that *voice* is sadly lacking in most enterprises as most choose *loyalty* whatever the injustices.

By understanding the relationship between *exit* and *voice*, and the interplay that *loyalty* has with these choices, organizations can craft the means to better address these issues, and thereby effect an improvement. Failure to understand these competing pressures can however lead to organizational decline and possible failure.

Readers can apply this concept to their own experience. We know from history that General Robert E. Lee hated slavery but felt loyalty to his home state of Virginia, and therefore did not answer the call of President Abraham Lincoln to head the Army of the Potomac, but did answer that of President Jefferson Davis of the Southern Confederacy.

The brilliant German physicist Max Planck, the inventor of the *quanta* of *quantum theory*, hated Nazism and anti-Semitism, but loved Germany, and was loyal to Adolf Hitler throughout the war as he saw many of his Jewish physicist colleagues lose their jobs, or worse. *Loyalty* was intrinsic to his German character, whereas Albert Einstein, a colleague and friend, chose *exit* rather than support Hitler's totalitarian regime, moving to the United States.

WHAT PRICE PATRIOTISM!

We acquire the leadership we deserve. We do so by voting as we do or failing to vote at all. *Everyone is a leader or no one is.* It is apparent that we live in denial, count on hope but leave courage to others. Reality is too messy. The crippling disease of Americans is optimism, crippling because it is not attentive to economic, social, political and military incongruities.

President Jimmy Carter sought reelection handicapped with similar economic circumstances to that of President Barak Obama, but he didn't see the role of the presidency as that of an actor.
Unceremoniously, Hollywood actor and California Governor Ronald Reagan, who replaced him, did.

Carter, Reagan, Obama, indeed, all presidents since the 1970s have promised "transparency," including President Clinton, but only President Carter attempted that practice. That one time he addressed the nation on television in a polo shirt and cardigan sweater (July 15, 1979) demonstrated that transparency is not something most Americans are inclined to favor.

Viewers prefer presidential euphemisms, or a *"hope rope a dope."* Machiavelli's *"The Prince"* (1532) provided rational justification. To win and stay in power, the Italian provocateur proclaimed, had little to do with virtue and less to do with transparency. Leadership, he claimed, was a cynical profession that had much more to do with using any means to a desirable end while giving quite the opposite impression.

The operational word "hope" is a powerful one because it challenges no one to do anything.
President Barak Obama used the operational word "hope" in his book, *"The Audacity of Hope"* (2008). Hope is not audacious; hope is passive. It is courage that is audacious and active. But courage demands risk, sacrifice, action, and we don't elect people who emphasize that operational language.

We are a passive and reactive society, not an active and engaged one. We react to crises; we don't anticipate them. The 2008 economic meltdown is simply par for the course.

Presidents Reagan, Obama, and Clinton knew what the Renaissance author was advocating, which was to be as clever as a fox, ruthless as a lion, but seemingly as docile as a lamb.

Leadership in the American Republic has devolved to platitudes. Banalities require convincing actors but seldom translate into prudent action. Such leaders astonish us with their glibness which paradoxically makes them more vivid with the eye test.

We equate *"brilliance"* with presentation skills; leadership with mesmerizing performance in debate. This is not unlike a phantom chasing shadows. It never occurs to us it is our own invention.

"Phantom" here is used in the Buddhist sense. The Buddhist would see this not as a person, but as a picture in the mind without blemishes. You cannot shake hands with a picture. A picture is a cold medium devoid of feelings or warmth other than our own projected into the image.

This makes the real, unreal, empty of individuality, and therefore a shadow of the mind.

The first electronics guru of the *Information Age* was Marshall McLuhan. He declared that *"The Medium Is The Message"* (1967), discerning that television was a cold medium and that the viewer injected his or her subjective warmth into that cold phantom object on the screen. The aim of television's engaging personality on the tube is to capture the viewer's attention with but one objective in mind: to manipulate that mind to be receptive to that personality's message. This aspect of *"prisoner of the mind"* has become our collective cage.

Notes:

1. After experiencing South African apartheid in 1968, while on assignment there for my company, I chose Albert Hirschman's *exit,* retiring from my executive position only in my mid-thirties. However, I'm sure it had no appreciable impact on my company. After a sabbatical of two years, I would go back to school to earn my Ph.D., then return to industry, once again as an international executive, living in Europe, only to *exit* again in my late fifties, primarily to write books and articles about my experiences, which happen to include Hirschman's attributes of *Exit, Voice, Loyalty.*

THIRTY TWO

WHAT WOULD YOU DO IF NOBODY EVER FOUND OUT?

The measure of a man's real character is what he would do if he knew he never would be found out.

Thomas Babington Macaulay (1800-1859), British poet and historian

THE MAJESTY OF HAVING A MORAL CENTER

There is so much we do that nobody ever knows about. It is the engine of enterprise that pulsates through most of us, and is essential if a society is to survive.

Yet, our society is obsessed with recognition, with getting credit, with winning awards of achievement and outstanding performance. But that is not what keeps society on an even keel, not what keeps a modicum of sanity carrying us through the day.

Most of us live lives of quiet desperation well below the radar, living courageously while giving the opposite impression, lives in which our private hell is apparent if anyone would notice. Were we not so stoic in our everyday pursuits, society would not exist, would not persist. It is this quiet normality of our lives that sustains a community, a country, a society. It is the lives of people of all shapes and sizes, occupations and preoccupations, joys and sorrows who keep pretty much to themselves, people who are largely invisible to the movers and shakers of the day who demand all the attention, recognition and get most of the credit.

People of the earth with a center and a compass, very reliable people, pay little heed to the movers and shakers, as they are too busy being and doing.

Recently, an Iowa farmer, close to ninety years old, died, and everyone wondered who he would leave his modest farm to. Well, his holdings were far from modest, and extended well beyond his farm. He remained a bachelor, stayed close to home, lived modestly, kept much to himself, and so it was a shock to learn he had been an astute investor.

This farmer had farm land worth more than $2 million across several counties, and yet he lived almost as if on subsistence. A church goer all his life, he left his $2 million estate to a number of Catholic churches spread out in several counties, churches he had visited in his long life, leaving dollar bequests ranging from $300,000 and more.

It was never necessary that he be found out; never necessary to proselytize his faith. So, I ask the question: what would you do if nobody ever found out?

It was never necessary for this Iowa farmer to make public his faith, never necessary to put himself in the frame. He was a man of the land, the land of his birth, the land that he nurtured and the land that nurtured his nature, while he quietly prospered for the effort.

One can only speculate how his spiritual and material side complemented each other. Once his will was revealed, after his death, he was found out. His faith and farming were love made visible. He epitomizes the words of Indian mystic Julal al-Din Rumi (1207-1273):

"Every one has been made for some particular work, and the desire for that work has been put into his heart."

Indian master Swami Brahmannda (1863-1922) adds:

"If you wish to work properly, you should never lose sight of two great principles: first, a profound respect for the work undertaken; and second, a complete indifference to its fruits. Thus only can you work with the proper attitude."

Chances are this farmer never read Indian mystics or masters, but his life and work were expressions of their words. Perhaps he thought he had only borrowed the land for a while and was returning it to God through his Roman Catholic Church.

Not a single parishioner of his church had any idea of his *"grand strategy."* His parish priest confessed he wasn't sure he even knew who he was.

My intention is not to single him out for praise or celebration. He is mentioned in the content and context of the living and working majority who have a subtext as well that may be similar to that of this Iowa farmer. One can imagine he relished the singular pleasure of quietly building his philanthropy in the shadow of these stormy times.

THIRTY THREE

THE WORLD IN DISORDER: AN EXCHANGE

"They who say all men are equal speak an undoubted truth, if they mean that all have an equal right to liberty to their property, and to their protection of the laws. But they are mistaken if they think men are equal in their station and employments, since they are not so by their talents."

Voltaire (1694-1778), author of *Candide* (1759)

WE ARE NOT ALL THE SAME!

This may seem self-evident, but many act as if we are all the same. No two individuals look alike, so it shouldn't surprise us that no two individuals think or act alike, much less are equally endowed with the same ability. Yet, we can become frustrated to the point of anger when people don't comprehend things as quickly as we do, or behave as we think they should.

Carl and Simon are two readers who regularly react to the postings of my missives. They however display a different take on what I have to say, which is not only quite all right, but to be applauded. Thinking gets us in touch with who and what we are, and in a way, *introduces us to ourselves.*

While everyone seemingly agrees that death and taxes are certainties, why are so many of us less comfortable with differing belief systems or such matters as the rich and the poor, the gifted and the common, the ambitious and the lazy, the fortunate and the luckless?

Could it be that we fail to accept ourselves as we are, and therefore have a problem accepting others as we find them? Do we not see that equal opportunity is not the same as equality? We have a right to equal opportunity, but we don't have the same talent, as Voltaire reminds us.

We are all different, unique, and should be happy that we are. Diversity of interests and talent makes for a dynamic and energetic society. We are bound to differ widely in skills, abilities, energy, passion, commitment, and drive. It is the nature of being human. Then there are those who "seize the day," and others who wait for the day to seize them. Admittedly, some are born into special circumstances that gives them a considerable edge. It happens!

On PBS television, Ken Burns presented a documentary on the Roosevelts, profiling the lives of Theodore Roosevelt, Franklin Delano Roosevelt and Eleanor Roosevelt. They came out of a patrician class as did Great Britain's Queen Elizabeth and her husband Prince Philip of Greece, as they were both great-great-grandchildren of Queen Victoria.

Intermarrying within the aristocracy has been common. Then we have the gentrified Sir Winston Churchill with an American born mother.   Cousins Theodore Roosevelt and Franklin Delano Roosevelt rose to the Presidency of the United States, while another cousin, Eleanor Roosevelt, became the wife of FDR, and the First Lady.

Perhaps less grand but nonetheless notable, we have the father and son, George Herman Walker Bush and George Walker Bush rise to be President of the United States.

Theodore Roosevelt took a passive pastoral nation to hegemony prominence in the early 20th century, while the Bush family bridged the 20th century with early 21st century with their presidencies. So, while we Americans claim to be a classless society, blue bloods commonly rise to the top in America's leadership roles.

Ken Burns' video history of the Roosevelt family is not a hagiography, but a balanced view of the family's heroics and flaws, frailties and vanities, which mirror our own national psyche.

For example, Theodore Roosevelt was compulsive to the point of madness with blind ambition. His real and imagined deficiencies coupled with his obvious assets finds his bust atop Mount Rushmore, along with George Washington, Thomas Jefferson and Abraham Lincoln.

Franklin Roosevelt, on the other hand, was a party animal. This prompted Supreme Court Justice Oliver Wendell Holmes to say *"He has a second-class intellect, but a first-class temperament."* As it turned out, that is what the nation needed in World War Two.

His wife, First Lady Eleanor, was stable, mature, balanced and effectively engaged in social and cultural issues. She was also insecure and suspicious of her husband's many flirtations. Quietly, she did amazing things for the poor and disadvantaged as well as military veterans and their families during the war while her husband, the president, took the bows. That said she was a notable asset to his four successive reelections to the presidency.

The Roosevelt's were born to wealth, status and privilege. They turned their attention to the service of the nation. We have not often seen their kind, nor their kind of leadership. Some would argue that FDR, with his comprehensive economic "New Deal" policy during *The Great Depression,* actually spawned our eventual national codependency on the Federal Government, rather than sponsoring our collective initiative to socioeconomic independence.

Franklin Delano Roosevelt was elected as president for the first time when I was born. I grew up captivated by his personality and his homespun warmth listening to his "fire side chats" on the radio. His picture was on the wall of our modest working class home along with Pope Pius XII, two equally patrician men of the times.

The president and the pope were groomed from birth for command. It was not necessary for them to define that role or assume that commitment. In contrast, our age is obsessively self-conscious of who leads and who is meant to follow. The consequence of this is palpably evident in the political gridlock of the United States Congress. In everyday life, it is simply manifest chaos.

We once took charge and defined the times. Now we wait for events to define ours.

For the past quarter century, I have been pondering this matter, looking back to see ahead, noting how often we repeat the same chronic problems and embrace the same tired solutions. These observations have been reduced to missives. Many respond to them sharing their views.   Such is the case of Carl and Simon. They have taken the time to think through what I have said and react to it based on their own values, beliefs and experience. I applaud them for it as I learn from them. In that sense, this process is a way of introducing us to ourselves.

In *"Meet Your New Best Friend"* (2014), I write:

We are all authors of our own footprints in the sand, heroes of the novels inscribed in our hearts. Everyone's life, without exception, is sacred, unique, scripted high drama, playing out before an audience of one, with but one actor on stage. The sooner we realize this, the more quickly we overcome the bondage of loneliness and find true friendship with ourselves.

Theodore Roosevelt struggled with this proposition of identity all his life, while his cousin, Franklin, never gave it much thought until he was cut down with polio in his thirties.

Life is always crying out to get our attention whatever our nature or the particularity of our birth.

CARL RESPONDS:

You are right, I am not angry. I find the ignorance of human nature interesting. I have learned many things from students and, hopefully, them from me.

While studying art, the concepts that were used to teach drawing came from a book *"The Natural Way to Draw."* I used that method in my drawing classes.

What I found was that just as everyone can learn to write, everyone can also learn to draw if they make the effort. However, just as it does not mean everyone who learns to write will become a great writer, so it is also true that everyone who learns to draw does not achieve the same level of success.

After I got my MA degree in art education, I started teaching art classes to 7th graders. One of the ideas pushed in the art education classes was that the teacher should put all the students' works on the bulletin board no matter the quality.

After the first two weeks, students started asking why certain pieces were on the bulletin board because they thought they were not very good. After that lesson from my students, I only put "A" work on the bulletin board. After that, students would work hard to get their work on the board. Interesting, huh?

For anyone who would disagree with that, I would respond that in sports as in everything else, everyone is not equal. Inequality, in that sense, is inevitable.

We can all learn something up to a point if we work hard, but everyone will not achieve the same level of quality.

That is the same in all parts of life including economics. If people are given things without effort, they will never work to achieve more. That is what I have learned, and that is how I teach.

SIMON RESPONDS:

These "welfare" discussions are so tedious. Less than 10% of the federal budget is allocated to the poor.

There are actually people who are living in cardboard boxes. Yes, there are other forms of welfare that are not included in my ten percent. That would be Social Security, Medicare (not Medicaid), and corporate subsidies.

Still, 10% is less than half the defense budget. It is also less than half of what the federal government pays in pensions.

That's the crux of my argument. "Taking from the rich" is not "giving to the poor." There's a bit of (well, maybe a lot of) narrow-mindedness that informs most of these arguments.

We tend to blame systems for things we don't like. It's not my fault seems to be the mantra favored by the have nots as well as the haves. In the end, every war, every disturbance, can be traced back to two things - money and religion. Money usually takes the lead and religion follows on as an excuse.

The reality is most of us work hard to get what we have. Others, through laziness or bad luck are trumped by the aggressors who experience good fortune and become the statistical outliers.

When those with good fortune are asked to pay a bit more in taxes to improve the infrastructure that allowed them to become rich, it's only fair, don't you think?

DR. FISHER COMMENTS:

If readers feel Carl and Simon seem to be talking past each other, it may be because they are commenting on the most sensitive subject of equality and inequality from their own experience and perspective.

When we wax with candor, our own personal biography surfaces and reveals what truly moves us to get up in the morning and "seize the day." It is such disclosure that is good for the soul.

It doesn't follow that anyone is right or necessarily wrong but it does show how hard it is for us to be on the same page discussing the same issues. Imagine the magnitude of this problem when we bring in the mix of different languages and cultural values.

The world is in disorder for reason. Peoples across the globe are being forced into this electronic age without the necessary cultural, economic or educational foundation. We see people on America's streets with iPhones and other electronic gadgets who cannot afford their rent.

We are moving to global interdependence and are exercised because people in the fast food service industry make less than $10 an hour, when more than 2 billion souls across the globe don't make $10 a day.[1]

Change starts with conversation. Expressing our views, voicing our concerns and articulating our beliefs openly provides a small window of opportunity to promote common understanding that eventually will benefit us all.

Notes:

1. For the 95% on $10 a day, see Martin Ravalli on, Shohua Chen and Prem Sangraula, *"Dollar A Day Revisited: World Bank"* (May 2008). These economists note 95% of developing country population people live lives on less than $10 a day. Using 2005 population numbers, this is equivalent to just under 80% of the world population, but does not include populations living on less than $10 a day from industrialized nations. Put another way, the blunt truth is that 80% of humanity lives on less than $10 a day.

THIRTY FOUR

THIS BUSINESS OF IDENTITY!

IF IT DOESN'T START EARLY, CHANCES ARE IDENTITY WILL BE LIKE RIDING A ROLLER COASTER!

"Unlike a drop of water which loses its identity when it joins the ocean, man does not lose his being in the society in which he lives. Man's life is independent. He is born not for the development of the society alone, but for the development of his self."

B. R. Ambedkar (1891-1956), Buddhist and Indian economist

IDENTITY AND THE WINE OF AGE

As I was shopping for school clothes with their mother, my nine-year-old twin grandsons, were full of questions as we stopped at MacDonald's.

Out of the blue, Keaton asked, *"Why do baseball players have so many tattoos?"*

"Some even have tattoos on their faces," chimed in Killian.

"My favorite player on the Tampa Bay Rays, Evan Longoria, colors his hair in streaks, wears it in a Mohawk, or sometimes shaves his head completely," observed Keaton. *"It's weird."*

"Yes, he's always changing his hair," agreed Killian. *"I think it's funny."*

I told the twins I didn't know why he did, or why most athletes do such things. Athletes tend to be superstitious, I know, and play their hunches. Should they be hitting for average or hitting home runs, they often attribute the success to the bat they are currently using, or what they were doing when the streak started, repeating that routine to the letter.

Likewise, when they are in a slump, they work on the problem by watching film, listening to coaches and teammates, hitting off a tee to check out their swing, or engage in some idiosyncratic behavior designed to lift them out of the nosedive.

As for the tattoos, sixty years ago, players such as Mickey Mantle, Ted Williams and Stan Musial, if they had tattoos, didn't flash them with authority as athletes do today. Tattoos have become close to mainstream for athletes if not the culture in general. Critics see them as self-destructive, while advocates see them as art, still others see them as the nation personality in identity crisis, especially in mid-life. In any case, those who have them will justify them while those that abhor them will look on them with disgust.

Not so long ago, the so-called "steroid era" found baseball players attempting to get an edge on competition by using banned substances to bulk up, increase leverage, bat speed and power, and enhance performance. These athletes were willing to sacrifice long term health for short term advantage, many of these athletes only in their fifties or sixties have paid the ultimate price by dying early.

What my grandsons' curiosity revealed was the consuming problem of identity, which starts about their age, 9.

"When you are my age," I said, *"and your own grandsons are at about your age now, it will give you an opportunity to talk to them*

about life lessons. They are formed at your age, but you have no idea then how important those lessons are at the time."

They looked at me curiously. *"I don't know what you mean, grandpa,"* said Keaton.

"That is because I haven't told you."

They were now paying attention, their ice cream cones dripping seemingly of no concern.

"What I share with you now will likely reside in the back of your minds to be brought up one day when you are my age, talking to your grandsons as I am talking to you now.

"Your grandfather has had a very easy life because, unknown to him when he was your age, his behavior as a nine-year-old would prove significant. It is what has made for a happy life."

"You work all the time, grandpa," Keaton declared, *"I'm interested in fun, not work."*

"I suppose you could call doing research, writing books and articles, work, but for me it is fun, the most fun I have had in my life."

"It is like school, papa. I like school," Killian added in support, *"but Keaton doesn't."*

Again, I felt we could wander off on a tangent, so I asked, *"Can I tell you what it was like when I was nine-years-old, and going into fourth grade like you are?"*

"Yes!" they said but with questioning wonder in their eyes.

"When I was your age, America was at war. They called it World War Two as there had been a World War One a generation before your grandfather was born.

"I grew up in what was called the Great Depression, meaning a lot of fathers were out of work, and families had to do with little. We got used to getting along with little, and then the war came, and the little we had was now rationed, which meant that even if you had money there was only so much sugar and meat and other foods you could buy.

"There was no MacDonald's, and even if there had been, few could afford to eat there. It was a different time, just as this is a different time for you two.

"What the future will be like when you are eighty-years-old is not known, but it will be different. What will be the same will be the problem of identity. That is a problem in every generation, and it is always the same problem."

"Identity?" Keaton asked, *"I don't know what that means."*

"It means knowing who you are."

"I know who I am."

"Are you sure?"

"Yes."

"How do you know?"

"I just know. I am Keaton Fisher. That is who I am."

"No, Keaton. That is your name. That is not who you are. You don't know who you are until you are challenged with life lessons that tell you who you are.

"Once they occur, and they will occur, if they haven't already, situations that don't at the time seem too important, but will in due course prove of great importance as you move into your teens, twenties, thirties, and all the way to your eighties.

"When I was a boy of nine going on ten, several things happened that I can look back on now and realize their significance. I'd like to share a couple.

"When I was going into the fourth grade, my da took me by the hand and marched me downtown to the Martin Morris Sporting Goods & Clothing Store to buy school clothes for me, like I have been doing for you two today.

"The clerk in the store had been a school chum of my da's and they talked and talked about the old days, and about classmates, while my da had me pick out pants and shirts, underwear and socks, sweaters and jackets, shoes and galoshes. When I was done, my da told the clerk to wrap it up, and charge him.

"The clerk looked at my da hesitantly, and said he'd have to check my da's credit. He did, and came back and said he was sorry, that only cash would do.

"My da's confident smile shriveled to a look of terror, an expression I had never seen before. It was as if he collapsed to my size, and was no longer in charge. I found myself saying, 'We don't want this stuff,' taking my da's hand and marching him out of the store.

"Once outside, his hands shaking so bad he could hardly light his cigarette. He was crushed, but I was defiant. I didn't know why

but I hated that clerk, hated that store, and hated everything that it represented."

"You did that?" Killian asked in disbelief.

"Yes, Killian, I did that, and it became a pattern."

"Pattern? Why do you use these big words grandpa?" asked Keaton, *"I don't know what you mean."*

"I mean it wasn't an isolated incident. For example, when the Courthouse Tigers, the guys I played baseball with over at the courthouse grounds, all went to the movies, I guess everyone planned on going to the Capitol Theatre where the comedians Bud Abbot and Lou Costello were playing. Next door the Rialto Theatre had a historical drama of the Northwest Passage. I wanted to see it, and said I'd meet them all after the movies ended.

"They called me a spoil sport, but I felt nothing of the sort. I wasn't going to a movie I didn't want to see because everyone else was, or doing so because they insisted I do."

"I would have preferred the funny show," said Keaton. *"I'd probably like the other movie,"* said Killian, *"but I'd want to be with everyone else. Would that be wrong?"*

"No, it wouldn't, Killian. At that early age, it wasn't a problem for me to go my own way.

"My reason for sharing this with you is that others, people you like, people who may fail to make wise choices, may persuade you to do what they plan on doing, drinking, smoking, doing drugs, cheating in school, misusing other people's things, all sorts of behaviors, only because they don't want to do these things alone.

"By having you do these things with them they justify in their minds that they are all right to do them, when they clearly are not. People don't like to do unwise things alone."

"Daddy talks about making wise choices. Is that what you mean?" asked Keaton.

"It goes beyond wise or right choices. I'm talking about identity. You mention Evan Longoria and his peculiar behavior. Kids see what he does and they copy that behavior because he is a famous baseball player, not realizing they are aping him at the expense of discovering their own identity."

"Daddy says you're different, grandpa," stated Keaton, *"Is that what he means?"*

"You'd have to ask him. My reason for telling you this goes back to what I said in the beginning. Your grandfather has had a very easy life and a happy one because of those lessons learned when he was your age."

The beauty of being a writer is that should they forget this conversation it will still be there in print somewhere long after their grandfather is gone. I suspect then it will bring a smile to their faces.

THIRTY FIVE

SELF-ESTEEM: AN EXCHANGE

Disciplining yourself to do what you know is right and important, although difficult, is the highroad to pride, self-esteem, and personal satisfaction.

Margaret Thatcher, longest serving British Prime Minister of the 20th century

Confidence has nothing to do with what you look like. If you obsess over that, you'll end up being disappointed in yourself all the time. Instead, high self-esteem comes from how you feel in any moment. So walk into a room acting like you're in charge, and spend your energy on making the people around you happy.

Marian Seldes, American actress

A READER WRITES:

Dr. Jim,

Happy New Year to you and Betty. Once again thank you so much for keeping me in the loop, as it were. I owe a great deal to you for opening my eyes in so many ways, for comforting me, and for reassuring me at times as I struggled to understand certain situations at work and at home. I think it's been almost 10 years since I first encountered your writing on the Statewave website. And, I thank God for the Internet!

This seems like as good a time as any to share this item with you. I have mentioned to you before my reservations about this

promoting of self-esteem in children by doting parents. I have seen some of the results and it's not pretty. Your "cage" metaphor is perfect for some of these people who develop this high self-esteem mantra without an accompanying work ethic, believing there is gain without pain or personal responsibility. It seems others have noticed what you and I have.

This Dr. Mezmer is a clever fellow certainly, witty and with a way with words. I however disagree with him that his mouse example illustrates the process of building self-esteem, but he's onto something.[1]

By my own definition he is talking more about confidence. It's all mixed together I think. Regardless, I thought you might like to see it and I'm a bit curious what you think of his point. I'll admit I've only scanned your essay quickly but I intend to read it through before saying anything more about this. But hey, thanks for writing it and for sending a copy to me.

Very best regards from Calgary.

Your friend, Henry

PS One comment concerning our children: As parents, we think we know what and who our children are and likely, as you say, we do not. But certainly, from the opposite standpoint, the same is true for our children. They know we are their parents, i.e., what we are, but do they ever think about who we are? Not that I can see.

But since at a certain age, they consider themselves quite grown up and extremely wise, isn't it apropos for a parent to suggest to these all-knowing people of the world that they really don't know "who" we are either and to stop projecting their limiting concept of us onto our persons. That is, stop treating us as father and mother and start seeing us for who we really are. That could be very liberating for parents. Can you write an article like that for our adult children to read? I hope so. Thanks and regards.

DR. FISHER RESPONDS:

Henry,

Thank you for your response.

I'm afraid children don't see their parents as persons (WHO WE ARE) until they become parents themselves, and then the shit really hits the fan. My children (all but one) are in their forties, and a little of that light is starting to break through.

Recently, a nice couple was visiting us. They have one of those monster mobile homes on wheels, for reason. They never learned to say "no" to their kids, who even though now married (and remarried in a couple cases) have failed to grow up, and are still attempting to take an easy ride off of "mom and dad." The monster mobile home on wheels is has become their getaway strategy.

One daughter, whom they thought was on a two-week vacation, literally moved in with them with her husband and two kids, and stayed for months. To reconcile the situation, what do you imagine they did? They gave them their house and built their own. This is only one of their excesses.

They gave another son a home and large piece of property, which he sold and took the profits to buy an even larger piece of property (none of the profits returned to his parents). Then he got into trouble on his taxes, upkeep and mortgage, and now he is at the point of foreclosure.

Guess what? He is looking for his parents to bail him out again, certain that they won't let him tank. Obviously, he fails to see the irony in this.

Then there is one of my uncles. He gave his four children each $20,000 in 1964. Still in good health although near eighty, he wanted to save his children inheritance taxes should his will be probated. He reasoned this was a generous alternative to possibly a messy situation.

Incidentally, that $20,000 in today's dollars represents about $150,000.

The interesting thing is that his children resented their father's late generosity, pointing out that he had been a tight wad all his life, and when they really needed the money for a down payment on their house or to start up a business, he wouldn't give them a dime. They failed to see their father's frugality was the reason he was able to be so generous in his dotage.

Notes:

1. The reader is referring to this excerpt from the blog of Dr. Mezmer's *"Bad Psychology"*: *Saturday, July 02, 2005: The steam in self-esteem, or how positive psychology gets it wrong.*

We are living in sensitive times, where the common cant is that if people were treated delicately, and with the proper affirmations, they would become like happy busy beavers and spin off with the frenzy of a whirling dervish all sorts of creative and useful things. In a phrase, it's all about building self-esteem, that 'can do' attitude that comes from constant encouragement.

Of course, discouragement is the most prevalent element of the school of hard knocks, or life in the real world. But no matter, as the 'happiness' or positive psychology movement insists, adaptability to the vicissitudes of the real world requires one to be steeped in the positive illusions bestowed by a lifetime of uninterrupted success. A continuously rewarding life that makes every effort good enough, and a twelfth place finish a cause for praise makes for a feel good paradise for children who live in a familial world that shadows reality. It certainly builds self-esteem.

Nonetheless, like a stock market bubble inflated by the proxy of demand, a sudden gust of reality can deflate all hopes, and be more crushing to the spirit than a lifetime exposed to the constant bite of reality. Whether man or mouse, the story is the same, as a mouse can certainly relate. Give a caged mouse his cheese to follow continuously every press of a bar, and he will expect to have cheese forever. However, if the schedule of reward is shifted to a bit of cheese after on average every fifth bar press, then the mouse's behavior would halt, unprepared as he was to the vicissitudes of fortune. On the other hand, if the mouse was always exposed to such variable schedule of reward, or inoculated by the fickleness of fortune, then he would be prepared to press the bar for much longer periods before he would get his cheese.

Ultimately, self-esteem is not about moving the cheese, but being prepared to at times not having any cheese. That is, a confidence about your prowess in prospering in a difficult world depends upon intermittent failure, that bar press or sales call or job interview that produces nothing. Self-esteem in other words depends upon having your self-image deflated from time to time, so that your point of view is always tempered by reality. Of course, it will make for transient happiness, but as our mouse would attest, it's necessary to prevent us from becoming permanently miserable.

Ultimately, to dissent from the pabulum of popular psychology, happiness is not the point, but an exclamation point that follows the frequent drudgery and heartbreak of being alive.

THIRTY SIX

REACTION TO THE "SUMMATION":

WHEN MEN WON'T WORK & THE WOMEN WHO CARRY THEM!

A READER WRITES:

Dr. Jim,

It is indeed very sad.

Our throwaway society now extends to its people. I've a brother who was let go at age 61 from a terrific executive job; the company then went bankrupt (COBRA Insurance).

He was educated, multi-talented, and "played by the rules" all his life, but today's companies simply refuse to hire people his age. (He and his wife are currently in the process of moving to Mexico.)

My sister with multiple sclerosis (with a master's degree) is a social worker in Wisconsin. Her livelihood is now jeopardized due to a punk governor who'd rather kiss the Koch Brothers' asses than complete his own college education!

I had to leave the room when a retired union-worker-nephew railed on and on at a family reunion about HIS employees {public workers} who belong to AFSCME and make "too much." - Such pomposity!

Thankfully, our children remain healthy and all draw paychecks, but their lives are full of stress and anxiety (48-58 hours per week), and they've hardly any of the leisure time that we enjoyed at their age.

A good friend's son, unable to secure decent employment, became "Mr. Mom" to his four children, and does so beautifully! Hopefully, it won't last forever, but they are making it work for them at present.

Dr. Jim, I guess I just want to say that people are doing now what most of us have always done… the best that we can, given what we have to work with!

Trouble is, there's precious little to work with today. It's sure as hell not a time to look for ways (via cruel budget cuts) to increase the misery index!

Thirty-seven other countries manage to afford healthcare for all and still not put seniors out on the street. If that one worry and expense was taken off Americans' plates, perhaps the multitude of other problems we have might get on the path to being solved as well. All the best,

J

DR. FISHER RESPONDS:

Dear J,

Your short note covers why the DOW Jones Industrials went down 280 points today, why real estate appears to be moving towards a double dip, why unemployment seems fixed at around 9 percent and is unlikely to change anytime soon.

True, countries such as France, Germany, Sweden, Norway, and Great Britain spend half as much as Americans do for healthcare yet they have universal coverage.

Incidentally, Germans take half as many MRI's as Americans do. Collectively, these 37 countries take less than half as many prescription drugs as Americans do, and go to the doctors half as often. You can imagine the savings. Translated, it appears we are something of a psychosomatic nation.

We don't often think it much less say it, but one reason there are so many medical tests, so many prescriptions, so many MRI's, EKG's and other expensive tests is because doctors write prescriptions for these procedures. It is one of the ways they inflate their incomes while not appearing to do so.

So, while we are blaming insurance companies and pharmaceutical companies for their extravagance, they have a willing complicit partner with many doctors.

That said we live in a country of hypochondriacs. People get a nosebleed and go to the doctors or the emergency room of some hospital. They fall down and sprain their knee or ankle and it is off to the professional to treat them. Beyond MRI's and the like, there are many people who elect for surgery because their doctor acts like a snake oil salesmen.

An entitlement mentality supports this cabal of medicine, pharmacy and insurance and then wonders why their insurance premiums keep going up and up. It is a kind of robbery that is totally legal if not ethical, and has become standard operating procedure since we are living longer, and we have Medicare and Medicaid, and now Obama Care.

Your sad communique reflects the frustration felt by most hard working Americans where work, workers and the workplace are changing, and so is the distribution of income. While everything else is changing, it is not likely this differential will change anytime soon.

Your brother is in an unfortunate predicament. It is what every worker fears once they hit the age of 55, but to his credit, he seems to be dealing with it in a creative way.

The fact is, and this should be our real concern, we have seven million Americans unemployed, another seven million underemployed, and another seven million or so who no longer have the energy or the inclination to look for work.

Like your brother, it is safe to say men in these three categories trusted management and national leadership to protect their jobs and their economic well-being.

This was not realistic if it ever was, but the idea was real in the mind. Workers came to believe that the government (state or federal), or by their employer would take care of them. This resulted in a complacent workforce counter dependent on others for their total well-being.

It has essentially suspended them in permanent adolescence believing they were owed a living because they showed up for work on time, kept their noses clean, and were loyal.

This is where the fallacy lay. An employer owes the worker only a day's pay for a day's work and no more unless he has a contract that states otherwise.

This is a harsh truth that workers knew during the *Great Depression* but every generation after 1945, and the end of World War Two, has been of another mind. Now, when economic stability is changing, when the nature of business is changing, when the rest of the world is becoming more competitive with the United States, economic stability and job security are changing as well.

Much as I have a problem with the corporate model, managers and leaders are not bad people, but are caught up in this same history.

The world has changed. More can get done with less people. Unemployment, in real terms not the published data, may hover around ten million unemployed for years to come. A new economic model needs to be created that includes continuous training and development for all workers all the time to stay on top of trends.

The days when a person can learn a skill and then coast for forty years on the job are over. School is never out in the future for anyone.

You say we have that model now? Yes, the cosmetic model, but cosmetology will no longer suffice in a world that operates beyond skin deep.

It is easy to forget that the Internet and the *Electronic Age* is only decades old. What will it be like in fifty years? Rome's collapse started with mass unemployment.

Imagine this, if we don't solve the problem of unemployment, what we see in Yemen, have seen in Tunisia and Egypt, and are seeing now in Syria could be around the corner for our country. Gated communities could become vulnerable to such attacks, as well as places of business.

Stability is not a given for the United States any more than it is for emerging economic powers such as Brazil, China and India. We have democracy going for us. Now, all we have to find is the leadership to sustain it.

You are right about the lack of leisure for Americans. Most companies provide vacations and sick leave for workers. The problem is Americans prefer to work than to take leave.

You say Americans can't afford to vacation? That may be true now. Americans didn't vacation in the boom years. They worked more, spent more, and accumulated more evidence of their success with boats and fancy cars, and other accouterments of success. Now, they are paying for that flamboyance.

Incidentally, I am not referring to *MEN WHO WON'T WORK* when considering men who play Mr. Mom. There is no more demanding job than being a house husband and prime caregiver of children. Ask any woman who has tried to juggle being mom, managing a career and being a confidante to her husband.

We muddled through our era, but the demands were of a kinder nature. The true heroes of our time are people such as your sister with multiple sclerosis, who didn't falter but stayed the course and focused on the possible, and for that attention she has shown the rest of us the way.

THIRTY SEVEN

SIX DEGREES OF SEPARATION, REALLY?

SEPARATION AND CONNECTION

There is a theory that no one in the world is separated from anyone else more than "six degrees." When you think about it, the idea does make some sense. We all have run into people who know people whom we know. Then there are other people we meet only to find that we not only know of them or of people with whom they are associated, but are related to them.

As incredible as that may seem, everyone is approximately six or fewer steps by way of introduction from any other person in the world. So there is more than a little truth to the idea that a chain of a friend of a friend to yet another friend can be made.

To connect any two people in six steps was a popular idea conceived by Hungarian playwright Frigyes Karinthy (1887-1938) in his short story, *Chains* (1929). He writes:

Everything returns and renews itself. The difference now is that the rate of these returns has increased, in both space and time, in an unheard-of fashion. Now my thoughts can circle the globe in minutes. Entire passages of world history are played out in a couple of years. Something must result from this chain of thoughts. If only I knew what! (I feel as if I knew the answer to all this, but I've forgotten what it was or was overcome with doubt. Maybe I was too close to the truth. Near the North Pole, they say, the needle of a compass goes haywire, turning around in circles. It seems as if the same thing happens when we get too close to God.).

Karinthy wrote this play when there were only 1.5 billion souls in the world. Now there are more than 7 billion. He died long before the jet age, or instant electronic communication across the globe with the Internet in this *Information Age.* Perhaps in his bones he knew something seemingly miraculous was on the horizon.

Irish American playwright John Guare (1938 -) took Karinthy's *"Chain"* and turned it into *"Six Degrees of Separation,"* which appeared on Broadway and in film. The film of *Six Degrees of Separation* (1993) explores the existential premise that everyone in the world is connected to everyone else in a chain of no more than six acquaintances, thus, "six degrees of separation."

BRINGING THE IDEA HOME TO THE PERSONAL

Dr. Donald Farr and I grew up in the same small city of Clinton, Iowa (33,000), going to different public high schools and different state universities in Iowa but never meeting. Our careers, although different, indicate a movement from the physical to the social sciences in something approaching lockstep. We even acquired Ph.D.'s in the same discipline: social industrial-organizational psychology.

Along the way, I wrote a book, *Work Without Managers* (1991). Living in Florida, I got a note from an author in New York City, William L. Livingston IV. He had seen my book at a book fair, and wrote, *"Send me your book and I'll send you a copy of mine."* His book was titled *The New Plague* (1986). That exchange established a twenty-two year personal and professional relationship that exists to this day.

Here is where the *"six degrees of separation"* spirals in another fashion.

Dr. Don taught human engineering in design for years and lectured at CSUN, and helped form the Human Factors Society back in the 1950s.

He worked in Aerospace on weapon systems and on space vehicles including the first space shuttle at NASA. He also worked on commercial nuclear power plants (redesign of control rooms), commercial product designs and system safety designs, building flow block diagrams and providing detailed failure analysis reports.

As you will see, while Dr. Donald Farr and I assumed similar careers, Bill Livingston was in the process of doing this as well perfecting his *Design for Prevention* thesis in a book. Even more incredible, he has a connection to Dr. Don in nuclear research but without the two ever having met.

As a psychologist, I have written about masculine (left brain) and feminine (right brain) thinking. Engineers and scientists I found have a preference for quantitative cognitive (left brain) thinking to subjective intuitive (right brain) thinking. Yet these two brains are complements and useful in the problem solving as such.[1]

Scientists/engineers, such as Dr. Donald Farr and William Livingston IV, have seen the merits of marrying the two sides of the brain to a common purpose.

*   *   *

Rita is a student of the occult, which suggests a right brain orientation. Having dabbled a bit in the arcane, I respond as I do. My fascination is that we have this bicameral mind, but tend to favor one lobe or the other. This is apparent in the following exchange.

437

A READER WRITES:

Dr. Jim,

Do note with interest your communication and participation. Your work most noble contributes to the benefit of mankind. Your expression makes an impression.

Dr. Don, your twin from another mother, like you shares his past and present work and whatever new endeavors he may choose.

So essential to keep the mind busy. Busy, busy busy! It helps the memory to engage, to process and to share.

Yes, every individual has the feminine and masculine side within them. The Female is known as the "Magnetic Pole," The Male is known as the '"Electric Pole."

Speaking of poles, I am not "pole dancing" tonight, but "pole casting" in the interest of knowing if you are still reading my e-mails as they drift into the Cloud with no rain of response. You must be busy, busy, busy! Am I right?

Dr. Jim, you mentioned in passing the book "Bhagavad-Gita." I study this book on a daily basis. I call it "Rita's Gita." Excellent material.

Indeed, I have several metaphysical books that I embrace as they are part of my mental attire.

Dr. Jim, what other metaphysical books do you study? Do you keep all my metaphysical books that I have given you in a special place? Are they quickly accessible, expressible and reachable?

I am not a lover of fiction. Does that tell you something about my lobe (left) preference? I have always appreciated facts to fiction. I know many women who do enjoy reading novels, but I prefer substance. Diversity and divergence is always appreciated in my convergence to something new.

Voice of Choice always in style.

Drs. Don and Jim, you gentlemen could be called "Parallel Pals" with congenial circuitry, oscillating, equivocating, vacillating and vibrating to new insights.

I always enjoy reading your missives.   It has been another Wonderful Wednesday.

Happy New Year to You and Yours,

Always,

Rita

DR. FISHER RESPONDS:

Dear Rita,

First of all, Happy New Year to you, too.   You make us all happier.

Yes, I read all your e-mails, yes, your metaphysical books that you have given me are in a safe space and place in my heart. And later, you will see listed some of the books I have read that you may have also read. If not, this book or these books may appeal to your interests.

You are quite perceptive in saying Dr. Don and I are *"Parallel Pals"* with congenial circuitry even though we have never met, but thanks to this medium we have gotten to know each other.

Often, I have written about another friend, William L. Livingston IV, whom I have met and have had a close relationship with for the past several years.

He is an author of several books, and like Dr. Don, a quintessential engineer, as well as a student of human nature and *Natural Law*. He writes:

"Sir James:

For Your Information!

Farr and I go back to the TMI (Three Mile Island) nuclear aftermath when human factors became big in plant operations. He was prominent then in the HF (Human Factor) field. I'm not sure we ever met but we were preaching to the same choir at the same events."

William Livingston built nuclear power plants in such places as Korea. Trained in science, he came to appreciate the daunting impact of human factors in the course of his work. He continues:

"My view is that the sciences, hard or soft, are constrained by the same institutional proclivities, enforced by the natural law I yammer about. Like me, Farr is one dude in a setting like this, and another dude when he is doing HF society stuff."

This is shared with you to acknowledge the special person Dr. Don is, from the testimony of another person equally employed. Dr. Don is a person who wears many hats with the acumen of science and humanity's touch to do what he does so splendidly well.

I go on about my humble beginning failing to note that Dr. Don grew up in similar circumstances to that of mine, although he lost his father when still quite young. He took a circuitous route to his achievements always helping people along the way. The behavioral side of his enterprise can be more demanding than pursuing the laws of science."

 Livingston concurs:

"Otherwise, I find the soft science institutions to be more brutal than the hard ones. Look how they treated you."

He is referring to my constant war with academia, which was similar to my war with the corporation. Author Charles D. Hayes in *"The Rapture of Maturity" (2004),* a book I recommend you read, writes perceptively about my inclination:

"Life is full of contradictions. James R. Fisher, Jr. provides an interesting example.   He is an expert on organizational psychology but has never found an organization where he fits in."

This brings me to another subject, that of the "outsider-insider" (me) to your metaphysical orientation of being unbothered by either disposition while joyfully participating in the sorrows of the world. Your energy and joy and perspicacity are revealed in your words.

Since returning from South Africa in 1969, you could say I have made an eclectic spiritual journey to apprehend that metaphysical side of my nature so as to balance it with my material side.

I am not a student of metaphysics as you are, although I have read widely on the subject. Being reared Irish Roman Catholic has been something of a handicap. Reading the works of scholars of the early Christian church (they are not mentioned here), I have been both enlightened and surprised to learn how much it is made up, or as you might say, fiction. That doesn't seem to make it

441

less relevant as there are 1.2 billion Catholics in the world, many of whom would defend Holy Mother Church to the death.

Trained in the hard and soft sciences, I find many writers in those disciplines have also flirted with metaphysics. In my rather extensive book collection, I suspect I have at least 500 books on this and related subjects. This has made me neither wise nor especially informed but only more interested in pursuing the matter with no closure in sight. Can you relate to that phenomenon?

Readers of my blog (peripateticphilosopher.blogspot.com) have told me (mainly respondents from other countries) that the mystical influence in my writing is apparent. For the curious, I will list books that I may have led to such influence:

- *Works of Aldous Huxley including "Brave New World," and "Point Counterpoint." Works of Alexis Carrel including "Man, the Unknown," and "Reflections on Life."*
- *"The Odyssey of the Self-Centered Self" by Robert Eliot Fitch*
- *All the published works of Kahlil Gibran including "The Prophet" and "The Madman."*
- *All the published works of Krishnamurti including "You are the World" and "Think on these Things."*
- *Most of Gurdjieff's works including "All and Everything" and "Meetings with Remarkable Men."*
- *"Power of Will" by Frank Channing Haddock*
- *"The Mythic Imagination" by Stephen Larsen*
- *"Going Home – Jesus & Buddha as Brothers" by Thich Nhat Hanh.*
- *"The Philosophy of Humanism" by Corliss Lamont* □ *"Teachings of Buddha" by B.D.K.*
- *Several works of C.S. Lewis including "God in the Dock" and "Abolition of Man."*

- *Several works of Michael Novak including "The Experience of Nothingness" and "Ascent of the Mountain Flight of the Dove."*
- *"Human Destiny" by Lecomte du Nouy.*
- *Works of James Redfield including "The Celestine Vision" and "The Tenth Insight."* □ *"Christ" by Edward Schillebeeckx.*
- *"The Unconscious Civilization" by John Ralston Saul.*
- *"The Amazing Secrets of the Masters" by Robert Collier.*
- *"The First Secret" by Lao Tze.*
- *"The Second Secret" by J. B. Priestley.*
- *"The Third Secret" by Alfred North Whitehead.*
- *"The Fourth Secret" by Michelangelo.*
- *"The Fifth Secret" by Buddha.*
- *"The Sixth Secret" by Buddha.*
- *"The Seventh Secret" by Montesquieu.*
- *"The Imitation of Christ" by Thomas a' Kempis.*
- *Several works by Joseph Campbell including "Mythical Image" and "The Hero with a Thousand Faces."*
- *Several works by Fritzof Capra including "The Tao of Physics" and "The Turning Point."*
- *"Awakening the Buddha Within" by Lami Surya Das.*
- *"The Wisdom of Eck" by Paul Twitchell.*
- *"Ego & Archetype" by C. G. Jung.*
- *All of P. D. Ouspensky including "Tertium Organum" and "In Search of the Miraculous" and "The Psychology of Man's Possible Evolution."*
- *"Radhakrishnan: The Man and his Thought" by S. J. Samartha.*
- *All of Alan W. Watts including "The Book" and "Does it Matter?" and "The Wisdom of Insecurity."*
- *"Flesh of Reason" by Roy Porter.*
- *"The Heresy of Self-Love" by Paul Zweig.*
- *"Existentialism" by Patricia F. Sanborn.*

- *Most of Jean Paul Sartre including "The Word" and "Situations."* □ *"Animal Faith and Spiritual Life" by Santayana.*
- *Vedanta or Hindu Upanishads.*
- *The Jewish "Torah."*
- *"Collectio Rituum" of Roman Catholicism.*
- *"The Zen Teaching of Huang Po."*
- *"The Seat of the Soul" by Gary Zukav.*

Isn't reading is a form of meditation? I know these splendid authors allow for no more than *six degrees of separation.* Perhaps it could be no other way. After all, we all they have the same bicameral mind, do we not?

It is nice to know you find my missive interesting and of some use, as I feel blessed to be connected to you, as I do all those others mentioned here.

Be always well,

Jim

SIX DEGREES OF CLOSURE

When I came back from South Africa in 1969, I was a very disturbed young man and took the drastic step of retiring. I found sanctuary at the Haslam Book Store in St. Petersburg, Florida where I spent many hours of many days over a two year period doing little else in a self-imposed sabbatical (1969-1971), reading books, playing tennis and teaching myself how to write, publishing one book (Confident Selling Prentice-Hall 1971), and introducing me to myself.

After South Africa, I chose my life to be one of continuous surprise. The only thing that has been orderly has been this avocation of writing. Otherwise, it has been a roll of the dice.

Mainly going forward as if walking blind, I uncovered a sense of resilience. Most of us have little sense of our true strength. Our spiritual side will not run dry if we take the time and care to replenish it in self-loving action.

Since a little boy, I have been writing if not always in words on paper, but in thoughts as a way to take me out of myself in the language of the mind. I took comfort in the words of D. H. Lawrence, who admitted, *"I never know when I sit down, just what I am going to write, I make no plan, it just comes, and I don't know where it comes from.* With such emphasis on spontaneity, I couldn't be discouraged, never worried what others might think. My focus was on uncovering my own sense of reality.

This gave me amazing freedom and my form of meditation. It is how I happen to write the poem for my book, *"In the Shadow of the Courthouse."* It was first composed in my head when I was about five-years-old but did not find the language to express it until I was middle aged.

THE COURTHOUSE POEM

"I have never lost my affection for this edifice (The Clinton County Courthouse). It was like a parent that never wavered, never changed. I am sitting here now, reflecting on the fact that it is forty-five years since I have spent any time with my old friend.

Painting of the Clinton County Courthouse, Clinton, Iowa by Carl H. Johnson ©, Galena, Illinois.

"If I were a poet, I would give it metaphorical significance, like a giant knight, standing ever at attention to protect my neighborhood from itself and from the dangers outside.

"If I were a poet, I would see it as a Greek god, an Adonis, a Zeus, a mighty warrior who never falters from its vigilance.

"If I were a poet, I would sing the praise of this frozen music, this enchanting melody which never varies in my head, this quiet dignity, this sculptured perfection, this sensible grace as common as a pair of old shoes.

"If I were a poet, I would wonder why we could have such stability, such reasoned continence against the harsh reality of tumultuous change, as it has not varied for me one iota from what it was a half century ago.

"If I were a poet, I would remark that the tower and the time and the psychology of its movement is frozen like magic so that wherever I go it is stop time to my mind.

"If I were a poet, I would tell the world that it has been so important in making this fumbling, stumbling, bumbling individual, called "me," to always feel a mystical anchor to my roots of being.

"If I were a poet, I would exalt its unique character with Vivaldi's 'Four Seasons" to dramatize how the earth around us may change, but the spirit within remains forever constant.

"If I were a poet, I would note that men live and die, but that this structure is immortal because it exists beyond nature.

"If I were a poet, I would sit here and wonder as I am now, over the happiness I feel for having the opportunity to once again ponder the regard I hold for it. And finally

"If I were a poet, I would want the world to know of the many lives that this edifice, this sentinel has influenced in the course of my fleeting life. How many young who are now old have been given succor and sustenance, and semblance of order in their lives because they have lived In the Shadow of the Courthouse?" Be always well,

Jim

Notes

1. To illustrate this "right brain"/"left brain" conflict in the engineer, I write in the engineer's *Short Circuit Newsletter* (Spring 1993):

The engineer has kept in touch with the technical, but generally shown an aversion, even contempt for the social. Yet his relations to both are critical to his success. Unwisely, he has assumed that the challenge of the technical world exceeds the complexities of the social. Actually, the reverse is closer to reality. Our knowledge of the vagaries of human nature differ little with those of Plato's time, while our knowledge of the universe far exceeds that known in the time of Galileo (p. 24).

THIRTY EIGHT

"ANIMAL FARM": The AMERICAN STYLE in the 21st CENTURY!

"Man is the only creature that consumes without producing. He does not give milk, he does not lay eggs, he is too weak to pull the plough, he cannot run fast enough to catch rabbits. Yet he is lord of all the animals. He sets them to work, he gives back to them the bare minimum that will prevent them from starving, and the rest he keeps for himself."

George Orwell, *Animal Farm* (1945)

A READER WRITES:

Hello Jim.

This may be somewhat off the topic but I suspect you have some insights into this phenomenon.

Yesterday I was trying to explain to a Japanese visitor why I thought "squeaky clean" Justin Bieber had recently become a "bad boy."

In my view at least, when one becomes a celebrity and the world adopts you as its own, your biggest battle is to remain grounded; to retain your sense of who you really are, your identity.

Perhaps young Justin Bieber has lost himself, at least temporarily. Or perhaps he is rejecting the image/role that was foisted upon him by the world.

If you have another view, I would like to hear it.

Bieber is not unique of course. Celebrities constantly fall from grace, but he is a mere child.

The world seems to enjoy placing certain people on a pedestal and then delights when they topple from the heights; unable or unwilling to live up to their appointed identity.

I would not care to be a celebrity. Such a struggle...

Take care of yourself... that back especially.

Albert

DR. FISHER RESPONDS:

Dear Albert,

Fortunately, I know who Justin Bieber is thanks to my three granddaughters, whereas my two grandsons don't seem to fancy him one way or the other. Four of them are nine, two sets of twins, and one six-year-old. Otherwise, I would not have had the foggiest idea who he was.

Even as a youngster, I wasn't into popular culture, and as Betty can tell you, I never remember the names of tinsel town celebrities on television or in film, authors is quite another matter.

I say this in order to qualify my limited perspective on this young man, who seems to me to have a lot in common with the "spoiled brat" persona of children of baby boomer parents of which I expect he is a grandson.

For the life of me, I cannot understand the draw of *"American Idol"* and like-minded programs where ordinary people quite often with little or no talent compete to become instant celebrities.

Did Justin Bieber rise to fame in this manner? I have no idea, but if he did, blame those addicted to celebrity consciousness as much for the aggravation.

The irony of our times, again from my vantage point, is that so many want to leave the comfort zone of the amateur for the professional at a time when the amateur is coming into his or her own in virtually all endeavors. This is not new.

Culture periodically attempts to unshackle itself from the absolutism of the established order.

This was the central theme of the fantasy allegory of Jonathan Swift (1662-1745) with *Gulliver's Travels* (1726) and George Orwell with *Animal Farm* (1946) and *Nineteen Eighty Four* (1949).

Both authors targeted readers with only a passing interest or comprehension of power, politics and history where the objective of the minority was to keep the majority down by the device of distracting subjugation.

Justin Bieber seems to be a current if unwitting ploy to that end.

Those in charge have mucked up the world as far back as the Romans. It is an age old device used to take the economic and political heat off those in power when prices are rising and unemployment has millions idling on the streets. This is a recipe for revolution or societal collapse. Roman emperors used the distraction of gladiators in the coliseum to entertain the masses, now we have the Justin Bieber's of the world. It is only an expedient measure as the inevitable invariably comes to pass. Rome fell like a thud. What will happen to our West?

Can you imagine the surprise when the Visigoths and Germans invaded Rome, laying waste to it, followed by nearly a thousand years of what would be known as "the dark Middle Age"?

Justin Bieber, child that he is, pampered child no less, seems to be a pawn in the hands of the puppet masters that control us all.

Swift and Orwell used satire to demonstrate this fact with their works having little instrumental or terminal impact in the long run.

The phantasmagoria of the Lilliputians in *Gulliver's Travels* and Pigs as the Old Major (Karl Marx), Napoleon (Joseph Stalin) and Snowball (Leon Trotsky) in *Animal Farm* have been today reduced to Disney productions.

Orwell is saying men exploit animals in much the same way as the rich exploit the poor.

Swift, an Irishman, is more focused on power and its corruption, given the struggle of the Irish with Great Britain.

Fast forward to our recent past. Wozniak and Jobs, Gates and others were amateurs, who created the electronic age, only to have it spin off into vacuous entertainment as personal media (Face book, et al) and 24/7 superfluous reporting called "cable news," further subjugating the majority to the whims of the minority.

These enterprising amateurs found their way in the dim light of garages when the bright lights of academia found no place for their kind. They were children who went against the grain of convention when the parents of society had lost their way.

We forget that science was born by amateurs of the clergy when the Church was omnipotent, and *The Inquisition* executed heretics for uncovering the truths of nature.

The parents of society always want to keep their children in place, controllable and docile according to parental dictates. Materialistic society has evolved with money the god of that control.

- Money is the tapeworm that traps people in self-rejection giving credence to celebrity as their social marquee.
- Money is what drives the Justin Biebers of the world into seeking and savoring meaningless idolatry at the expense of personal worth and comfortable identity.
  ☐ Money is the phantom that if you don't have it you pay for it at every hour of the day with petty humiliation and unnecessary discomfort.

Consequently, should you not have money, you beg, borrow or steal to pay to see a Justin Bieber performance or buy his DVD's or books or apparel or facsimiles of him for yourself or your children.

Whenever celebrity is idolized, that synthetic identity is typically manifested in behavior and nuance by the admirer and can in time become a person's synthetic identity at the expense of his authentic identity. We saw it with "The Beatles" a few generations ago, when John Lennon announced that *The Beatles* were more popular than Jesus.

"Bigger than Jesus" was Lennon's controversial remark made in 1966. He told a reporter that Christianity was in decline and that the Beatles had become more popular than Jesus Christ. The comment drew no controversy when originally published in the United Kingdom. Anger flared up, however, in Christian communities when it was republished in the United States five months later. It was the arrogance of ignorance which has become epidemic.

My *Animal Farm* is the current workplace where I find much in common with Swift and Orwell.

That said constant is the retreat from adulthood into the juvenile of every age. We can write about it but not change it. No, the world of celebrity is not a kind place, nor a safe place to be. Identity cannot be found in mass adulation, or found without struggle.

Authentic identity is the ultimate power which has nothing to do with money or status, but everything to do with contentment.

Jim

THIRTY NINE

IT'S HARD TO BE SELF-CONFIDENT WHEN OUR CULTURE MAKES US FEEL OTHERWISE!

ORGANIZATIONAL DEVELOPMENT (OD)
Intellectual Capital & the Power of People!

The Fisher Paradigm © ™ is a diagnostic tool of organizational development (OD). It is primarily an intuitive rather than a cognitive determiner. There are no algorithms to master, no mathematical verifications to replicate, yet it can be a useful tool in attempting to find the source of our collective frustration.

OD grew out of a need to bring some order to the invasive chaos in complex organization. Management attempts to give it direction and purpose while management itself is becoming increasingly anachronistic.

OD reveals the subtle cues to organizational behavior through intuitive reflection. Corporate memory and identity can be faulty or no longer relevant. OD assesses and identifies any drift to dysfunction.

The corporate memory depends on qualitative values (culture) and spiritual vitality (Consciousness). This can lead to the counterintuitive idea that the less instrumentally driven the more terminally relevant the organization is. That is:

- Total reliance on vertical thinking and cognitive reasoning can demonstrate a chronic dependence on crisis management, circular argument, and critical thinking in the problem solving. This calls for the complement of lateral thinking, intuition and creative thinking.

- If you take a system apart and operate each of those components in such a way that every component is working as well as it might, then one thing is certain. The system as a whole will not behave as well as it can. This is counterintuitive thinking to *Machine Age Thinking* but is absolutely essential to systems thinking.

OD engages intuition while still utilizing its cognitive arsenal. The Fisher Paradigm © ™ suggests that the unconscious is key to moving beyond rational explanatory limits.

ORGANIZATIONAL CULTURE & CONSCIOUSNESS

The Fisher Paradigm©™ uses a simple typology to determine the dominant culture in the organization in terms of its consciousness. To wit:

The Culture of Contribution. People in this culture are engaged, not management dependent, but collaborative partners with management. Workers are confrontational and conflicts are normal fare, but managed. This is "conscious competence" as work is not management dependent, but goal centered.

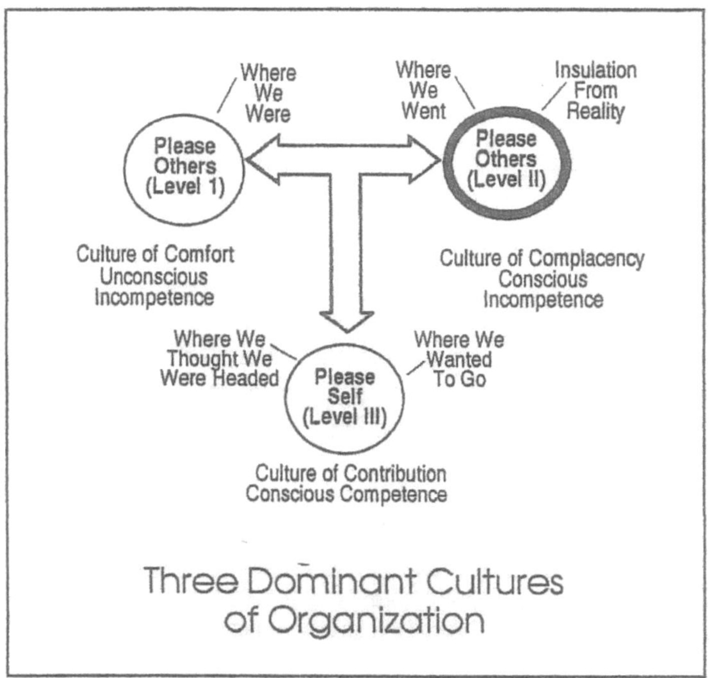

To assess the organizational culture, this formula should prove useful:

- The structure of work determines the function of work;
- The function of work creates the dominant workplace culture;
- The workplace culture dictates the dominant organizational behavior;
- The dominant organizational behavior establishes whether the organization will prosper and grow, or vegetate, flounder and decline.

INTRODUCTION OF AN IDEA

Most leaders are using the Fisher Paradigm©™ but are unaware of that fact. This author argues everything revolves around learned experience. Formal education can enhance, but can also impede that experience if the dominant culture is not a worker friendly climate for learning. Learned experience has two components:

- Immanence – something "inside the individual."

- Transcendence – something "outside the individual."

Consciousness contains more than what is assumed. Feelings have no specific language, and therefore feelings can be misinterpreted because of cultural programming. The inclination is to explain feelings away rather than to explore their relevance to the problem.

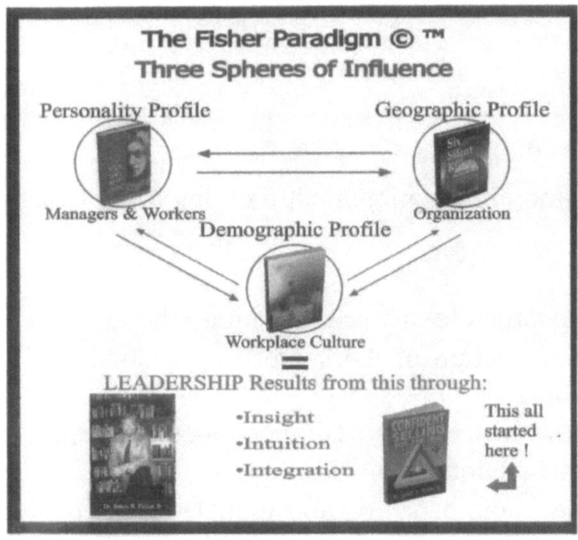

Visual used in seminar, AQP Conference, New Orleans, 2001.

We talk too much and think too little. Instead of allowing feelings to speak to us, we rush to describe them. This has resulted in an explanatory society that imposes limits on understanding.

Feelings too often are treated as facts. When obsessed with feelings instead of what has occurred, the situation is unlikely to be sensed correctly. Alas, we have a plethora of explanatory models that are greatly influenced by how a situation feels. As a result, we are more disposed to defend sacred biases than to get inside and neutralize them, more apt to search for rather than create a solution, more likely to imitate what has worked elsewhere than discover what will work for us.

We prefer rule-of-the-thumb justifications to thinking through our problems, to assume what is evident rather than to question its validity. Meanwhile, our senses struggle to breakthrough false assumptions. This is when intuition comes into play:

"Did I really sense what I believe I sensed, or am I fooling myself?"

When faced with this dilemma, the tendency is to reject the intuition instead of mounting some type of action falling back on what is accepted and expected in order to be consistent with what everyone says, "is" so.

This is a pardonable offense in most cases, but not for the OD practitioner. When OD ignores the forces of intuition, and looks only for the rational explanation "outside itself," OD surrenders insight to a total dependence on cognitive methodology. Both the cognitive and intuitive are relevant and necessary, but without OD gauging the intuitive sense of the situation, chances are the dominant culture and the consciousness level of that culture will not be detected.

CONSIDER CUBE AS IMAGE OF THIS PHENOMENON

A cube has six sides but we can never actually see more than three. Our immanence or "something inside" tells us there are three faces, not a cube itself. But if we embrace our transcendence or "something outside" in clear subjective reporting, we know we are looking at a cube. We don't say, "I

am looking at three faces but deduce that I'm looking at a cube."
So, it is not false to say that our perceptions contain more than
meets the eye.

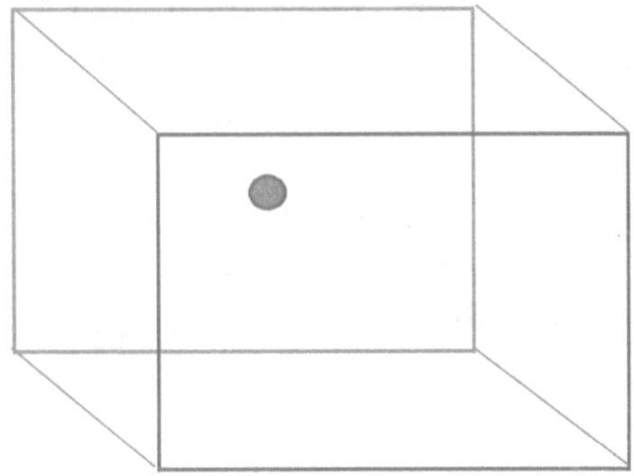

WHERE IS THE CIRCLE IN THE CUBE?

Innate transcendence contains within itself the ultimate
significance of learned experience, that is, we demonstrate
sufficient courage to embrace what we know is there but not
there, that is, cannot be seen.

The OD practitioner with diverse training, experience and
background in such distinct fields as psychology and sociology,
engineering and history, personnel and manufacturing is in
possession of a repertoire of tools to encourage speculation as to
the significance of transcendence in his work.

Simply possessing these attributes is not nine-tenths of the law.
OD often requires penetrating the barrier of his own cultural
programming to get to the essence of a thing.

The individual grows from the "outside-in" rather than the
"inside-out." Parents, teachers, preachers, friends, relatives,
peers and so on define the individual and what that individual

perceives as true, just and right before learned experience kicks in to refute or confirm that programming.

To become oneself, and to discover one's essence, rebellion is often required from the norm. Einstein demonstrated this rebellion in challenging the 300-year reign of Newtonian physics. More recently Nobel Laureate Richard Feynman playfully reinvented quantum mechanics and grew to be at odds with the very community that idolized him.

Both these accomplished scientists relied more on their internal dialogue than the constraints of their academic training and cultural programming to define themselves and orchestrate their minds to new scientific truths.

The Fisher Paradigm©™ acknowledges these inevitable barriers, and proposes a model meant to engage insight, promote intuition, and integrate conceptual understanding with common sense. Such understanding is only possible when transcendence is realized.

The Fisher Paradigm©™ promotes this understanding by postulating that learned experience centers around three discrete spheres of influence:

- Personality Profile

- Geographic Profile

- Demographic Profile.

These are offered as profiles (see previous graphic) or spheres of influence, recognizing that these spheres are constantly bombarding our senses comparable to the three invisible surfaces of the cube that are not seen but are inevitably there.

CASE IN POINT

Few would argue the discovery of the "DNA fingerprint" has been one of the more remarkable discoveries in recent times.

James Watson and Francis Crick were co-discoverers of the DNA molecule. That enormous breakthrough was managed through conventional painstaking laboratory research. This is well documented in Watson's bestselling book, *"The Double Helix"* (1969). The methodology was representative of what we expect from scientists.

Not so for Kary B. Mullis, Nobel laureate for Chemistry, 1993. Mullis departs from the furrowed brow stabbing in the dark of this mystifying lot to be more like everyman, and weird everyman at that. Since winning the Nobel Prize in Chemistry with Michael Smith of Canada in 1993, he has been criticized for promoting ideas in areas in which he has no expertise such as his denial of the AIDS epidemic, climate change, and his belief in astrology.

His discovery was that of the polymerase chain reaction (PCR), which redefines the world of DNA, genetics, and forensic science. Known more widely as a surfer, a bar hop, strip club patron, and veteran of Berkeley's rebellious 1960s, he is perhaps the only Nobel Laureate ever to describe a possible encounter with aliens.

A scientist of boundless curiosity, he refuses to fit the mold of "scientist," or to accept any proposition based on secondhand or hearsay evidence, preferring to embrace the chiaroscuro of life in all its shades and patterns, not from a distance but as part of him. Incidentally, with Michael Smith simultaneously discovering the polymerase chain, it is likely he would agree that we are all separated by "six degrees of separation."[1]

In his book *"Dancing Naked in the Mind Field"* (2000), he challenges us to question the authority of scientific dogma and every other kind of authority as he reveals the workings of an uncannily original scientific mind. His words fit comfortably in the *Fisher Paradigm© ™*. He writes:

"Suddenly, I knew how to do it.

'Holy shit!' I hissed and let off the accelerator. The car coasted into a downhill turn. I pulled off. A giant buckeye stuck out from the hill. It rubbed against the window where Jennifer, my girlfriend was asleep. I found an envelope and a pencil in the glove compartment. Jennifer wanted to get moving. I told her something incredible had just occurred to me. She yawned and leaned against the window to go back to sleep.

"We were at mile marker 46.58 on Highway 128 (Malibu, California), and we were at the very edge of the dawn of the age of PCR. I could feel it. I wrote hastily and broke the lead. Then I found a pen. I confirmed (my intuition). I must have smiled. I could still smell the buckeyes, but they were drifting a long way off. I pulled back onto the highway, and Jennifer made a sound of approval that we were underway again.

"About a mile down the canyon, I pulled off again. The thing had just exploded again. A new and wonderful possibility. Not only could I make a zillion copies, but they would always be the same, that was important. That was the almighty, the hallelujah! Clincher.

"The hell with Jennifer. I had just solved the two major problems in DNA chemistry. Abundance and distinction. And I had done it in one stroke.

"I stopped the car at a nice comfortable turnout and took my time working my way through the consequences. The simple technique would make as many copies as I wanted of any DNA

sequence I chose and everybody on Earth who cared about DNA would want to use it. It would spread into every biology lab in the world.

"I would be famous, I would get the Nobel Prize."[2]

The Fisher Paradigm©™ is common yet rare. It is common because the innate capacity for intuition is available to everyone, rare because intuition goes against societal cultural programming in this cognitive age.

If anything, society kills the intuitive drive. Shameless intuition is too incomprehensible to contemplate as evident in the Washington Post's tactless assessment of *"Dancing Naked in the Mind Field"*:

"Kary Mullis, perhaps the weirdest human ever to win the Nobel Prize in Chemistry, has written a chatty, rambling, funny, iconoclastic tour through the wonderland that is his mind."

The critic focused on the person demonstrating little interest in or curiosity about how Mullis, a highly trained scientist, stepped out of the stereotype of a scientist and made this incredible breakthrough. Dancing naked in the mind field, indeed.

Dr. Kary Mullis was considered by his scientific colleagues to be a flake, if not incompetent for the ways he behaved against how he was expected to behave as a scientist. Thus he was not only able to think outside the box but beyond the limits of what the Scots like to call the multitude.

Mullis was a free man in an age of unctuous conformity, which ironically has become more awkwardly evident in the scientific community than in such expected self-conscious institutions as theology, philosophy and academia.

Notes:

1. Duncan J. Watts, one of the principal architects of network theory, uses this premise in *"Six
Degrees: The Science of A Connected Age,"* W.W. Norton & Co., New York, 2003.
2. Kary B. Mullis, *"Dancing Naked in the Mind Field,"* Vintage Books, New York, pp. 6-8.

FORTY

WHEN THE INCIDENTAL BECOMES THE ACCIDENTAL BECOMES THE NORM THERE IS NO CHANCE FOR SELF-CONFIDENCE!

"It [the mind] can make a heaven of hell or a hell of heaven. In our constant search for meaning in this baffling and temporary existence, trapped as we are within our three pounds of neurons, it is sometimes hard to tell what is real. We often invent what isn't there. Or ignore what is. We try to impose order, both in our minds and in our conceptions of external reality. We try to connect. We try to find truth. We dream and we hope. And underneath all of these strivings, we are haunted by the suspicion that what we see and understand of the world is only a tiny piece of the whole.

"Some people believe that there is no distinction between the spiritual and physical universes, no distinction between the inner and the outer, between the subjective and the objective, between the miraculous and the rational. I need such distinctions to make sense of my spiritual and scientific lives. For me, there is room for both a spiritual universe and a physical universe, just as there is room for both religion and science. Each universe has its own power. Each has its own beauty, and mystery."

Alan Lightman, *The Accidental Universe: The World You Thought You Knew* (2014)

ATONALITY AS METAPHOR TO TROUBLED SOUL

The *"game of life,"* which sociologist Irving Goffman wrote about in *"The Presentation of Self in Everyday Life"* (1959), more than fifty years ago, still resonates with poignancy.

Goffman *"On reality and contrivance"*:

If a performance is to come off, the witnesses by and large must be able to believe that the performers are sincere ... we find that a rigid incapacity to depart from one's inward view of reality may at times endanger one's performance.

I have witnessed senior management lying through their teeth in addressing the troops as far back as the 1960s. That same discordant sound still vibrates through the cockles of my mind from the political stump to the church pulpit.

We have seen this on display with the recent scandals associated with General Motors over faulty ignition switches. Engineers lied to management; management lied to their boards; their boards lied to investors, and Wall Street, far from guiltless, acted as dissembling agent to the commercial global world.

Goffman *"On teams"*:

In a recent study of the police, we learn that a patrolling team of two policeman, who witness each other's illegal and semi-illegal acts and who are in an excellent position to discredit each other's show of legality before the judge, possess solidarity and will stick by each other's story, no matter what atrocity it covers-up or how little chance there is of anyone believing it.

This sounds ancient, but is it?

A lad told me recently of his father, an attorney, who has made a habit of taking tickets his wife, daughter and son have gotten for traffic violations, and because he once was a police officer himself, uses his influence so that those police officers, who wrote the tickets, are sure not to show up in court when these traffic violations appear on the court's docket. Consequently, they are dismissed for lack of corroborating evidence. This recently extended to the lad's girlfriend who got a ticket for a violation on university grounds, and was told "not to worry, it was being taken care of."

Imagine how the tens of thousands of Floridians feel who have gotten tickets for speeding or being clocked and pictured going through red lights.

Florida collects over $100 million dollars a year in revenue from these cameras at red lights, alone. Who profits? The companies that install the cameras, not the State of Florida that gets all the grief for having them. Go figure!

Longshoreman turned philosopher Eric Hoffer once said, *"If you want to understand a society, study the games they play and how they play them."*

Now we have America's new national pastime, the National Football League (NFL) superseding what once was the private domain of Major League Baseball, demonstrating the ambivalence and dodgy morality of infallible authority, once the domain of the Roman Catholic Church.

Take the Ray Rice incident. This NFL football player hit and knocked out his then girlfriend (now his wife) at the Revel Hotel and Casino, Atlantic City (New Jersey), February 15, 2014 in the casino elevator. Hidden elevator cameras captured the entire episode. Rice, 27, literally knocked out his girlfriend, Janay Palmer, 26, her falling unconscious to the floor, with him then dragging her limp body out of the elevator onto the tile floor.

Millions saw this video on Facebook, cable television or network news. Later, before a blanket of television cameras backed by his National Football league teammates of the Baltimore Ravens, Ray Rice apologized insincerely to a multimillion fan base watching on television and across the nation and the world.

The NFL commissioner Roger Goodell met with Ray Rice and his fiancé, and gave the football player a two game suspension. The commissioner claimed he gave such a light suspension because Ray Rice was "ambiguous" in recapping the incident. That was May. The commissioner's assessment of Rice's remarks turned out to be a lie.

Ray Rice had actually told Commissioner Goodell unequivocally that he had hit his fiancée in the elevator and knocked her unconscious.

In September, the celebrity news website TMZ released the video of what happened inside that elevator to the shock of the nation. It should not have been shocked given the millions who saw the video on television with Rice dragging his lifeless unconscious fiancée from the elevator.

It was the aftermath of this incident that was handled so poorly it became like clashing cymbals. Stephen A. Smith of *First Take* on ESPN sports channel, a commentator who often is quite perceptive, was so cavalier and insensitive with his reaction to the Ray Rice affair that he was suspended for a week from broadcasting. NFL Commissioner Roger Goodell received no comparable sanction.

As Goffman would say: *We want to believe what we want to believe despite what our minds and better senses tell us.*

Goodell has been riding the NFL economic bandwagon if precariously ever since, that is, until the police revealed this past week that the video inside the elevator was sent to the National Football League headquarters several months ago. Denial is never far from self-deceit and cover-your-ass.

Now, we come to where the rubber hits the road.

Roger Goodell in his ten years as NFL commissioner has grown the NFL to eclipse all other national sports in popularity, audience, and most of all, revenue.

Goodell has made NFL owners super rich. While NFL football players stand united behind Ray Rice, many know it could be them in the dock next, thinking, *"There go I but for a little luck."* Now owners stand united in support of Goodell, their most beneficial meal ticket to power and greed. Incidentally, these 32 appreciative owners pay commissioner Goodell $40 million a year.

This shows the ugly head of capitalism where there are no rules, no laws that cannot be breached. The concern is not with what is ethical and moral, but what can be done within legal constraints. This is the blurring of lines between the systems of these two clashing values.

It is unlikely that Arundhati Roy's book *"Capitalism: A Ghost Story"* (2014)" is on any NFL owner's library shelf. Roy tells a chilling story of how money in India trumps social justice and what we take as being moral and decent.

From poisoned rivers, barren wells, clear-cut forests to hundreds of thousands of farmers unable to feed their families choosing to escape punishing debt with suicide, it is a ghost story only too familiar in Third World countries in Africa and South America, as well as parts of China.

India is a nation of 1.2 billion souls, but the country's richest people own assets equivalent to one-fourth of India's Gross Domestic Product (GDP). There are ghosts nearly everywhere you look in India, Roy reports, with hundreds of millions attempting to survive on two dollars a day

Capitalism: A Ghost Story examines the dark side of democracy in contemporary India, and shows how the demands of globalized capitalism have subjugated billions of people to the highest and most intense forms of racism and exploitation.

When you think that our children and young adults are addicted to surreal games, to fantasy football, and to other activities without meaning or consequence, you sense how the incidental becomes the accidental becomes the norm.

FORTY ONE

SELF-ESTEEM NOTWITHSTANDING, IT IS WHAT AND WHO YOU ARE THAT COUNTS!

"If the growing child's self-concept is sufficiently insulted, the craving for self-esteem may be so intense as to foster a rigid adherence to whatever mechanisms are immediately efficacious .... Maturity is not reached until one seeks primarily to satisfy one's own valid inner standards; whereas the pride ridden is often preoccupied with what others think about him, and with the impression he makes."

Samuel J. Warner, *Self-Realization and Self-Defeat* (1966)

THE OWNED SELF AND ACQUIRED SELF

Is it nature or nurture that drives behavior? Whatever side of this argument you prefer, what we are remains constant. We cannot escape our "own self" or essence as this is what we are at birth. It is our biological inheritance, our genetic code, our DNA. It is what cannot be changed or taken from us. It is our *"real self."*

Who we are, however, constantly changes. It is our nurtured self. It is a product of our culture and conditioning, our programming. This is our *"acquired self."*

It is reflected in our maturity, discipline, focus, performance, stability, and ability to handle adversity. Think of it as something we rent, like a dwelling, and like a dwelling we can move out, and choose another dwelling.

Some people change their *"acquired self"* or personality all through their lives. We may see this personifying insincerity as with chameleons described earlier. More likely, however, such people are simply adjusting to the current company they keep. It behooves them to move and behave consistent with that company in order for it to work favorably for them.

On the other hand, professional actors find a socially esteemed role by escaping their own identity by playing other characters. Novelists do the same. Indeed, people in caring roles from educational to therapeutic to scientific gravitate to professions that allow such escape while having these assumed roles esteemed if not envied.
What we are feeds into who we think we are and should be. So, there is overlapping between the *"real self"* and the *"acquired self"* for us all.

Psychologists see who we are in terms of our personality. They then describe this learned behavior with a complex and convoluted nomenclature complete with nuance and aberration to represent another syndrome. Psychiatrists then medicate the individual to neutralize these aberrancies in an effort to control the symptoms without addressing the malady.

It is not easy being human. It has been difficult throughout human history to comprehend what we are (our inherent character) with who we are (our personality).[1]

Indeed, psychologists are careful to see that no phase of who we are escapes developmental and/or ameliorating attention from childhood to adulthood to parenting.

When we interact with each other, the child, the adult and the parent are all actively present in our personality, registering our level of maturity at the moment.

So, who we are is a thinking, behaving, and feeling being bringing all of this to fore in our interactions with each other.

Many have attempted to interpret this dynamic and reduce it to manageable concepts.

- Eric Berne did so with *"Games People Play"* (1964) reducing Sigmund Freud's Ego (*Reality Principle*) to the adult, Super-Ego (*Morality Principle*) to the parent, and the Id (*Pleasure Principle*) to the child, demonstrating how these three states are active in the psychology of our relationships.

Berne's nomenclature swept the American continent like a panacea. Now, behavior could be reduced to palliatives.

- Thomas A. Harris in *"I'm OK – You're OK"* (1967) used Berne's transactional analysis (T/A) to construct four classifications to show positions we take with respect to our egostates:

  (1) I'm not Okay-You're OK

  (2) I'm Not Okay-You're Not Okay

  (3) I'm Okay-You're Not Okay

  (4) I'm Okay-You're Okay

These positions are consistent with Berne's Parent (P), Adult (A), Child (C) or PAC.

Then John M. Dusay came along with *"Egograms: How I See You and You See Me"* (1977). Egograms differentiated transactional analysis a step beyond that of Berne and Harris with "The Parent" differentiated to the "Critical Parent" and the "Nurturing Parent," "The Child" to the "Free Child" and the "Adapted Child," while "The Adult" remained the same anchoring the middle.

This was followed by an insightful study, *"The Nurture Assumption: Why Children Turn Out the Way They Do"* (1998) by Judith Rich Harris. Author Harris subscribes to the dictum that peer pressure and not parental influence dictates adolescent behavior.

HOW THIS PLAYS OUT IN A MACRO SENSE

Who we are and what we are were once assumed to be interchangeable. If our father was a farmer and our mother was a homemaker, we would work the family farm and marry a farm girl and she would be a homemaker like our mother. The same was true of the factory worker, teacher, doctor, or lawyer.

The battle of nature and nurture, the nurturing parent or critical parent is personified daily on network television with entertaining therapists such as "Dr. Phil." He feels there is too much *nurturing parent* and so he amalgams tough love into the *critical parent* to popular applause and probity.

Oprah Winfrey, on the other hand, feels there is too much *critical parent* and so blends her enabling love with a large dose of *nurturing parent*. Both are popular, and both appeal to who we are, "right now," without a backward glance to what we are, and cannot escape being, and so the dilemma.

These talking heads are in the self-esteem business and appeal to the feeling side of our personality. They are parent surrogates for those participating and the many listening are not used to anyone listening to them, including their parents.

Who we are and have become is looking for answers to what went wrong with what we are. Of course, no fault of these commentators, they are fulfilling a need with a bit of synthetic love and ephemeral advice for those looking for answers in all the wrong places. It doesn't stop there.

- More than a half century ago, parents abandoned the role of parenting their children with both mother and father becoming full-time breadwinners. This meant leaving children to their own devices and to fend for themselves.

The parents were having too much fun working and playing and neglecting their traditional role as parents.

- Parents, too, didn't want to grow up because they didn't want to grow old. It became fashionable to be eternally young. The cosmetic and plastic surgery industry became booming businesses.

Moreover, self-esteem books became a publishing bonanza. Self-worth no longer had to be earned but something acquired (see Nathaniel Brandon's *The Psychology of Self Esteem*, 1969).

- So, while children had the pleasures of behaving with the freedom of adults without adult constraints, their incipient maturity was at risk as they were not yet ready to handle such freedom.

Meanwhile, rather than children modeling their parents' behavior their parents commenced to model their children's behavior:

- This was apparent in dress, manner, speech, tastes and attitude with little awareness at the absurdity of it all.

Education became a factory with the academic curriculum more resembling products of an assembly line in a manufacturing facility.

Even more bizarre, educators became the critical parent while corporate managers became the nurturing parent with corporations assuming the role of the workers care giver and care taker. The workplace came to resemble a recreational facility more than a place of productive work.

The unintended consequences was a totally dependent workforce to corporate management. In the 1980s, when times were good, management flirted with the idea of lifetime employment and benefits and entitlements while management failed to see that worker efficiency had little to do with worker effectiveness.

Workers came to expect to be educated on the job, not seek education on their own time, even with the company paying for their tuition and books. Showing up for work on time was made more important than what was accomplished in a daily routine. Workers came to feel they were "owed" a job and a living wage.

Management unwittingly created a *Culture of Comfort* of management-dependence, which devolved to a *Culture of Complacency* with workers counter dependent on the workplace for their total well-being. This has led to arrested development of workers with everyone losing.

The unhappy irony is that workers don't want to grow up, and management would prefer them as children than to have them challenge its authority as adults in the *Culture of Contribution*.[2]

HOW THIS PLAYS OUT IN A MICRO SENSE

From birth onward, we experience joy and disappointment, all the while being told by others what we are as we experience these events. So, it is not surprising that our true vocation gets lost in the translation.

We grow from the outside-in until we rebel and find a peaceful marriage within between our *"real self"* or essence and our "acquired self" or personality.

A FATHER REFLECTS

I lost my daughter when she was 17. The pain was so sharp that it crippled me emotionally. I thought I knew who she was, but I could not fathom what she was apart from what I expected her to be. I didn't recognize the changes in her, only saw her in terms of smooth surfaces with no bumps or bruises. I guess I expected her to transition from a little girl into a grown women without any messy fluidity between the blissful stage of childhood and the mature stage of adulthood. I wasn't ready for her to become a person.

For 10 years, I never saw her, but then she had the maturity to come back to her father. She is now the mother of two lovely children, a boy and a girl. She still models, and is still beautiful in her forties. We play tennis, grab a bite to eat occasionally and share our love of her children.

The teenager years are difficult for both parents and teenagers. It is impossible for children to remain what parents believe them to be, when they are trying to find out who they are in terms of what they are. Equally difficult, teenagers have trouble being honest with parents because they are struggling to be honest with themselves. Parents forget that children grow up with that tape recorder in their heads that Eric Berne's refers to, echoing voices of the Parent, the Child and the Adult.

The genetic code is what they are and can be. They are like the acorn that James Hillman describes in "The Soul Code" (1996) that must grow down into fertile soil in order to rise up to become the mighty oak. We as parents make this natural process unnatural by projecting our own fears, our obsession for being in control, confusing the roles of critical and nurturing parent, and failing to realize neither one is any longer valid nor reliable.

FALLACY OF THE "COMPARING AND COMPETING"

When personality (who we are) becomes more dominant than our essence (what we are), we are likely to chase ambition at the expense of our true nature in a *compare-and-compete* frenzy.

This is likely to find us experiencing little pleasure in what we are doing or where we are going, always wanting to be somewhere else doing something else. The dominant code of our restless society sponsors this synthetic culture that serves no one, except its exploiters.

Since most of us are unlikely to become rich or famous, we can imitate those that do by buying the cars they promote, purchasing homes that resemble theirs, and living inauthentic imitative lifestyles that become caricatures of who we actually are.

Few question this competing idolatry. Indeed, we take pride in being a competitive society. Comparing and competing destroys the individual or who he is. It puts the focus on others at the expense of grasping one's own essence.

Psychiatrists Willard and Marguerite Beecher write in *"Beyond Success and Failure: Ways to Self-Reliance and Maturity"* (1966):

"Competition enslaves and degrades the mind. It is one of the most prevalent and destructive forms of psychological dependence. Eventually, it produces a dull, imitative, insensitive, mediocre, burned-out, stereotyped individual devoid of initiative, imagination, originality, and spontaneity."

If we don't get sidetracked along the way, we can realize our potential and satisfy our destiny, but it is not an easy journey. We will encounter many potholes that must avoided which necessitates being alert to that possibility.

What we are with who we are in harmony can produce a happy, healthy and satisfying life. When who we are (personality) dominates at the expense of what we are we are likely to become superficial and rootless.

In that case, what we are (essence) is out of balance with who we are (personality). We are unlikely to be comfortable in our own skin and seek to escape that discomfort through celebrity worship or the achievements of others, resigning ourselves to a second-hand identity and lifestyle.

In such a state, we can develop a self-negating attitude. We don't need to learn new skills as we are already smart enough. We don't need to meet new people because what can they teach us? We don't talk to people outside our specialty because they are too thick to understand. We are suspect of global warming so we drive our SUV tanks, dump our spent batteries in the garbage, think nothing of throwing our trash in a vacant lot, and see no point in voting as elections are rigged anyway.

To restore balance, we must get beyond comparing and competing, living second-hand lives, waiting for someone else to take the lead, and criticizing doers instead of having the gumption to do something! We are mired in conflict, which leaves little energy to focus on who we are to pursue what we are consistent with our gifts and spirit.

When children reach a certain age, they want to separate themselves from their parents, not emulate them. They want their own identity, which is unlikely to differ much from their parents once given the room to explore wider horizons.

Where we are or eventually appear to go is where we likely should be, for if we cannot envision ourselves being somewhere else doing something else chances are we're not likely to ever get there.

PERSONAL REVELATION

My rebellion was postponed until after I was married and had a family. It happened while I was a young executive in South Africa during apartheid.

It never occurred to me that a society 80 percent black could be subjugated to draconian practices by the 20 percent white population in a democracy, yet that is what I experienced.

It was 1968. Moreover, my Roman Catholicism seemed complicit by omission to the Afrikaner government's policy of the separate development of the races. That didn't sit well with me.[3]

Suddenly, my life made no sense to me. I resigned a promising career with a wife and four small children to support. For the next two years, I read books, wrote one, and when nearly broke, went back to school full-time to pursue a Ph.D., consulting on the side.

You might say I have been rebelling ever since as it has been a tortuous road to integrate what I am with who I am to discover my authentic self. This finds me a writer today who hopes to help readers make whole the two sides of their divided self. Once self-worth is established then self-esteem will follow, but not before. That has been my experience.

Notes:

1. This "shrinking of America," that is, turning life's adventure, purpose and meaning over to psychologists, psychiatrists, psychotherapists, or social therapists for relevance is one of the themes of *Time Out For Sanity!* (2015). Madness has been manufactured into a consumable product with a willing market in the modern personality. People wonder, *"Is this all there is"* (to life)? An army of will confection merchants are at the ready to answer that question.
2. The significant impact of culture and the changing nature of work, workers and the workplace are salient themes of *Work Without Managers: A View from the Trenches* (2014).
3. *A Green Island in a Black Sea: A Novel of South Africa during Apartheid* (2014) explores how the clash of cultures can be troubling to the point of catastrophe for the naïve

person who has bought into a value system that, clearly, his own society no longer believes in. Had he taken a "time out" and rebelled in his adolescence, he wouldn't be faced with this quandary in his thirties.

FORTY TWO

THANK GOD FOR DIFFERENCES!

"Management deals best with what it knows, which means people are often managed as things. People do not behave, react, or forgive the way things do, which is the basis of conflict. Relationships imply conflict. As sociologist Georg Simmel observed, conflict can be the very glue, which binds people to a task. Yet conflict is considered a pejorative. Disagreement is considered disruptive when it is a vital precursor to agreement. Managed conflict keeps the organization on course and is essential to its health."

James R. Fisher, Jr., *"Six Silent Killers"* (1998), p. 119.

CONTINUITY AND DISCONTINUITY

A MIND SELF-IGNORANT OF ITSELF

After reading the novel *"Train"* by Pete Dexter, winner of the National Book Award for *"Paris Trout,"* I could not find his books on the shelves of either Barnes & Noble or Borders.

Thanks to the Internet I was able to order all his published works at discount prices, which made me wonder how could someone write so well, so honestly and poignantly and not have an audience. I answered my own question.

It was another nail in the coffin of our current cultural discontinuity. But that is not why I am writing this today. I am writing about the marvel of television that despite all its inanities manages to connect us to the continuity of "minds alive" on noncommercial television's Public Broadcasting System, or PBS and C-Span and its *"Book Beat,"* as it is better known, proving not everyone is asleep.

That said commercial television has its merits for a baseball fan. To take a break from reading, I checked the baseball games on television – Cincinnati Reds and Chicago White Sox, Boston Red Sox and Atlanta Braves – and during a commercial break, I wandered over to C-Span. There I caught Jay Wesley Richards lecturing on his book, *"Money, Greed and God"* at the Enterprise Institute.

Richards is an advocate of *"intelligent design,"* which rejects the theory of natural selection, or Darwinian evolution, arguing that the complexities of the universe and of all life suggest an intelligent cause in the form of a supreme creator. In contrast, Darwinian evolution is the theory of evolution by natural selection.

It was first formulated in Darwin's book *"On the Origin of Species"* in 1859. Darwin, and others discovered that Nature represents a process by which organisms change over time out of necessity for survival. These changes are manifested in heritable, physical or behavioral traits.

Richards is a passionate young man with a point of view, an educated perspective, and a convincing way of presenting his argument. Knowing that he was an apologist for *"intelligent design,"* I wondered if I would have listened to his ideas on capitalism (which he sees as the solution not the problem), missing an opportunity to experience an engaged mind. I must confess I might have done so. If I had, it would have been my loss.

We don't grow wiser only listening to those who espouse what we already know to be true, or think to be so.

He covered a lot of territory that I have considered often with a different slant but honestly not from his point of view. He reads

Ayn Rand (*on selfishness*) the same way I've read her, but has a different appreciation of greed and interpretation of self-interest even though my sentiments are similar. I feel uncomfortable bringing a theistic point of view into my thinking and writing although, I suspect, Richards has had similar training to that of my own.

This is further evidence that our cultural moorings influence how ideas and information are processed, then interpreted and become assimilated into our thinking. Stated another way, we are never freely engaged no matter how disciplined or structured or how arduous our training. Ideas seem to always be tainted by our initial exposure to and in life.

It is difficult to get out of the cage of our cultural programming, which is most apparent when we give matters of some discontinuity a rational twist to continuity, often not realizing we are doing so. Social psychologist Leon Festinger might suggest our views were tainted with a bit of *cognitive dissonance.* He claims we are inclined to process new information so that it fits comfortably in our minds with what is already there; otherwise, it is likely to be rejected. [1]

Richards breaks down words into their Latin origins, and defines them in those etymological terms. For example, *"altruism"* does not mean *"selflessness"* but *"other directed,"* from the Latin "alter." An individual doesn't abandon *"self-interest,"* but is *"other directed"* to promote self-interest in relating to significant others. This is consistent with Freud's *"quid pro quo,"* or something gained for something given. In such terms, self-interest is not only critical to success, but essential to survival.

The author demonstrates his finesse in making this connection, while intrinsically establishing a different set of biases to my own. So, his connection in one sense becomes a disconnection in another sense to my thinking, or his continuity leads to discontinuity between us. Simply put, he believes in *"intelligent design"* and I believe in Darwinian evolution.

Clearly, we can we speak a similar language but differ widely in its application, interpretation and meaning.

The irascible curmudgeon Christopher Hitchens in January 2008 had a debate on *"intelligent design"* with Richards. Hitchens loves combat, his opponent loves congenial discourse. What an odd couple! On stage was Richards, boyish, clean cut and well groomed and Hitchens, overweight, disheveled needing a shave and haircut. Hitchens is the darling of agnostics and atheists of the liberal left, and Richards, a passionate defender of theistic Christian conservatism.

It is refreshing to see television sponsoring discussions of people of ideas, allowing them to have free reign in that climate. This exposure may reduce the screws of intolerance a twist or two.

We live in an age where people off the rails of conventional norms have difficulty being heard. It is even more difficult for them to get into print much less find an audience. Kudos to C-Span and PBS for providing this small window compared to the panoramic screen that commercial television offers to our collective lowest common denominator. As long as we have this small window, ideas will not die.

Richards referred to a book about *"bees"* in which he described how combative, self-interested, and conflicting were these bees, while being terribly productive. An experimenter introduced a chemical to make the bees less aggressive, and the hive fell apart.

Edward O. Wilson at Harvard has been telling us for years that the smallest creatures on earth, insects, behave precisely as man, or is it the other way around? [2]

Anyway, conflict has been a thesis in my books on organizational development (OD). Managed conflict and polite confrontation is the glue that holds workers on task. It is harmony that leads to discontinuity and functional collapse, not conflict. Harmony is the antithesis of productivity, and like the bees, dissolves cohesiveness.

We have had eighty years of increasingly harmonious organizational life, thanks to the auspices of Human Resources (HR) management. The faulty thinking that this entails goes back to 1927 and Elton Mayo's study of the Hawthorne Works of Western Electric in Chicago. The study found that manipulation of various hygiene factors – changing the lighting, moving workstations, or changing working conditions – resulted in increased worker productivity.

This led HR to give workers everything but the kitchen sink, which first created the *Culture of Comfort,* which then led to the *Culture of Complacency* at the expense of the *Culture of Contribution.* The latter is necessary to generate productive work.

How bizarre that this quest for continuity can lead to discontinuity was revealed by the experimental program at Bethlehem Steel and the Aluminum Company of America (ALCOA). These two major companies launched in the 1960s a furlough experiment with their veteran workers. John Strohmeyer writes about this in *Crisis in Bethlehem* (1986) showing how it all went awry.

The plan was for Bethlehem Steel and ALCOA to give senior workers 13-week paid furloughs every five years when these workers were already the highest paid in American industry, and had more entitlements and benefits than nearly any other American workers. Strohmeyer refers to this *"as the crippling goose that laid the golden egg."*

The masterminds of this program envisioned the furlough experiment to be an effective way to induce workers to greater productivity and more effectively manage manpower requirements. It was anticipated that many of these workers would use this "paid for free time" to pursue educational opportunities (which these companies also paid for), travel and enrich their lives, or pursue favorite hobbies they never had time for before. What do you think most of them did?

They acquired second jobs to increase their income. This led to something approaching a nightmare. When workers returned to their regular jobs, because they needed the additional income to maintain their new standard of living, many attempted to manage two jobs, performing poorly on both.

Instead of seeing the futility of this, and how they were equally responsible for the continuity leading to discontinuity, they took their wrath out on management.

From an insightful point of view, there was some merit to this, as these workers exposed the fact that they were behaving at work mainly as dependent twelve-year-olds in fifty-year-old bodies.

These companies had unwittingly developed a counter dependency that was only exacerbated by this intervention. In assuming responsibility for their total well-being, workers became obligingly suspended in terminal adolescence. No thought was given to how this program might rupture and/or reinforce this dependency. It was telling evidence of how vacuous the idea was and how clueless was the management of these workers' psychology.

The experiment compressed rather than broadened these workers' horizons while diminishing them as proud and engaged workers.

Work was all they knew and what they knew came to fill the void of the 13-week furlough.

We are so late smart when it comes to understanding what makes us tick and what does not. Continuity and discontinuity are normal fare in the life of the individual and in the collective life of the workplace, and by extension, society.

Remember this, whether you are an advocate or adversary of *the theory of evolution* or *"intelligent design,"* you can learn a lot about yourself, especially in the other thinker's camp.

No one has a monopoly on ideas. But there is no better way of understanding oneself than to entertain ideas outside the realm of one's own thinking and experience.

The steel and aluminum workers in the 13-week furlough experiment were as self-ignorant and on automatic pilot as those workers in 1927 at the Hawthorne Works of Western Electric in Chicago. Those in the social and behavioral sciences have been misreading ordinary people for a century now, and management has been unwittingly their sponsor. May I remind you that management is still in charge?

Notes:

1. Leon Festinger, *"A Theory of Cognitive Dissonance,"* Stanford University Press, Stanford, CA. 1957.
2. Edward O. Wilson in *"Naturalist,"* Inland Press, Washington, D.C., 1994. Wilson gives a definitive appraisal of the dynamic world of ants, which has more than a little in common with our own. More specifically, if you would like more pragmatic information about bees and colony collapse disorder, see Dominique DeVito's *"Beekeeping: A Primer on Starting & Keeping a Hive,"* Sterling Signature, New York, 2010, pp. 137-140. We are having a critical problem maintaining the desirable productive bee population, critical to plant growth and development.

FINAL WORD

Gazing out of the window of my study, having put these missives into this framework, it makes me think of the power of words.

It is only when you put things into words that you begin to grasp reality; and of course images create that reality. This, in a way, is more important than reality itself because all we see of reality is its images, and we do that through a collection of words. That allows us to comprehend the world and our place in that world.

It is why books such as the Bible, Torah and Koran are believed to hold timeless truths.

Even when we question the reality of ourselves, it is usually someone else who paints that portrait of us with words, someone else who puts us under the spotlight if only for the moment.

This eclectic presentation taken from more than 1,200 missives on my blog (peripateticphilosopher.blogspot.com) demonstrates the phenomenological path this writer has taken through a simple quest to understand the core of our individual and collective identity.

If that is felt to a lesser or greater degree by the reader, and the reader feels more confident joining this quest, then it has served its purpose as it has introduced you, the reader, to yourself in a new way.

Be always well,

James R. Fisher, Jr., Ph.D.

ABOUT THE AUTHOR

Dr. Fisher sees himself as a peripatetic philosopher, intrigued by the eclectic images and imagery he encounters. He doesn't claim to be a systematic observer but an intuitive and insightful recorder of his time having worked and lived on four continents (North and South America, Europe and Africa).

Dr. Fisher is trained in the physical and behavioral sciences and uses this window to share what he has learned from the experience.

This is his twentieth book in the genre of social/industrial psychology. He lives with his wife, Betty, in Tampa, Florida and may be reached by e-mail (thedeltagrpfl@cs.com).